Setting the Agenda

The News Media
and
Public Opinion
(3rd Edition)

未名社科·媒介与社会丛书（翻译版）

议程设置

新闻媒体与舆论
（第三版）

〔美〕马克斯韦尔·麦库姆斯
（Maxwell McCombs） 著
〔智〕塞巴斯蒂安·瓦伦苏埃拉
（Sebastián Valenzuela）

郭镇之 徐培喜 译

北京大学出版社
PEKING UNIVERSITY PRESS

著作权合同登记号　图字：01-2021-1851

图书在版编目(CIP)数据

议程设置：新闻媒体与舆论：第三版/(美)马克斯韦尔·麦库姆斯,(智)塞巴斯蒂安·瓦伦苏埃拉著；郭镇之,徐培喜译.—北京：北京大学出版社,2023.10

(未名社科·媒介与社会丛书：翻译版)

ISBN 978-7-301-34323-4

Ⅰ.①议…　Ⅱ.①马…②塞…③郭…④徐…　Ⅲ.①大众传播—研究　Ⅳ.①G206.3

中国国家版本馆CIP数据核字(2023)第157237号

Setting the Agenda: The News Media and Public Opinion, Third Edition
Copyright © Maxwell McCombs and Sebastián Valenzuela 2021
First published in 2004 by Polity Press
This edition is published by arrangement with Polity Press Ltd., Cambridge
Simplified Chinese Edition © 2023 Peking University Press
All rights reserved
简体中文版由北京大学出版社有限公司出版发行

书　　　名	议程设置：新闻媒体与舆论(第三版) YICHENG SHEZHI: XINWEN MEITI YU YULUN(DI-SAN BAN)
著作责任者	〔美〕马克斯韦尔·麦库姆斯(Maxwell McCombs) 〔智〕塞巴斯蒂安·瓦伦苏埃拉(Sebastián Valenzuela)　著 郭镇之　徐培喜　译
责任编辑	陈相宜
标准书号	ISBN 978-7-301-34323-4
出版发行	北京大学出版社
地　　　址	北京市海淀区成府路205号　100871
网　　　址	http://www.pup.cn
新浪微博	@北京大学出版社　　@未名社科—北大图书
微信公众号	北京大学出版社　北大出版社社科图书
电子邮箱	编辑部 ss@pup.cn　　总编室 zpup@pup.cn
电　　　话	邮购部 010-62752015　　发行部 010-62750672 编辑部 010-62753121
印　刷　者	大厂回族自治县彩虹印刷有限公司
经　销　者	新华书店
	650毫米×980毫米　16开本　19.25印张　250千字 2023年10月第1版　2023年10月第1次印刷
定　　　价	79.00元

未经许可，不得以任何方式复制或抄袭本书之部分或全部内容。
版权所有，侵权必究
举报电话：010-62752024　电子邮箱：fd@pup.cn
图书如有印装质量问题，请与出版部联系，电话：010-62756370

献给贝齐

马克斯韦尔·麦库姆斯

献给特雷、西蒙、卡米洛和圣地亚哥

塞巴斯蒂安·瓦伦苏埃拉

前言　消息与余留

唐纳德·肖（Donald L. Shaw）
戴维·韦弗（David H. Weaver）

即使在小时候，我们也能凭本能知道，一则消息（例如一声哭泣）会激起某种反应。这部综合性著作清楚地表明，许多消息，特别是来自新闻媒体的消息，不是随机产生的，而是由记者和其他人依据自己的优先考虑，按照从最重要到最不重要的顺序依次排列的。受众不得不循此顺序阅读、观看、倾听和学习。议程提供了优先顺序，而不仅仅是信息。

在个人生活中，我们活在真实的世界里，有家人、朋友、街道地址，有工作、学校、医院，有沙漠和山脉。而在公民生活中，我们却活在想象的世界里，我们从其他人（包括媒体）那里了解这个世界。当然，这两个世界是有所重叠的，从接触的世界到想象的世界，是一个连续体。来自其他方面的信息，包括传统媒体和社交媒体的信息，提供的都是有优先顺序的议程。媒体的优先次序显而易见：报纸以大字标题突出最重要的话题、总统选举结果或摧毁一切的龙卷风。电视节目以热点问题开头，甚至会打断常规节目，播出"突发新闻"。社交媒体启动某个话题，并一直关注它，直到把其他人聚集到这个信息网络中，就像阁楼上一张不断扩大的蜘蛛网。

议程设置通常被描述为这样的现象：新闻界告诉我们该思考什么

对象(what to think about),而不是该思考什么内容(what to think)。我们早就知道,媒体的报道可以放大话题,甚至放大人物,就像19世纪的巴纳姆(P. T. Barnum)把一个实力不俗的歌手珍妮·林德(Jenny Lind)变成了世界巨星——"瑞典夜莺"。一条消息的力量,或者说一个以这种或那种方式放大了的声音的力量,几个世纪以来已经为人所知;但是,研究议程设置的学者列出了产生这种现象的许多方式,以及与之相关的跨越时间、民族和政治制度的具体证据。传播学者马克斯韦尔·麦库姆斯和塞巴斯蒂安·瓦伦苏埃拉查阅了大量文献,并以一种教师和学者都可以使用的方式将其编成一卷。这是一本有关议程设置的教材与重要学术著作。

议程设置的学术渊源由来已久。七十年前,斯坦福大学的威尔伯·施拉姆(Wilbur Schramm)凭借自己的著作和收集到的有关媒介与大众传播的重要洞见,或多或少可以说发明了"大众传播"这一学术领域。这些文献成为早期的学术文本和研究指南。初始阶段,新闻学学者从事法律和历史研究(现在仍然如此),同时也借鉴社会学和社会心理学的方法。他们还采用了内容分析这种天然属于新闻学研究的方法。几十年前,先后任教于斯坦福大学、北卡罗来纳大学和得克萨斯大学的韦恩·丹尼尔森(Wayne Danielson)同俄亥俄大学的吉多·斯坦普尔(Guido Stempel)等人开始将文本内容与计算机联系起来,找到了将研究样本扩大至大量人群的方法。施拉姆很早就勾勒出了一个消息传递模式,消息传递的方向是由传播者到达受众,带有一个较弱的反馈回路。它曾经是,现在也仍然是一片有待发现的天地。

借助内容分析,人们可以向后看,阅读消息,辨别受众甚至文化的细节;但也可以向前看,更准确地展望在受众那里产生的效果。当然,相关过程也包括阅读消息本身。麦库姆斯及其同事的议程设置研究,比以往任何时候都更准确地将内容分析与受众效果联系了起来。人们可以作出预测,这是建立理论的第一步。如果有时间和资源,我们可以追溯历史：一位瑞典歌手的声音如何从小镇和城市的礼堂弥漫到各地，进入听众想象的空间，甚至在一个多世纪后的今天，回声依旧。议程自有其余留。议程设置研究提供了概念，也提供了工具，既有前瞻，又有回顾。甚至可以这样说，我们站立之处，也是基于消息本身。

对麦库姆斯和唐纳德·肖的原创文章的引文分析表明，议程设置概念的发展，伴随着在一段时间里对它所代表的简单想法（有认知刺激，就有认知反应）的抵抗，在当时，即20世纪50年代和60年代，态度改变是主导范式。我们记得读过一篇文献综述，详细描述了这种抵抗，就像大西洋海滩上退潮时留下的线条，从：（1）消息没有余留，到（2）有轻微但属人为的余留，到（3）有余留，但我们早就知道了，再到（4）消息会有影响，但大多数微不足道，可以用其他原因解释。这篇文献综述暗示，这就是说，议程设置研究并不重要，至少对那些最关注态度和行为变化的人来说是如此。议程设置的第一篇论文基于针对1968年总统选举的查普希尔研究，但它遭到了新闻教育协会（Association for Education in Journalism，AEJ；现为AEJMC）的拒稿。该文直到1972年才在《舆论季刊》上发表，只稍有修改。

但是，也许正是因为概念的简洁，议程设置研究仍在继续。到目前为止，全世界已有500多篇文章、大量书籍和数千篇论文（讨论议程设置）。麦库姆斯和肖1972年的文章在谷歌上的点击量超过了100万。现在，议程设置有了不同的研究分支，如属性议程设置、媒体间议程设置和议程融合等，还有其他许多。通过对第二层面和第三层面议程设置的研究，人们可以看到媒体消息的属性是如何在受众的头脑中再生的，并且可能想知道，在一些国家，对传统媒体和社交媒体的内容制作者加紧控制究竟意味着什么。美国已经有了第一位推特总统，但可能不是最后一位。还有证据表明，受众会将传统媒体和社交媒体的信息搅在一起，力求找到一种令人感觉舒服的混合体，但这个混合体却不一定是准确的事实。约翰·弥尔顿（John Milton）提出的抗辩理由假定,真理终将战胜谎言,虽然我们可能正滑向一个后事实社会。即使果真如弥尔顿所言(真理终将战胜谎言),媒体仍然据有根据事实或者观点设置议程的权力。

议程设置有时可能是一个复杂的社会话题,其影响范围远远超出了新闻媒体和受众。西弗吉尼亚大学的丽塔·科利斯特拉(Rita Colistra)探讨了议程削减(agenda-cutting)的重要性。想想看,在美国历史上的某些时期,南方的白人报纸不刊登关于非洲裔美国人活动的新闻,除非与犯罪或事故有关。日本人似乎无视其在第二次世界大战中的侵略者角色,而德国人则在他们的历史书中承认了自己的所作所为。历史是一个重要的议程设置者。如果你没有出现在当代生活的新闻议程上,你就不存在于公民文化中,至少对那些不认识你的人来说是这样。

议程设置有积极行动的一面。试想,如果新闻媒体引发了一场关于气候变化(或者倡导消灭贫困和创造机会)的常规性地方运动,会怎么样?记者们可能定期进行相关报道。随着时间的推移,受众会更多地思考这些话题,尽管仅此一点并不能保证公民行动。议程设置是促进社会变化的必要的第一步。告诉人们去思考什么是一种相当强大的力量。这不正是老师、父母、宗教和政治领袖、老板甚至朋友应该做的事吗?

议程设置研究有时采用复杂的方法,但"传播者向接收者传递消息"的概念始终是其简单的核心。本书将文献和研究领域组织成清晰的部分,使这一学科的力量和演变条理分明。这个版本(第三版)是与众不同的,因为这本书就像这个领域一样,已经进化了。没有人像马克斯韦尔·麦库姆斯(现在加上了塞巴斯蒂安·瓦伦苏埃拉)那样了解议程设置研究。他们对议程设置研究的描述一点一点地浮现出来,就像在一个"我是什么?"的页面上追踪数字一样。这本书的第三版是迄今为止最完整的故事,对我们理解议程设置过程作出了重要的贡献。

我们很高兴,在过去的半个世纪里,我们与我们的学生、学生的学生及其他许多人一起,成为这一传播研究潮流的贡献者。戴维·韦弗记得,在1973年研究社会心理学时与麦克斯(马克斯韦尔·麦库姆斯的昵称)一道创造了"导向需求"的概念,提出了相关性与不确定性在信息搜寻中的重要意义。令人兴奋的是,从1972年的夏洛特研究得到的数据,无论是在媒体的接触方面还是在议程设置相关性的强度方面,都如此符合导向需求模型的预测。

唐纳德·肖还记得,在北卡罗来纳查普希尔的那个下午,麦克斯走入门厅,说他们投给 AEJ 的关于议程设置的论文被拒绝了。怎么办?一种选择是把论文扔进垃圾桶,然后去做其他的事情。毕竟,常识早就表明,新闻确实有影响。谁需要对议程设置进行精确统计?麦克斯却有不同的想法。所以,他告诉今天的学生,当你的学术论文或文章遭到拒绝时,仔细审视你的想法:或许你真的能成气候呢。

唐纳德·肖,北卡罗来纳大学
戴维·韦弗,印第安纳大学

序　言

如今,当人们讨论政治与舆论时,议程设置已经成为一个常用词语。什么是公众应该关注并为此采取行动的核心问题？"议程设置"这一词组概括了所有社群有关这个问题的持续对话与辩论,这些社群可以小至地方社区,也可以大到国际舞台。在大多数关于这些话题的对话中,新闻媒体都发挥着重要的,有时是具有争议的作用。对于新闻媒体这种持久而广泛的影响,如果还有人存在疑问,那么可以再参考一下《纽约时报》对20世纪英国报业巨头比弗布鲁克(Beaverbrook)男爵的描述。比弗布鲁克被描绘成"一个和首相一道用餐并为国家设置议程的人"[1]。还可以参考《纽约时报》前主编麦克斯·弗兰克尔(Max Frankel)对自家报纸的描绘：

> 它是那些最聪明、最有才华、最具影响力的美国人的"内部刊物",这些人处于美国权力的顶层。虽然人们可能会轻视或批驳这份报纸的专栏作家与评论家的意见和观点,但是他们不能抛弃它的每日新闻套餐。这些新闻框定了美国严肃人士的智慧与情感议程。[2]

大众传播媒介机构的急剧增长与快速扩张现已成为当代社会一个不容置辩的特征,也是最近一百年来社会的核心方面。19世纪主要孕育了一大批报纸和杂志;20世纪则增添了电影、广播、电视与有线电视,媒介交叉重叠,无处不在;20世纪末又迎来了互联网;而在21世纪，各种新传播技术万花筒式的多变组合（最值得注意的是移动社交媒体），继续让经由媒介的传播和人际传播以及各种媒介及其内容之间的传统界限日益模糊。这些新的渠道重新定义了"大众"（mass）传播，并扩大了这种传播在社会中的议程设置作用。大众传播曾经意味着大规模地扩散相同的消息，特别是通过报纸、电视和广播。而新的传播渠道，如脸书（Facebook）、优兔（YouTube）、照片墙（Instagram）和推特（Twitter）等，社会上使用它们的人数量众多、比例甚大，在此意义上，它们仍然属于大众（massive）规模的传播；但就流通的消息而言，这些渠道却是个人化的。

虽然现在人人都在谈论媒介景观中这些新兴技术的冲击，但是，传播的巨大社会影响早在马克·扎克伯格（Mark Zuckerberg）创立脸书之前几十年就已经显现。在《制造总统，1972》（*The Making of the President, 1972*）一书中，美国记者西奥多·怀特（Theodore White）将新闻媒体为公众注意力设置议程的能力描绘为，"一种在别的国家只有暴君、牧师、政党以及官僚才享有的权威"[3]。自从怀特发表了这番令人信服的洞见以来，世界各地的社会科学家详细阐述了新闻媒体及不断扩张的各种传播渠道，影响我们的政治、社会及文化议程的许多方面的能力。

在有关这种影响的智力图谱中，最引人注目且记录完备的一个成员，便是大众传播的议程设置理论，这也是本书的主题。很少有理论刚诞生就羽翼丰满的。理论通常始自一种简明扼要的洞见，其后，经过各种探索者和调查者多年耕耘，不遗余力地细化和解释，这一智力领域的轮廓才逐渐清晰起来。议程设置理论的形成正是如此。这个理论源自一个简单的假设，涉及大选期间新闻媒体影响公众对社会与政治议题的关注的效果；由此出发，这个理论逐渐扩展，又纳入了许多新的命题，如与这些效果有关的心理过程，塑造传播议程的影响因素，媒体信息中特定要素的冲击，以及这种议程设置过程的各种后果。这样,议程设置理论便超越了传统的新闻媒体的效果研究,成为描绘公共事务相关信息通过不断增加的过剩传播渠道持续流动并产生效果的一张详细图谱。

现今这种理论形式的议程设置思想的直接来源是,研究者在1967年初某日对《洛杉矶时报》头版新闻报道编排的不经意观察。那一天有三条重要新闻:国际新闻,是在英国郡议会选举中工党出人意料地败给了保守党;国内新闻,有一条关于华盛顿政界的丑闻正浮出水面;地方新闻,是大洛杉矶地区主持一个大型联邦资助扶贫项目的主管被解职,而这一项目是约翰逊总统发起的"向贫困宣战"运动的基石。毫不奇怪,《洛杉矶时报》将地方新闻作为头版头条,而将其他两条新闻置于不那么显要的头版次席。如果没有其他两条新闻,这三条新闻中的任何一条都能轻易地登上头版头条。正是这一点引起了加州大学洛杉矶分校几名年轻教员的猜测性交谈。在世纪广场酒店大厅,某次周五下午举行的"青年教师茶话会"上,我们边喝边聊这一话题。我们想知道,如果某条新闻被安排到一个不显眼的位置,那么这个事件带来的冲击会不会因此而减少。这种猜测基于先前各种分散的观点与经验研究的结果,大众媒介对公众的影响这一问题撒下了议程设置理论的种子。

对议程设置思想的正式说明始于那一年秋天,当时我转到北卡罗来纳大学查普希尔分校,在那里遇见了唐·肖(Don Shaw),由此开启了我们五十多年的友谊与专业合作。我们对议程设置思想进行正式调查研究的最初念头,完全基于在洛杉矶时关于新闻报道编排的那些猜测。我们尝试根据既有报纸对同一条新闻完全不同的编排方式设置一次实验。在北卡罗来纳州,《夏洛特观察家报》是一份广受尊重的报纸,它一天中要出一系列不同的版本:早间各版针对距离夏洛特较远的地点,最后一版则为本市居民提供新闻。这种多个版本的设计方式会造成一种结果,即某些新闻在一天中的早些时候可能占据头版的显要位置,在接下来的版本中可能退居头版的次要位置,有时会完全退出头版。我们一开始打算利用各种版本之间的差异作为实验的基础。但是后来发现,新闻的每日编排极不稳定,无论是在新闻的主题上,还是在报纸位置的安排上,均无规律可循,因此,我们无法系统地比较它们对公众感知产生的影响。

尽管遇到了这样的挫折,但理论的想法仍然迷人,我们决定改换路径,尝试另外一种方法:对1968年美国总统选举中那些犹豫不决的选民进行一次小规模的调查,同时,对这些选民所使用的新闻媒体如何编排选举中的重大议题进行系统的内容分析。选择那些犹豫不决的选民作为样本是基于这一假设:相对于广大选民而言,这些对选举感兴趣但还没有决定把选票投给谁的人,可能最容易受到媒体的影响。这就是"查普希尔研究"(Chapel Hill Study),亦即现在公认的议程设置理论的起源。[4]

查普希尔研究的基本贡献在于"议程设置"这个词语本身,它使这个关于媒体影响的概念立即在学者中流行起来。已故的史蒂夫·查菲(Steve Chaffee)曾回忆说,在1968年新闻教育协会(AEJ)的年会上,当我第一次向他介绍我们进行的议程设置研究时,虽然这个新词还很陌生,但他马上就理解了我们研究的焦点。

因为唐纳德·肖接受过历史学训练,所以人们料想我们会记下创造出"议程设置"一词的准确时间,诸如"8月初某个周二的下午"之类的记录。然而,讽刺的是,无论是我还是唐纳德·肖,都没有记住我们想到这个名字的准确时间。1967年,我们从全美广播业者协会(National Association of Broadcasters,NAB)申请到了一小笔资金,部分用于支持调查,在申请书中我们并没有提到"议程设置"这个词。但是在1969年我们向这个协会提交的有关查普希尔研究结果的报告中,却使用了这个词,就好像一直在使用它似的。"议程设置"这个词应该是出现在1968年的某个时点[5],而且毫无疑问,查菲是最早承认"议程设置"有用性的"裁判者"之一,除了直接参与查普希尔项目的那些人之外,也许他是认识"议程设置"概念的第一人。谷歌全球书籍词频统计器(Google Books Ngram Viewer)也提供了进一步的引证资料,显示1968年是"议程设置"一词被系统使用的第一年。第一章将会叙述查普希尔研究的细节,以及议程设置思想的一些关键性知识先导。

在1968年查普希尔调查取得成功之后,套用夏洛克·福尔摩斯(Sherlock Holmes)的话来说,显然,游戏开始了。关于媒介对舆论会产生什么效果的问题,人们发现了充满希望的解决线索,至少能够撩开这块神秘面纱的一角。接下来,许多"侦探"开始追踪这些线索,力求解释媒介如何影响公众的注意与感知,解释媒介、媒介内容以及媒介受众的各种特点如何调节了这些影响的效果。福尔摩斯侦破的案例被整理成厚厚的九大卷宗,与此非常类似,在议程设置的巨大知识网络中,人们也按时记录下各种各样的线索与联系。然而,由于传播研究中的观点市场在很大程度上是自由放任的,所以,对传播媒介议程设置作用的详尽阐释并不总是以一种整齐有序或系统的方式进行的。多年来,很多"侦探"在各种各样的地理与文化背景下处理了大量案件,累积了不少证据,这里增加一点,那里又增加一点。解释议程设置思想的新理论概念也在这个知识网络中不断出现,一会儿在这一部分,一会儿在那一部分。

许多年来,研究侧重的是公众议题议程。特别是新闻媒体公布的民意测验结果,作为大众意见的表达方式,通常被人们视为公众意见(舆论)。议程设置理论产生于描述与解释新闻媒体就当时的议题对公众意见所产生的影响。这种研究经常采用盖洛普民意调查自20世纪30年代起便一直使用的一个开放式问题:"什么是这个国家当前面临的最重要问题?"这是因为,基于这个问题的民意调查,记录了数十年来公众与民意测验组织者关注的几百个议题。[6] 2020年,也许是现代历史上的第一次,对于"最重要问题"(MIP),全球作出了完全一致的回答:冠状病毒危机。

议题议程之外,议程设置理论也涵括公众对政治候选人及其他公众人物的意见,尤其是这些人在公众心目中的形象,以及大众媒介在塑造这些公众形象方面所起的作用。这些更大的话题议程既包括公众议题,也涉及公众人物,标志着一种重要的理论延伸:从传播过程的开始阶段,即媒介与公众关注并认为重要的话题,转移到其后的阶段,即媒介与公众感知与理解这些话题的细节的方式。这些阶段又为考察媒介在态度、观点和行为方面的议程设置效果打开了新的局面。

近几十年,对议程设置效果及其后果的调查已经延展到公共事务领域之外,研究者也在探索不同的环境如体育、宗教和企业经营中的议程设置作用。所有这些媒介对公众的影响本书都有所记录,不仅以理论的方式,而且以世界范围内经验证据的方式予以展现。

自 1968 年创始性的查普希尔研究以来,我们对议程设置的认识之历史演变是零散的。与此相反,本书各章力求系统有序地展示我们在这些年里获得的新知,并努力整合各式各样的证据——无论是历史与地理场景的分殊,还是媒介与话题的混杂,抑或调查方法的多样。本书的核心目的在于展现这幅整合后的图画,用约翰·帕夫利克(John Pavlik)的话来说,就是创作一部议程设置理论的《格氏解剖学》(*Gray's Anatomy*)[7]。构成这幅图画的大部分证据来自美国,因为议程设置理论的创始人——唐纳德·肖、戴维·韦弗[8]与我——都是美国学者,并且直到最近,大部分实证调查都是在美国进行的。但是,读者也会看到来自西欧、东亚、拉丁美洲以及中东地区的大量证据。议程设置理论的巨大优势之一,就在于这种证据的地理与文化多样性,它们验证了传媒影响社会的最主要方面。

除了对我最好的朋友与长期的研究伙伴唐纳德·肖和戴维·韦弗不胜感激之外,本书的成果还要归功于世界各地的许多学者,他们创造了记录于此的大批积累性文献。其中,塞巴斯蒂安·瓦伦苏埃拉是杰出的拉丁美洲学者,他作为合作者,与我一道完成了第三版的编写。塞巴斯蒂安是位于圣地亚哥的智利天主教大学传播学院的副教授,他为《议程设置》这本书带来了重要的国际声音,延续着得克萨斯大学奥斯汀分校的学者过去三十年来为议程设置研究作出的重要贡献。

议程设置理论是一幅复杂的学术图谱,仍然处于演化之中。虽然本书的重点是基于经验研究的以媒介为中心的地图,也就是我们现在所知的媒介在舆论形成方面的作用,但是后面几章也讨论了媒介影响发生的更广阔背景。媒介的议程设置效果一直是学者研究的一座宝矿,我已经开采了超过五十年,但仍然有许多财富尚未挖掘出来。然而,即使是现有的学术探索图谱,也已经确认了令人振奋的新领域,而当代公共传播系统的变化也为细描这幅图谱创造了无穷的新机遇。

即便在最初的公共意见领域,除了描述与解释媒介如何影响我们对公共事务的观点之外,仍有很多问题值得思考。对于新闻工作者来说,我们现在讨论的现象,即新闻媒体的议程设置作用,就推进何种议程而言,仍然是一个严肃而至关重要的伦理问题。提供"公众有必要知道的"新闻是新闻专业主义话语库中一个反复出现的短语。然而,媒介议程真的能呈现公众需要知道的事务吗?[9]美国广播公司(ABC)的新闻节目《夜线》(*Nightline*)的执行制片人曾经产生怀疑,他问道:"我们有什么资格认为自己应该为这个国家设置议程?是什么让我们比周围的人更聪明?"[10]在很大程度上,新闻基于讲故事的传统,但好的新闻并不仅仅是讲个好的故事,而是要讲述那些意义重大、有益公民的故事。[11]媒介的议程设置作用将新闻及其讲故事的传统与公共意见领域联系起来,对社会而言,这种关系具有重要的影响。媒介景观的扩展及新闻和政治传播的演变提出了关于舆论形成的重大问题。

马克斯韦尔·麦库姆斯

得克萨斯大学奥斯汀分校,2020年3月

目　录

第一章　影响舆论　/ 001
　　一、我们关于世界的图像　/ 003
　　二、当代的经验证据　/ 004
　　三、积累的证据　/ 008
　　四、在其他议题上的重复验证　/ 017
　　五、原因和结果　/ 018
　　六、一种新的传播景观　/ 021
　　小　结　/ 028

第二章　现实与新闻　/ 030
　　一、怪异的图像　/ 031
　　二、考察议程设置效果的角度　/ 040
　　三、内容与接触　/ 043
　　四、过去年代的议程设置　/ 043
　　小　结　/ 045

第三章　我们头脑中的图像　/ 047
　　一、政治候选人的画像　/ 050

二、全国选举中的候选人形象 / 051

三、地方选举中的候选人形象 / 054

四、视觉形象与属性 / 057

五、议题的属性 / 059

六、雄辩论据 / 062

七、议程设置与其他传播理论 / 066

八、属性议程设置与框架建构 / 067

小　结 / 070

第四章　议题和属性的网络 / 072

一、联想式记忆 / 074

二、候选人和属性的网络 / 074

三、网络议程设置的累积证据 / 077

四、一种新的格式塔视角 / 079

小　结 / 079

第五章　议程设置为何发生 / 081

一、关联性与不确定性 / 082

二、议程设置效果的出现 / 084

三、关联性 / 087

四、有关公众议题的个人经验 / 090

五、个体差异 / 093

六、顺带学习 / 096

七、议程融合 / 097

小　结 / 100

第六章　议程设置如何起作用 / 101

一、公众议程的承载容量 / 103

二、公众议程的多样性和暂时性　/ 105

三、教育与议程设置　/ 107

四、解释显著性的转移　/ 110

五、效果的时间框架　/ 113

六、显著性测量的多样性　/ 117

小　结　/ 120

第七章　塑造媒介议程　/ 122

一、总统与国家议程　/ 124

二、补贴媒介议程　/ 127

三、俘获媒介议程　/ 130

四、三种选举议程　/ 135

五、地方选举中的媒介议程　/ 137

六、地方议题的属性　/ 138

七、选举三要素　/ 139

八、更广阔的图景　/ 140

九、媒体间议程设置　/ 142

小　结　/ 147

第八章　议程设置的后果　/ 150

一、铺垫舆论　/ 153

二、属性议程与意见　/ 155

三、形成意见　/ 158

四、影响行为　/ 159

五、财经新闻的议程设置作用　/ 164

小　结　/ 165

第九章 传播与社会 / 167

　　一、传承文化 / 169

　　二、议程设置的新战场 / 171

　　三、其他文化议程 / 173

　　四、概念、领域和场景 / 175

　　五、议程设置理论的继续演化 / 177

注　释 / 179

参考文献 / 235

索　引 / 261

第三版译后记 / 281

第一章　影响舆论

美国幽默作家威尔·罗杰斯（Will Rogers）喜欢在他的讽刺性政治评论的开头说这么一句话："我知道的所有事情都是从报纸上读来的。"这句评论是对我们所拥有的关于公共事务的大部分知识与信息的简洁概括，因为我们关注的议题和产生的担忧大多都与个人的直接经验无关。很久以前，沃尔特·李普曼（Walter Lippmann）就在《舆论》（*Public Opinion*）一书中指出："那个我们必须在政治上与之打交道的世界，我们摸不着，看不见，也想不到。"[1]在罗杰斯与李普曼的时代，日报是人们获知公共事务的主要来源。今天，虽然我们已经拥有极大扩充了的全套传播渠道，但是核心的问题依然不变。对于公众议程上几乎所有的事情，公民接触的只是二手现实，这种现实是由新闻工作者对这些事件与局势的报道建构而成的，而这些报道反过来又被使用者借助数字和移动媒体放大、转化并加以评论。

社会学家罗伯特·帕克（Robert Park）同样捕捉到了我们与新闻媒体的双向关系，并以新闻的"信号功能"（signal function）这一令人尊崇的短语简练地描述了这种情形。[2]新闻每天提醒我们关注自己无法亲身经历的大环境中的最新事件与变化。但是新闻媒体所做的事情，远远超过告知重大事件与议题的范围。通过日复一日的新闻筛选与呈现，新闻工作者聚集我们的注意力，影响我们对当前什么是最重要的事件的认识。新闻媒体这种确认关键议题和话题并影响它们在公众议程上的显著性(重要性)的能力,后来就被称作新闻媒体的议程设置功能。

新闻媒体每日提供大量线索,表明各种话题在当日议程上的相对重要性。报纸的头版头条报道、一篇报道在网站上的位置、一篇报道的长度,甚至一篇报道所获得的社交媒体互动量,都能传达出某些话题在新闻议程上的重要性。电视新闻议程的容量十分有限,因此,即使只是被电视晚间新闻简要提及,也是一个强烈的信号,足以表明某个话题的重要性。更多的线索还体现为新闻播报中的位置、报道时间的长短。对于所有传播媒介来说,日复一日地重复某个话题,是凸显其重要性的最有力的信息。

公众利用这些来自新闻媒体的显著性线索去组织他们自己的议程,并决定哪些是最重要的议题。时间长了,新闻报道所强调的议题就成为公众认为最重要的议题,新闻媒体的议程就在相当程度上成为公众的议程。换句话说,新闻媒体在很大程度上设置了公众的议程。在公众中建立这种显著性,将新闻中的某个议题、事件、公众人物或者重大因素置于公众议程,使之成为公众关注和思考的焦点,甚至成为公众采取行动的契机,这是舆论形成的初始阶段。

对舆论的讨论通常围绕观点的分布进行:多少人赞成,多少人反对,以及多少人还没有作出决定。这就是新闻媒体及大量新闻受众对民意测验深感兴趣的原因,在政治竞选时期尤其如此。但是,在考虑观点的分布之前,我们需要知道哪些因素位于舆论的中心。人们会对许多事情形成看法,但是对他们而言,真正重要的事情只占少数。新闻媒体的议程设置功能,便是它们对某个关注对象(例如一个争议性话题,或者一位政治候选人)在新闻中的显著性的影响,以及对相当多的人是否认为这个对象值得自己关注并形成看法的影响。

虽然有许多议题在竞争公众的注意,但只有少数议题最终成功地获得了关注。而新闻媒体对我们的认知——什么是现在最重要的议题——发挥了重要的作用。在专业新闻媒体机构中,这并不是蓄谋已久、有意为之的,如同"要有一个议程"的说法。试图产生特定的影响,属于党派媒体、宣传、广告和所谓"假新闻"网站以及其他寻求说服的传播形式的领域。[3]专业新闻媒体志在告知,而非说服。它们的议程设置作用并不是来自说服的努力,而是一种不经意的影响,因为新闻媒体必须在其关于当前最重要的新闻的报道中选出并强调几个主题。

专业新闻媒体对新闻客体的显著性及有关这些客体的特定观点的影响之间存在差别。伯纳德·科恩(Bernard Cohen)曾观察到并总结了这种差别,他指出,新闻媒体在告诉人们"怎么想"(what to think)方面可能并不成功,但是在告诉人们"想什么"(what to think about)方面则异常成功。[4]换句话说,新闻媒体可以为公众的思考与讨论设置议程。有的时候,新闻媒体所做的超过了这一点;而另外一些时候,新闻媒体则未能做到这一点。因此,我们有必要在后面的章节扩展科恩那令人信服的观察。但是首先,让我们更细致地考虑舆论形成的最初阶段:抓住公众的注意力。

一、我们关于世界的图像

李普曼是现在我们简称为"议程设置"的思想的知识先祖。在他于1922年出版的经典著作《舆论》中,开篇第一章就叫作"外部世界与我们头脑中的图像"。虽然李普曼并没有使用"议程设置"这一词语,但是在这一章中他概括了议程设置的想法。他的论点是,新闻媒体作为我们了解直接经验之外的大千世界的窗口,决定了我们有关那个世界的认知图式。李普曼主张,舆论的反应并非针对真实的环境,而是针对新闻媒体创造的拟态环境(pseudo-environment)。

在初版问世一个世纪之后,《舆论》一书目前仍在印刷。这本书提供了一连串引人入胜的轶闻证据,以支持其理论。例如,在书的开头,李普曼讲述了一个令人信服的故事："1914年，在一座海岛上，住着一些英国人、法国人与德国人。"第一次世界大战爆发已逾六周，但直到一艘邮轮来到这个岛屿，这些朋友才知道他们彼此成了敌人。[5]李普曼写作此书是在20世纪20年代，他是在用时新的例子补充自己在序言中提到的柏拉图洞穴寓言。李普曼用自己的话说出了苏格拉底的观点："不管我们对所处环境的认识是多么间接……只要我们相信头脑中关于环境的图像是真实的，我们便将它认作环境本身。"[6]

二、当代的经验证据

现在，关于传播媒介议程设置作用的经验证据已经证实并详细描述了李普曼粗线条的观察。当议程设置命题最初提出的时候，它遭遇到的是传播学者中流行的有限效果范式，亦即认为大众媒介在改变人们认知和态度方面效果有限的理论。与之相反，议程设置研究显示，新闻媒体在短期内具有强大的、直接的效果，不是影响人们思想的内容（what to think），而是影响人们思想的对象（what to think about）。

不过，作为一种关于舆论形成的理论，议程设置的实证研究很晚才流行起来，远远迟于李普曼的著作。《舆论》出版于1922年，而对大众传播如何影响舆论的最初科学调查发生在十多年后。而整整五十年后，首次明确针对大众传播议程设置功能的调查研究的成果才得以出版。

关于大众传播对舆论的效果的系统分析始自1940年美国总统选举，这是建立在科学调查之基础上的实证研究。当时，社会学家保罗·拉扎斯菲尔德（Paul Lazarsfeld）与其哥伦比亚大学的同事、民意调查专家埃尔莫·罗珀（Elmo Roper）合作，对俄亥俄州伊利县的选民进行了七轮采访。[7]调查结果不仅出乎大众预料，而且令学者感到意外，这些调查以及接下来二十年在其他地区进行的后续调查研究，并没有发现多少大众传播影响人们的态度和观点的证据。伊利县调查二十年后，约瑟夫·克拉珀（Joseph Klapper）在《大众传播的效果》（*The Effects of Mass Communication*）一书中宣布了所谓的最小后果定律（Law of Minimal Consequences），并盛行一时："大众传播通常不是受众效果的必要和充分的原因；而是居于一系列中介性的功能和影响中，并通过它们起作用。"[8]

然而，20世纪40年代和50年代进行的这些早期社会科学调查确实发现了许多证据，证明人们从新闻媒体处获取了信息，尽管这些信息并没有改变他们的观点。选民也的确从新闻中学到了东西。而从新闻业的角度看，确保人们获得信息是比说服人们接受特定观点更加核心的问题。多数新闻工作者更关心告知信息。说服是社论版的事情；然而，即便在社论版，告知信息仍然是核心问题。此外，即使在最小后果论被广泛接受而成为传统智慧之后，许多社会科学家的心中仍有一种挥之不去的疑问，他们认为重大的媒介效果并非没有，只是尚未被发掘或者测量出来而已。此时，在检验媒介效果方面，研究范式转换的时机已经成熟，这种转换就是从关注说服转向关注传播过程更早阶段的告知。

在李普曼之后，社会科学领域的其他作者也提出过这样的观点：新闻媒体影响人们将什么视为时下相关议题。[9]不过，直到1968年，在美国总统竞选期间，北卡罗来纳大学新闻学院的两位年轻教授在查普希尔市开展了一次小型调查，这一观念才得到了适当的实证检验。他们的核心假设是："大众媒介"通过影响议题在选民中的显著性来为政治竞选设置议题议程。两位教授，也就是唐纳德·肖和马克斯韦尔·麦库姆斯，还为大众传播这种假定的影响拼造了一个名字："议程设置"。[10]

检验这个关于议程设置的假设，需要比较两组证据：一组描述公众议程，即查普希尔选民最关注的系列议题；另一组描述这些选民使用的新闻媒体中的议题议程。如框1.1所示,议程设置理论的核心论点是:随着时间的流逝,新闻中强调的那些方面将会变成公众认为重要的议题。换句话说,媒介议程设置了公众议程。与最小后果论相反,这是一种传播对公众产生强大因果性效果的论断——显著性由媒介议程转移到公众议程。

框 1.1　新闻媒体的议程设置作用

媒介议程	公众议程
新闻报道模式	公众的关注
最突出的公众议题　　→	最重要的公众议题

议题显著性的转移

为了确定1968年总统选举期间查普希尔的公众议程,调查者通过随机抽样对那些尚未作出投票决定的选民进行了调查。由于这个议程设置新假设与当时关于大众媒介效果的主流观点背道而驰,调查者只访问了那些犹豫未决的选民。原因在于,如果在最适宜的条件下,亦即在这些尚未决定投票给谁的选民中,还不能发现议程设置效果的话,那么就没有什么理由再到一般大众中去探究这个问题了——因为在竞选活动中,公众对某个政党的长期心理认同及选择性认知的过程通常会削弱大众传播的效果。

在调查中,研究者请这些犹豫未决的选民指出当前他们认为关键的议题,不管总统竞选人对这些议题的观点如何。按每个议题有多少比例的选民提及进行排序,这些序列议题就构成了公众议程。应该注意的是,按照公众提及议题的频率进行排列,比仅依据公众的关注程度将系列议题分为高、中、低三档要准确得多。

研究者还对这些选民使用的九种主要新闻来源进行了内容分析。这些新闻来源包括五份地方与全国性报纸、两家电视网与两份新闻杂志。各个议题在媒介议程上的排列顺序取决于近几周来关于它们的报道数量。尽管这项研究并非首次将民意调查与内容分析结合起来评估特定媒体内容的影响,但同时使用这两种方法测量大众传播效果在当时还比较罕见。

在1968年美国总统竞选期间,五个议题主导了媒体与公众的议程——外交政策、法律和秩序、经济、公共福利、公民权利。查普希尔的选民对这些议题的排列顺序与之前二十五天这些议题在新闻媒体上的排列顺序几乎完全对应。而在未作出决定的选民中,这五个关键竞选议题的显著性与它们近几周在新闻报道中的显著性实际上是完全相同的。

不仅如此,与作为大众传媒有限效果论的思想基石的"选择性认知"相比,议程设置概念所表达的媒介具有强大效果的观点更能解释议题在公众议程上的显著性。要明白,议程设置并非回到原先的魔弹(magic bullet)或者皮下注射(hypodermic needle)等媒介万能效果论,也不是将受众视为消极等待新闻媒体设定程序的机器人。但是,议程设置理论确实给新闻媒体指派了一种为公众议程倡导议题的核心作用。或者借用李普曼的话说,新闻媒体提供的信息在建构现实图像方面发挥了关键作用。不仅如此,正是新闻媒体提供的总信息集,影响了我们关于现实的各种图像。

与此相反,选择性概念将核心影响力归于个体,并根据媒体内容与个体已有的态度和观点的契合程度将其分成不同层次。从这种观点出发,研究者常常假定,新闻媒体很少能改变个体的议题优先次序,因为个体会尽可能去接触支持自己想法的信息,并搜寻自己早已视为重要的议题的相关新闻。例如,在选举中,一般会预测选民会将最大注意力投向他们偏爱的政党所强调的那些议题。

那么,公众议程最可能反映哪一种情况呢?是议程设置理论假设的那种结果,即选民接受新闻中全部的议题议程,还是选择性认知理论假设的那种结果,即选民接受自己所偏爱的政党提出的议题议程?

为了回答这些问题,那些犹豫未决但又有一定倾向(虽然还未达到坚决支持某一候选人的程度)的选民被分成三个小组:民主党的支持者、共和党的支持者,以及乔治·华莱士(George Wallace)的支持者——华莱士是那场选举中的第三方候选人。对于这三组选民中的每一组,研究者都采用哥伦比亚广播公司(CBS)电视网中的新闻报道进行配对比较:选民小组的议题议程与CBS的所有新闻报道对比;选民小组的议题议程与CBS播出的这个小组所偏爱的政党和候选人的新闻报道对比。接着,对全国广播公司(NBC)、《纽约时报》以及一家地方日报重复了这种形式的比较。最后,需要对比十二对相关关系:三个小组乘以四种新闻媒体。

在每一组关系中,哪一对相关性更强?是将选民与所有新闻报道相比较的议程设置相关性更强,还是将选民与他们所偏爱的政党和候选人的新闻报道相比较的选择性认知相关性更强?结果发现,在十二对关系中,八对支持了议程设置假设;一对没有发现差异;只有三对支持了选择性认知假设。关于媒介强大效果的一个新视角站稳了脚跟。

三、积累的证据

查普希尔研究发表一年之后,西奥多·怀特在系列作品《制造总统》(The Making of the President)的最后一部中,细致地描绘了新闻媒体的议程设置作用。摘录见框1.2。自1968年总统选举期间在查普希尔开展小规模研究至今,关于新闻媒体议程设置作用的独立学术作品已经积累了500多篇,涵盖六大洲,涉及政治和非政治场景、各种各样的媒介和数十个议题。[11] 2011年,《舆论季刊》在纪念创刊七十五周年时指出,查普希尔研究是该刊引用最多的文章。[12] 到2020年3月,这篇文章仅在谷歌学术(Google Scholar)上的引用次数就超过了12 000次。一些作者甚至提到了"议程设置重器"(agenda-setting juggernaut)[13]，以凸显议程设置概念在探究新闻工作者及其生产的新闻的影响时的人气。还有一份学术期刊专注于扩充议程设置理论，就是《议程设置杂志》(*The Agenda-Setting Journal*)，这在新闻研究中可能是独一份。

框1.2　新闻的权力

美国报业的权力是与生俱来的。它为公众讨论设置议程；这种横扫一切的政治权力任何法律都不能限制。它决定了人们谈论与思考什么——这是一种在别的国家只有暴君、牧师、政党以及官僚才享有的权威。

在美国，如果没有新闻界事先为公众的头脑做好准备，任何国会的重大立法、任何对外冒险、任何外交行动和任何伟大的社会改革都不会成功。当新闻界抓住某个重大议题并将其抛入讨论议程的时候，它是自主行动的——环保事业、民权事业、终止越战以及作为高潮的水门事件，都是首先被新闻界提上议程的。

——《制造总统》，西奥多·怀特

在这个国家的首都的舆论河流中，《华盛顿邮报》非常像一头鲸鱼，哪怕是它激起的最小水花，也不会毫无反响。没有任何其他报纸能够像《华盛顿邮报》主导华盛顿那样主导一个城市……虽然有一些人抱怨，自本杰明·布拉德利(Benjamin C. Bradlee)于1991年9月从总编辑的位置上退休之后，这份报纸便失去了活力，但《华盛顿邮报》所具有的对国家政治议程的影响力似乎并未被削弱；对这个永远有不满人群、领导者和奋争者聚集的城市，该报近乎神秘的重要性并没有减少。

——《纽约客》(1996年10月21日和28日)

尽管发表了大量研究成果，但议程设置理论的基本思想仍然是简单易懂的：这个理论关联到一种过程，经由这个过程，新闻媒体认为值得关注的各种元素(如议题、公众人物、公司或者政府机构)以及用以形容这种元素的属性，往往也会被公众认为值得关注。更重要的是，议程设置的基本假设已被广泛的研究记录下来。最近的元分析(亦称荟萃分析，是以一种有意义的统计学方式汇总分散的研究结果的技术)发现，媒介议程与公众议程之间的平均相关系数为+0.49。[14] 考虑到人类沟通现象的平均效应的估计值不过+0.21[15]，便可看出这

一数字的意义。这些强有力的证据的集合,记录了媒介议程与公众议程的时间先后顺序与因果联系的更多细节。以下便是这些证据的一个样本。

1. 1972年夏洛特市的美国总统选举

查普希尔研究的调查面很窄,仅针对投票意向未明的查普希尔选民和他们在1968年秋季选举活动中使用的媒体来源。为了找到议程设置的新证据,调查者在1972年总统选举期间扩大了调查范围,从北卡罗来纳州夏洛特市的所有选民中抽取了具有代表性的样本,在夏秋两季分三次检验了选民使用新闻媒体的情况。[16]研究者确认了在选举年议程设置的两个不同阶段:在夏季与初秋,日报是主要的动员者。《夏洛特观察家报》以巨大容量——几十个版面,而电视网新闻只有半小时——在最初的几个月里影响了公众议程。电视新闻则没有做到这一点。不过,在竞选活动的最后一个月,无论是地方报纸还是电视网,都没有发现什么支持议程设置效果的证据。

除了记录地方报纸对公众的议程设置影响之外,横跨夏秋两季的对这次选举活动的观察还排除了相反假设的存在,证实并非公众议程影响报纸议程。因为只要在两个或更多时点观察媒介议程与公众议程,就有可能同时比较交叉时滞相关系数,这是测量这两种竞争性因果假设的强度的。例如,第一时点上的报纸议程对第二时点上的公众议程的影响,可以与第一时点上的公众议程对第二时点上的报纸议程的影响进行比较。在夏洛特研究中,议程设置的假设胜出。

1972年总统竞选活动的议题议程包括三个与个人非常相关的议题,即经济、毒品和旨在促进公立学校种族融合的校车接送问题,还包括四个与个人关系较远的议题,即水门丑闻、美苏关系和美中关系、环境及越战问题。所有这七个议题在公众议程中的显著性都受到地方报纸新闻报道方式的影响。

2. 1976年美国三个社区的总统选举

1976年,对整个总统竞选年的深入研究,再一次凸显了新闻媒体的议程设置作用在一年中不同季节的变化。[17]为了捕捉这些变化,从2月到12月,研究者在三个差异很大的社区对选民小组进行了九次访谈。这三个地方是:新罕布什尔州的莱巴嫩市,这是一座小城镇,每个选举年度民主党与共和党都在此地召开预选会,推举总统候选人;印第安纳州的印第安纳波利斯市,这是一座典型的美国中等城市;伊利诺伊州的埃文斯顿市,位于芝加哥市郊,主要是高档住宅区。同时,研究者对三家全国电视网及这三个地区的地方报纸的选举报道进行了内容分析。

在全部三个社区中,春天预选时电视与报纸的议程设置作用都是最大的——这个时段选民刚刚开始接触总统竞选活动。在接下来的时间里,新闻媒体对公众议程的影响呈下降趋势,尤其体现在七个与个人关系较远的议题的显著性上,即外交事务、政府公信力、犯罪、社会问题、环境与能源、政府支出与规模及种族关系。在整个竞选过程中,选民都相当关注与个人关系较大的议题(如经济问题),不管报纸或者电视对这些问题的态度如何。当议题直接影响到人们的生活的时候,人们更可能依靠自身经验而非新闻媒体报道作出判断。

尽管对公众议程上的议题的详细检验有助于我们了解新闻媒体议程设置作用的各种变化,但具体议题因选举而异,因此需要一些汇总性的统计数据,这可以让我们在不同场景下比较议程设置作用的大小。议程设置研究者在说明新闻媒体的议程设置作用时最常用的测量方法是相关性统计。这些统计数据准确地总结了媒介议程与公众议程之间在议题排列顺序上的对应程度。就媒介议程而言,哪个议题被报道得最多,哪个次之;就公众议程而言,哪个是公众认为最重要的议题,哪个次之;等等。

11 　　这些相关性统计数据的数值范围可能从+1.0(完全对应)到0(完全无关)再到-1.0(对应关系完全相反)不等。议程设置理论预测,媒介议程与其后的公众议程之间存在一种高度正相关关系。

　　利用这些相关性统计数据总结1976年对三个社区总统选举长达一年的密切观察所取得的关键成果,我们发现,在春季预选期,即电视与报纸的议程设置影响都达到顶峰时,全国电视的议程与其后的选民议程之间的相关系数为+0.63,这属于显著相关。相反,三家地方报纸的议程与阅读它们的选民的议题议程之间,相关系数仅为+0.34;而此时还是报纸作用最强的时期。尽管流行的观点认为,是电视深刻地影响着社会生活的方方面面,但我们最好先不急于依据这个特定发现对电视与报纸的影响力下定论。在本章的最后部分,我们将对各种传播媒介发挥的议程设置作用进行更慎重和全面的描述。

　　1976年对整个大选年的深入研究提供了另一个机会,来比较议程设置理论的核心假设(是媒介议程影响了公众议程)和与之竞争的因果假设(是公众议程影响了媒介议程)。如前所述,在春季,全国电视的议程与其后的公众议程之间的相关系数为+0.63;而在同一时期,公众议程与其后的全国电视的议程之间的相关系数却仅为+0.22。对照罗泽尔-坎贝尔基线(Rozelle-Campbell baseline,表明随机产生的统计预期值),两者之间的差异被进一步放大。此例中的罗泽尔-坎贝尔基线数值是+0.37。媒介议程设置的相关系数远远大于基线数值,而相反假设的公众议程设置的相关系数则小于基线数值。虽然报纸得出的议程设置的相关系数是相当小的+0.34,但是相反假设的公众议程设置的相关系数更小,仅为+0.08(此例中的罗泽尔-坎贝尔基线数值也是+0.08)。因此,对比之下,媒介议程设置的优势仍然非常明显。在两种情况下,因果影响的相关性证据皆证实:是报纸与电视的议题议程影响了公众的议题议程。

　　最初探测大众传播媒介议程设置作用的这些经验研究覆盖了连

续三届美国总统竞选。研究选举,并非假定议程设置的效果仅限于选举,而是因为全国选举为检验媒介效果创造了一个自然的实验室。在全国选举期间,有关公众议题和其他政治方面的消息不断涌出,如果这些消息可能产生任何重要的社会效果,那么必然在选举日之前显现出来。

除了选举具备的研究媒介效果的这些优势之外,还有一种关注大众传播在全国选举中的作用的持久学术传统,这也有助于议程设置研究。拉扎斯菲尔德及其同事是这种传统的开创者,首先是在1940年,他们进行了针对美国总统选举的伊利县调查;其后是在1948年美国总统选举期间,他们对纽约州的埃尔迈拉市进行了调查。出于这些原因,探索议程设置的最初研究都是在选举背景下进行的。

但是,新闻媒体的议程设置作用既不局限于选举,也不局限于美国,甚至也不局限于广义的政治传播范畴。美国总统选举研究仅仅是个起点。议程设置现象,是传播过程的一个持续和不经意的副产品。在选举与非选举的场景中,在国家与地方的层面上,在世界范围内的各种地理环境下,甚至在持续增加的超越政治传播的广泛议程中,人们都发现了这种现象的存在。不过,下面我们将聚焦于议题议程,这是传播媒介议程设置作用被研究得最透彻的领域。

3. 对公民权利的全国性关注

从1954年至1976年,在包含六次总统选举的二十三年里,公民权利议题的显著性在美国起起落落,但其起伏规律与新闻报道的模式非常吻合。[18] 在20世纪50年代至70年代这三十年里,盖洛普共开展了27次民意测验,其中将公民权利列入国家面临的"最重要问题"的美国人所占的比例,由0到52%不等。将公民权利在公众议程上的显著性的这种持续变化,与27次民意测验之前一个月《纽约时报》头版的新闻报道相比较,结果发现,两者之间的相关系数达到突出的+0.71。即便排除了之前月份新闻报道的影响,相关系数仍然为+0.71。这是有关媒介议程设置作用的特别有说服力的证据。也应当注意,公民权利议题在公众中的显著性主要反映了前一个月新闻报道的重点,这是公众对媒介议程相对短时间内的反应。在这二十三年的研究中,媒介议程在时间上早于公众议程,又为媒介议程影响公众议程这一因果关系的论断提供了进一步的证据——公众议程在相当程度上来自媒介议程。

4. 英国人和美国人对外交事务的关注

显然,新闻媒体是大多数人获知外交事务议题的主要信息来源。在英国和美国,外交事务的显著性均随媒体关注程度的高低有规律地起落。[19]自1990年到2000年,外交事务在英国公众中的显著性与《泰晤士报》上有关外交事务的文章数量之间的相关系数高达+0.54。外交事务在美国公众中的显著性,自1981年到2000年,在二十年间(其中有十年与英国重合)与《纽约时报》上外交事务相关文章数量之间的相关系数也达到+0.38。除了两份报纸上单纯的文章数量发生作用之外,那些报道本国卷入其中的外国新闻内容也对公众议程产生了额外的影响。

5. 德国的舆论

研究者在1986年全年对德国公众议程与媒介议程之间的关系进行了每周对比,结果发现,电视新闻报道强烈地影响了公众对五个不同议题的关注:能源的充足供给、两德关系、欧洲政治、环境保护和国防。[20]

在能源供给议题上,这些议程设置的效果显现了出来。1986年初,这个议题在新闻议程与公众议程上的显著性都很低。但是到了5月,这个议题在新闻议程上迅速升温,公众议程在一周之内同样跟进。

新闻报道由每周几条增加到每周十几条,又猛增到每周一百多条。关注能源供给充足性的公众则从仅占人口的15%,猛增到25%到30%之间。当后来新闻报道减少时,对德国能源供给表示关注的公众数量也随之减少。

同一年,在其他11个议题上,并没有体现出议程设置效果。如前所述,公众并非消极接受媒体安排的集合机器人。在某些议题上,媒体报道的方式与公众的关注之间产生了共鸣;在其他一些议题上,则不存在共鸣。

6. 瑞典选举中的议程设置

在2006年瑞典全国选举期间,一项追踪失业议题的固定样本研究在这个北欧国家发现了明显的议程设置效果。[21] 当新闻媒体集中报道失业问题时,公众也将"失业"列为重要的议题。在那些更关注政治新闻的人中,这种议程设置效果更加明显。

7. 路易维尔市的舆论

至此,在讨论新闻媒体的议程设置作用时,我们检验的例子大都基于大选或者全国范围的舆论表现。然而,在地方公众议题上也存在议程设置效果。我们首先介绍一座美国城市的长期舆论趋势,然后对整体议程以及议程上的八个独立议题的趋势进行分析。[22] 当研究者将肯塔基州路易维尔市自1974年直至1981年的公众议程与《路易维尔时报》的新闻报道进行比较时,发现公众议程与新闻议程之间的总体相关系数为+0.65。然后,进一步分析八个议题在这八年中各自所受关注的起起落落,结果发现排在新闻议程最前面的四个议题产生了强大的议程设置效果,这四个议题是:教育、犯罪、地方环境和地方经济发展。

尽管新闻媒体对很多议题产生影响,但它们并不能完全控制公众议程。在《路易维尔时报》的议程上,排名第五与第六的议题分别是公共娱乐和医疗保健,这两个议题是反向议程设置的例证,也就是说,公众的关注为新闻媒体设置了议程。对另外两个例子的详细分析也表明,媒体的影响力并非无往不胜。长期以来,地方政府的新闻是地方报纸传统上的主要内容,但是公众对地方政府的关注并没有受到新闻报道趋势的影响。也许,地方政府的消息或任何类似的其他话题,大量持续的相关报道只会变成模糊一片的白噪声,起不到信息流的作用。不仅公众对地方政府的关注不受任何新闻界议程设置的影响,而且,新闻报道的趋势也未体现任何反向议程设置的作用,尽管那些年地方政府在公众议程上排名第六。

8. 西班牙、日本和阿根廷的地方舆论

1995年春季,在西班牙潘普洛纳市的公众议程上,失业与城市拥挤(尤其是周末时的老城区)居于前列。[23]研究者将公众议程上的六项主要关注议题与前两周的地方新闻报道相比较,结果发现了高度的对应性。公众议程与地方主流日报之间的匹配程度为+0.90;与潘普洛纳第二大日报的匹配程度为+0.72;与电视新闻的匹配程度则为+0.66。

在拥有32万居民的日本东京都町田市,针对1986年市长选举的一项研究也发现了议程设置效果。[24]该市公众议程上一共有七个议题,将这个公众议程与町田市四家主要报纸的报道进行比较,结果得到了一个虽不突出但也算是显著的相关系数:+0.39。这项研究虽然在年龄、性别和受教育程度不同的选民中没有发现强度的变化,但本书第五章提出的一种心理因素的确提供了对这种相对较低的相关性的解释。

在1997年布宜诺斯艾利斯大都市区的立法机关选举中,也发现了地方层面的议程设置效果。[25]当年9月,在当时的四大议题上,公

众议程与布宜诺斯艾利斯五大报纸的联合议题议程之间的相关系数为+0.20；而到了10月接近选举日的时候，两种议程在四大议题上的对应性却飙升至+0.80。这一增长表明公众在选举活动接近尾声的几周内从新闻媒体那里学到了很多。

1998年，在阿根廷一个主要政治联盟挑选总统候选人的预选中，研究者进一步发现了议程设置效果的有力证据。在当时的六项主要议题上，选举时期的公众议程与前一个月的报纸议程之间的相关系数为+0.60；与电视新闻之间的相关系数甚至更大，为+0.71。[26]

四、在其他议题上的重复验证

相似的证据还来自20世纪80年代的系列研究，即在41个月的时间里对美国11个不同议题的单项分析，结果表明新闻报道对舆论趋势的影响会发生变化。[27]在对11个议题中的每一个进行分析时，媒介议程基于电视、报纸和新闻杂志报道的混合；公众议程则来自13次盖洛普民意测验中对国家面临的最重要问题的回答。在这些分析中，显然可以看出两种模式。首先，除了一个议题之外，媒介议程与公众议程在其他议题上均呈正相关，这些议程的中位相关系数为+0.45。在道德议题上则呈负相关，这很容易解释：因为新闻媒体很少提出道德议题。

对于这一时期除道德外的其他10个公众议题来说，所有相关系数都是正向的。这显示了相当程度的议程设置效果。然而，两种议程之间联系的强度也存在明显的差异。这要求我们注意，对于当今的最重要问题，在媒体报道之外，也存在其他影响公众感受的因素。本书第五章和第六章将讨论各种心理与社会因素。这些因素在公众与传播媒介围绕时下议题进行的每日交流中具有重要意义。它们能够提高或者限制媒介发挥影响的程度。

五、原因和结果

此处回顾的证据,加上在世界各地进行的其他领域的许多研究,都证实了媒介议程与公众议程之间存在因果关系。证明这种因果关系的第一个必要条件是,在假定的原因及其结果之间存在显著的相关性。全球范围内数百个议程设置研究都满足了这种证据条件。

证明这种因果关系的第二个必要条件是,有时间先后顺序。在时间上,原因必须先于结果。在早先的查普希尔研究中,研究者就已经留意并列两种议程的结果,将民意调查获知的公众对当前议题的关注与新闻媒体在访谈之前几周及调查进行时的报道内容进行比较。[28]在接下来的两场美国总统选举中,议程设置效果的证据来自固定样本研究。1972年总统选举期间,研究者分别于6月和10月在夏洛特市进行了两轮调查采访与内容分析,在选举之后,马上又进行了第三轮采访。[29]在1976年总统选举期间,从2月到12月,研究者对三个不同社区先后进行了九轮采访,并对全年的地方报纸与全国电视新闻进行了内容分析。[30]这两次固定样本的设计都对媒介议程与公众议程之间关系的时间顺序进行了详细的检测。

此处回顾的议程设置效果的其他证据,来自各种非选举的情况,也包括历时性研究。这些设计可以对媒介议程与公众议程之间关系的时间顺序进行详细检测。对美国公民权利议题的研究跨越了二十三年的时间[31];还有11项重复验证的此类研究出现于20世纪80年代,研究者在41个月里对单项议题进行了分析[32];在德国,1986年的一项深入研究对五个议题进行了逐周分析[33];研究者还在八年时间里对路易维尔的八个地方议题展开了分析,既有总体的,又有个别的[34]。

议程设置效果的所有这些证据都建立在"现实世界"的基础上,也就是说,基于随机抽样的民意调查和对实际存在的新闻媒体的内容分析。这些证据显示了在广泛背景下的议程设置效果;它们之所以极具说服力,正是因为它们描绘了现实世界中的公众意见。然而,对议程设置理论的核心命题(媒介议程影响公众议程)而言,这种现实描摹并不是最佳的证据,因为对媒介议程和公众议程的这些测量与许多未受控制的因素联系在一起。

要证实新闻媒体是产生这些效果的原因,最好也是最没有争议的证据来自实验室中的控制实验。在这种环境中,理论上的起因可以得到系统控制,受试者被随机安排到不同形式的控制条件下参与实验,然后研究者对各种结果进行系统比较。来自实验室的证据提供了媒介议程影响公众议程之因果链条中的第三条,也是最后一条,即表明媒介议程的内容与公众对此议程的反应之间存在一种直接的功能性关系。

在实验室里,研究者让受试者观看经过剪辑以强调特定公众议题的电视新闻节目,结果是国防、污染、军备控制、公民权利、失业以及其他一些议题的显著性发生了改变。[35]研究者采用了各种控制手段,以确认某受控议题显著性的变化事实上来自受试者与新闻议程的接触。例如,在一个实验中,一些受试者观看的电视新闻节目强调了国防,而控制组所观看的电视节目中并没有与国防相关的内容。比较结果发现,国防议题在测试组受试者中的显著性变化远远大于控制组中受试者的变化。相反,在其他七个议题上,这两组受试者在观看新闻之前与之后都没有明显的差异。

有两个实验调查了网上新闻对个人议程的影响,更新了实验室研究的因果证据。其中一个实验比较了国际议题在《纽约时报》印刷版与网络版的读者中的显著性。虽然在读者中,印刷版比网络版体现出更强的议程设置效果,但两组读者与没有看过《纽约时报》的控制组相比,差异却更加明显。实验者认为,"互联网新闻的当代化身正在巧妙地,但却必然地改变着新闻媒体设置公众议程的方式"[36]。因此,这些实验为将来进一步探索议程设置的过程开启了一扇新门。另一个实验让受试者收看 CNN 播出的新闻或者访问 CNN 的新闻网站,然后让他们回忆头条新闻并对重要议题进行排序,[37]结果显示,电视新闻对观众的影响要强于网络新闻的影响。当然,可以争辩的是,网页形式并不总能保留媒介议程的显著性线索。

近年来,研究者也采用实地实验的方式,在实验室之外检验新闻媒体的议程设置效果。这种设计的长处是,由于测量结果来自现实世界而非实验室,因此实验设计强大的内在效度与同样强大的外在效度相匹配。最知名的实验是由哈佛大学的加里·金(Gary King)及其同事开展的。[38]经过三年的谈判,他和他的同事成功招募到几个新闻机构参与实验,包括著名的出版物《国家》杂志与《赫芬顿邮报》。其后,在一年半的时间里,每次两到五个媒体,采用不同的组合方式,自愿就11 个广泛选题(如移民、气候、教育等)中的任一个同时撰写故事。每一组故事都由这些媒体在连续两周内的一周予以报道。这些报道的影响是通过比较刊登故事的"处理"周与没有出现这些故事的"控制"周的结果来测量的。每当他们启动这种实验程序,研究者都对推特上的对话内容自动进行分析。通过检验与所选择题目相关的推特讨论,研究者发现,在故事出现后的一周里,讨论增加了 60%。马修·根茨科(Matthew Gentzkow)在《科学》杂志上评论这个实验时总结说,这一研究"提供了迄今为止关于媒介议程设置作用的最坚实、最有说服力的数据点之一"[39]。

虽然实验室研究有时被批评为人造情境,但是它们为新闻媒体的议程设置作用提供了重要的补充证据。议程设置效果的完整证据,既需要实验的内在效度,即对媒介议程和公众议程进行的严格控制和测量;也需要内容分析和调查研究的外在效度,即其设计足以保证我们的发现超越直接观察到的现象,能够推广到现实世界更广泛的情境中。从这两方面的证据来看,议程设置理论的一个主要贡献在于,将特定的媒体内容与它在公众中产生的效果明确地联系在一起。

六、一种新的传播景观

近几十年来,随着传播渠道的大量扩展,特别是互联网站点和个人化社交媒体的持续增长,我们已经进入一个议程设置研究的新时代,需要为三个主要的研究问题寻找答案。

1. 网络媒体会对公众产生议程设置效果吗?

在20世纪90年代和21世纪初的大多数时间里,对网上媒介议程设置效果的关注都集中于这样的问题,即新闻网站、博客、电子公告牌、竞选网站和搜索引擎等如何影响传统媒体——或者被传统媒体所影响,这种现象通常被称为"媒体间议程设置"。一般而言,证据显示了主流媒体与网络媒体之间的双向关系,两类议程相互作用、彼此强化。[40]随着21世纪头十年中期社交媒体平台及新的党派喉舌的到来,这些关于议题议程互惠作用的最初发现大部分得到了验证。[41]

在关于媒体间议程设置的比较研究中,鲜少有研究记录下网上媒介议程对公众议程产生的效果。不过,针对这一问题的一项初步的概述性研究,却发现了对议程设置基本假设的强大支持证据。[42]例如,在2010年美国参议院选举期间,对竞选网站的一次分析发现,候选人网站在印第安纳波利斯选民中成功地影响了七个议题的显著性。[43]转向对网上新闻媒体进行研究,如前所述,已发现CNN网络版的读者增加了对一系列国家议题的关注;而在一次实验室研究中,阅读《纽约时报》网络版的受试者也增加了对外交事务的关注。[44]在韩国,两个非传统的网上新闻社——OhmyNews(哦!我的新闻)和PRESSian(报料人)——影响了公众对美国军车导致两个女孩死亡事件的关注,这一争议事件引发了大规模的反美抗议活动。[45]网络媒体和传统媒体的议题议程的同质性,无疑有助于数字渠道对公众的优先选项施加强大的影响,我们将简要讨论一下这个话题。[46]

随着过去几十年社交媒体的兴起,研究者已将关注焦点置于脸书和推特等社交平台在影响公众议程方面所起的作用。在西班牙进行的一项研究,借助传统的"最重要问题",检验了通过脸书消费新闻的行为是否与背离集合性公众议程的个性化议程有关。[47]将受众调查与网页追踪的数据相结合,作者们发现:个体越多地使用脸书作为获取新闻的门径,他们提及公众议程上前两个议题的可能性便越小(当时公众议程上的两大议题是失业与腐败)。尽管统计结果是显著的,但效果却很小。特别是,那些不使用脸书看新闻的人在回答"最重要问题"时,有47%的可能提及失业与腐败;在一般脸书用户中,这种可能性降至35%。然而,对比调查对象提及的全部"最重要问题",统计结果却显示,脸书的影响并不显著。

另一项研究[48]分析了美国36家新闻媒体与随机抽取的不同使用者两年内所发推文的相互影响。首先,在媒体机构与不同类型的使用者(即关注推特的公众、一般公众、民主党支持者和共和党支持者)群体之间,关注议题的相关系数从+0.55到+0.79不等。这意味着,在议题议程之间存在中度到有力的相关关系。其次,最重要的是,时间序列分析可以建立因果关系:究竟相关性是源自新闻媒体在推特上设置公众议程的能力,还是反过来,来自公众的讨论对其后的新闻议程的影响?结果是相当一致的:

> 值得注意的是,在每一案例中,以媒体关注的变化来预测之后所有受众关注的变化都更加可行,而不是相反,由此可以确认:媒体机构在引导政治关注方面发挥关键作用。[49]

总而言之,现有研究确认了从媒介议程到公众议程的显著性转移。这种证据不仅发现于传统的新闻媒体机构,也来自新的互动性数字平台。[50]也就是说,只要人们还使用媒体,媒体内容为公众的关切设置议程的潜力便始终存在。

2. 网络媒体激增削弱了传统媒体的议程设置作用吗?

近几十年来,传播景观正在转型,先是有线电视,紧接着是卫星电视,加入了传统的大众传播媒介队伍;现在,网站和个人化的社交媒体又急剧增加。随着传播景观的转变,一些观察家已经预言:我们在过去半个多世纪里所观察到的议程设置效果将会减弱,如果不是完全消失的话。[51]这个预言的论据是,大量互动式媒体带来的无数内容加剧了对注意力的竞争,于是挑战了传统新闻在人们日常媒介使用中的地位。[52]然而,尽管对这种可能性的猜测十分流行,但迄今为止,占压倒优势的证据却告诉我们,媒介议程设置的作用仍在持续。借用马克·吐温(Mark Twain)给美联社的著名电报中的话,就是——关于议程设置已经死亡的报告是极为夸张的。

一项广泛的历时性研究分析了《纽约时报》自1956年至2004年报道的公众在盖洛普民意调查中对"国家面临的最重要问题"的回答,结果表明:这些效果的强度虽有变化,但并未发现随着时间的推移而清晰可辨的趋势。[53]在更近的一项时间序列分析中,这一发现得到了验证。来自瑞典的这个研究收集了1992—2014年的媒体内容和舆论资料,同时,作者们就12个不同政治议题的相关公众意见分析了整体层面和个体层面的议程设置效果。研究结果显示,在2014年,亦即存在很多可选媒介的年代,传统的新闻媒体在设置公众议程时仍然像1992年一样具有影响力,而那时的选择则非常有限。[54]同样,在智利进行了一项研究,对广播电视从2001年到2016年的议程设置能力进行了历时性分析[55],发现媒介议程和公众议程之间的相关系数平均为+0.75。不仅如此,也并没有出现直线下降的趋势——如果说2001年的相关系数徘徊在+0.90的话,那么到了2016年,它还停留在强有力的+0.80。

另一种追踪因数字渠道激增而发生的议程设置效果的变化的方式,是通过群组分析(cohort analysis)对比不同世代的个体对媒介议程影响的易感性。虽然在新的传播媒介环境中,不同世代的人使用媒介的方式的确出现了分化,但对北卡罗来纳州和路易斯安那州进行的全州范围的调查发现,议程设置的效果在青年、中年和老年世代中的差异很小。[56]年轻的成年人更依赖互联网而较少关注传统媒体,但这种现象对议程设置效果强弱的影响不大。特别令人信服的是,在路易斯安那州对互联网的高度使用者和低度使用者的议题议程与本州主要报纸的议题议程进行的比较研究。互联网低度使用者的议题议程与报纸议程之间的相关系数是+0.90,而在互联网的高度使用者中,相关系数是+0.70。

与此类似,比较《纽约时报》的议题议程与老中青三个世代在1976年至2004年全部美国选举年的议题议程,在长期趋势中并没有发现与新媒体的出现相关的拐点。[57]总的模式是,一种议程设置强效果贯穿始终,一代人与一代人之间没有太大的差异,尽管他们使用媒体的方式已然不同。在这些年里,青年一代与媒介议程之间的相关系数中位数为+0.77,数值范围在+0.55至+0.93之间。35—54岁的中年人与媒介议程之间的相关系数中位数是+0.79,数值范围在+0.66至+0.93之间。55岁及以上者与媒介议程之间的相关系数中位数是+0.77,数值范围在+0.61至+0.93之间。

不仅如此,前面讨论过的元分析[58]也显示,研究成果出版的年份并不是预测议程设置效果强度的重要指标,这意味着,传统的新闻媒体(它们是这篇元分析论文所使用的文章中研究最多的媒体)的影响力像以往一样强大。

过去几十年里议程设置效果的强度,以及它们在当今环境中的持续强度,都来自媒介和公众长期的行为方式。在最初的查普希尔调查中发现的媒介议程之间的高度同质性持续至今。巴勃罗·博奇科夫斯基(Pablo Boczkowski)不仅在布宜诺斯艾利斯的主要报纸与网络报纸的新闻议程中看到了高度的同质性,而且发现,自 1995 年到 2005 年,这些新闻议程越来越相似。他将这种趋势归因于,现在能从网上和电视上得到的新闻严重过剩,强化了新闻工作者长期以来形成的关注竞争对手的职业习惯。[59]在公众中,强大的议程设置效果源于公民渗透(civic osmosis):个人持续接触来自众多传播渠道的浩瀚信息海洋。[60]詹姆斯·韦伯斯特(James Webster)和托马斯·克西翁热克(Thomas Ksiazek)对尼尔森公司 2009 年 3 月从 1000 户家庭采集到的电视和互联网数据进行了网络分析,他们提到:

> 我们发现 236 家媒体的受众高度重复,这意味着公众的关注存在重叠现象,而非由忠实受众组成隔绝的群体。[61]

对多数人而言,接触新闻的范围从习惯性地刻意关注某些新闻渠道,转向在日常生活中偶然地接触其他新闻渠道。而这些新闻渠道的同质性带来的结果则是,公众对时下主要议题的高度共识。

3. 与传播格式塔(整体)的集合影响相比,特定传播渠道的效果如何?

长期以来,对媒介效果的兴趣,常常伴随着对不同传播渠道取得这种效果的相对能力的迷恋。议程设置的研究也不例外。一旦人们了解了议程设置的基本思想,他们马上就会问:哪种媒介最能设置公众议程? 在 20 世纪后半叶,研究的注意力特别指向印刷媒体与电视媒体的比较。现在,对大量社交媒体的研究也加入了这个行列。对这一问题的最好回答是:"视情况而定。"不管是所有这些渠道同声齐唱,千部一腔,鲜有差别;抑或是其中一两个渠道在影响力方面明显地超越其他渠道;在这样那样的情况下,形势相当不同。即使在差异的确存在的地方,多数渠道也都对这种议程设置的效果有所贡献。我们是在一片新闻与信息的汪洋大海中游泳,传播渠道的格式塔意味着,总体效果大于部分之和。

然而,在这些年检验媒介效果的研究中,一直存在着强调个别媒介甚于媒介集体的倾向,尤其是在关于媒介效果和政治极化的文献中。这是议程设置文献中在"属性议程设置"标题之下的一批研究成果。例如,在2012年美国大选背景下进行的一项研究发现,与中立的广播网(CNN和NBC)相比,党派渠道(如福克斯新闻网)更强调候选人的情感属性(如道德、领导力、关爱、智慧和忠诚),由此产生了不同的议程设置过程。[62]这种研究路径证实,人们受到他们所选择使用的媒体的影响。这样看来,受众的极化以及随之而来的碎片化并未减弱个体层面的媒介效果。

与此相反,"公民渗透"的概念强调了媒介的集体作用。新媒体激增为这种传播格式塔增加了丰富多样的动态渠道。我们畅游于其间的,是潮流越来越多的海洋。我们有必要了解这片海洋中的各种潮流,既包括促进了传播的活水,也包括污染了海洋的污秽。总而言之,我们需要了解作为整体的信息海洋,它是怎样随着时间的推移而变化和更替,又是如何影响到公众议程的。从我们这个领域出现的最早期直到现在,大量的经验证据表明,人们一直从这种传播格式塔中获得新闻和信息。在进行基准式的1940年伊利县研究时,拉扎斯菲尔德及其同事便在人们使用的各种大众媒介中发现了相当多的重叠。

> 高度接触某种传播媒介的人也更倾向于高度接触其他媒介。很少有人大量接触一种媒介而极少接触其他媒介。[63]

尽管在回答调查问题时,人们可能举出特定的新闻媒体作为他们主要的消息来源——例如,早晨多数时间阅读的报纸,多少有些规律地收听的广播或者收看的电视新闻——但是,人们远非与更大的新闻环境绝缘。在1996年西班牙的全国选举中,人们对所使用的主要媒体的议程的同意程度,与他们对这家媒体主要竞争者的议程的同意程度高度相似。[64]例如,将《纳瓦拉日报》作为主要新闻来源的选民,与该报议程设置之间的相关系数为+0.62;而他们对竞争性的地方报纸的赞同程度则为+0.57。经过18组对比,不同媒体相关系数的中位数差异只有0.09。

回到前面对日报在当前世代中的议程设置效果的比较:

> 尽管证据表明年轻世代不像年长世代一样常常接触传统媒介,的确,他们使用互联网明显更多,但那种径直认为媒介的多元化导致我们所熟知的公众共同议程终结的观点,支持的证据很少。相反,年轻人不同的媒介使用习惯似乎根本没有显著地影响议程设置的效果。[65]

在2006年瑞典的全国选举期间,杰斯珀·斯特龙巴克(Jesper Stromback)和斯皮罗·基欧瑟斯(Spiro Kiousis)测量了九种主要新闻媒体的日常新闻使用的影响。他们分析了包括报纸、电视和广播在内的混合数据后发现:

> 关注政治新闻对公众感知到的议题显著性产生了明显的和相当强烈的影响;对政治新闻的关注,比对广播和电视上各种特定新闻节目的关注,或者对不同报纸的关注,都更为重要。[66]

这一发现并未否认存在更有力量和更具影响力的报纸、广播电视台和网站。然而,站远点去看,却是更宏大的汇集传播声音的格式塔确定了我们的社会肌理。更常见的是,传播的主要效果产生于媒介的集体作用及公民渗透的持续过程。公民渗透的一个重要方面,便是公众可接触到的新闻渠道数量众多。当个人被问及本地或者全国面临的最重要问题时,回答者提到的不同问题的数目与本地区媒体声音的多寡显著相关。[67]

小　结

本章列举的远非所有关于新闻媒体对公众施加议程设置影响的积累证据,但却是涵盖广泛的一个证据样本。此处展示的例子描述了在美国、英国、西班牙、德国、日本和阿根廷等各种全国和地方的背景下,不同媒介在选举期和较平静的政治时期,对许多全国和地方议题的议程设置效果,从1968年直至今天。最近的研究也记录了娱乐媒体的议程设置效果,例如奥普拉·温弗里(Oprah Winfrey)的日间电视脱口秀节目。[68]

当然,还有其他一些重要的影响因素塑造着个人的态度与公众的意见。我们对某个议题的感知,可能源于我们的个体经验和普遍文化,或者源于我们接触的传播媒介。[69]舆论的趋势是随着时间的推移由新的世代、外部事件和传播媒介共同塑造的。[70]然而,关于议程设置效果的这些累积证据支持的一般命题依然是,新闻工作者确实对受众头脑中关于世界的图像产生了重要的影响。

在大多数情况下,这种议程设置作用是传媒无意中造成的副产品,因为它们每日必须关注若干新闻话题。而大量媒体将关注投到少数几个议题上,便向受众传达了一个明确的消息,即什么是当前最重要的议题。议程设置将我们的注意力引向舆论形成的早期阶段,那时议题刚刚出现并首次引起公众的关注,在这种情况下,新闻工作者负有一种强烈的道德责任,需要谨慎地为自己的议程选择议题。

本章列举的议程设置例子,以理论的术语说明了议题的显著性从媒介议程向公众议程的转移。在接下来的章节中,我们会看到,议程设置作为一种关于显著性转移的理论,并不仅限于从媒介议程到公众议程的转移,甚至也不限于公众议题的议程。当代社会中有许多议程。除了定义舆论形成背景下的各种议程之外,这种关于显著性转移的思想已经被应用于很多其他场合。第八章就讨论了几种新的、更广泛的应用方式,将议程设置理论扩展到了政治传播领域之外。但是首先,我们将为我们这幅关于媒介议程对公众议程的因果影响的理论地图添加进一步的细节。

第二章　现实与新闻

一些新闻工作者拒绝承认媒介对公众存在任何议程设置作用。他们说:"我们只是报道新闻,也就是世界上正在发生的事。"一些批评议程设置观点的人也持有相似的假定,他们声称,公众只是对他们周围的环境作出反应而已,媒介也是一样。也就是说,媒介议程与公众议程之间的联系是虚假的。然而,李普曼却认为,新闻媒体是"外部世界与我们头脑中的图像"之间的桥梁,在论及新闻媒体的这种作用时,李普曼引进了"拟态环境"的概念,指称存在于我们头脑中的关于世界的图景——一种与现实相比总是不完整且通常不准确的图景。李普曼断言,我们的行为是对这个拟态环境的反应,而非对真实环境的反应。在对传播媒介的议程设置效果进行了几十年社会科学研究之后的今天,积累的证据进一步强调了李普曼在真实环境与拟态环境之间作出区分的重要性。

这种区分并非声称新闻全为凭空杜撰——绝非如此。新闻工作是一种基于可验证的观察的经验活动。多年来,全球新闻界出现重大丑闻,就是因为不能遵守这一职业伦理。然而,每日发生的事件及情势经过新闻机构的职业透镜折射,常常就是另一幅世界图像,一种拟态环境。如果以更加系统的方式细究起来,这种拟态环境与真实环境相去甚远。许多事件与情势都在努力吸引新闻工作者的注意。但新闻工作者既没有能力采集到这些事件的所有相关信息,也没有必要将有关事件的所有情形都告知公众,因此,他们凭借一套传统的职业规范来指导自己,撷取每日环境中的新闻。结果便是,新闻媒体呈现的不过是更大的环境中很有限的一部分情景,就像通过某些现代建筑物的狭窄窗口看到的一样,只是极为有限的景观。如果窗户玻璃的透明度不高,光滑度欠佳,这个比喻就更为传神了。

一、怪异的图像

《纽约客》杂志有一张著名的封面图,戏仿曼哈顿区居民对整个美国的认识。在这幅呈现整个国家的地图上,凸显着一个非常大的纽约市,另一侧则是相当大的加利福尼亚州,中间各州都紧紧地挤在一起,几乎不存在。还有一幅相似的地图,画的是得克萨斯人对美国的认识。当然,图上主要是一个巨大的得克萨斯州,其他47个州都被画得小小的,挤在边缘。这两幅心理地图都与人们在学校中学到的美国地图不同。它们虽然夸张,但却是美国人活生生的心理反映。下面,我们将思考几个经验例证,看看新闻媒体刻画的世界"地图"以及随后在公众中出现的观点,是如何与讽刺纽约人和得克萨斯人的著名图画有异曲同工之妙的。

1. 美国舆论的十年

在整个动荡的20世纪60年代,美国在广泛议题上的全国舆论一再证实现在我们已经非常熟悉的一种模式,即新闻媒体产生重要的议程设置效果。[1]在这十年的民意调查中,当盖洛普公司要求美国人指出国家面临的"最重要问题"时,越南战争、种族关系与城市暴动、校园骚乱和通货膨胀等议题总是居于公众议程的前列。将20世纪60年代公众议程上所有14个主要议题的显著性,与《时代周刊》《新闻周刊》《美国新闻与世界报道》三大杂志对同样议题的报道相比较,结果显示出高度的一致性:新闻议程与公众议程之间的相关系数为+0.78。

有批评意见认为,媒介议程与公众议程之间的这种高度相关是误导性的,因为媒体与公众都不过是在对"外部世界"作出反应。为了反驳这种观点,雷·芬克豪泽(Ray Funkhouser)主要采用《美国统计摘要》的数据,创建了一个历史议程。例如,越南战争的显著性,是以美国在20世纪60年代投入的兵力的大幅度变化来测量的。像这样将"现实控制"引进分析,极大地凸显了议程设置过程的力量。数据显示,媒体对越南战争、校园骚乱和城市暴动的报道数量达到顶峰的时间,要比这些事件达到历史高峰的时间提前一两年。在报道顶峰出现的年份,所有这些议题的实际情形通常都与其他年份没有什么差别。在某些情况下,当问题显示好转时,对问题的报道却增多了;或者是,当问题增多时,报道数量却下降了。芬克豪泽发现,"媒体报道的模式与任何议题的现实情况都不存在一一对应的关系"[2]。简言之,20世纪60年代的媒介议程与公众议程在保持高度相关的同时,却都与这一时期的历史趋势存在距离,且不甚相关。

此处将"历史现实"纳入分析是特别重要的贡献,尤其证明了媒介对公众议程产生效果的因果关系。因为证据有力地反驳了认为新闻的报道与公众的关切都仅仅是对现实世界作出反应的那种批评,说明媒介构造并呈现给公众的是一个拟态环境,而这个拟态环境明显塑造了公众看待世界的方式。

2. 制造危机

1973年秋天,德国报纸呈现出多幅怪异图像,与超出个人直接经验的大环境有关。[3]自9月上旬到12月下旬,每周报纸对本国石油供给量的负面陈述都超过了正面消息。不仅如此,在10月至11月,将当时的局势描述为一场"危机"的报道稳步增加。直到1974年1月和

2月,关于危机的讨论才收住势头,新闻报道对局势的评估出现了正面与负面平衡的情况。

那么,在那个秋季与冬季,德国真的发生了一场能源危机吗?触发这些新闻报道的是阿拉伯国家在秋季早期采取的提高油价与联合抵制的一系列措施,主要针对美国和荷兰。事实上,德国在当年9月和10月的石油进口量均明显高于前一年的同期,11月的进口量同比则基本持平。尽管宣称"一场石油危机正在到来"并无事实基础,但是德国的五家报纸——三家覆盖主要政治光谱的全国性精英报纸和两家小报——从当年9月直到第二年的2月共发表了1400多篇有关石油和石油产品的供给的文章,足以让这种"危机"的形势出现在公众议程上。

在11月开展的一系列民意调查中,超过三分之二的受访车主担心出现燃油供给的严重短缺。在12月,随着负面报道数量的减少,担心燃油短缺的人数也减少到受访车主的二分之一,后来又减少到大约三分之一。

根据报纸的描述,能源形势的显著性在德国公众中激发了强烈的行为反应。购买石油产品的行为在10月份数量猛增。石油与柴油燃料的销量同比增长了7%,重燃油增长了15%,轻燃油增长了31%。虽然10月的石油进口量超过了去年同期,11月的石油进口量与去年同期基本持平,但是由于需求量非比寻常的激增,零星地区确实出现了石油短缺的情况。在接下来的几个月里,石油销量大幅降低,不难预料,主要原因在于消费者之前的囤积。

1973年发生在德国的这场石油"危机"源于需求的急剧增长;而刺激需求增长的,是密集的报纸报道,而并非现实中供给的严重短缺。在这种情况下,报纸的议程设置效果超出了在公众中制造显著性与提高关注度的范围,即几百项研究所证实的通常的认知效应,还包括一种行为效应,即消费者根据自己对形势的判断作出了个体反应。

3. 对毒品问题的全国关注

相似的情况出现于 20 世纪 80 年代的美国。《纽约时报》在 1985 年底"发现"了毒品问题,并发表了第一篇相关报道(总共发表了一百多篇),此后,公众对毒品的关注持续升温。[4] 在《纽约时报》的带领下,第二年《新闻周刊》也刊发了有关这一议题的封面报道,随即两大全国电视网进行了特别报道,全美的报纸都卷入了毒品报道的浪潮。不难预测,公众对毒品问题的关注度也随之上升。

《纽约时报》的这种议程设置效果,主要体现在对其他新闻媒体、公众以及联邦政府的影响上,效果因 1986 年中期体育明星与毒品有关的死亡事件而得到巩固,如全美篮球运动员伦·拜亚斯(Len Bias)和职业橄榄球运动员唐·罗杰斯(Don Rogers)。但是,这些戏剧性事件只不过是维持了业已存在的媒介议程而已。在新闻媒体中,毒品议题日益显著,随后公众对毒品议题的关注也相应增加。这是一个"纯粹"由媒体设置议题议程的突出例证,因为在所有这些月份中,毒品的实际使用量并没有任何变化。毒品问题之所以在全国议程上出现,源自新闻工作者对某种形势的认知,而非公众对现实变化作出的反应。

但是全国的关注是爆炸性的。布什政府发动了一场重大的媒体宣传活动;作为对此的回应,《纽约时报》的报道与舆论关注的程度在 1989 年都达到了顶峰。1989 年 9 月,63% 的美国公众认为,毒品是国家面临的最重要问题——这可是一个天文数字。而一年之后,持这种观点的公众就只有 9% 了。由新闻媒体、总统和普通公众构成的议程设置三重奏反映了一系列不断变化的复杂关系。[5] 然而,这个三位一体的组合与外部世界的关系通常是脆弱的,它对公众议题投以关注的时间往往也是不确定的。[6]

4. 罪行恐惧

另外一个例子发生在 20 世纪 90 年代。在这个例子中,一个公众议题的议程设置过程同样完全缺乏任何重要的现实依据。1992年,得克萨斯民意调查询问公众什么是国家面临的最重要问题,从框2.1的答案中我们可以看到,只有2%的人提及犯罪行为。到了1993年秋天,15%的人的答案是犯罪。接下来,在1994年上半年的两次民意调查中,超过三分之一的得克萨斯受访者提到了犯罪。这样的关注度高得异乎寻常,因为盖洛普民意调查自20世纪30年代开始询问这个问题,问过不知道多少次,但是极少发现公众对某个问题如此关注。在1995年和1996年初,对犯罪的关注程度多少有些下降;但即便是在那时,仍有大约20%的得克萨斯人认为犯罪行为是国家面临的最重要问题。

框2.1 关于犯罪的报纸报道与公众关注

时间段	得克萨斯民意调查* %	达拉斯与休斯敦报纸中关于犯罪的文章数量	
		总数	剔除对辛普森和赛琳娜的报道
1992年夏	2	173	173
1993年秋	15	228	228
1994年冬	37	292	292
1994年春	36	246	246
1994年夏	29	242	216
1994年秋	22	220	205
1995年冬	24	233	207
1995年春	21	248	211
1995年夏	19	212	200
1995年秋	15	236	126

*这是在得克萨斯民意调查中认为犯罪是国家面临的最重要问题的受访者比例。

来源:Salma Ghanem, 'Media coverage of crime and public opinion: an exploration of the second level of agenda setting', unpublished doctoral dissertation, University of Texas at Austin, 1996。

具有讽刺意味的是,当公众对犯罪的关注上升到不同寻常的高度时,现实的犯罪统计数字却表明,同期的犯罪率实际在下降。当然,面对下降的犯罪率,刺激公众关注程度提升的原因很可能是新闻媒体的犯罪报道。框2.1还记录了1993年晚期、1994年和1995年得克萨斯两大报纸《达拉斯晨报》和《休斯敦纪事报》对犯罪主题的密集报道模式。在所有九个时间段里,犯罪报道的数量均超过了1992年夏季,当时公众中也很少有人表现出对犯罪的关注。

详细分析框2.1中记录的这些趋势,可以发现,得克萨斯主要报纸中犯罪报道增加的模式在之后的舆论中得到了反映。[7]在整整两年半的时间里,公众将犯罪认作主要社会问题的关注趋势与媒体犯罪报道的密集模式之间的相关系数为+0.70。即便考虑到这一时期发生过两起耸人听闻的重大犯罪事件,新闻报道与公众对犯罪的关注之间的高度一致性依然成立。1994年夏天,新闻媒体开始在世界范围内大量报道辛普森(O. J. Simpson)杀妻案。辛普森是著名的橄榄球明星,后来成为体育评论员,他被指控在洛杉矶的一条人行道上捅死了他的妻子及其朋友。1995年春季,在得克萨斯州非常有名的西班牙裔歌手赛琳娜(Selena)被谋杀。从1994年夏季一直到第二年秋季,在所有犯罪报道中,对这两起谋杀案的报道占到总量的将近六分之一。有人可能会认为,对这两起耸人听闻的谋杀案(其中一起实际上就发生在得克萨斯)的报道可以解释得克萨斯公众对犯罪问题的高度关注。但是,即便从分析中剔除了所有关于辛普森和赛琳娜案件的新闻报道,媒介议程与公众议程之间的高度一致性仍然存在,相关系数为+0.73。

在芝加哥、费城和旧金山的日报读者中,也发现了公众对报纸犯罪报道的相同反应模式。这三个城市都各有两家竞争性的报纸,它们的犯罪报道风格与方式完全不同,一种比较克制,另一种则比较大胆。在所有这三个城市中,将大量新闻篇幅用于犯罪报道的报纸的读者显示出来的罪行恐惧,都要高于另一份报纸的读者。[8]

在此,报纸并不是唯一的肇事者。电视的作用或许更大,它更多的是通过娱乐节目而非新闻报道的方式,在观众中培植一种对罪行和暴力的恐惧。乔治·格伯纳(George Gerbner)及其同事将这种世界观命名为"邪恶世界综合征"(the mean world syndrome)。通过多年来对电视受众的深入研究,他们得出结论说:"电视上会频繁出现暴力行为,几乎无法避免,因此,长期接触电视,易于使人将世界想象成相对邪恶和危险的。"[9]这种娱乐电视节目会设置一种长期议程的断言得到了相当多证据的支持。

另一项研究广泛考察了华盛顿特区的地方电视犯罪新闻报道的效果[10],不仅补充了对美国地方报纸犯罪新闻的调查,而且推进了对娱乐电视节目在犯罪与暴力方面的涵化效果的研究。研究的结果通常与议程设置理论和涵化分析有关。前一种结果是,人们指认犯罪是最重要的问题;后一种结果则是,人们产生了成为犯罪受害者的风险感和夜间独行的恐惧感。这个研究除了让受试者接触地方电视新闻(内含大量暴力内容)之外,还测量了三组现实情况,作为研究结果的预测变量。这三组现实情况是:作为犯罪受害者的直接经验,地方街区犯罪率,以及身为某个犯罪受害者的朋友、邻居或者亲戚。在观看地方电视新闻与将犯罪认作华盛顿都市区面临的一个重要问题之间,存在非常密切的联系;但是,只有一种现实情况影响到了受试者对华盛顿都市区犯罪问题严重程度的看法,那便是地方街区的犯罪率。相比之下,观看地方电视新闻与涵化分析预测的任何结果都没有联系,但是几乎一半的现实测量明显地关联到对罪行的恐惧感。

在智利对电视报道犯罪议题进行了一次类似的分析,所发现的议程设置和涵化效果大都可与美国调查的结果相比拟。[11]尤其是,对收集到的2001年至2012年的舆论数据、电视新闻和犯罪率进行的一项时间序列分析发现,四家主要广播电视网的犯罪新闻报道量对罪行恐惧及指认犯罪为智利面临的最重要问题的公众比例具有独立的效果,这种效果超出了犯罪受害率和经济不安全趋势的影响。不仅如此,在2001年至2006年,虽然犯罪受害率实际上是稳定的,但黄金时段的新闻节目报道犯罪的时间却增加了一倍,于是,指认犯罪为最重要问题的人数也增加了一倍。个体层次的数据验证了这种集合层次的分析。在采用了几种统计控制手段(例如"作为犯罪受害者")后,这种关系再一次被证明属实。

早在当代大众媒介引发公众对犯罪的关注之前很久,20世纪初的小报新闻时期就有这样一句名言:"你给我30分钟时间在警察局浏览犯罪报告,我就能给你创造出一股犯罪浪潮。"简言之,公众对犯罪行为的恐惧和对犯罪作为一个社会问题的担忧,与媒介议程之间的联系不逊于与现实存在的犯罪活动的联系——如果不是更多的话。

正如《纽约时报》一篇社论观察到的:"放大恐惧要比减轻恐惧容易得多,这是人类生存的一条简单真理。"[12] 在这个例子中,社论评论的对象是2001年夏天的一批新闻报道,包括《时代周刊》大肆渲染的鲨鱼袭人封面故事。但是海洋科学家迅速指出,那年夏天鲨鱼袭击人类的数量一点也不反常,只是媒体注意到了零星的事故并集中报道罢了。《纽约时报》的这篇社论还揭示,与此相比,从1990年到1997年,美国有28名儿童被跌落的电视机砸死,这个数字是整个20世纪葬身大白鲨之口的人的四倍。在电视机前看电影《大白鲨》或者《鲨卷风》,可能比在海里游泳更加危险。

5. 发现环境问题

一项研究仔细考察了1970年到1990年关于环境问题的美国舆论,发现这些问题在公众议程上的显著性趋势,与针对空气和水污染进行的三项"现实"测量所得的统计数据之间没有关系。[13] 相比之下,66次盖洛普民意调查测得的公众对最重要问题的回答,与《纽约时报》的环境新闻之间却存在实质性的联系,无论是就报道的长度还是突出程度而言。在剔除现实测量之后,公众的关注与《纽约时报》报道的长度之间的相关系数为+0.93,与报道的突出程度之间的相关系数为+0.92。从1970年到1990年,这类报道的长度与突出程度都有了很大的提高;而"现实"测量的统计数据却表明,总体的污染程度实际呈下降趋势。

斯图尔特·索罗卡(Stuart Soroka)进行了一项突破性的议程设置动力分析,即追踪加拿大1985年至1995年的焦点议题,环境议题也是其中之一。[14]除了测量新闻报道、舆论和现实世界指标(如二氧化碳排放)之外,研究者还将决策者对环境问题的关注纳入考量。这种方法对媒介设置公众议程的能力实施了更为严格的测试。统计结果描绘了一幅所有议程相互影响的复杂图画,但是,一致的结果是:在控制了现实世界的趋势后,新闻媒体对环境的关注同时引导了公众和政策制定者对这一议题的注意。这种情况在20世纪80年代末特别明显,其时,新闻媒体、公众和政策议程对环境的关切均迅速上升,直到20世纪90年代才逐步平缓。

6. 警报发觉

总体来说,对舆论的这些描述告诉了我们大量事实,既反映了新闻工作者的自由裁量权,也表明了媒体在描绘现实方面有时会存在的偏差。这些例子涉及的情形非常多样。自1970年到1990年,当时空气污染和水污染的情况逐渐改善,公众却基于日益增多的环境问题报道表现出了担忧。20世纪90年代出现了相似的情形:尽管现实中的犯罪现象呈减少的趋势,但是在日渐增加的犯罪报道面前,公众对犯罪问题忧虑不已。同样的趋势也可以在21世纪初的智利看到。20世纪80年代,虽然现实中的毒品问题与先前相比根本没有什么差异,但是美国的公众意见却对越来越多的毒品报道作出了反应。同样的模式也反映在对鲨鱼袭击的报道以及对德国石油供给的报道中。而在20世纪60年代，无论是新闻报道的趋势，还是公众对主要议题的关切程度，与这些议题的现实情况都没有关系。

在所有这些例证中，公众对形势的反应都让人想起一种"警报发觉"（alarmed discovery）现象，这是指公众对议程上的新议题作出的最初反应。安东尼·唐斯（Anthony Downs）的"议题关注周期"理论就描述了这种现象。[15]上面讨论的新闻媒体对各种议题的呈现也可以称作一种"警报发觉"，这是因为，当新闻开始强调其中任一议题的时候，在现实世界中异常情况还没有发生呢。实际上，这些都是在现实世界中进行的自然实验，由此产生了强有力的因果证据，足以证明新闻媒体对公众意见的议程设置影响。

二、考察议程设置效果的角度

世界各地对议程设置效果的探索从各种角度考察了这种传播现象。一个由四部分组成的模型系统地描述了这些研究的角度。因为这个模型是应国际传播协会主席艾弗里特·罗杰斯（Everett Rogers）之邀，在墨西哥的阿卡普尔科城会议上最初提出的，所以被称为阿卡普尔科模型（Acapulco typology）。这个分类系统是由两个二分维度确定的。第一个维度区分了看待议程的两种方式：关注焦点既可以是界定议程的全系列议题，也可以缩小为议程上的单个议题。第二个维度区分了测量公众议程上议题显著性的两种方法：描述整个群体或特定人口的集合测量与描述个人反应的个体测量。这两个维度结合在一起便描绘了关于议程设置的四种不同角度，如框2.2所示。

> **框 2.2　阿卡普尔科模型：考察议程设置的四种角度**
>
> | | 公众显著性的测量 | |
> | --- | --- | --- |
> | | 集合数据 | 个体数据 |
> | 关注焦点 | | |
> | 整体议程 | 角度 I
竞争 | 角度 II
机械 |
> | 议程上的单个议题 | 角度 III
自然历史 | 角度 IV
认知画像 |

角度 I 包含整体议程，使用对全体样本的集合测量来确定这些议题的显著性。议程设置研究中最早的查普希尔研究采用的就是这个角度。在那场美国总统选举中，媒介议程与公众议程由五大议题组成。研究者通过两类集合测量，确认了这些议题的相对显著性。对于媒介议程来说，这些议题的显著性由每个议题的新闻报道数量决定；对于公众议程而言，议题显著性由认为政府应该就某议题采取行动的选民的占比决定。这个角度被命名为竞争（competition）角度，因为它检验的是为获得议程上的位置而彼此竞争的一批议题。在议程设置方面，其他一些对全部竞争性议题进行研究的案例，牵扯到接下来的两场美国总统选举，日本、阿根廷与西班牙的地方舆论，以及在整个 20 世纪 60 年代美国舆论的趋势。

角度 II 的思路与早期集中于整体议题议程的议程设置研究相似，但是将重点转移到了每个人的议程上。角度 I 涉及的是系统层面，角度 II 涉及的则是个体层面，然而，当个体按照要求排列一系列议题时，几乎没有证据表明这些个体排序与新闻媒体对这些议题的强调之间存在任何对应关系。[16] 这种角度被命名为机械（automaton，或机器人）角度，因为它对人类行为持负面看法，实际上是回归到了大众媒介效果的皮下注射理论。尽管媒体能够影响个体对某些议题的重要性的看法，但是媒体的整体议程即便可能，也极少被个体完全复制。

角度Ⅲ将关注的焦点置于议程上的单个议题,但是与角度Ⅰ相似,使用的是集合测量的方法,以确定某个议题的显著性。通常情况下,这些显著性测量是指,关于某个议题的新闻报道总数与将这个议题认作国家面临的最重要问题的整体公众比例之间的关系。这个角度被命名为自然历史(natural history)角度,因为它意在研究,随着时间的变化,单个议题的显著性从媒介议程向公众议程转移后的对应程度。前面已经讨论过采用这个角度的研究案例,包括考察美国二十三年间的公民权利议题,对路易维尔市八年中八个不同议题的观察,以及对德国的16个议题为期一年的深入研究。

角度Ⅳ又是聚焦个体的,但是将观察范围缩小到单个议程项目的显著性。这个角度被命名为"认知画像"(cognitive portrait),体现在议程设置的实验研究中。这些实验在受试者接触新闻节目之前与之后,分别测量单个议题对于个体的显著性,其中对各种议题的接触量进行了控制。

这些观察议程设置现象的不同角度增强了我们认识这种媒介效果的信心。角度Ⅰ提供了大量证据,有效地、全面地描述了在某些具体的时点上新闻媒体内容与舆论之间丰富多变的混合。这个角度力求按照世界的本来面貌描述事实。角度Ⅲ提供了对单个议题自然历史性的有用描述,代价却是忽视了这个议题存在于其中的更加广阔的社会背景。然而,了解单个议题在较长一段时间里的动态,非常有助于理解议程设置发挥作用的过程。对于我们理解议程设置的动因,角度Ⅳ也作出了重要贡献。从理论的视角看,利用角度Ⅲ与角度Ⅳ获得的证据对于阐释议程设置理论绝对不可或缺,它们能解释这种现象如何发生以及为什么会发生。但是,议程设置理论的终极目标又让我们回到角度Ⅰ,即在各个社区(共同体)与国家的生活中全面考察传播与舆论的关系。

三、内容与接触

议程设置研究聚焦于显著性从一处向另一处的转移,通常是从媒介议程到公众议程。阿卡普尔科模型已经确认了用来测量这种显著性转移的各种研究设计的不同类别。请注意,我们检验过的这些设计和案例均强调媒介议程的内容与公众议程的内容之间的比较。在大多数议程设置研究中,经常接触新闻媒体的情况是被假定的而非测量得到的。不过,一小部分基于注意的研究记录了关注新闻媒体的水平与议程设置效果的强度之间的明确联系,补充了上述基于内容的议程设置研究。[17]

一项对2006年瑞典全国选举的研究,从这种基于注意的角度扩展开来,调查了每日使用新闻的行为对公众议程的影响,其测量范围横跨九个主要新闻媒体。结果发现:"关注政治新闻对公众感知到的议题显著性产生了明显的和相当强烈的影响;对政治新闻的关注,比对广播和电视上各种特定新闻节目的关注,或者对不同报纸的关注,都更为重要。"[18]同样,我们之前讨论过的在智利对媒体使用与犯罪感知的研究也发现,观众越关注电视新闻,越可能将犯罪视为国家面临的最重要问题。[19]

四、过去年代的议程设置

虽然"议程设置"一词直到1968年才被创造出来,但是在那之前很久,这种现象就已经存在。在最终组成了合众国的英属殖民地,在1776年《独立宣言》发表之前的四十年里,殖民地报纸对地理的关注和对地名的重视程度变化极大。[20]从1735年到1744年的十年间,亦即独立之前几十年的初期,大约三分之一的地名指的是盎格鲁-美利坚大家庭中的某地,要么是不列颠,要么是北美。而《独立宣言》发表之前的十年里,三分之一的地名只是指北美。在最后的两年(1774年和1775年)中,整整一半的地名仅关涉北美。1763年之后,将"英属十三殖民地"认作独立一体的报纸符号有了极大的增长,更表明了报纸在争取政治共识方面的议程设置作用。从那时起,报纸上全部"英属十三殖民地"符号中的大约四分之一将殖民地指称为一个单一共同体。18世纪殖民地报纸的这种地理议程帮助一个新国家确立了文化与政治身份认同。

到了19世纪晚期,进步时代的改革家极力推崇新闻媒体的议程设置作用,相信这种权力的行使乃是民主政治的核心。19世纪90年代,不仅在芝加哥和圣路易斯,而且在其他大城市,市政改革家都学会了这种方法。[21]以芝加哥为例,19世纪90年代末涌现的所有公众议题,在那十年的多数时间里,都显著地反映在报纸议程上。这个时期,报纸持续密集报道的一个议题是市区有轨电车的规制,结果是这个议题多年来在地方选举中占据主导地位。关于这个议题的讨论如此之多,以至于直到1899年,所有的市长候选人都还觉得,有必要将有轨电车的规制作为竞选宣传的主要议题。[22]

在19世纪和20世纪之交的美国政治的其他地方,著名的堪萨斯报纸编辑威廉·艾伦·怀特(William Allen White)利用他的报纸《恩波里亚公报》推行一种反民众主义的议程。虽然很难断定这个报纸的议程对其时当地公众议程的精确影响,但是珍·福克茨(Jean Lange Folkerts)总结说:

> 怀特为他的读者设置了一个议程,否认1895年到1900年间农民遭遇了经济困难,因为怀特不喜欢他们提出的制度修补建议,他也担心企业家会失去控制权,以及东部资本遭受损失。[23]

本章前面提到,新闻媒体影响舆论焦点的证据包括对整个20世纪60年代动荡十年的观察。[24]第一章则回顾了从1954年到1976年美国公民权利议题的演变。[25]虽然这两个20世纪的例子都只是历史的细枝末节,但它们却是有用的基准性研究,因为它们拥有自己的优势:在一个相当长的时间段里,对新闻媒体的内容与系统测量的舆论进行了比较。大多数历史研究(此处是指20世纪30年代民意调查发展起来之前进行的所有研究)都不具备这种优势。不过,基于大量确认议程设置理论的当代证据,爱德华·考迪尔(Edward Caudill)总结说:"历史结果是,报刊的议程可能是舆论的合理指南,影响范围超出了报刊的直接读者。"[26]当然,他也注意到,此处存在局限和限制,特别是要求大众传播广泛存在,并且能够与对其意见感兴趣的民众建立富有意义的联系。[27]

小 结

我们头脑中的图像有着广泛的来源。在帮助我们认识周围世界的各种知识渠道中,新闻媒体的作用尤其突出。议程设置理论描述和解释了新闻媒体在当今多数重要议题上建立共识的作用。第一章回顾了大量证据,表明媒介议程的强调与之后公众议程的重视之间存在高度的一致性。为了排除对媒介议程与公众议程之间这种因果关系的任何怀疑,议程设置假设被引入实验室进行检验。本章回顾了更多证据,表明现实世界发生的事件,与新闻媒体对这些事件的描绘及公众对这些事件的认知之间存在相当程度的独立性,从而进一步巩固了媒介议程设置公众议程这一命题。对于20世纪60年代的广泛议题、70年代的石油供给议题、80年代的毒品议题、70年代到90年代的环境议题、90年代到21世纪头十年的犯罪议题,以及21世纪初的犯罪议题和鲨鱼袭人议题,事件的媒介议程与历史议程大不相同。更近一些,列表还包括了所谓的"假新闻"("fake"news),亦即为达到政治或其他自肥目标而有预谋地制造可核实的虚假新闻报道。这是议程设置研究的一个主要领域，因为证据表明，专业新闻媒体已被传染，正在转运虚假新闻网站的议程。[28]然而，在所有这些情况中都存在强大证据，表明是新闻媒体及其对这个世界的描绘设置了公众议程。

我们近些年来获得的关于新闻媒体议程设置作用的知识，反过来也被用于增进我们对历史的理解。如果说议程设置理论所描绘的当代舆论动态可推论过去，那么学者们就可以利用对报纸和杂志的内容分析来书写过往的舆论史。这种历史分析与当代舆论阐释的结合提供了丰富的理论前景，有助于人们理解新的政治实践的迅速演变，而这些实践是与新传播技术和全球媒体机构联系在一起的。

阿卡普尔科模型界定的两个角度为这种理论前景提供了重要的概念支持，这两个角度是系统层面的自然历史角度与个体层面的认知画像角度。两者都提供了一种特写式的图景，呈现了议程设置过程发生作用的方式。从这两个角度收集到的见识，可以进一步纳入区分更加精细的理论图景，在这个图景中，媒介与公众围绕持续变化的混合议题进行复杂的互动。在阿卡普尔科模型中，这个更广的角度叫作竞争角度，其关注的是一系列议题。议程设置调查始自"现实世界"情境下的查普希尔研究，对于志在理解公众意见的学者与公民来说，这种角度始终是根本的角度。

最后，在21世纪，《纽约时报》的专栏作家威廉·萨菲尔（William Safire）响应李普曼的拟态环境思想，对现实与新闻的关系进行了简洁的概括："而在政治中，被新闻界和公众广泛接受的就是真实的。"[29]

第三章 我们头脑中的图像

李普曼指出,新闻媒体是"我们头脑中的图像"[1]的主要来源。由这一雄辩论点衍生了议程设置这个强壮的知识后代。议程设置是一个社会科学理论,它相当详细地描绘了传播媒介对我们头脑中关于政治与公共事务的图像的影响。其核心的理论观点是,媒介图像中的显著元素不仅会成为受众图像中的显著元素,而且会逐渐被公众视为至关重要。

在前面几章,焦点是有关公众议题的各种议程。然而,从理论上讲,这些议程可以由任何种类的一组元素组成,既可以是一系列议题,也可以是多位政治候选人、若干竞争性机构,或者其他任何东西。在实践中,迄今为止,全世界有几百项议程设置研究,绝大多数都将主要关注点放在由公众议题组成的议程上。在这些议程设置研究中,核心的发现是新闻对议题的强调程度影响了公众对这些议题的重视程度。不过,即便是在1968年美国总统选举期间进行的创始性的查普希尔研究中,也只发现大约三分之一的新闻报道与议题有关,其余报道强调的是竞选活动中的事件和政治策略,以及候选人的信息。[2]

几十年来,公众议题一直是议程设置理论研究压倒性的焦点,这是有充分理由的。首先,用议程设置这个比喻来说明一个由公众议题组成的议程,非常合适,它在新闻媒体与舆论之间建立了一种牢固的、明确的理论联系,任何对新闻、政治和舆论感兴趣的人都能看到这种明显的关联。其次,在有关选举的社会科学研究中,存在一个强大的规范性传统,非常强调议题对知情舆论的重要性。最后,业已成熟的民意调查实践,其重点就是社会议题,它还提供了测量公众议程最为常用的方法论。

虽然议程设置关注的是议题的显著性,而不是民意调查的传统焦点,即赞同与反对意见的分布,但议程设置与舆论研究的核心领域是相同的,都是时下重要的公众议题。李普曼在《舆论》一书中探索通过新闻媒体将外部世界与我们头脑中的图像连接起来,这种想法经由议程设置研究取得了量化的经验成果。[3]

如果完全抽象地思考这个理论比喻中的关键术语"议程",那它扩展到议题议程之外的潜力就变得清晰起来。在关于大众媒介议程设置作用的大多数讨论中,每个议程上的分析单元都是一个客体,即一个公众议题。然而,从议程设置的角度看,分析的客体并不仅限于公众议题。在美国和世界上其他国家大选之前的政党初选中,人们最感兴趣的客体是那些在政党内部争取总统提名的候选人。在这种情况下,议程就是一个由候选人组成的议程,在整个政治竞选时节,候选人在媒介议程与公众议程上的显著性都会相当不同。在加拿大议会中,另一种议程,也就是下议院议员质询政府部长的问题的议程,也反映出报纸的议程设置影响,特别是在敏感的议题上,如国家统一的问题。[4]有许多客体在努力吸引新闻工作者与各种受众的注意力,这些竞争优先地位的客体都可以定义一个议程。

无论是以公众议题、政治候选人,还是以其他项目来确定议程,此处所使用的客体(object)一词都与社会心理学家所用的态度客体(attitude object)意义相同。客体是我们的注意所指向的事物,或者我们对之持有态度或意见的对象。传统上,在关于议程设置的讨论中,客体一直是某个公共议题。但是,能够构成媒介议程和公众议程的客体的种类实际上是无限的,从公司到国家,再到其他现象。

除了客体议程之外,还有另一层面的议程设置需要思考。议程上的每个客体都有许多属性(attributes),即充实每个客体图像的那些特点与性质。正如不同客体的显著性存在差异一样,每个客体不同属性的显著性也有所不同。当然,这些属性的范围可能极为不同,它们可以是像"左撇子"这样具体的描述,也可以是像"文学天才"这样宽泛的形容。在议程设置理论中,属性是个总体称呼,涵盖了表征某个客体的全部性质与特征。

不管是选择某些客体加以关注,还是选择某些属性来描绘这些客体,都体现了强大的议程设置作用。新闻议程及其系列客体的一个重要组成部分就是属性,这是新闻工作者及随后公众思考与谈论每个客体时都会想到的。

新闻的这些属性议程影响公众议程的方式,便是议程设置的第二层面。第一层面当然是指客体显著性的转移。第二层面则是指属性显著性的转移。框3.1显示了大众传播媒介议程设置作用的这两个方面。

在范围更广泛的传播过程的理论背景下,传统议程设置关注的是传播过程中一个关键的早期阶段,即获得注意的阶段。[5]某个议题、某位政治候选人或其他话题出现在公众议程上,就意味着它已经充分曝光,并在相当程度上引起了公众的注意。属性议程设置聚焦的是传播过程中接下来的一个阶段,即理解的阶段。李普曼将这个阶段描述为在我们的头脑中形成图像。这个阶段的焦点是,议题、政治候选人或话题的哪些方面在公众中变得显著。

在"注意"与"理解"之间进行这种理论区分非常重要。虽然媒介消息携带的信息,通常既与议程设置过程的第一层面有关,也与第二层面有关,但是这些信息施加的影响却有本质的区别——一个是客体的显著性,另一个是特定属性的显著性。不仅如此,议程设置效果的这两个方面并不总是一道产生的。在评论资深政治家H.卡尔·麦考

尔(H. Carl McCall)2002年竞争纽约州州长的候选人资格时,《纽约时报》指出:

> 虽然67岁的民主党候选人麦考尔先生已经有三十年的从政经历,但是选民并不了解他。民意调查显示,虽然选民可能知道他的名字,但却对他没有印象。[6]

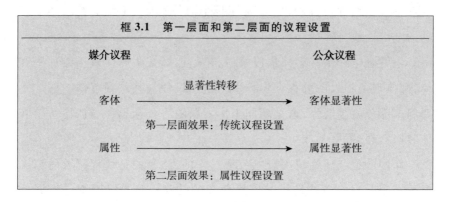

框3.1　第一层面和第二层面的议程设置

在拓宽了议程设置的视角之后,就有必要修改伯纳德·科恩那句关于传播媒介影响力的名言了。在简洁地概括了议程设置与早期媒介效果研究之间的差异后,科恩指出,新闻媒体在告诉人们怎么想方面可能并不成功,但是在告诉人们想什么方面则异常成功。[7]明确注意到第二层面议程设置作用的研究却进一步提示,对于一些客体,媒介不仅告诉我们想什么,而且告诉我们怎么想。这种结果是否表明,媒介有时候的确也在告诉我们应该怎么想?如同我们将要看到的,证据响亮地给予了正面的回答。

一、政治候选人的画像

尽管人们对科学的普遍印象以重大发现为中心,但是,将多数社会科学的发展形容为一种不断演化的过程,还是更合适一些。在这个演化的过程中,隐约可见的事物逐渐变得清晰起来。李普曼的名言

"我们头脑中的图像"逐步被阐释和拓展,并且在精确而严密的证据的支持下成为一种社会科学理论,这一案例就特别适于说明这种过程。自1968年的查普希尔研究开始,绝大多数这类证据都涉及有哪些公众议题被纳入了议程。用李普曼的话来说,这种证据的焦点是我们头脑中的这些图像与什么有关。随着时间的推移,人们的注意力转移到了属性议程设置上来,将它作为一个额外的影响因素,证据的焦点是这些图像的实际细节。

这种客体议程与属性议程之间的理论区分,即框3.1中描述的第一层面和第二层面的议程设置,特别清晰地体现于选举场景中。此时,得票数的列表显示出一个有关候选人的议程。用议程设置的术语来说,那些竞争政治公职的候选人是一些客体,这些客体在公众中的显著性可以受到新闻报道与政治广告的影响。关于"知名度"的竞选研究,以及其他一些测量客体显著性的方法,描述的就是这些候选人在公众心目中的相对显著性。竞选经理的任务则日益变成确保候选人获得新闻媒体的报道和设计政治广告,从而提升候选人在选民中的显著性。[8]然而,这些媒体宣传活动在很大程度上超越了提升客体显著性的目标,而通常包括为候选人树立一种形象,其中特殊的属性必须特别醒目。事实上,许多政治策略家假定,选民之所以选择某些候选人,是基于他们的特定形象,而不是因为他们兜售的那些议题立场。

在20世纪70年代,一些学者已经勾勒出我们头脑中关于政治候选人的部分图像(这些图像的起源是新闻媒体);但在那时,它们始终是一些关于议程设置的孤立的、奇特的证据碎片。直到20世纪末,新的理论探讨才促使人们重新审视以前的草图,并勾勒出新的素描。[9]

二、全国选举中的候选人形象

选民头脑中关于1976年美国总统候选人的图像,简洁地描绘了议程设置的第二层面及其对属性议程的关注。这一年,时任总统杰拉尔德·福特获得了共和党内的总统提名,而民主党则有 11 位有抱负的总统候选人在春季预选时积极竞争党内的总统提名。这次的候选人实在太多了,选民难以一一了解他们,而且大多数美国选民并不热心政治。这里显然可以提出一个问题,即选民心目中竞选者的形象在多大程度上是由新闻报道塑造的。研究者将纽约州北部民主党人对候选人的描述与《新闻周刊》的属性议程(1 月初这份杂志简要介绍了 11 名候选人的特点)进行比较,结果发现了证实媒介影响存在的重要证据。[10]

在这些证据中,尤其具有说服力的是,关于候选人属性的媒介议程与选民议程之间一致性的增强,即从 2 月中旬的 +0.64 增加到 3 月底的 +0.83。这说明,选民不仅了解了媒介议程,而且在预选的数周内,通过进一步接触新闻报道,了解得更为深入。

吉米·卡特从预选竞争中胜出,代表民主党人挑战在职的共和党总统杰拉尔德·福特。对伊利诺伊选民的一个总样本进行分析,还有更多证据表明,选民从新闻媒体那里了解了这两个人的情况。[11]在《芝加哥论坛报》选举报道的属性呈现与伊利诺伊选民对卡特和福特两人的属性描述之间,发现了惊人的一致性。

在整个选举年度,媒介的属性议程与其后公众的属性议程的交叉时滞相关系数中位值为 +0.70。根据 14 个不同的特征来界定,这些属性议程包括能力、同情心和政治信仰等广泛的特征。因为交叉时滞相关系数同时考虑到了新闻媒体对选民的影响及选民对新闻媒体的影响,所以得到的证据特别明确:施加影响的方向是从媒介议程到公众议程。

随着积累的证据越来越多,情况也越来越清楚:只要政治体制与新闻媒体具备合理的开放性与自由度,媒介的属性议程设置影响在世界各地的选举中都会发生。在 1996 年西班牙大选期间收集到的广泛证据,极好地表明了这些媒介效果在不同文化环境中的存在。[12]

1996年,西班牙保守的人民党的候选人何塞·玛丽亚·阿斯纳尔(José María Aznar),成功地挑战了在职十二年的社会党首相费利佩·冈萨雷斯(Felipe González)。这次选举中还有第三位候选人,即代表极左翼党派联合阵线的胡里奥·安奎塔(Julio Anguita)。在西班牙潘普洛纳的选民中,有证据表明,主要的新闻和广告媒体对这三个候选人的公众形象产生了重大影响。

在新闻媒体与选民对候选人的描述中,有五个实质属性:对争议问题的立场和政治意识形态;正式资格和生平资料;个性;资质感知与评估性判断;正直(基于对候选人"腐败"或"不腐败"的直接描述)。在对候选人属性的描述中,之所以要注意最后一种,是为了把握那次全国选举中的一个重大议题:政府腐败以及与此相关的争议,即时任首相冈萨雷斯是否也卷入了腐败问题。

这次研究还超越了先前在美国选举中对属性议程设置的检验,将属性议程的范围扩大,既包括实质属性,又包括情感语气(基调)——这是第二维度的属性。新闻媒体与选民在形容这些候选人时的语气被分为正面、负面或中性。语气当然是政治传播中一个特别重要的方面。

在对第二层面议程设置效果的严密测试中,这些描述的实质类别与情感语气被合并成一个5×3的描述矩阵(5个实质类别×3种语气类别)。首先,根据一项在选举之后对潘普洛纳选民进行的调查,为三个候选人各列了一个描述矩阵。其后,根据对两份地方报纸、两份全国报纸、两档全国电视新闻节目以及电视政治广告的内容分析,列出了另外21个描述矩阵(7家媒体×3个候选人)。这次在西班牙的研究还增加了政治广告,它被纳入新闻媒体的组合,是来自西班牙的证据的一个新特点。

将选民心目中的候选人"画像"与各种传播媒介对候选人的 21 种描述作比较,得出了非常惊人的结果。首先,所有 21 组相关系数都是正向的。尤其突出的是选民议程与报纸议程之间的比较,无论是本地的还是全国的报纸,相关都非常明显。例如,选民的属性议程与地方报纸《纳瓦拉日报》的属性议程在冈萨雷斯身上的相关系数为+0.87,在阿斯纳尔身上的相关系数为+0.82,在安奎塔身上则为+0.60。就全国性报纸《国家报》而言,三人各自的相关系数分别是 +0.84、+0.83 和+0.86。

在关于候选人属性的选民描述与两份地方报纸的属性议程的所有六项比较中,相关系数中位数为+0.70。在选民与两份全国报纸的所有六项比较中,相关系数中位数为+0.81。在选民与两档全国电视新闻节目的六项比较中,相关系数中位数为+0.52。在对选民与公共电视节目中的政治广告进行的三项比较研究中,相关系数中位数为+0.44。

进一步分析发现,这些大众传播媒介传递的消息克服了公众选择性认知的问题,即一般人强调自己喜欢的候选人的正面属性和对立面候选人的负面属性的那种倾向。在这项研究中,随着选民与报纸、电视新闻及政治广告的接触增多,他们对其他候选人的正面评价和对自己喜欢的候选人的负面评价都相应增加,[13]这说明选民确实从媒体那里学到了东西。这一研究关于媒介属性议程设置的证据之所以特别引人注目,是因为它在民主政治环境下,将大量的、多元的新闻渠道与对三名大选候选人丰富的实质性和情感性描述结合了起来。

三、地方选举中的候选人形象

让我们将视线延伸到亚洲背景下的一次地方选举。在 1994 年中国台湾地区台北市长选举中,研究者发现了属性议程设置的进一步证据。[14]研究者将三个市长候选人在选民心目中的形象与台北报纸和电视台对这些人的描述进行了比较。属性议程包括12个类别,分别代表广泛多样的个人与政治特征。选民心目中的候选人形象与《中国时报》《联合报》的属性议程之间的相关系数分别从+0.59到+0.75不等,这六项比较的相关系数中位数为+0.68。与持反对立场的报纸《自由时报》的所有比较都没有发现重大相关,与电视新闻的所有比较也是如此。就台北的电视台来说,选民都明白,所有三家电视台当时都在当局以及长期掌权的国民党控制之下。有一个例子,就是某部门拥有一家电视台40%的股份。在这些例子中,属性议程设置并没有发生,进一步证实了我们前面的观察,即议程设置效果的出现需要一个自由开放的媒介系统。

回到西班牙的政治场景。在潘普洛纳1995年的地方选举中,研究者从实质属性和情感语气两方面分别考察了五个政党候选人的形象。[15]公众的媒介接触被分为三种程度(无接触、有些接触、充分接触),研究者将由此产生的候选人公众形象与地方电视新闻、两份潘普洛纳报纸新闻的描述相比较。对所有候选人的每一次比较都构成一组,这与调查1976年竞争美国民主党内总统提名的候选人形象的做法相似。在框3.2中,对于实质属性(从意识形态、资格、个性等方面对政治候选人的描述),人们在报纸和电视上接触越多的政治信息,媒介议程与公众议程的匹配程度就越高。尽管在三种程度的接触上模式是完全相同的,但关键的区分在于对媒介政治信息全无接触还是至少有些接触。对候选人的情感描述呈现了同样的模式,如框3.2所示。至少从报纸和电视上获取了一些政治信息的人对候选人的描述方式与新闻媒体的报道方式非常相似。不接触媒介传递的政治信息的人对候选人的情感描述与新闻媒体的情感描述的匹配程度则弱得多。

框 3.2	西班牙地方选举中的属性议程设置	
实质属性		
对不同媒介中政治信息的接触程度	报纸	电视新闻
无接触	+0.74	+0.81
有些接触	+0.90	+0.91
充分接触	+0.92	+0.92
情感属性		
对不同媒介中政治信息的接触程度	报纸	电视新闻
无接触	+0.49	+0.56
有些接触	+0.88	+0.86
充分接触	+0.79	+0.83

来源:Esteban López-Escobar, Juan Pablo Llamas and Maxwell McCombs, 'Una dimensión social de los efectos do los medios de difusión: agenda-setting y consenso', *Comunicación y Sociedad* Ⅸ (1996): 91–125。

与涉及公众议题显著性的传统议程设置效果的累积证据并行,关于属性议程设置和政治候选人公众形象的证据,主要基于对民意调查结果与新闻媒体及政治广告内容分析的比较。[16]这种证据的优势在于,能够描绘一幅政治传播的代表性画面;局限性则在于,需要证实媒介议程与公众议程之间存在确定的因果关系。在第一章中我们已经注意到了这个问题并进行了讨论,强调了实验室实验提供的补充证明媒介议程与公众议程之间存在因果关系的证据的重要性。幸运的是,实验室证据表明,在属性议程设置与政治候选人的公众形象之间也存在因果关系。

在一次实验室实验中,研究者让一半受试者阅读一篇报纸报道,这个报道虚构了一个非常腐败的美国政治候选人。另外一半受试者则阅读另一篇媒体报道,这篇报道将这个候选人描述为一个道德高尚的人。其后,采用一个开放式问题和一个闭合式等级量表进行调查,测试这些接触了相反特征描写的个体受试者对候选人的描述。结果，在开放式问题和闭合式等级量表的回答中都发现了重大差异。向两个实验组提出的问题都是："假设你的朋友从另一个州来拜访你，他不了解这个候选人，你会怎样向你的朋友描述这个候选人？"在对这个问题的回答中，研究者发现，即便是仅仅短暂地接触一篇新闻报道，也能导致明显的差异。在让两组受试者对候选人的诚实、真挚程度及可信度打分时，也发现了同样的差异。在实验室的控制条件下，等级量表与开放式问题都记录了第二层面议程设置效果的存在。[17]

四、视觉形象与属性

虽然许多议程设置研究都考虑到了电视新闻，但这些新闻的实际视觉内容还是很少得到关注。在一次独创性研究中，雷尼塔·科尔曼（Renita Coleman）和斯蒂芬·班宁（Stephen Banning）[18]检验了2000年美国大选中电视新闻对布什和戈尔的视觉描绘所反映出的情感议程。他们对两位候选人的非语言行为（面部表情、姿态、姿势）进行了内容分析，发现戈尔比布什得到了更多的正面行为镜头，而布什比戈尔得到了更多的负面行为镜头。

这些图像被拿来与2000年美国国家选举研究的结果作比较。美国国家选举研究（American National Election Study，ANES）针对上述两位竞选者进行了调查：有一组问题是询问被调查者，对候选人是否感到"愤怒"、"满怀希望"、"害怕"或者"骄傲"；另一组问题是询问被调查者，在何种程度上可以用七个正面或者负面的词语来形容布什和戈尔。这些问题的得分加在一起，便形成了对某位候选人一个正面的和一个负面的情感属性指标。

比较这些媒介属性议程和公众属性议程，结果发现了视觉信息的影响的适度证据。就布什而言，媒介和公众在正面和负面属性议程上都呈显著相关(两项都是+0.13)。但就戈尔而言,媒介和公众只在正面的属性议程上显著相关(+0.20)。正如作者总结的:

> 虽然非语言线索的效果可能比某些语言线索的效果要小,但效果还是显著的[……]视觉可以发挥虽不突出但仍然很重要的作用,在政治过程中助力印象的形成。[19]

在许多发达的民主国家都很常见的群体极化环境中,第二层面的议程设置已经成为可以用来解释党派媒体影响力的合理说明。与传统新闻相比,党派媒体极力报道己方支持的候选人的正面属性和己方反对的候选人的负面属性。于是,党派媒体更容易在受众中强化极化的属性议程。例如,在一项对2012年美国选举的分析中,研究者采用ANES的调查结果,将《NBC晚间新闻》(NBC Nightly News)、CNN《安德森·库珀360度观点》(Anderson Cooper 360°)和福克斯新闻《布雷特·拜尔特别报道》(Fox News Special Report with Bret Baier)提及竞选者巴拉克·奥巴马(Barack Obama)与米特·罗姆尼(Mitt Romney)五大特征的频度,与观众对同样特征的想法作比较。[20]这些特征包括道德、领导力和智识等方面。研究所得的三个结果值得注意。第一,内容分析显示,三个节目对两名竞选者的正面和负面属性给予了极不均衡的展示。正如可以预料到的,福克斯明显倾向于支持罗姆尼,反对奥巴马;而CNN略微倾向于反对罗姆尼。NBC则相反,采取了一种最平衡的正负两面报道议程。第二,这种不平衡的媒介议程与观众关于两位竞选者的属性议程非常一致。这种发现尤其适用于福克斯特别报道的观众。第三,福克斯新闻的属性议程的效果最可预见——对罗姆尼的正面态度与对奥巴马的负面态度,这是一种特别能被属性议程设置解释的极化效果。相反,研究者发现NBC的晚间新闻具有一种非极化的效果——它的观众越是接受节目的属性议程,他们就越不可能对任何一位竞选者抱有极端看法。所有这些关系都是在控制了党派认同、政治利益和其他变量的条件下发现的,因此,所有结论都站得住脚,相当有力。

媒介对政治候选人公众形象的影响是属性议程设置的一个非常直观的例子。我们大部分关于政治候选人的知识——从他们的政治意识形态到个人品行等一切方面——都来自新闻报道与媒体广告的内容。这些属性议程设置效果在各种各样的地理与政治背景下都得到了验证。对全国候选人,我们有来自美国与西班牙的证据。对地方候选人,我们有来自西班牙的进一步证据,以及来自中国台湾地区的证据。美国的实验进一步补充了这些源自实际选举的证据。

五、议题的属性

议题显著性一直是传统议程设置理论关注的中心,但它也可以延伸到第二层面。与所有其他客体一样,公众议题具有多种属性。在新闻中,以及在人们思考与谈论议题时,这些议题的某些方面(也就是议题的某些属性)得到强调。不仅如此,某个特定议题的显著属性通常还会随着时间而变化。接下来我们会看到,经济议题尤其如此。近几十年来,经济议题在许多国家都是一个反复出现的重大议题。有的时候,经济议题的显著属性是通货膨胀;其他时候,经济议题的显著属性却是失业或预算赤字。在新闻媒体如何塑造时下相关议题的舆论方面,属性议程设置进一步扩充了我们的知识。

在1993年日本大选期间,研究者同时检验了第一层面和第二层面的议程设置,结果再一次证明了议程设置理论跨越文化背景的有效性,以及在两个明确区分的认知层次上的有效性:一个是对客体的关注,另一个是对客体属性的理解。[21]这项研究从传统的议程设置假设开始,首先考察了密集的新闻报道对"政治改革"议题显著性的影响。这个议题占两份主要的全国性报纸与三家电视网的议题报道量的80%以上。政治改革的议题几乎垄断了整个新闻议程,在这种情况下,比较这个议题在媒介议程与公众议程上的排序的传统做法并不可行。

当然,这些比较背后的假设是,媒介议程与公众议程的高度相关性源自人们与媒介的接触。在日本的这次选举中,联系这两种议程的行为(媒介接触)得到了明确的测量。研究者将受试者媒介接触的测量结果与他们对政治的关注兴趣结合起来,形成了一个政治新闻专注度指数,结果支持了事先假设的命题,即媒介议程上的一个显著议题在公众中的显著性与这些公众对政治新闻的投入程度呈正相关。受试者对电视新闻的专注度与政治改革议题的显著性之间的相关系数为+0.24;专注于报纸的,相关系数为+0.27。

事实上,在议程设置的第二层面上,电视新闻与报纸均提及体制相关改革,次数是提及道德相关改革的两倍,这便创造了对新闻媒体设置属性议程的平衡预期。首先,公众议程上体制相关改革的显著性应该与人们对政治新闻的关注程度呈正相关,因为政治体制是改革议题在新闻中被强调的方面,亦即属性。相反,没有什么理由期待公众议程上道德相关改革的显著性与人们对政治新闻的专注度明显相关,因为新闻较少关注政治改革的道德属性。

这两个假设都得到了验证。对于政治改革的道德方面,相关性几乎为零(电视为+0.05,报纸为+0.09);对于政治改革的体制方面,电视新闻的相关系数为+0.20,报纸新闻的相关系数为+0.26。值得注意的是,第一层面与第二层面议程设置的效果,无论是报纸新闻还是电视新闻,相关性数据几乎相同。

在选举之外,一个复杂的议题,如经济,相关的新闻报道和公众观点也可能包含许多不同的方面或属性。与经济这个总话题相关的一系列属性,可以是当前的具体问题,也可以是这些问题产生的原因及解决这些问题的办法。另外,还有范围更小的系列属性,例如,对一些经济问题解决方案的赞成与反对意见。对于这两组属性,在美国明尼阿波利斯市的公众中,发现了报纸的议程设置效果,但电视新闻却没有。[22]对于具体的问题,如与总体经济话题相关的原因与解决办法,报纸议程与公众议程之间的相关性特别高(+0.81)。至于对经济问题解决方案的赞成与反对意见,两种议程之间的一致性只是稍微低一些(+0.68)。报纸聚焦于经济问题的特定方面影响了公众看待经济的方式。

环境是另一个在广度与复杂度上可与经济比拟的当代议题。作为一个公众议题,环境既可以是国际问题,也可以是颇受地方关注的问题;既可以是抽象关切的问题,也可以是具体关心的问题。日本两家主要日报的新闻报道明显影响了东京居民对全球环境问题的关注模式。[23]1992年6月,联合国环境与发展会议在里约热内卢召开。在这次会议召开之前的四个月里,《朝日新闻》与《读卖新闻》对全球环境八个方面的报道都稳步增加。这八个方面涵盖广泛,从酸雨、野生动物保护到人口爆炸和全球变暖等问题。

在东京居民中,这些媒介议程产生了显著的议程设置效果。早在2月,报纸属性议程与其后的公众属性议程之间的一致性就达到了+0.68。到了4月初,两者之间的一致性提高到+0.78,这是最高值,并且一直持续到5月中旬。在联合国环境与发展会议召开之前与会议进行的那几周,两者之间的一致性有所降低,反映了时滞现象,这也是议程设置中涉及学习过程的部分。在日本发现的时滞现象与在美国发现的全球环境议题中许多方面的情况相似。[24]关于议程设置效果的时滞问题,更多细节将在第六章讨论。

我们思考与谈论公众议题的方式,受到新闻媒体报道这些议题时所呈现的"图像"的影响,这方面的证据不断积累。在媒介呈现中突出的议题属性在公众头脑中也变得明显起来。这是对最初的议程设置观点的重大扩展。最初的议程设置观点强调,新闻媒体塑造公众议程的能力表现在,它会影响到公众认为哪些议题更为重要。然而,是属性议程确认了一个议题,并且在某些情况下,引导公众意见倾向于特定的角度或者选择某种解决方案。为某个议题设置属性议程是政治权力的一种体现。在任何议题上,能够控制政治辩论的角度,就是对公众意见最大的影响。

六、雄辩论据

正如乔治·奥威尔在《动物农场》一书中所描写的居民关系,某些属性要比其他属性"更平等一些"。某些属性要比其他属性更可能经常进入媒介信息;某些属性要比其他属性更容易被受众注意到并记住。[25] 在对某条消息的解读中,某些属性也会被认为比其他属性更加切题,更有意义。一个客体的某些特点可能引起公众的共鸣,从而成为雄辩的论据(compelling arguments),增强正在讨论的议题、人物或话题的显著性。

客体的某种属性可能成为增强显著性的雄辩论据,这种观点为议程设置的学术地图增加了新的内容。在本章前面部分,框3.1用两条连接媒介议程和公众议程的带箭头横线说明了议程设置的第一层面和第二层面。媒介议程上的客体显著性影响公众议程上的客体显著性,而媒介议程上的属性显著性则影响公众议程上的属性显著性。框3.3为那张图谱增加了另外一条连接线,一条连接媒介议程属性显著性与公众议程客体显著性的带箭头斜线。也就是说,当媒介议程强调某个客体的某种特殊属性时,可能直接影响到这个客体在公众中的显著性。媒介议程对客体的某种描述方式可能比其他方式更有说服力,因而更容易创造客体在公众中的显著性。到目前为止,客体在公众中的显著性主要是由这个客体在媒介议程上出现的频率来解释的。媒介议程提及的客体并没有根据媒体赋予客体的属性种类来划分层次。

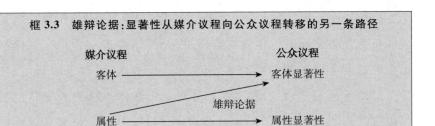

现在，对框3.3中的带箭头斜线，我们已经掌握了新的证据。这是一种被称作雄辩论据的关系，是议程设置过程的一个重要方面。[26]第二章讨论了20世纪90年代早期得克萨斯州的一种情况。在那个时期，新闻中密集的犯罪报道在公众中引发了对犯罪问题的令人惊讶的高度担忧，人们将犯罪视作国家面临的最重要问题。框2.1详列了新闻报道与公众关注的这种并行趋势。

具有讽刺意味的是，当时，一方面是公众对犯罪的担忧达到异乎寻常的高度，但另一方面，得克萨斯州的实际犯罪率却在下降，并且已经连续下降了好几年。难道只是因为犯罪是一个"热键"议题，一经新闻报道强调，就能让公众以爆发性的特殊方式作出反应？还是新闻报道包含了特别雄辩的论据，能够增强犯罪作为社会议题的显著性？对这种情况，除了传统的议程设置效果之外，还有没有其他的解释？

研究者考察了新闻报道对犯罪问题的各种呈现方式，揭示了与公众的担忧关系特别密切的两个角度（"对普通人构成威胁"和"发生在本地"），其强度实际上超过了犯罪报道对公众的总体冲击。[27]在这两个报道角度下，普通人与新闻所描述的犯罪行为之间的心理距离都很小。虽然得克萨斯人对远方的谋杀案或作为新闻主打内容的大量传统犯罪报道并不感到焦虑，但他们确实担心遭遇驾车枪击、光天化日之下被抢劫以及本地犯罪。特别是，得克萨斯人对犯罪的显著认知，亦即是否将犯罪问题认作全国面临的最重要问题，主要与新闻报道所呈现的两种情况的频度强烈相关。一个是新闻中描述的犯罪行为是否让普通人觉得个人安全受到了威胁(相关系数为+0.78),二是犯罪行为是否实际发生在得克萨斯州(相关系数为+0.73)。新闻报道中的这两个属性都能解释犯罪议题的显著性,同时也解释了,甚至更好地解释了公众议程与那一时期媒介整体连珠炮般发布的犯罪报道之间的关系(+0.70)。这些属性便是提升犯罪议题显著性的雄辩论据。

雄辩论据是新闻报道能够影响客体在公众中的显著性的特殊属性。关于雄辩论据的这种影响,还有其他证据。一项美国舆论研究分析了20世纪90年代联邦预算赤字是否显著的问题,结果发现了强大的议程设置效果。[28]从1994年到1996年,在18个月的时间里,全国19份主要日报新闻报道的频率,足以解释在这个议题上的85%的显著性方差。进一步分析这个议题的四个具体方面,发现其中的两个方面(政治领导者之间的非对抗性对话、赤字问题上的政治冲突)是公众关注预算赤字的雄辩论据。将这一对属性加入分析,可以解释联邦预算赤字在美国公众中的92%的显著性方差。虽然这些雄辩论据,即联邦预算赤字这两方面的显著性,对增加这个议题在美国公众中的显著性只作出了轻微的贡献,但这是一个难得的机会,可以同时观察到第一层面和第二层面的议程设置的独特效果。而在媒介消息与公众传播中,议程设置过程的这两个组成部分通常被捆绑在一起,在实践中大多不可分割。

雄辩论据可以造成极其不同的结果。在1990年德国大选期间,虽然媒体仍然大量报道原东德地区存在的问题,但这一议题在选民中的显著性大幅下降。[29]这是一种议程缩减效果(agenda-deflating effect),这种现象在发行量很大的小报《图片报》的读者中表现得尤为明显。《图片报》对德国统一的报道采用了高度乐观的框架。在这个例子中,雄辩论据便是对德国统一议题的正面语气,这个属性降低了该议题在公众议程上的显著性。

从理论上说,雄辩论据是媒体报道公共议题的某个方面(或者说属性),它能够强烈影响公众议程和政策议程;而焦点事件[30]可以被认为是雄辩论据的戏剧化形式。例如,2011年由地震和海啸导致的日本核反应堆事故所造成的灾难性后果,成为一个重要的因素,促使德国决定立即关闭本国17个核反应堆中的8个,而这是全国四分之一电力的来源。另一个捷克共和国的研究探讨了焦点事件在争议问题上的这种作用,涉及的是归还被没收的教会财产[31];焦点事件是关于一处特定资产(St. Vitus Cathedral,圣维特大教堂,在布拉格)的一次审判,这次审判得到了新闻媒体的大量报道。在分析中,媒介议程被分为三部分:仅针对归还财产这一议题的报道、仅针对教堂审判这一议题的报道、结合审判与归还两个议题的报道。就公众议程上归还财产议题的显著性而言,合并两个议题的新闻报道比单纯报道归还财产的新闻所产生的议程设置效果要强很多,而单纯报道教堂审判的新闻对公众议程中归还财产议题的显著性并没有影响。

由议题的显著性转向竞选者的显著性,对1980年到1996年美国民主党和共和党总统候选人的一系列深入的验证性研究,确认了两种属性,即道德品质与领导能力,是候选人在公众中的显著性的雄辩论据。[32]将这两种属性放到《纽约时报》《华盛顿邮报》《新闻周刊》《美国新闻与世界报道》这四个新闻媒体的议程中去检验,结果发现:就道德品质而言,在媒介的属性显著性与各党派候选人在公众印象中的显著性之间,八对关系中的六对显著相关,数值范围从+0.66到+0.98;就领导能力而言,八对关系中的四对显著相关,数值范围从+0.80到+0.87。

在许多例子中,这些新闻报道对世界的看法极大地影响了公众头脑中的世界图像。但情况并非总是如此!一项范围广泛的研究深入考察了美国媒体与公众对公共事务的看法,虽然确认了五个主要方面——冲突、经济、人情味、无力感和道德,但是媒介与公众在显著性方面的一致性却只有+0.20。[33]然而,在这种情形下,媒介议程设置影响的缺乏似乎并不像+0.20这个总指标数所表明的那么突出。如果从议程上拿掉"冲突"这个在媒介议程上排第二而在公众议程上排最后的方面,那么,媒介与公众在其余四个方面的一致性就是+0.80了。[34]可见,虽然新闻媒体是公众获取公共事务信息的主要来源,但公众并非总是消极地任由媒介摆布的机器人。

因在新闻报道中强调各种不同的属性而对公众产生影响,对这种影响的关注是一种媒介批评新思路的基础。传统的媒介批评检验新闻报道的内容是否准确与平衡;而这种媒介批评的新思路则基于属性议程设置的理论,考察媒介消息中的强调方式与语气类型,以及这些属性议程与公众思想和行为的共鸣。

七、议程设置与其他传播理论

五十多年来,议程设置理论之所以能够持续发展,是因为它与社会科学中各种其他思想共通共融。在大众传播对公众的影响方面,学者们已经构建了一个日益精细的学术图谱,在这个过程中,议程设置理论也吸纳并融合了其他一些传播学概念与理论。

议程设置理论吸纳的概念包括地位授予(status conferral)、刻板印象形成(stereotyping)、形象塑造(image building),以及门径掌控(gate-keeping,亦即把关)。地位授予是指在受到媒体大量关注之后,个人的显著性相应增长。[35]这种对"名人"的概念化明确了第一层面议程设置的一种情况,这里的客体是某个人。刻板印象形成与形象塑造涉及属性的显著性,属于议程设置的第二层面。[36]把关概念描述并解释了新闻从一个媒体组织向另一个媒体组织的流动,这个概念在20世纪80年代早期就与议程设置理论建立了联系。在那个时期,学者们提出了"谁设置了媒介议程?"[37]这个问题,并借此开启了绘制智识地图的新方向。通过对这个问题的回答,学者们已经确认了一个巨大的关系与影响的网络,我们将在第七章详细讨论。

对议程设置理论的补充包括涵化分析(cultivation analysis)与沉默的螺旋(the spiral of silence)。从大众传播认知效果的长远角度来看,涵化分析检验了媒体尤其是电视娱乐节目所引出的各种视角的显著性。[38]在这些视角中最著名的是"邪恶世界综合征",它展现了一幅关于我们周围世界的悲观图景。这种症状产生的原因,就是电视上播出了过多的犯罪内容。[39]议程设置理论与沉默的螺旋[40]研究的是大众传播媒介的受众两种貌似非常不同的行为:前者涉及人们对世界的认知再现,后者则关系到人们参与公众议题讨论的意愿。但是,这两种观点实际有一个共同的心理基础:每个人都会监测自己所处的社会环境。[41]这种监测的一种结果是公众议题议程,另一种结果则是与别人谈论当下议题的频度。

议程设置与其他各种传播概念的联系,可以比拟为航空业中寰宇一家(One World)、天合联盟(SkyTeam)与星空联盟(Star Alliance)几大系统之间的联系:各自独立的航空公司联合起来,以获得全部市场份额。这种理论概念的演化性整合反映了传播学领域的成熟。

八、属性议程设置与框架建构

对议程设置第二层面即属性议程设置的解释,也可以与另外一个主要的当代概念建立联系,那就是框架建构(framing,亦即架构)。属性议程设置与架构都聚焦于媒介消息中关注的客体,如议题、政治人物或者其他话题,是如何再现的。属性议程设置与架构也都在努力探索,对一个客体某些方面和细节的强调,在何种程度上能够影响人们对那个客体的认识和感觉。不过,试图超越一般陈述,对属性议程设置与框架建构进行融合,却是很困难的,原因在于架构的诸多定义存在分歧。结果是,有时属性和框架是同义的概念;有时属性与框架是交叉的概念;还有的时候,它们是完全不同的概念。

我们从议程设置与框架建构相同的用法开始讨论。在1996年的总统提名竞选中,研究者使用计算机内容分析的方法对四名共和党候选人的各种属性进行了详细分析,从候选人的竞选宣传和《纽约时报》《华盛顿邮报》《洛杉矶时报》对竞选的报道中确认了28个属性类别。[42]尽管是从议程设置角度出发的研究,关注的是候选人发出的新闻通稿和媒体新闻报道的属性议程,但在文章标题中焦点却被描述为"候选人的框架建构"。与议程设置的研究设计不同的还有,这篇发表的文章并没有将竞选新闻通稿中对候选人的描述与记者在新闻报道中对候选人的描述进行比较。议程设置理论建议增加进一步的比较研究,以确定候选人发布的新闻通稿对新闻议程的属性议程设置效果。在得克萨斯大学举行的一次关于议程设置理论的研讨会上,计算结果显示,这项框架建构研究得出的证据有力地支持了属性议程设置的影响,反映在其中三个候选人身上的效果分别是+0.74、+0.75和+0.78,而在领跑并最终获得提名的罗伯特·多尔(Robert Dole)身上,议程设置的影响则为+0.62,虽然稍低,但仍不失强健。

一项对日本经济困难的民意调查研究,则用一种创造性的眼光看待框架与属性之间的这种交叉关系(也是理论联系)。[43]基于框架是低阶属性的捆绑工具这一观点,研究者在分析中还采用了问题性情境(problematic situations)的概念,指一种可以将具体的社会议题和关切转化为一系列更广泛的认知类别的思考角度。[44]研究者对《每日新闻》在52周内的报道进行了内容分析,确认了新闻报道中有关国家经济困难的12个清晰的方面,亦即属性。然后将日本经济困难的这些属性放入问题性情境,进行民意调查,询问公众对于这12个方面的问题有何看法。最后对这些项目进行因素分析,结果发现,之前在理论上确认为问题性情境的四个宏观框架(分别是机构/制度价观的崩溃、个人价值的丧失、局势的模糊和迷惑以及社会冲突)可以涵括所有12个项目。

对于《每日新闻》经济报道的属性议程设置效果,研究者既从低阶属性(议题的12个方面),也从宏观框架(四个问题性情境)进行了测试。结果发现,随着公众接触越来越多的新闻,在高低两个层次上,报纸议程与公众议程之间的一致性都增长了。在低阶属性层面,低、中、高程度的新闻接触与媒介议程之间的相关系数分别是+0.54、+0.55和+0.64。在宏观框架层面,三种不同接触程度的相关系数分别是+1.00、+0.80和+1.00。虽然这两个系列的相关系数存在数值差异(那无疑是因为类别数量的不同,前者是12,后者是4),但无论是在微观属性方面,还是在宏观属性方面,都存在议程设置的效果。

最近,有学者回顾架构研究并得出结论:"媒介效果研究应该抛弃'框架建构'这一作为若干不同的媒介效果模式的总称的通用术语,而采用那种更精确的术语,在等值(equivalence)和强调(emphasis)两种框架建构之间作出区分。"[45]虽然这个述评是针对架构的,但这种区别揭示了议程设置与框架建构之间的相似性和非相似性。强调性框架与议程设置理论的属性显著性相似。例如,全球变暖议题可以用经济、政治或者个人生活方式来框定,具体做法取决于新闻对这些角度的强调。在议程设置研究中,这些框架可能被概念化为议题属性。然而,等值的框架却与议程设置理论的任何方面都截然不同。综述所谓的"等值性框架",也可以指"修辞性框架"(rhetorical frames),指的是用两种方式说同一件事情,会产生不同的结果。

有一个经典的案例,是丹尼尔·卡尼曼(Daniel Kahneman)与阿莫斯·特沃斯基(Amos Tversky)的一项实验。在这个实验中,他们分别从存活率和死亡率两个不同的角度来发布消息,说明同一种情况,结果产生了极为不同的反应。[46]另一个人们熟悉的例子是"还有半杯水"和"只剩半杯水"的口语表述。当然,用属性的方式来说,这两种表达说明的是杯子装水的同一种情况。除了属性与强调性框架交叉的情况之外，议程设置与框架建构是传播学研究中界限清晰的不同理论路径。

小　结

媒介在展示公共事务的大千世界时强调的显著元素，往往也成为我们个人世界图像中的显著元素，这个议程设置理论的普遍命题起初测量的是对时下议题的关注度。研究者对媒介议程所强调的议题与公众议程上逐渐显现的议题进行比较。这些比较一次又一次地证实：媒介议程与公众议程的议题排名高度一致。借用李普曼的话说，在"图像是关于什么的"问题上，存在高度的一致性。这是议程设置的第一层面。

在这些图像的实际细节方面，也存在高度的一致性。将大众媒介对政治候选人和公众议题的描述与公众对这些客体的描述进行比较，结果显示了"图像"内容的高度一致性。大众媒介中的显著属性往往也会成为公众头脑中的显著属性。这是议程设置的第二层面。在这个层面，媒介内容中关于公共事务的特定方面与舆论的形成存在明确的联系。两个层面的议程设置都反映了媒介在传播过程的早期阶段对舆论形成的重大作用，亦即效果，既包含受众在最初层面对消息的关注，也包含其后他们对消息主题的理解。[47]

公众思考这些问题的方式（"怎样想"的问题）既包括认知的元素，也包括情感的元素，而这一过程与公众"想什么"的问题以及他们的态度和观点又紧密地交织在一起。在《美国政治中的议程与不稳定性》(*Agendas and Instability in American Politics*)一书中，弗兰克·鲍姆加特纳(Frank Baumgartner)和布莱恩·琼斯(Bryan Jones)发现，在舆论和公共政策发生重大转变之前，这些议题的显著方面常常会率先在公众中出现重大的转变。他们的个案研究包括核能、烟草、杀虫剂、汽车安全等问题。[48]

讽刺的是,属性议程设置的这些结果又将我们带回到媒介影响人们态度和观点的老传统上了。这是20世纪40—50年代大众传播实证研究开始的地方,也是此后一代学者几乎完全放弃的领域——他们报告说,媒介几乎不产生任何明显的效果。议程设置理论的出现是对这种狭隘判断的回应。第八章将会根据新近的理论进展,重新审视这种判断。

第四章 议题和属性的网络

在议程设置研究中,议程通常被认为是,一系列离散的议题(或其他客体)及其属性,根据媒体报道或民意调查中公众提及的频率进行排序。然而,在新闻中,议题和属性是捆绑在一起的。在一家新闻网站的主页上,一篇关于重大科学突破的报道可能会与健康生活方式的特稿争夺版面和关注度。重要事件和"软新闻"一道显示,没有任何明确的线索可以确定哪个更为重要。同时,一名政治记者可以在同一篇报道中突出候选人的许多不同特征。在所有这些例子中,只有通过历时性的系统分析,才可能确定哪些议题或属性在新闻议程上处于更高的位置。基本的议程设置研究提供了一种简单明了的方法,那就是计算一个话题在新闻中被报道的次数。而属性议程设置研究通过对媒体突出报道的新闻议题进行更加细致的分析,关注并探索那些议题的哪些属性如何确切地影响到公众意见。不过,基本的议程设置研究和属性议程设置研究是以分离的观点看待议题和属性的。沿着这个方向更进一步,就是我们现在所说的网络议程设置,它研究的是特定议题和属性绑定而成的"束"(bundles),它们构成了新闻,并显现于公众的思考和对话中。

在第三章,我们检视过"雄辩论据"的概念,首次从理论上确认了媒介将其议程诸元素之间的关系转移到公众议程上的那种能力。这个概念认为,新闻媒体可以将某个客体和某种属性绑定,使它们同时在公众心目中变得显著。一些其他的束也值得考虑。

孙和韦弗(Son and Weaver)对媒介的客体和属性议程的扩展,考虑到了新闻媒体向公众展示候选人及其情感属性时的新闻背景。[1]他们对2000年美国总统选举进行了研究,探讨了这样一个问题,即哪些新闻来源的候选人显著性和哪些新闻来源的候选人属性显著性,可以预测公众对每个候选人的意见变化,无论是即时的,还是累积的。研究发现,第一层面和第二层面的议程设置对候选人在全国民意测验中排名的影响基本上都是累积的,而不是即时的;不同的新闻来源产生了截然不同的效果。对于候选人的显著性而言,记者的分析和民意调查的排名有很强的累积效应。就候选人属性的显著性而言,候选人本人的言论及竞争对手党派成员的陈述都对民调结果有很强的累积效应。其他新闻来源则很少或者几乎没有影响。

这一扩展的视角建议将客体和属性显著性的传统度量与新闻要素结合起来,后者或者是新闻来源,或者是写作风格,这些都是新闻报道的特征。根据李普曼的"我们头脑中的图像"的观点,无论是雄辩论据的概念,还是新闻故事特征和传统衡量标准(客体和属性显著性)的整合,都提出了一个问题:"媒介能在多大程度上转移一幅综合图像的显著性?"

一些心理学家和哲学家认为,人们的心理表征是以图画、图示或者制图的方式运作的。也就是说,受众根据这些元素的相互关系将客体和属性绘制成网状图。从这个角度看,新闻媒体是将一系列元素之间的关系的显著性传递给了公众。这些系列可以是媒介或公众议程上的客体、媒介或公众议程上的属性,也可以是客体和属性的一种组合,也就是说,一组完全整合的客体和属性(包括媒介消息的属性)。媒介议程和公众议程上各种元素之间关系的集合,就是议程设置的第三层面。[2]这个层面研究的焦点是客体和/或属性的整个网状系统(networks)的显著性转移,而不仅仅是第一层面和第二层面所考察的离散元素的显著性。

一、联想式记忆

网络议程设置的理论核心是记忆的网状联想模式。认知心理学、哲学、地理学和传播学等各种学科的学者以相似的方式将这种联想式记忆模式理论化,但名称各不相同。例如,联想网状模型(associative network model)[3],认知图绘(cognitive mapping)[4],以及扩散激活模型(spreading activation model)[5]。这些联想模型并非如第一层面和第二层面的议程设置理论所暗示的那样,将我们的心理表征以层级或线性的结构方式概念化,而是认为表征是作为各种元素构成的网络来运作的。[6]在公众议程的网状模型中,个体的认知表征呈类网状结构,其中每个特定的节点通常都会连接到其他许多节点。这种网络中的一个节点可以指信息的任何单元:客体及其属性,目标、价值观和动机,情感或情绪状态,甚至是基模或框架那样的宏观单元。[7]

以政治传播为例。当一个人考虑某个政治候选人并引用某些属性来描述他时,并不需要清楚说明按照候选人属性的显著性排列的等级。作为替代,各种各样的属性可以构成一个网状图像,描述个人心目中的候选人形象。新闻媒体正是这些认知网络的主要信息来源。正如我们在第一章中提到的,新闻媒体可以决定我们关于世界的认知图式。

二、候选人和属性的网络

媒介是否能捆绑各种元素,使其在公众心中变得显著?对此的最初探索[8]采用了一项早期研究的数据,那项研究基于对政治候选人离散属性集合的传统分析,发现了很强的属性议程设置效果。在对得克萨斯州四名州一级政治候选人的选民形象开展的原创研究中[9],媒介属性议程和公众属性议程之间的总体对应关系为+0.65。进一步运用网络分析统计技术,对媒介议程与公众议程的属性绑定模式进行分析（即考察第三层面议程设置效果）,其相关系数为+0.67,这一结果在统计上与最初的分析非常相似。当然,这些议程的网络化表征显示出更为丰富的属性图像。这些得自绑定式选举数据的结果与2010年州长选举期间收集到的新数据[10]进行了复验,得出的相关系数为+0.71。

为了进行第三层面议程设置研究,最初的步骤是将数据排列为一个矩阵,显示成对属性在同一篇新闻文章（媒介网状属性议程）中出现的频率,以及每对属性在受访者对候选人的描述（公众网状属性议程）中出现的频率。矩阵展示了媒介内容分析所发现的10种属性同时出现的情况,见框4.1。根据调查对象对候选人的描述,构建了同样的10个属性同时出现的相似矩阵。

框4.1 候选人属性矩阵

	A	B	C	D	E	F	G	H	I	J
A		4	2	3	3	0	1	2	0	3
B	4		9	11	7	5	7	2	4	17
C	2	9		7	6	3	4	1	2	8
D	3	11	7		6	4	3	1	1	12
E	3	7	6	6		1	1	1	1	8
F	0	5	3	4	1		3	0	2	6
G	1	7	4	3	1	3		1	2	5
H	2	2	1	1	1	0	1		0	1
I	0	4	2	1	1	2	2	0		2
J	3	17	8	12	8	6	5	1	2	

（A=领导力;B=经验;C=能力;D=可信度;E=道德;F=关爱;G=沟通技巧;H=对家庭/背景、出身和种族/族群的自豪感;I=非政客;J=对候选人个人资质和性格的"其他"评论。）

来源：Lei Guo and Maxwell McCombs, 'Network agenda setting: A third level of media effects', paper presented to the International Communication Association, Boston, 2011.

这些矩阵是对数据进行网络分析的输入部分。我们的研究用的是 USINET(一种社会网络分析软件),其他研究则使用了 R 语言或类似软件。软件计算了两个矩阵之间的相关性,并绘出了潜在的网状结构。首次网络议程设置研究[11]检查过的媒介网状属性议程和公众网状属性议程都呈现在框 4.2 中。

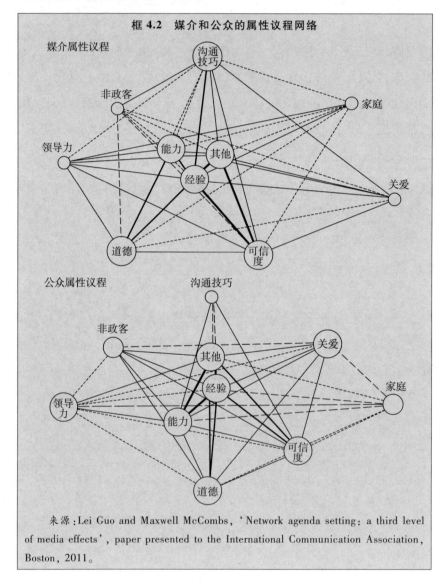

框 4.2　媒介和公众的属性议程网络

来源:Lei Guo and Maxwell McCombs, 'Network agenda setting: a third level of media effects', paper presented to the International Communication Association, Boston, 2011.

除了衡量媒介网状属性议程与公众网状属性议程的对应程度,也就是计算相关性之外,网络分析还详细显示了媒介的和公众的属性议程网络中各属性的点度中心性(degree centrality)。具体说来,点度中心性是指网络中的一个节点(特定的属性或客体)与网络中所有其他元素之间连接(联系)的数量。例如,在由客体(如议题)组成的网络中,网络分析细致呈现了每个客体在媒介和公众的议程网络中的点度中心性。在网状环境中,点度中心性是对这个网络中每个元素显著性的度量。

在框4.2中,能力和经验这两个属性与网络中的其他属性有许多联系,因此具有较高的点度中心性得分。相反,非政客这一属性的点度中心性得分较低。还要注意,图中节点连接线的粗细显示出元素之间连接的数量。

三、网络议程设置的累积证据

随后的一项研究检验了横跨五年的网状议题议程,超越了在政治竞选期间对网状属性议程的密切关注。[12]研究者对2007年至2011年五年间皮尤研究中心(Pew Research Center)的卓越新闻项目(Project for Excellence in Journalism, PEJ;这个项目对48个美国新闻媒体每周报道最多的话题进行内容分析,从而获得媒介网状议题议程),与盖洛普民意调查每月询问的"最重要问题"的结果(公众网状议题议程)进行比较,结果发现整个时期媒介议程与公众议程之间的相关系数从+0.65到+0.87不等。除此之外,一项交叉时滞相关分析表明,在大多数情况下,媒介网状议题议程影响了公众网状议题议程。将五年中所有媒介网状议题议程与公众网状议题议程合并进行比较,得到的相关系数为+0.81。

在美国,对网络议程设置的最初探索依循议程设置更早阶段的研究趋势,也主要集中于竞选活动。在2012年巴拉克·奥巴马和米特·罗姆尼竞选总统期间,一项创新研究[13]调查了新闻媒体在推特上绑定不同议题的方式,以及这些绑定方式如何影响了推特用户对选举议题的讨论。研究分析了17周的竞选活动,其中有15周,奥巴马的支持者的网状议题议程与报纸和广播电视频道的网状议题议程呈正相关。同时,罗姆尼的支持者的网状议题议程在17周中有13周与传统媒体的网状议题议程显著相关。将奥巴马和罗姆尼的支持者的网状议题议程与新媒体(例如微软全国广播公司[MSNBC]、福克斯新闻,以及在这些媒体工作的记者的个人账号)的相应议题议程进行比较,结果也都得到了验证。其他基于网络的议程设置研究也已经在最近的美国大选背景下进行。[14]

在美国之外,一项研究[15]将网络议程设置模式应用于2012年中国台湾地区领导人选举期间收集到的数据,研究者比较了媒体(报纸和电视)报道中议题和候选人属性的网络与用同样方式测量的公众意见网络。就像对奥巴马和罗姆尼的研究一样,台湾地区媒体和公众网状议程之间的整体关联也是正向和显著的,特别是在属性(而不是议题)层面。

网络议程设置研究也重复并延伸了对政治之外的活动的检验。在中国香港地区进行的网络分析基于网络议程设置初始研究的类似方法,比较了媒体关于两个不同议题的新闻报道和民调的公众反应。在这两个案例中,证据都显示了在第三层面上强大的属性议程设置效果。还有一项关于伊拉克战争的网络属性议程研究,比较了美国、中国和波兰的新闻报道。[16]另一项研究关注所谓的"技术博客"和传统新闻媒体有关技术话题、技术产品和科技公司的网状议程。[17]还有一项实证研究比较了绿色和平组织、新闻媒体及脸书对某一环境议题的行动者及其属性的讨论的网状议程。[18]

四、一种新的格式塔视角

虽然第三层面议程设置及其网络分析统计方法是近年来出现的议程设置理论的新面向,但它其实是源自早期的议程设置研究的某种格式塔观点的延伸。我们所指的格式塔,是混合了重大公众议题和新闻媒体呈现给公众的新闻话题的集合体。这种格式塔视角也描述了公众在接触媒介议程时所体验和吸收的那些观点。

在议程设置研究最初的日子里,雷·芬克豪泽将20世纪60年代整整十年的新闻报道的主要议题,与公众反映的美国这十年面临的最重要议题进行比较,发现了高度的相关性,相关系数为+0.78。[19]最近,斯特龙巴克和基欧瑟斯[20]又发现,对政治新闻的关注总量(亦即对媒体报道格式塔的关注),而不是对特定新闻媒体的关注,预示着选民在投票时认为最重要的议题的显著性。

采用网络分析方法的议程设置研究为该理论在当前媒介环境中的应用注入了新的活力。如第一章所述,多年来,人们一直认为,议程设置的效果取决于传统新闻媒体的命运。许多观察家指出,随着电视、广播和报纸的同质性议程被数字媒体的异质性议程所取代,议程设置效果出现的可能性已经减少。然而,网络议程设置研究在纳入源自推特、党派网站和其他非传统媒体的数据后,却也发现了显著性从一组议程转移到另一组议程的有力证据。[21]不仅如此,网络分析路径还激发了新一轮关于议程设置的跨国研究,[22]而这一直是其他传播理论的受限之地。

小　结

传统的第一层面和第二层面的议程设置研究考察了离散的消息元素(议题或其他客体及其属性)从媒体向公众的转移。然而,将媒介议程视为网络化元素的集合,一个格式塔,并考察这些元素之间的联系,可以更全面地了解媒介呈现的内容和公众的体验。

在我们理解媒介对舆论的影响方面,采用网络分析方法已被证明是一个重要的进步。新闻报道提供的关于候选人、议题及其各自属性的认知地图和情感指南,影响着媒介使用者有关"外部世界"的心理图像——媒介所传递的客体和属性的集合,往往也会出现在人们的头脑和对话中。

第五章 议程设置为何发生

在高中物理课上,你可能学过一条科学原理,叫作"大自然不容真空"。同样的命题也适用于人类心理。在我们每个人心中,都有理解周围环境的需求。[1]每当我们发现自己处在一个新的环境,也就是说认知一片空白时,就会有一种不安的感觉;直到我们不断探索这个环境并在脑海中形成了图像,这种感觉才会消失。回忆你刚上大学的第一年,你可能走进了一个全新的、陌生的校园,开始了一次新的知识航程。或者回忆你刚刚搬到一座新城市的经历,甚至仅仅是访问一座新城市,尤其是去外国城市的经历。在这样的情况下,新去的人会产生一种了解身边环境的导向需求。大学会举办内容广泛的新生引导活动。出版商也发现,为游客提供指南类书籍,包含地图册、饭店和餐馆名录,以及其他各种向导性信息,其实有利可图。

在市民生活领域,也有许多让公民感到需要指导的情境。在政党挑选提名竞选公职者的预选中,有时会有十几个候选人。因为是党内的预选,所有的候选人都属于同一个政党,所以选民经常使用的指导线索,即政党归属,在这里意义不大。在这种情况下,许多选民都感到自己非常需要引导。这种情况还出现在债券选举(bond elections)和其他全民公投中,党派标签在此完全没有指导意义。此外,在许多基层公职选举中,出现的都是非党派的,常常也很陌生的候选人。在所有这些情况下,选民通常会转向新闻媒体寻求指导,他们或者依靠手边的新闻报道获得与形势相关的信息,或者直接依赖报纸社论形成自己的观点。[2]当然,在获得指导的需求程度方面,并不是每个选民都一样。一些公民在作出选举投票决定之前喜欢搜集大量的背景信息,也有一些人只是想要一条简单的引导线索。"导向需求"(need for orientation)是一个心理学概念,它描述了在希望获得引导线索和寻求背景信息方面的个体差异。

这些经常在选举情境中显示出来的行为模式,是心理学家爱德华·托尔曼(Edward Tolman)提出的"认知图绘"(cognitive mapping)理论的一个缩影。[3]之前我们遇到的一个相似观点是李普曼的拟态环境概念,李普曼认为这种拟态环境是我们头脑中关于世界的图像,而并非世界本身。这两种观点的共同之处在于,我们会形成关于外部环境的地图,虽然在许多时候这些地图是极为粗略、高度浓缩的。罗伯特·莱恩(Robert Lane)通过检验我们"从政治环境中获取意义的努力",强调了这种绘图行为的目的性本质。[4]莱恩将这些努力的根源分别归结为人类的天性、童年的社会化过程和正规教育。"导向需求"这个心理学概念是戴维·韦弗在1972年关于议程设置的夏洛特研究中引进的,如我们在第一章中总结的,它描述了人们寻求意义的这种努力,为显著性从媒介议程向公众议程的转移提供了一种心理学解释。

一、关联性与不确定性

从概念上讲,个体的导向需求可以通过两个次级概念来界定:关联性与不确定性。它们相继发生作用。关联性(relevance)是界定导向需求的初始条件。不管怎么说,在许多情境中,尤其是在公共事务领域,我们大多数人并没有心理方面的不适感,也不会有导向需求,因为我们觉得这些与我们没什么关联。亚美尼亚或者新西兰的国内政治很难激起多数欧洲公民或者北美公民的兴趣。同样的道理也适用于当前的许多议题,甚至在我们自己的国家也是如此。有许多议题只与全体公众中的一小部分有关。在这些与个体关联性低甚至不存在关联的情境中,导向需求也很低。

然而,不管出于什么原因,只要个体感到某个话题与自己关联性很高(为简单起见,关联性在这里只分高低),那么他下一个必须考虑的因素便是话题的不确定性(uncertainty)。在框 5.1 中我们可以看到,不确定性是导向需求的第二个,也是继关联性之后的界定条件。情况常常是,个体已经获得了他关于某个话题想知道的所有信息,那么,他的不确定感便很低。许多公众议题,公众对于它们的意见在很长时间里都非常稳定,就属于这种情况。在这种情况下,人们通常并不会无视新闻媒体;但他们关注新闻报道,主要是为了获知身边环境是否发生了重大改变。[5] 在这种高相关性和低不确定性的情形下,导向需求处于中等水平。

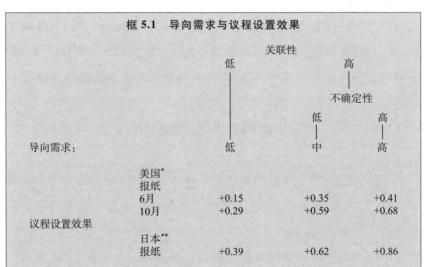

框 5.1　导向需求与议程设置效果

		关联性		
		低	高	
			不确定性	
			低	高
导向需求:		低	中	高
议程设置效果	美国*报纸			
	6月	+0.15	+0.35	+0.41
	10月	+0.29	+0.59	+0.68
	日本**报纸	+0.39	+0.62	+0.86

* 来源:David Weaver, 'Political issues and voter need for orientation', in *The Emergence of American Political Issues*, ed. Donald Shaw and Maxwell McCombs (St Paul, MN: West, 1977), pp. 107–119。

** 来源:Toshio Takeshita, 'Agenda-setting effects of the press in a Japanese local election', *Studies of Broadcasting*, 29(1993): 193–216。

在其他时候,关联性与不确定性都比较高。这种情况经常出现在政党预选时期,因为这时出现了许多公众不熟悉的候选人,而且政党归属这个最简单的引导线索也不管用了。对于刚刚进入公众议程,基本上算新的议题来说,也是如此,例如最近一段时期美国关于医疗保险改革的广泛辩论。对于许多美国人来说,这个议题的复杂性与含义的广泛性导致了高度的关联性与高度的不确定性。用理论术语来说,这些公民的导向需求很高。

相反,对于1998年比尔·克林顿总统和莫妮卡·莱温斯基的性丑闻,大多数美国人并没有导向需求。虽然多数人觉得总统的这种个人行为应该受到谴责,但大多数人同样认为,这种行为与他的总统职位没有关系。即便新闻媒体咬住丑闻报道不放,但是一次又一次的调查数据都显示,人们对克林顿作为总统的工作表现评价很高。[6] 从特朗普第一次受到弹劾调查的例子中也能观察到同样的趋势。尽管有密集的负面新闻报道,但从2019年10月调查启动开始,到2020年1月参议院宣判他无罪为止,特朗普的支持率始终稳定在40%—45%。[7] 有时,公众对媒介没有什么导向需求,也没有感到必须去关心媒介的议程。

二、议程设置效果的出现

个体在公共事务领域的导向需求越高,他们就越可能关注大众媒介的议程。[8] 例如,1972年美国总统选举期间,在北卡罗来纳州夏洛特市的选民中,导向需求高的那部分人中有79.8%经常通过看报纸、收看电视节目及阅读新闻类杂志来获取政治信息。相较而言,导向需求中等的那部分人中只有62.5%经常使用大众媒介获取政治信息。而在导向需求低的那部分选民中,这个比例仅为47.4%。

这个概念还解释了教育与接触大众媒介议程之间众所周知的关系。[9] 2000年美国总统预选时,在得克萨斯选民中,受教育程度既与收看候选人在有线电视上的辩论高度相关,也与导向需求的存在高度相关——界定这种导向需求的具体方法是询问人们是否觉得竞选议程上有任何与自己相关的议题。对这些关系的详细分析显示,导向需求是一个干预变量,可以解释受教育程度与收看候选人辩论之间的联系。受教育程度是对个人的公共事务认知取向粗略的背景预测指标;而收看候选人辩论则是高度具体的信息搜寻行为。受教育程度越高(尤其是到了大学或大学以上水平),就越可能产生导向需求;这种心理需求继而又与收看辩论的行动联系在一起。

在选举期间,选民经常从新闻媒体与政治广告中获知大量关于候选人的信息及其在各种议题上的立场。这种学习行为包括对媒介议程的明显采纳,与选民的导向需求水平直接相关。在框 5.1 关于导向需求的概念图示下面,是对 1972 年美国总统选举时在夏洛特选民中出现的议程设置效果的总结。[10]在夏季竞选活动成形期间,以及其后秋季竞选期间,议程设置的效果随着导向需求的提高而一径增长。如果将选举比喻成一个开放式的公民课堂,那么议程设置效果从 6 月到10 月的增长支持了"课堂"这个比喻:这一阶段学生们正在做功课。

我们在第一章讨论过的日本市长选举研究中也发现了议程设置效果的相同模式。[11]如果将这些日本选民按导向需求水平分成不同的级别,那么,议程设置效果的力度也随着需求度的上升而一径增长,框 5.1 显示了这一趋势。如前所述,在这些选民中,媒介议程与公众议程之间的相关系数为+0.39,总的结果适度,但为正相关。与大多数研究发现的证据相比,这个相关系数很低。

但是,框 5.1 也显示,对于那些导向需求为中等的选民来说,其议程与媒介议程之间的相关系数却为+0.62;而对于那些导向需求很高的选民来说,相关系数更是达到惊人的+0.86。进一步检验这次选举的证据,可以解释+0.39 这个相对低的总体相关数值。这是因为,受访的大部分选民导向需求较低,而这种选民大约占了 57%。只有 21%的选民导向需求较高。在这种情况下，导向需求这个概念便为媒介议程与公众议程之间这种较低的总体一致性提供了一个简明的解释。由于导向需求较低，大部分选民缺乏关注或者采纳媒介议程的动机。

"导向需求"这个概念还解释了在最早的查普希尔研究中媒介议程与公众议程之间近乎完美的匹配。[12]查普希尔研究中发现的总体相关系数高达+0.97，这个相关性极大地鼓励了研究者对议程设置现象的进一步探索。虽然"导向需求"这个概念作为议程设置理论的一部分，是在查普希尔研究完成几年之后才提供解释的，但是追溯起来，十分清楚的是，最初的查普希尔研究所获得的议程设置证据，完全基于那些导向需求较高的选民。回顾整个研究过程可以发现，查普希尔的受访人完全是根据注册选民的名单随机选择的。也就是说，总统选举及其议题议程对这些人来说是具有关联性的。他们是注册选民，而且是尚未决定支持哪个总统候选人的选民。整个样本都是由这些尚在犹豫中的选民组成的。用理论术语来说，所有这些选民心中都有高度的不确定感。高度关联性和高度不确定性决定了高度的导向需求，这是可以预言媒介议程与公众议程之间存在高度一致性的理论条件。尽管查普希尔研究得到的相关系数+0.97非常高，但是在导向需求高的日本选民中得到的相关系数是+0.86，相形之下，+0.97并不是一个高不可攀的天文数字。

关于导向需求概念的有效性，还可以在框5.2中发现其他证据。这里的证据表明，选民的导向需求越高，就越觉得有必要获知总统竞选人在这些议题上所持的立场。[13]换句话说，这个关于求知欲的一般概念，解释了选民对某类特定信息在兴趣程度上的差异。选民对相对不知名的竞选者吉米·卡特在各种议题上的立场均表现出较大兴趣，超过了对寻求连任的在职总统福特的立场的关心，这一发现进一步验证了导向需求这个概念的有效性。

一项研究发现，在美国中西部的一个地方环境议题上，公众头脑中的图像与地方报纸对一个大型人工湖开发的六个方面的报道也有很强的相关性(+0.60)。[14]与前面描述的第一层面议程设置的客体显著性的模式相同,报纸的属性议程与公众头脑中的图像的一致性程度也随着公众导向需求的增加而上升。对导向需求低的市民而言,他们的属性议程与报纸的属性议程的匹配度只有+0.26;而在有较高导向需求的人那里,这种匹配度是+0.77。我们再次看到,导向需求的增加促成了对媒介议程更多的获取行为。

框 5.2 导向需求与对政治信息的平均兴趣水平

	导向需求		
	低	中	高
福特的议题立场	4.8*	5.5	5.7
卡特的议题立场	5.0	5.6	6.3

*最大值=7

来源:David Weaver and Maxwell McCombs,'Voters' need for orientation and choice of candidate: mass media and electoral decision making', paper presented at the American Association for Public Opinion Research, Roanoke, VA, 1978。

三、关联性

关联性是确定导向需求的关键概念。一个话题或议题与个体的关联性有很多来源。近年来,这些多样化的关联性来源已经得到相当细致、透彻的阐述。有一项创新性的研究,调查了八个不同的宏观和微观议题,从全球变暖到个人健康,采用了一套含13组两极词语的语义差别量表,测量那些议题的关联性。[15]对这些数据的分析揭示出三种深层维度:

社会关联性维度——使用无关联/有关联、不重要的/重要的这些标准来测量;

个体关联性维度——例如，对我而言是重要的/对我而言是不重要的、与我无关的/与我有关的；

情感关联性维度——例如，无聊的/有趣的、刺激的/不刺激的。

西班牙社会学家费尔明·博萨（Fermín Bouza）对个体关联性与社会关联性也进行了同样的区分：

个体始终保有一个重要的个人利益领域，在一定程度上，它与个体认为的公共利益或所有人的利益相分离。个人利益领域与公共利益领域之间的这种明确区分，标志着一块区域的存在，我将它定义为"政治传播的影响区域"［……］因为在这个区域，个体感到国家利益与自身利益有明显的重合。[16]

研究者利用社会关联性、个体关联性与情感关联性之间的理论区分，巧妙地组织了得克萨斯州的两次全州民意调查的数据。这两次调查是为了探明被访者在回答盖洛普调查广泛使用的"最重要问题"（什么是这个国家当前面临的最重要问题？）时，为何会提及某个特定的议题。[17]对一系列后续问题的分析是为了探究受访者在回答"最重要问题"时所提及议题的回响，结果确认了稳定地构成一组的议题关联性的五个来源，这与理论上的区分相吻合：

社会关联性维度——公民责任和同侪影响；

个体关联性维度——自身利益和业余爱好；

情感关联性维度——情感激发。

塞巴斯蒂安·瓦伦苏埃拉采用了另一种观察议题的个体关联性的途径，指出罗纳德·英格尔哈特（Ronald Inglehart）的物质主义和后物质主义价值观[18]与议程设置效果有很强的关联。[19]瓦伦苏埃拉利用了一项对全加拿大主要日报的内容分析、2006年加拿大全国选举的调查数据和一项原创性实验研究，他发现，无论是在集合层面还是在个体层面,具有物质主义价值观的人都比具有后物质主义价值观的人显现更突出的议程设置效果。例如,在集合层面,媒介议程与公众议程之间的相关系数,物质主义者为+0.55,后物质主义者为+0.35。这些发现与这样的状况是一致的,即媒体明显更多地报道物质主义的议题(如经济和犯罪),而较少报道后物质主义的议题(如环境和政治改革的情况)。[20]

对新闻中的客体的情感也很重要。尽管西方思想有贬抑感情而突出理性的传统,但神经科学家长期以来一直认为,感情与认知是交织在一起的。在议程设置领域,乔安妮·米勒(Joanne Miller)发现,新闻触发的特定情感解释了人们对议题重要性的判断。[21]她的实验测量了受试者在阅读犯罪新闻报道时触发情感(如感到愤怒、自豪、充满希望和快乐,以及悲伤和恐惧)的程度。其中,只有悲伤和恐惧的感觉对议程设置的效果产生了调节作用。无论是对情感激发作用的总测量,还是对六种情感反应联合产生的效价的总测量,均未能解释接触犯罪新闻与指认犯罪为国家面临的最重要问题之间的联系。然而,负面情绪的产生的确让人更有可能将犯罪视为最重要的问题。

这种新兴的阐释关联性概念的格式塔(完形),是议程设置研究中的一个主要趋势的例子。借用物理学的术语,这种对关联性概念的重新检验代表了一种"向心"(centripetal)趋势,也就是说,学者们将注意力转向内部,以期进一步解释议程设置理论的基本概念。

这种趋势的另一个例子,是由约尔格·马特斯(Jörg Matthes)开发出来的系列量表,通过调查问题测量导向需求。[22]对应于第一层面的议程设置,使用等级量表测量人们对客体本身的导向需求,例如,"持续关注这个议题对我很重要";另外的等级量表测量第二层面的议程设置效果,既包括所在意的客体的实质属性("我想要彻底了解特定细节"),又包括可见于述评和社论的新闻评论所反映出的客体的情感属性("我很看重对这个话题的评论")。我们可以汇总这三个系列的测量,为每个问卷回答者创建一个导向需求的单一得分。

在对德国失业议题的一次调查中,马特斯发现,基于这种复合测量方法得出的导向需求的强度可以预测基本的第一层面议程设置效果。然而,导向需求强度却不能预测第二层面的媒介议程设置效果,特别是在失业议题的情感属性上。[23]

一次控制实验比较了传统的导向需求测量方法与这些新的测量方法在预测议程设置效果方面的强度差别。结果发现,传统的测量方法有更强的预测能力。不过,将传统方法与新方法的第一维度(直接联系到第一层面议程设置的维度)的测量结果相比较,却显示出这两种测量非常相似。[24]

四、有关公众议题的个人经验

新闻媒体并非我们了解公共事务的唯一来源。个人经验,包括与家庭成员、朋友和同事的谈话,也让我们知晓许多议题。当然,主导来源会因人而异,因事而异。对于一个经济议题,如通货膨胀,直接经验几乎总是主导来源。如果在经济方面出现了明显的通货膨胀,那么个人在日常购物中便会发现。我们不需要新闻媒体提醒我们注意这个问题,也不需要新闻媒体驱散我们对其重要性的任何不确定感。相反,对于国家的贸易赤字等经济议题,新闻媒体可能是我们获得指导的唯一来源。还有许多其他公众议题,尤其是在外交事务领域,个人的亲身经验极其有限,甚至根本没有。用理论术语来说,一些议题是强制性的(obtrusive),也就是说,它们不容商量地闯进我们的日常生活,被我们直接体验到。其他议题是非强制性的(unobtrusive),我们只是在新闻报道中与它们相遇,而不会在日常生活中接触到它们。[25]

一项加拿大研究考察了新闻媒体对三个公众议题的显著性的议程设置影响,发现根据强制性与非强制性议题的区分,能够预测结果的不同模式。[26] 框 5.3 显示,在 16 个月的时间里,有关通货膨胀的新闻报道模式与这个议题在加拿大公众中的显著性之间,只有很低的一致性(+0.28)。但是,在国家统一这个抽象而非强制性的议题上,却存在极高的匹配度(+0.96)。我们稍后会很快回到第三个议题,即失业问题,凭推想它似乎是个强制性议题,但这里的实证结果(+0.67)却更接近对非强制性议题的预期。不过,首先让我们来检验一些从美国得到的支持强制性与非强制性议题之区分的其他证据。

框 5.3　在强制性议题与非强制性议题上的议程设置效果(自然历史角度)

强制性		非强制性
加拿大*		
通货膨胀 +0.28	失业 +0.67	国家统一 +0.96
美国**		
犯罪 +0.19	失业 +0.60	污染 +0.79
生活成本 +0.20		毒品滥用 +0.80
		能源 +0.71

  *来源:James Winter, Chaim Eyal and Ann Rogers, 'Issue-specific agenda setting: the whole as less than the sum of the parts', *Canadian Journal of Communication*, 8, 2(1982): 1–10。
  **来源:Harold Zucker, 'The variable nature of news media influence', in *Communication Yearbook 2*, ed. Brent Ruben (New Brunswick, NJ: Transaction Books, 1978), pp. 225–240。

在对美国十年舆论的研究中,也发现了同样的结果——舆论与新闻报道在非强制性议题上具有高度一致性,而在强制性议题上则只有低度一致性。[27]框 5.3 显示了在污染、毒品滥用与能源这些非强制性议题上的高度相关性,以及在犯罪、生活成本这些强制性议题上的低度相关性。在美国地方层面,路易维尔研究中发现的议程设置模式也表明,媒体报道在强制性议题上缺乏影响力,这在第一章中已经总结过了。在这个研究中,虽然媒介议程与公众议程之间的总体相关系数为+0.65,但是,详细比较各个议题在这两个议程上的排名,可以发现,

"两个议程之间的重大差异表现在道路维护、医疗保健、法庭审理、排水系统、大众交通等人们很可能具有直接经验的议题上"[28]。

所有这些关于强制性与非强制性议题之间差异的证据都基于对单个议题的分析。按照阿卡普尔科模型的分类,这些都是属于自然历史角度的证据。不过,从竞争角度考虑整体议题议程的研究,也发现了能够得出相同结论的证据。框 5.4 显示了一系列比较,其中,媒介议程与公众议程上的议题都被分成了两组,一组是非强制性议题议程,另一组是强制性议题议程。[29]非强制性议题议程包括七个议题:政府可信度、政府开支、外交事务、环境与能源、犯罪、种族关系、社会问题。强制性议题议程包括四个与经济有关的议题:失业、税收、通货膨胀、经济总体状况。在框 5.4 中,所有对非强制性议题的测量均表明存在强大的议程设置效果。相关系数中位数在+0.67 与+0.74 之间。与此相反,在强制性议题上,媒介议程与公众议程之间几乎没有什么对应关系。相关系数中位数只在+0.20 与+0.32 之间。

框 5.4 在强制性议题与非强制性议题上的议程设置效果(竞争角度)		
	强制性议题议程	非强制性议题议程
新罕布什尔州		
报纸	+0.32	+0.67
电视新闻	+0.33	+0.74
印第安纳州		
报纸	+0.06	+0.60
电视新闻	+0.06	+0.59
伊利诺伊州		
报纸	+0.20	+0.95
电视新闻	+0.32	+0.95

来源:David Weaver, Doris Graber, Maxwell McCombs and Chaim Eyal, *Media Agenda Setting in a Presidential Election: Issues, Images, and Interest* (Westport, CT: Greenwood, 1981).

对新闻媒体关于强制性与非强制性议题的报道,公众之所以会作出差异如此明显的反应,一般可以用"导向需求"这个概念作出解释。因为强制性议题是指那些一定会闯入人们日常生活的议题,所以在许多情况下,个人经验就足以引导人们对身边形势作出判断,额外的导向需求相应较低,由此能够预测在这种情况下媒介议程与公众议程之间较低的相关性。而另一方面,在非强制性议题上,亲身经验并不能提供充分的指导。对此的理论假设便是,媒介议程通常是主要的导向来源,人们赖以减少他们心中的不确定感。

五、个体差异

当强制性与非强制性议题的概念被引入议程设置理论时,这种区分最初被当作一种简单的二分法。人们认为,议题要么是强制性的,要么是非强制性的。框 5.4 就是这种研究的典型代表。但是,框 5.3 已经预示了一种更巧妙的概念处理方法,根据这种方法,强制性与非强制性被当作一个连续体的两个端点。[30]考察公众与任何议题的相遇,都可以发现他们在亲身经验方面的个体差异。

现在,让我们回到前面讨论强制性/非强制性证据时暂时搁置的失业议题。这个议题表明,将强制性与非强制性概念作为一个连续体的两极而非简单的二分法来对待,是非常重要的。对于那些失业者或者认识失业者的人来说,这是一个强制性议题。但是对于大学终身教授、富裕的专业人士和许多其他人来说,失业是个抽象的非强制性议题。在失业以及其他许多议题上,人们的亲身经验差别极大。在框 5.3 中,失业经验的范围反映在方框的中间位置,位于连接强制性和非强制性以表示一个连续体的直线下方。虽然这两个相关性数值是在不同时期分别从美国与加拿大测得的,但它们非常相似。这说明,在这些时段,对于大多数北美人来说,失业议题基本上是个非强制性的议题,虽然并非人人如此。[31]

一项针对美国选民的固定样本研究,详细考察了与议题相关的亲身经验方面的个体差异。这项研究要求选民指出"美国联邦政府应该采取行动予以应对"的最重要问题。[32]分析集中在三个主要议题上:在失业议题上,通过调查受访者的个人或家庭就业情况,区分强制性与非强制性议题;在通货膨胀议题上,通过调查受访者的家庭收入情况,区分强制性与非强制性议题;在犯罪议题上,通过调查受访者夜间走在自己街区时的安全感程度,区分强制性与非强制性议题。

在认为议题具有强制性的那些人中,研究发现的证据为理论假设提供了支持,即他们主要通过与这些议题的接触来满足自己的导向需求,媒介并非重要的影响来源。高媒体使用者(较多使用媒体的人)并不比低媒体使用者(较少使用媒体的人)更有可能提及这三个议题中的任何一个。更多接触报纸和电视新闻也并没有提高这些议题在这个群体中的显著性。

然而,在认为议题具有非强制性的那些人当中,证据支持了另一个理论假设,即他们主要通过接触大众媒介来满足自己的导向需求,媒介的影响力也随着媒介接触量的增加而增强。对于这类选民来说,议题的显著性在高媒体使用者那里比在低媒体使用者那里要高。

在影响公众议题的显著性方面,大众媒介与亲身经验并非总是独自发挥作用。有证据显示,接触媒介的频次与对公众议题的亲身经验可以并行发生,共同影响公众议题。例如,在纽约州锡拉丘兹市(雪城)关于犯罪问题的民意调查中,在得克萨斯人对由13个议题组成的媒介议程的认同程度上,都发现了这种证据。[33]在雪城那些经常观看地方犯罪新闻的人中,地方犯罪议题的显著性更高,从而支持了议程设置的基本假设。在得克萨斯,媒介使用频率是公众与媒介议程保持一致的最佳预测变量。但是,在这两个调查中,对议题的亲身经验也是一个重要的因素,能够预测犯罪问题在雪城调查中的显著性,以及得克萨斯公众议程与媒介议程之间总体一致的程度。这两项研究的地理背景很不相同，一个是美国东北部的中型城市，一个是美国西南部面积很大的州，但两项研究都证明：媒介使用与亲身经验联合产生了强大的议程设置效果。例如，在雪城，对于那些经常接触电视和报纸上的地方犯罪新闻报道且对罪行有一些亲身经验的人来说，犯罪作为一个地方议题的显著性最高。在得克萨斯州，人们越是频繁使用新闻媒体，越是亲身参与公众议题，公众议程就越能反映媒介议程。

媒介使用和亲身经验与议程设置效果之间的这种正向并行关系，似乎与框 5.3 和框 5.4 中的证据相矛盾。然而，更深层的问题是，这个结果与前面调查的基本假设也不符。早期所有关于强制性与非强制性议题的研究都隐含这样的假设：对于个体导向而言，媒介消息与个体经验提供的线索是相互冲突的。于是，有关这些理论假设的反面证据也促使人们去说明一个更详细的理论地图。可以考虑这样一种可能性，即与某个议题有关的经验并不总能提供可满足个人心理需求的指导，因为人们在使用媒介与卷入议题的程度方面都存在个体差异，与此相伴的是，满足个人导向需求所需的信息量也存在相当大的个体差异。对于一些个体来说，可能是与某个议题有关的经验，而不是要满足导向需求，驱动他们在大众媒介上搜寻更多的信息，以验证问题的社会重要性。[34]对某个议题变得很敏感，可能会让这些个体成为特别适合研习媒介议程的学生。

在议题敏感度方面存在的个体差异，可与本章开头引用的莱恩有关正规教育的话联系起来。用莱恩的话说，正规教育影响人们"从政治环境中获取意义的努力"。在这方面，这里已经提到得克萨斯人令人意外的行为（高媒体使用），而得州人的受教育程度明显高于全国平均水平。未来对导向需求深度与广度的确切测量将能厘清亲身经验与媒介使用在议程设置过程中的作用。

得克萨斯研究的证据[35]还引入了"个人交谈"这个我们至今尚未

详细考察的传播渠道。在这些接受调查的得克萨斯人中,谈论公众议题的频率,既与媒介使用的频率存在正相关关系,也与对这些议题的亲身经验存在正相关关系。尽管谈论公众议题只是伴随其他许多行为产生的,在决定人们与媒介议程的一致程度方面并没有独立的作用(无论是正面的还是负面的作用)。还有一项研究调查了较依赖人际传播与较依赖新闻媒介的两类人是否具有相同议程的问题,也报告了类似的结果:在这两个群体的议程中没有发现明显的差异。[36]

谈论公众议题的行为没有发挥明确的影响,这大致代表了在研究议程设置过程中有关交谈作用的累积证据的平均状态。[37]有时,交谈强化了媒介议程的影响。[38]在德国进行了一项田野实验,研究者在杂志上发表了一篇有关某个新议题的文章。除了测量由文章引发的人际讨论之外,还测量了两天后这个议题在公众中显著性的变化。[39]研究发现,文章产生了一种连锁效应,首先是增加了对议题的谈论,其后又提升了议题的显著性,甚至在最初没有读过文章的人中也是如此。而在其他时候,交谈是与媒介相反的导向来源,它能够减少媒介的影响。[40]

六、顺带学习

导向需求、议题非强制性和亲身经验,是人们接受媒介议程的可能性的重要决定因素。对媒介的关注也是如此,正如我们在第二章中看到的,这里关注指的是接触媒介信息之后积极处理媒介内容的过程。[41]然而,由于新闻无所不在,脸书、推特和照片墙等社交媒体平台的兴起又强化了这一点,关注是否仍然是产生议程设置效果的必要条件,已经不那么清楚了。

在过去的十年中,这方面的研究一直围绕着"顺带(偶然、附带的行为)学习"(incidental learning)的概念在发展。对特定客体、人物或者形势的顺带学习,更可能发生于信息无所不在的环境中。[42]在当今的媒介环境中,各种议程高度冗余,增加了公众了解媒介议程的可能性,即便是在他们接触新闻不多的情况下。在德国,有两个实验研究显示了议程设置过程中顺带学习的作用。[43]其中的一个研究,要求参与者在两周内每天都访问同一个新闻网站。实验用的议题按照报道的频次(每日出现或者偶尔出现)和展示的显著性(头条新闻或简短报道)区别呈现。结果显示,对于那些并未亲身介入议题的受试者,顺带了解的线索(例如新闻的格式)也足以产生议程设置的效果;于是,这种对新闻议程的顺带学习转而帮助议题快速从媒体流向公众议程。在第一章中描述过的加里·金及其同事[44]在现实世界中的实验,发现公众议程在六天之内便会反映出新闻媒体的议程。总之,媒介议程与公众议程之间显著性的转移,既可能是积极行动的结果,也可能是顺带发生的现象。我们将在第六章讨论显著性转移的问题时重新回到这一结论。

七、议程融合

议程融合(agenda-melding/agendamelding),是晚近融入议程设置理论的一种思路,它进一步解释了公众议程的创建。大多数议程设置研究都聚焦于新闻媒介对公众议程的影响,而议程融合却将议程设置的这些效果纳入了包括其他来源的更为广泛的学习过程。正如唐纳德·肖等学者注意到的:

> 议程融合是一个过程。它发生于我们的头脑中。它将来自更广阔世界的消息混合到心灵舞台上的个人剧目中。传统媒体与社交媒体都在发挥作用,就像我们与他人在所有层次上的互动一样。我们的价值观与经验提供了吸引碎片并将它们聚拢一处的磁石。[45]

这种媒介议程设置与其他个体互动的结合所产生的结果是,构建了一种个人现实,它使我们每个人都能舒适地生活在想象的公民社区。

在"议程融合"概念中,一个关键步骤就是要在主流的传统媒体与各式各样的社交媒体之间作出划分,后者代表了对时下议题和话题截然不同的观点。区分纵向媒体与横向媒体是一种有用的办法。[46]纵向媒体(如报纸和电视网新闻)寻求的是到达社会许多不同的层面,以打造深厚的受众基础,建构广泛的社会议程。相反,横向媒体主要围绕特定观点和特殊兴趣,找到同质性的受众。在互联网上,带有某种政治倾向的社交媒体追求保守派受众,另有一些则寻找自由派受众。换句话说,纵向媒体传播的是与大多数公众相关的议程,而横向媒体则面向一小部分公众传播议程,通常反映的是某种自由派或保守派的观点。典型的情况是,这些横向媒体利用社交平台,允许信息来回流动,在这个过程中发送者和接收者都可以对消息的框架有一定程度的控制。横向媒体的这些强大反馈回路日益突显,是近几十年来不断扩展的媒介景观演化出来的主要特征。

议程融合将个体议程截然不同的来源(反映相反观点的纵向媒体和横向媒体)结合在一起,对于理解议程设置过程是一个富有成效的贡献。议程融合强调"受众并非被动地吸收媒介议程,而是主动为之,即便可能是无意识的。受众将媒介议程与个人关于公民社区的图像融为一体"[47]。

传统的议程设置研究,检验了媒介议程与公众议程之间的关系,在过去的半个世纪里,通过数百项实证研究的成果确立了研究领域。然而,这个领域仍然存在进一步解释各种变量的巨大空间。对媒介—公众议程关系的元分析发现,这些相关系数的平均数徘徊在+0.50左右。[48]这意味着,它只解释了因变量中25%的方差,因而为发现其他预测因素和解释变量留下了广阔的区域。

在2016年美国总统选举中,议程融合研究发现,推特的积极使用者的议题议程,不仅与纵向媒体,而且与横向媒体的议题议程高度对应。[49]选举日之前,民主党人和共和党人的推文都与纵向媒体的议题议程高度一致(民主党人为+0.96;共和党人为+0.97)。就横向媒体而言,相对于民主党人与民主党消息来源的一致性(+0.75),共和党人与共和党消息来源的一致性(+0.87)更高。所有的一致性都很强大,而民主党人和共和党人与各自横向媒体的匹配程度却比他们与纵向媒体的匹配程度稍微差一点。

在使用网络分析方法(详见第四章)再度分析2012年总统选举数据的一项验证研究中,也发现了同样的模式,只是在使用本党横向媒体时出现了相反的情况:在那次选举中,较之共和党人,民主党人与其新闻来源之间显示出了更高的一致性。[50]

民主党媒体对民主党人的显著影响与共和党媒体对共和党人的显著影响均显而易见。但是,在民主党人和共和党人反映本党横向媒体议程的显著性转移程度上,对比两个客体(在此情形下,是党派横向媒体)的数值,它们体现了理查德·卡特(Richard Carter)所称的"适切关系"(pertinence relationship)。[51]就候选人而言,2012年是民主党的奥巴马对共和党的罗姆尼,2016年是民主党的希拉里·克林顿对共和党的唐纳德·特朗普。在前一种情况下,可能是民主党人觉得更需要了解奥巴马,因为他当时是政治舞台上相对新的面孔;在后一种情况下,或许共和党人觉得更有必要深入地了解2016年的新来者特朗普。

这些议程融合的结果,乃基于纵向媒体议题议程、保守派横向媒体议题议程和自由派横向媒体议题议程三者之间强大的相关性。在2012年,这三种媒体议程的相关系数中位数是+0.83,2016年这些议程的相关系数中位数是+0.65。这些是当今媒介议程同质性的现实例证,而这种同质性早在最初的查普希尔研究中就被发现了。应该清楚的是,议程融合并非议程设置的另一个层面,而是一种过程,它为进一步解释个体如何建构其个人议程铺筑了道路。

小　结

　　导向需求是"大自然不容真空"这个科学原理的认知版本。[52]在公共事务领域,个人的导向需求越高,他或她就越有可能关注携带丰富的政治与政府信息的新闻媒介议程。[53]这个概念还确认了那些更可能从媒介议程转移到公众议程的议题,也就是那些与个体有关但非强制性的议题。如果一个非强制性议题引起了公众的共鸣,那么人们的导向需求将会是中度到高度。相反,在强制性议题上,导向需求可能大部分会通过个人经验得到满足。但是有时候,亲身经验会刺激获取更多信息的欲求,于是人们会转向大众媒介,寻求更多的引导。

　　导向需求为议程设置效果因何产生提供了一种细致的心理解释,它是议程设置效果最突出的偶发条件,是增加或者限制这些效果强度的因素。偶发条件的概念是20世纪70年代早期作为议程设置理论的第二个方面提出的。第一个方面当然就是研究媒介议程与公众议程之间的基本关系,那是由查普希尔研究开创的。区分议程设置研究的这些方面,并非标志着一条道路的终结和另一条道路的开端。相反,它们是在时间上平行的持续探究的道路。早期阶段发展起来的这两种议程设置研究持续至今,增加了新的偶发条件,例如议题的强制性、亲身经验和顺带学习。这些条件也出现在新的环境中,尤其是互联网与社交媒体渠道的持续涌现。对这些渠道而言,议程融合的概念可能会被证明特别有效。

第六章 议程设置如何起作用

媒介的议程设置效果广泛。研究者在美国的各类小城镇与大城市都观察到了这种效果。在国外，从日本东京到西班牙潘普洛纳这样判然有别的城市，从阿根廷到德国这样完全不同的国家，均发现了这种议程设置效果。现在总共有500多项关于议程设置的实证研究[1]，其中很多研究都效仿最早的查普希尔研究，实施于政治选举期间；其他一些开展于非选举时期的研究，也对舆论进行了监测。在过去超过五十年的时间里，研究讨论的公众议题丰富多样，涵盖了经济、公民权利、毒品、环境、犯罪、各种外交问题，以及其他几十种公众议题。现在，议程设置的研究主题远远超出了公众议题的范围，包括公众人物，越来越多的其他各种客体，这些客体的属性，以及所有这些客体及其属性结成的网络。这说明，议程设置是媒介传播的一种强大而广泛的效果，这种效果来自媒介的特定内容。

对许多人而言，议程设置理论最令人吃惊的地方，是媒介议程效果发生在地理特征与文化背景相差甚远的广泛地区。美国的文化和政治与西班牙的文化和政治背景极为不同，但是近些年来，在那些地方都发现了多样的议程设置效果。若将视线从西方转到东亚和南美的年轻国家或地区，文化和政治上的反差更为明显，但我们也观察到了这种议程设置效果。

若干年前，在中国台湾地区召开了一次研讨会，讨论这种最初发现于美国但获得了广泛国际验证的媒介效果。会议得出结论,认为议程设置效果(显著性从媒介议程到公众议程的成功转移),可以发生于任何政治体制和媒介系统相对开放的地方。当然,在现今世界,任何国家或地区都不存在完全开放的政治系统,没有哪个地方在成年人口中完全贯彻了"一人一票"的原则。[2]但是,前面提及的例子,说明美国、西班牙等地的政治体制属于比较开放的系统,在那里,选举的作用的确重要,它实际上决定了政治历史的走向。不仅如此,绝大多数成年人都能够合法地参与到选举中来。这些国家或地区的媒介系统(或至少媒介系统的主要部分)也比较开放,换句话说,媒体是新闻与政治表达相对独立的来源,不受政府的主导。在这两种开放性都具备的地方,公众会接受新闻媒体议题议程相当大的一部分。[3]

对1994年台北市长选举的观察[4],强调了开放原理的有效性,这可以解释议程设置效果的广泛出现。在那场选举中,台北市有三家电视台参与报道,所有这三家电视台都在某种形式上受当局与长期掌权的国民党的控制。不出所料,对电视新闻的研究并没有发现议程设置效果。虽然处于不同的文化背景,但是此处仍然可以借用美国政治科学家科依(V. O. Key)的那句名言:"选民不是傻瓜!"[5]相反,在台北两大主流日报中发现了很明显的议程设置效果。虽然像世界上多数新闻媒体一样,这两家报纸均带有特定的政治倾向,但它们是独立经营的企业,不受当局或国民党的任何直接控制。在其他政治与文化因素基本不变的情况下,台北的这个例子可以有效地比较开放与封闭两种媒介系统的不同影响。

在世界各地以开放的政治与媒介系统为标志的公民领域里,舆论的潮流生生不息。随着时间的流逝,单项议题的显著性伴随传播媒介与公众注意力的变化而起起伏伏。上一章展示了这个过程的几个重要的心理方面:包括导向需求的概念,它解释了人们在关注媒介议程时的个体差异;也包括强制性议题和非强制性议题的区别,说明媒介之外的个人经验能够在公众议程的形成中发挥作用;还有顺带学习的概念,它解释了这样的现象,即使在人们很少注意新闻内容的情况下,议程设置的效果也可能发生。此处,我们将罗列这种舆论产生过程的更多方面,如议题如何出现在媒介议程上,然后又是如何转移到公众议程的。我们将考虑公众议程的容量、议题为了在这个议程上占有一席之地而进行的竞争,也将考察这个公众议程演化的时间跨度。

一、公众议程的承载容量

为了在媒介议程、公众议程和决策议程上获得一席之地,各种议题之间会展开激烈竞争,这是议程设置过程中最重要的方面。在任何时刻,都有几十个议题在争夺公众的注意。但在一段时间里,社会及其机构只能关注几个议题。新闻媒体、公众和各种公共机构的注意是一种非常稀缺的资源。

人们关于议程设置的最早洞见之一,就是公众议程的容量有限。多年来,公众议程在任何时候通常只能容纳五到七个议题的说法,被接受为一种经验性的概括,并被认为是心理学家乔治·米勒(George Miller)提出的"魔法数字 7 ± 2"定律的另一个例证。米勒这一影响广泛的经验概括,描述了千差万别的感知过程的容量限度。[6]

其后多年时间里积累下来的证据却提示我们,议程设置的容量甚至更小。在盖洛普全国抽样调查中,对于调查的著名提问("什么是这个国家当前面临的最重要问题?"),公众只在几个问题上表现出可观的支持度。从 1997 年到 2000 年,在 10 次盖洛普民意测验中,当问及最重要问题时,只有一半的民意测验发现,公众议程上有多达五个议题的公众支持率超过 10%。一般认为,至少要达到这个水平,才能说议题引起了公众的广泛关注(显著)。[7] 五个议题当然是米勒定律中的下限。纵览所有 10 次民意测验,公众议程上的议题数量在两个到六个之间。另一项研究是对 1954 年到 1994 年的各种趋势的分析,同样基于盖洛普民意测验中对"最重要问题"的回答。结果发现,美国公众议程的容量没有发生变化。[8] 此外,为了更新这一描述,有研究者对 1975 年至 2014 年盖洛普调查的数据进行了分析,结果显示,虽然在此期间美国出现了媒介渠道激增、社交媒体兴起、精英极化的现象,但公众议程的容量实际上却几乎保持不变,平均而言,在对"最重要问题"的回答中只有三个议题的提及率达到 10%。[9] 这种趋势不独美国为然。例如,2017 年"拉丁美洲晴雨表"(Latinobarómetro,拉丁美洲年度民意调查项目)对 18 个拉丁美洲国家的公众进行了"最重要问题"的调查,结果发现,只有四个议题获得了超过 10% 的答复。[10]

公众议程容量的这种紧缩特点可以用公众拥有资源的有限来解释,资源的限度包括时间限制与心理容量。多数媒介议程容量的有限性甚至更加明显,报纸的篇幅有限,广播电视新闻的时段有限,甚至表面上拥有无限容量的互联网也不能改变这种资源的有限性。"卓越新闻项目"在美国收集的 2012 年新闻报道指数(News Coverage Index)的数据显示,在所考察的 12 家网站中,只有四大话题的新闻洞(除去广告之后保留的新闻报道空间)超过了 10%。[11]

在任何社会和任何时刻,所有这些对公众议题议程的限制,都可以归结为议程设置过程的一种零和博弈(zero-sum game)。零和博弈的观点强调了各种议题为获得媒介与公众的注意而展开激烈竞争,一个议题的崛起大多以另一个议题的衰落为代价。[12]

历史上,这种有限的议程容量和各种议题激烈竞争的一个结果,便是只有几个长期受到关注的问题才能在舆论中占据核心位置。例如,在美国,第二次世界大战结束之后的几年里,外交事务与经济议题占据着中心位置,而且外交事务几乎总是处于主导地位。虽然其他议题也不时获得公众的大量关注,但这两个议题可以说主宰了美国的公众议程。[13]

二、公众议程的多样性和暂时性

尽管公众议程在任一时刻都只能承载少数几个议题,但不论是议题的多样性,还是这些议题的支持者的相对规模,始终存在波动。有时,对三个议题的关注大体均衡,而在其他时候,一两个议题主导着数个次要议题。在美国,从20世纪50年代到80年代,公众议程的多样性下降了。然而,从20世纪80年代到21世纪头十年,随着时间的流逝,公众议程变得越来越多元。[14]特别是2008—2009年经济衰退之后,情况更是如此。[15]

尽管在此期间公众议程的容量保持不变,但议程上议题的多样性却增长了。有什么因素能够解释这一现象吗?这一谜题的部分答案是教育水准的提升。在美国,从1954年到2014年(包含了对美国公众议程进行分析的年头),人们就学的平均年限增长了56%,从8.5年增加到13.3年。[16]

在《理性选民》(*The Reasoning Voter*)一书中,塞缪尔·波普金(Samuel Popkin)观察到:

> 教育并不是通过拓展选民的"深度",而是通过延伸选民的广度来影响政治的。教育增加了公民认为与政治相关的议题数量,增加了公民将自己的生活与国家和国际事件联系起来的数量,由此发挥了影响政治的作用。[17]

他的观察认可了一种广为记载的情形,那就是大多数人,甚至是受教育程度较高的人,也很少拥有关于公众议题的详尽、深层的知识。那些受教育程度较高的人的确更多地阅读报纸,确实更经常地与家庭成员、朋友、同事讨论新闻。但波普金认为,这种行为的主要结果是,受教育程度较高的人"将拥有关于更广泛主题的有限信息,包括距离日常生活经验更远的全国性事件和国际事件的信息"[18]。这种教育施之于公众议程的更广泛效果,日益明显地表现为公众议程上议题多样性的增长。

如前所述,在第二次世界大战期间、战后直至1960年,国际事务这个单一类别的议题主导着公众议程。但是在之后的二十年间,即20世纪60年代和70年代,一系列更大范围的议题凸显出来。国际议题仍然在议程之上,主要是越战与冷战,但是经济议题与公民权利议题也获得了大量关注。在20世纪80年代和90年代,公众议程继续宽泛化与多样化。有四个主要议题获得了10%以上的公众关注——工作机会、个人经济议题、法律与秩序、国际事务;另有四个次要议题与经济的其他方面和国内议题有关,各自获得了5%到10%的关注。[19]

议程的容量保持稳定,再加上公众议程上议题的多样性持续增长,导致议题的生命周期更加短暂——现在,某些议题在公众议程上来来去去,较之前几十年更替更加迅速。换句话说,对议程设置过程中这些方面的问题的合理解释,便是教育的扩展性影响与有限议程容量的约束性影响发生了碰撞,结果是产生了一个变化更快、更不稳定的公众议程。在20世纪50年代,国际事务这个单一类别占据了中心舞台。但是到了20世纪60年代和70年代,成批的议题开始生长,主要议题与次要议题共享舞台(至少在某些短暂的间隔时间内),这种趋势一直持续到80年代及以后。"到20世纪90年代中期,一个议题在四到六个月时间内从议程上掉落下来的可能性大约是1975年时的两倍。"[20]在框6.1中,我们可以看到,长期统治公共事务的"巨星"仍然在公众议程上扮演主要角色,它们在舞台上闪耀的时间通常超过两年。然而,过去二十年的趋势不太明显,因为一些证据显示,一个议题从议程上掉下来的可能性相比它20世纪90年代的顶峰时期已经减少了。不过,显然,美国公众议程上的主要议题(经济和政府事务)现在仍不时与一系列新生的其他议题,如环境、教育、医疗等,分享舞台上的聚光灯。虽然这些新生的议题出现的频率不及主要议题,在舞台上停留的时间也不那么长久,但是在公众议程容量有限的情况下它们仍然有一席之地,这就支持了这样一种理念:教育水准的提高拓展了公众对时下议题的看法,从而对公众议程产生了影响。

框 6.1 主要议题在公众议程上的停留时间		
	每个周期的平均停留时间(以月计)*	周期数量 1954—1994*
个人经济议题	47.4	7
政治与政府	40.8	8
亚洲	27.8	4
总体外交政策议题	25.2	13
政府开支	21.8	5
俄罗斯与东欧	19.3	4
工作机会	15.1	14
总体经济议题	14.0	5
法律与秩序	10.3	12
技术	8.7	3

*一个周期是指一段时间,始自首次有10%或更多的人在回答"最重要问题"时提及这个议题,然后持续下去,直到低于10%。

来源:Maxwell McCombs and Jian-Hua Zhu, 'Capacity, diversity, and volatility of the public agenda: trends from 1954 to 1994', *Public Opinion Quarterly*, 59 (1995): 495—525。关于这十个类别涉及的特定议题的历时性细节,请看文章的附录A。

三、教育与议程设置

关于正规教育在议程设置过程中的作用,进一步的洞察来自对五种人口特征(年龄、受教育程度、收入、性别和种族)的比较,这些人口特征经常出现在民意测验中。一项研究的做法是,从一些地方报纸的消息中选出报道极多或极少的话题,混合在一起,选定斜跨美国(从佛罗里达到太平洋西北地区)的三个社区,在将近1000名受试者中测试这些议题的显著性。[21]结果发现,只有一个人口特征与这些议题的显著性相关,即那些接受较多正规教育的公民的回答更加紧跟媒介议程。教育经历的这种首要地位在整个政治与公共事务领域都是引人注目的。

不管人们是在处理认知问题(如判断政治信息是否真实或评估概念有多复杂),还是在处理动机问题(如对政治的关注程度和对政治事务的情感投入程度),抑或是在处理实际行为问题(如任何一种政治参与,从政党工作到投票等),受教育程度的差异在任何地方都具有普遍的解释力。[22]

教育具有双重效果,既能提高个体对新闻媒体的关注程度,又能让他们感知到反映在新闻中的范围更广的议题。但是从另一方面来讲,受教育程度较高似乎并没有增强个体对新闻中偏颇做法的抵御能力。与较少受教育的人相比,受到良好教育的人在接受媒介议程时并没有表现出更明显的提出争辩或建立心理屏障的倾向。[23]

然而,人们必须留意不去夸大教育与个体差异在议程设置过程中的作用。为了进一步确认教育相对于媒介消息在决定公众议程方面的能力,研究者比较了1977年到1986年的四个议题(通货膨胀、失业、国际问题和政府开支)在美国公众中的显著性与全国电视台在这十年里的报道模式。[24]研究者在不同的人口亚群体中分别观察这四个议题中每个议题的显著性变化,而这些人口亚群体则依据受教育程度与家庭收入来界定。研究者预测,在受教育水平较高的群体中,四个议题都会有更高的显著性。家庭收入也被用来测量人们对这四个议题的敏感度,因为研究者假定,通货膨胀和失业与高收入家庭关系不大,而国际问题和政府开支与高收入家庭的关系则较强。

从 1977 年到 1986 年，这些议题的显著性都发生了极大的变化。每个议题都呈现出既有高峰又有低谷的模式，不管是在媒介议程上，还是在所有收入与教育亚群体中，都有明显的升落起降。与此相反，不同人口亚群体之间的差异却极小。

具体到每个议题在媒介议程上的显著性与其在公众议程上的显著性之间的吻合程度，对于其中三个议题——通货膨胀、失业和国际问题——所有人口亚群体在一段时间里都呈现出相似的轨迹，与电视新闻报道数量的变化保持一致。虽然人口特征的差异很大，但是，从统计学的角度看，以受教育程度和家庭收入界定的个体差异只解释了2%的显著性差异，而不同年份则解释了37%的显著性差异。"换句话说，媒介议程设置效果并非体现为在不同个体中创造出各异的显著性，而明显地表现为推动所有个体的显著性随着时间的推移提高或者降低。"[25]

最后，在第四个议题（政府开支）上，没有看到什么议程设置效果，对此需要做一个重点注释。在所考察的十年中的最后三年，虽然电视新闻对政府开支关注很少，但议题在大多数公众中的显著性却直线上升，并且一直维持在高水平。这个议题在公众中的高度显著，可以用我们所知道的公众议程容量有限和某些议题反复出现作出部分解释。在最后这三年，即从 1984 年到 1986 年，经济的另外两个方面——失业与通货膨胀——在媒介议程与公众议程上的显著性都很低。回想一下，在 20 世纪下半期，失业曾是公众议程上长期徘徊的主导议题之一，通货膨胀也频繁出现。政府开支勉强可以算作一个次要议题，只是偶然出现在舆论舞台上。这个议题之所以在 1984 年到 1986 年走向舞台中央，可能是因为失业和通货膨胀这两个议题在这一时期的多数时间里离开了舞台。这再一次让我们注意到了公众议程容量的强力约束。

四、解释显著性的转移

在当代议程设置研究中,有两种相反的趋势:一种是离心(centrifugal)趋势。在这种趋势下,议程设置研究不断延伸到新的领域,包括第四章讨论的第三层面议程设置和将在第八章讨论的一系列不同场景。另一种则是向心(centripetal)趋势。在这种趋势下,研究者们正在回归本源,寻求进一步解释理论的关键概念。竹下俊郎(Toshio Takeshita)聚焦于从媒介议程到公众议程的"显著性转移"这个核心概念,确认了有关转移过程的两种清晰的理论路径:一种叫作刻意的认知投入(deliberative cognitive involvement),另一种则更为随意,叫作偶然卷入(incidental involvement)。[26]

议程设置双重过程的提出,让人想起了说服研究中的详尽可能性模型(Elaboration Likelihood Model, ELM)。该模型假定,存在"中心"和"边缘"(外周)两种不同的处理劝说性信息的路径。[27]这两种路径都可以产生说服作用,但意味着非常不同的认知努力程度,因而在态度改变的持续时间上会有不同的后果。在第五章中,我们已经看到,产生议程设置效果也有两种不同的路径——一种是关注媒介的主动路径,另一种是顺带学习的被动路径。[28]随后的研究进一步探索了议程设置传统中的双重过程的思路。

研究者在德国做了两个实验,以检验这种议程设置双重路径。他们要求受试者在一段时间内自由选择一家新闻网站,浏览自己想要阅读的内容。[29]通过观察受试者的电子日志文件,研究者确认了受试者在与实验有关的关键议题上阅读新闻报道所花费的时间。在受试者访问网站之前,研究者已经测试了他们对受控议题的投入程度。日志文件表明,投入程度越高的受试者,阅读的新闻报道越多。

实验结果还表明,如果认知努力程度较低——阅读的新闻数量不多,媒体线索(出现在网站上的次数、是头条新闻还是简短报道)便会极大地影响其后受试者对议题重要性的判断。相反,如果认知努力程度较高——阅读新闻数量较多,媒体线索便不会影响接下来受试者对议题重要性的判断。

引人注目的是,实验研究发现,"只要媒体在强调某个议题方面下足了功夫,那些投入程度较低(事先并不认为这个议题重要,也没有花费较多时间阅读议题相关报道)的人,会与那些投入程度较高(对这个议题比较上心,也会认真阅读新闻报道)的人,在同等程度上认为议题具有重要性"[30]。

在美国进行的两个实验进一步验证了信息处理的双轨路径——议程提示(agenda-cueing)和议程推理(agenda-reasoning)——所带来的议程设置效果。这些实验还引入了一个测试效果强度的偶发条件,也就是对把关的信任(gatekeeping trust)。与传统上更为普遍使用的测量媒介信任度或可信度的方法不同,把关信任是一种特殊的信念,即相信新闻报道是记者们按照重要性排列某些问题的系统化努力的结果。[31]

高度的把关信任增强了媒介议程在议程提示的情况下的效果。换句话说,那些对媒介把关信任程度较高的人认为,在确认什么是当下最重要的议题时,相信新闻报道的方式是合适的,自己可以采用这种认知捷径,不必亲力亲为。然而,在议程推理的情况下,那些把关信任程度较低的人则认为,在确认什么是当下最重要的议题时,新闻报道的模式并非深思熟虑、仔细推敲的结果。因此,他们会依靠新闻中的特定内容自行判断议题的重要性。

德国的实验检验了对媒介内容的在线处理过程,而美国的实验则考察了基于记忆的媒介内容处理过程,两者在理论上相互补充,丰富了对议程设置效果的解释。

还有一项在科索沃进行的实地研究,进一步解释了这些理论路径。该研究回到更早的导向需求定义,考察了导向需求的组成部分即关联性和不确定性等影响因素,由此创建了一个2×2的类型模式。[32]这种新思路与此前的概念化方法不同。此前的方法合并了模型中两个高—低单元格,以此测量中等导向需求。新思路则在这两个高—低格之间作出了理论区分。高关联性和低不确定性被定义为"中等导向需求—主动"类型,在这种情况下,人们可能期待从党派新闻媒体那里获得指点,以强化他们的既有倾向。相反,低关联性和高不确定性被定义为"中等导向需求—被动"类型,在这种情况下,人们可能依赖那些报道较为平衡的(独立性)新闻媒体,以减少不确定性。[33]

正如研究者所料,与具有中等导向需求却被动的公民相比,那些具有中等导向需求而主动的公民接触具有党派倾向的电视、广播和报纸更多,这个发现也可作为解释选择性认知的证据。然而,这些具有中等导向需求却主动的公民同样更加关注独立性的电视、广播和报纸。继而,在这些具有中等导向需求而主动的公民中,还发现了最强大的属性议程设置效果,具体表现为针对科索沃七个政治机构的属性调查,属性包括腐败/公平、不诚实/诚实、低效/高效,以及自私/关爱。在这些公民中发现的效果要远超在具有低导向需求、高导向需求和中等导向需求但被动类型的群体中的效果。

在新的传播环境中,随着传播渠道的增多,人们对选择性接触产生了相当大的兴趣。在一项实证研究中,娜塔莉·斯特劳德(Natalie Stroud)对选择性接触作出了细致的解释,她发现有三分之一的美国公众显示出党派行为模式,其特征是只接触那些跟他们想法相似的政治信息来源,而不采用任何跟他们想法不同的信息来源。[34]当然,更多的公民可能严重依赖与自身想法相同的消息来源。

根据科索沃研究的结果,也许存在一些不同的议程设置路径。对于那些并没有较多投入党派政治的公民,这个路径可能基本上属于那种总体的议程设置过程,这种过程自查普希尔研究以来我们已经探索了数十年。但是,对于高度参与党派政治的公民来说,很可能的是,那些非常强大的议程设置细分过程在发挥作用。这种可能性的证据在其后林迪塔·卡马伊(Lindita Camaj)的研究中可以看到。她在最初的科索沃发现的基础上精耕细作,再次对2012年美国大选使用了内容分析、抽样调查等研究方法。[35]她发现,具有高导向需求的人更可能从提供均衡新闻报道的电视节目中获取信息,具有中等导向需求而主动的人则更倾向于从党派电视节目中获取信息。有意思的是,具有中等导向需求和主动倾向的个体也像具有高导向需求的人一样,更可能收看电视网上的新闻。这意味着,较之非党派人士,党派人士往往不仅使用党派媒体,同样也使用独立媒体和主流媒体。

议程设置效果的独特理论路径所产生的证据,由于抗衡性的研究设计而得到充实:在德国,研究者进行了基于注意力的实验,在实验中由受试者决定接触的模式;在美国,不仅在实验中开展了基于内容的测试(研究者明确操纵受试者接触到的议程提示和议程推理的刺激),还对媒介内容与调查数据做了交叉分析;在科索沃,研究者采用了内容分析和问卷调查等研究方法,实施了实地调查。在这些研究的各自情境中,双轨路径都导向了明显的议程设置效果。

五、效果的时间框架

按照早期神话般的皮下注射理论,媒介的效果是立竿见影的。那种观点认为,媒介消息被注入受众的头脑,就像给病人打针一样,总能即刻见效。不过,在20世纪40年代至50年代,随着那些被概括为"最小后果定律"的经验研究证据的积累,支持皮下注射理论的观点消失了。[36]据此,威尔伯·施拉姆等传播学者声称,媒介真正重要的效果可能需要极长的时间才能显现出来,就像洞穴中钟乳石与石笋的形成过程那样,要经过亿万年一点一滴的积累。也就是说,媒介的效果可能强烈而巨大,但是在对较短时段的分析中无法体现出来。

在这样的背景下,问题便是:媒介对某个议题的关注,要经过多长时间才能转化为这个议题在公众议程上的高度显著性？难道真的需要心理上相当于亿万年的时间吗？或者说,从聚焦态度与观点的变化转到聚焦传播过程的更早阶段,例如关注焦点的形成和对重要性的感知上,有可能发现相对短期的媒介效果吗？

回顾一下,在二十三年的时间里,美国公众对公民权利议题的关注的升降,反映出了媒介在上一个月对同一议题的关注。[37]这说明,议程设置的效果虽然远非立刻发生,但相对来说还是短期的。关于议程设置的实验已经表明,所测新闻报道和公众广泛关切的时滞可能在数周之内,甚至只有几天。[38]当然,这就产生了如何概括这种议程设置过程情况的问题。我们已经知道,在不同的议题上,议程设置效果的强弱可能存在差异。不过,就议程设置效果发生的时间框架(时间表)而言,也有两项此类研究提出,议题显著性从媒介议程向公众议程的转移,通常需要四到八周的时间。

在一项对20世纪60年代到70年代的舆论趋势的历时性分析中,研究者分别在三个议题(污染、滥用毒品和能源)上捕捉到了公众议程与上个月全国电视新闻议程之间的相关性,相关系数中位数为+0.66。[39]另外,通过三轮固定样本研究,研究者发现,在环境议题的显著性方面,公众议程与前两个月三家地方报纸议程之间的相关系数中位数为+0.77。[40]公众议程通常反映前一两个月的媒介议程。而所有三项调查既涉及报纸与电视新闻,又涵盖各种不同议题,调查得到的相关性很明显且高度趋同。于是,我们对上述观点的可靠性就更有信心了。

在个人高度参与新闻的条件下,议程设置效果产生的时间间隔会更短。[41]在1996年美国总统选举期间,研究者对个人如何在互联网上讨论四个公众议题(移民、医疗保健、税收和堕胎)进行了监测。从9月直到11月大选之后的一周,人们在网上讨论四个议题的频数,被用来与《纽约时报》、路透社、美联社、CNN以及《时代周刊》围绕这些议题的新闻报道进行比较。关于移民议题的公众讨论立即对新闻报道作出了反应。在医疗保健与税收议题上的公众讨论出现稍长的间隔，但在一周之内效果也是明显的。在四个被考察的议题中，只有关于堕胎议题的讨论与新闻报道的模式无关。这种结果很可能是因为，这个议题在本质上具有高度争议性和情绪性。对于显著性的确受到新闻报道影响的三个议题来说，其时间框架要比传统新闻媒体的议程设置效果的时间框架短得多。这个结果并不让人吃惊，因为互联网是公众议程凸显的部分，只有那些对某个议题非常感兴趣的人才会以行动来回应。[42]

所有这些关于议程设置效果时间框架的证据，都基于一种对单个议题在公众议程上的显著性随时间流逝的变化的追踪分析。在阿卡普尔科模型中，这类分析被认为属于自然历史的角度。显然，还可以考虑其他角度，尤其是竞争角度，这一角度讨论的是为了在议程上占有一席之地而展开竞争的全部议题的情况。就分析来说，考察单个议题以了解其自然历史的基本过程是有用的；然而，竞争角度却提供了一个现实世界的写照，在这个世界上，总是有各种各样的议题在不断变化。那么，从竞争的角度看，什么样的时间框架会将媒介议程与公众议程联系起来？一项对议程设置效果的时间框架的研究，全面调查了包含11个公众议题的议程，以及一系列新闻媒体，从本地电视新闻、地方报纸到全国电视新闻节目和周刊新闻杂志。[43]

虽然这些新闻媒体在要报道多少周的新闻才能与公众议程完美对应上存在差异，但是这种差别比较小，与观察个体议题时所发现的时长基本相同：媒介议程与公众议程完美对应的时间间隔范围从一周到八周不等，中位数为三周。无论是哪一种媒体，议程设置的效果都很可观。如果我们的基准是从议题的自然历史角度确定的间隔即四到八周，那这项基于竞争角度的研究发现的间隔时间便居于这个基准范围内较短的那一端。

在德国进行的一项新近研究发现了更短的时间间隔。[44]这项研究采用了2009年至2014年收集的数据,进行了更精密的时间序列分析,发现媒体报道与公众最高回应之间的时间差在一天到两周之内。"尽管存在各种不同的情况,但是议程设置效果通常在七八天内达到高峰,电视新闻比报纸表现出效果要快些,但消退得也更快一些。"

然而,考虑到在媒介议程和公众议程上全部议题的复杂性,可以说重大议程设置效果发生的时间间隔仍然比较短。在相对较短的几周时间里,新闻媒体所报道的话题的显著性就被大量公众吸收了。

很久以前,保罗·拉扎斯菲尔德将大众传播描述为一个非正式课堂,在这个课堂里,学生不断进进出出。而且,这个非正式课堂与正式课堂的情况相似,一些学生虽然出席,但并不总是全神贯注地听讲。尽管如此,人们确实从大众媒介那里获得了知识。他们得知了各种各样的事实,并将其中的很多事实与他们对各种客体的认识和态度结合在一起。他们还获知了当前最重要的议题,将新闻媒体的议程融入他们有关社会所面临的关键问题的议程。

新闻媒体是教师,它们主要的传播策略就是大量重复。近几十年来,新的传播渠道激增,但这种重复的次数看起来不仅没有减少,反而增多了。我们的媒体教师不厌其烦地一遍又一遍重复某些话题,有时重点强调,有时则一带而过。当我们询问国家当前面临的最重要问题时,公民学生回答的主要是一到八周内从课堂上学到的课程内容。当然,在多数情况下,课程并非在八周之前突然开始的,但是,最近几周的报道模式显然对公众的影响最大。

硬币都有两面,也有实证证据反映了媒介学习另一面的情况,即信息衰退和在任何学习模式中都会发生的遗忘。如果我们不像在信息获取上那样下功夫来研究学习的这一面,那么学习衰退的时间框架就缺乏应有的关注。[45]议程设置效果的衰减点,被定义为媒介议程与公众议程之间的显著相关性消失的那个时间点,范围从八周到二十六周不等。在德国的调查研究中,一些效果消退得更快,甚至不到一周时间。[46]

关于议题在公众议程上的停留时间的这些结论,基本上都来自对经验研究的概括。它们既包括学习的增益(议题获得更多的公众关注)的过程,也包括学习的衰减(议题从公众视野中消失)的过程。我们之所以知道这些时间框架,是因为各类社会科学家对这个问题的探索产生了较为一致的数据,尤其是关于议题在公众议程上显著性上升的方面。但是经验概括不如经验发现来得合理,因为那些发现植根于明确的理论背景。

在这个方面,议程设置理论的现状与更大范围的媒介效果相关文献没有什么区别。考察传播理论方面两份内容全面、使用广泛的文章索引,发现在这个领域里,学者对各种媒介效果发生的时间框架都缺少关注。[47]这既是一个理论缺点,也是一种进步的机遇。

在早先对时间相关概念的讨论中,有一个议程设置效果理论框架的雏形。[48]这些概念既包括某个议题从出现在媒介议程上到出现在公众议程上所需要的时滞长度,也包括两个议程之间产生最佳效果(即最强联系)所需要的时间跨度。[49]在关于议程设置过程的观点中,还有一个更大的理论框架,叫作零和博弈。[50]但是,在这方面的工作仍然任重道远。

六、显著性测量的多样性

从方法论的角度看,各种各样的研究设计以及客体和属性显著性的测量方法不断涌现出来,大大超过了原创的查普希尔研究,从而极好地支撑了议程设置理论。

> 方法论技巧……近些年来发展迅速。起初,它限于程序性的等级相关分析,后来进一步扩展,纳入了最精密的结构

方程模型,以及横截面数据分析和多轮固定样本调查。研究者还使用测量总体舆论的时间序列分析、自然场景实验设计和深度个案研究来探究议程设置。鉴于围绕议程设置研究的活动如此之多,我们可以得出结论:它是议程设置领域最受追捧的模式之一。[51]

用以确定媒体对公众议程的议程设置效果的各种测量也有方法论上的优势。通常,这些效果是通过测量公众对盖洛普公司问题的回答而得到的。自20世纪30年代起,盖洛普民意调查总是询问美国公众:"什么是这个国家当前面临的最重要问题?"[52]这种方法对测量议题的显著性非常有效。[53]在一项全州调查中,研究者以分票设计比较了各种版本的公众议程,考察了使用"社会参考框架"的公众议程和使用"个人参考框架"的公众议程的差异,以及使用"问题"(problem)而不是"议题"(issue)的措辞带来的效果差别。结果显示,"最重要问题"指标具有互换性,不论是采用不同的参考框架,还是选择不同的措辞,都能带来答案的改变。[54]

虽然这个关于最重要问题的提问——以及其他测量议题显著性的开放式问题——依然被广泛使用,但在测量公众议程的客体和属性议程设置效果方面,也涌现出其他许多创造性的方法。如对《纽约时报》的网络版和印刷版进行实验比较,是对关于最重要问题的传统提问的补充,也增加了对显著性的测量。这种测量方法进一步要求受试者识别和回忆报上出现的新闻报道,并对这些新闻报道的不同类别的重要性进行排序。[55]在另一项实验中,研究者在测量种族主义的显著性时,使用了涉及三个不同方面的五级量表。这三个方面是,议题的重要性,与朋友讨论的程度,还有对政府采取更多行动的需求。[56]也请回顾我们在第五章中讨论过的一系列实验,这些实验使用含13组两极词语的语义差别量表,测量议题的显著性,并确认关于显著性的三种深层维度。[57]甚至在线使用谷歌搜索引擎的查询活动也被作为测量公众显著性的指标。[58]

为了分析纽约州雪城公众对于地方犯罪议题的意见,研究者不仅使用了传统的等级量表,还使用了一种行为测量方法,从而确认了议题的显著性:

> 思考雪城地区的犯罪问题,这里有一份从 1 到 10 的量表,1 表示对你个人不重要,10 表示对你个人最重要,你如何给犯罪问题打分?你对自己成为犯罪受害者的担心程度如何?你是根本不担心,有点担心,还是非常担心?[59]

在美国中西部有一个人工湖开发项目,研究者采用了三种不同的方式,以探明这个环境议题的各种属性的显著性。[60]研究者使用了两个开放式问题,第一个问题是询问人们对这个议题的哪些方面最感兴趣,第二个问题是询问人们对哪些方面讨论最多。第三种测量显著性的方法是成对比较,也就是研究者将属性列表中所有可能的成对组合展示给受访者,要求受访者从每个组合中选出自己认为最重要的那个属性。从一组受访者那里得到的系列判断,可以建立一个显著性的等距量表。例如,在框 6.2 中,我们可以看到,在美国中西部人工湖开发项目上,三种测量属性显著性的方法记录下了非常相似的属性议程设置效果。这些重复测量得出的相似性,有力地证明了这些效果的存在及其测量方法的有效。

框 6.2　属性议程设置效果比较(基于三种测量某环境议题在公众中的属性显著性的方法)

开放式问题		成对比较量表
"最感兴趣的方面"	"讨论最多的方面"	
+0.60	+0.61	+0.71

来源:David Cohen,'A report on a non-election agenda setting study', paper presented to the Association for Education in Journalism, Ottawa, Canada, 1975。

让我们回到用开放式问题测量显著性的方法。世界各地对候选人形象的属性议程设置的分析,均采用了最早在 1976 年美国总统选举研究中使用的一个开放式问题:"如果你的一些朋友长期在外,并不熟悉这些总统候选人,你会如何向他们介绍(某个候选人)?"[61]

最后,近期针对客体与属性议程设置的一些调查已使用"无应答"(non-response)来反向测量显著性。这种方式尽管存有争议,却被称为所有测量显著性方法的基础。举例来说,对于某个公众人物没有任何观点的人越少,那么这个候选人在公众中的显著性就越高。[62] 又如,对于某个公众议题的特定方面没有任何观点的人越多,那么这个属性在公众中的显著性就越低。[63]

在当前的传播环境中,存在大量关于公共事务的公众传播渠道。从方法论上讲,社交媒体提供了丰富的来源,可以对公众议程进行非介入式测量,并与内容分析这种具有长期优势的非介入式测量法并驾齐驱。如今,我们能够获得在没有研究人员介入的情况下产生的媒介议程和公众议程的数据,这些数据与调查数据相比具有明显优势。正是采用这种非介入式的测量,研究者对同性婚姻议题进行了富有创造性的时间序列分析,以比较芝加哥和亚特兰大的地方媒体和全国媒体的议程设置效果。[64] 在新的媒介环境中,计算机自动化也具有相当大的潜力。例如,对自动编码情感辞典(Lexicoder Sentiment Dictionary,LSD)的一项评估便推荐人们使用软件包来编码情感属性议程。这种软件编码方法是一个巨大的进步,超越了琐碎且时常不可靠的对语气进行编码的传统方法。[65] 随着采用计算方法的传播研究增多,应用计算机辅助技术进行内容分析和社会网络分析,特别是在测量网状议程从新闻媒体向社交媒体使用者转移的研究中,也越来越常见。[66]

小　结

公民参与到有关公共事务的不间断的学习过程中。他们对民意测验中"最重要问题"的回答通常反映了过去几周的媒介教程。议程设置效果通常是这个过程的结果。在很大程度上,效果是由媒介消息的特点决定的;只在很小程度上,是由这些消息接收者的特点决定的。公众传播,包括许多新的社交媒体上的传播,都是一个过程,在这个过程中高度重复的消息被广泛散布。这些消息的许多特点影响到究竟会有多少人去关注消息,并且至少理解消息的部分内容。

最终,媒介传播是个体受众与媒介消息之间的一场交易,在这场交易中,个体差异可能显得至关重要——从某种意义上讲,传播效果是一系列层层叠加的个人经验。不过,虽然没有哪两个人的经验完全相同,但个体特点迥异的人却常常拥有高度相似的体验。对于想要建立一种传播效果简约理论的我们来说,这就非常幸运了。

第七章　塑造媒介议程

越来越多的证据表明,新闻媒体对公众产生议程设置影响。随着这些证据的积累,20世纪80年代早期的学者提出了这样的问题:"是谁设置了媒介议程?"一条理论研究的新路径开始探索塑造新闻媒体议程的各种因素。在这条新的求索道路上,媒介议程成了因变量,也就是需要得到解释的结果。

而直到此时,在我们的议程设置理论研究中,媒介议程还一直是自变量,被当作塑造舆论的关键原因要素。框7.1描述了一种更广泛、更全面的议程设置过程模式,其中也包括先在于媒介议程的主要议程。考虑到媒介议程的起源,可以想到其他许多议程,例如立法机构或其他公共部门关注的议题和政策问题的议程(这属于新闻媒体常规报道的范围),或者政治活动中的竞争性议程,还有通常由公共关系专家提出的话题议程。现代社会中存在很多有组织的议程。

"剥洋葱"这个比喻非常有助于我们理解所有这些其他议程与媒介议程之间的关系。媒介议程是洋葱的核心,围绕它的洋葱各层则代表了在塑造媒介议程过程中起作用的多种影响因素。这个比喻还描述了这一过程的顺序特点,即外层因素的影响反过来又受到更接近核心的各层的影响。这颗洋葱的详细结构由很多层次组成。例如,帕梅拉·休梅克(Pamela Shoemaker)和斯蒂芬·里斯(Stephen Reese)的影响层次模型便确认了五个塑造新闻媒体内容的清晰层次,从主流文化

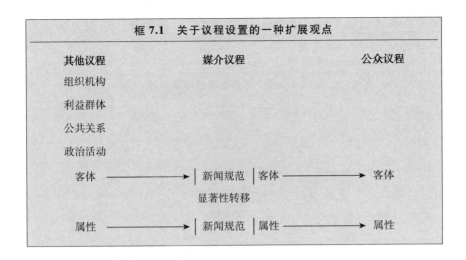

到个体新闻工作者的心理。[1]洋葱的一些中间层次描述的是新闻机构的行为与新闻专业规范，它们共同构成了新闻社会学，这是一个学术领域，议程设置理论在20世纪80年代开始与之合流。[2]

本章勾勒了三个基本层面，以回答"是谁设置了媒介议程?"这个问题。如框7.2所示，在这颗理论洋葱的最外层，是关键的外部新闻来源，例如美国总统、日常公关活动、政治活动的努力，有线下的，也有线上的。再深入一层，是各种新闻媒体之间的互动与影响，现在通常将这种现象称作媒体间议程设置。例如，社交媒体如脸书和推特，现在是媒体间互动的重要竞技场。这些互动在很大程度上确认并强化了社会规范与新闻实践。这些规范与实践是紧靠洋葱核心的层面，它们为最终塑造媒介议程确定了基本规则。

就新闻媒体的议程而言，专业规范和实践是最具决定性的因素，这一点对任何从事过新闻工作的人来说都是显而易见的——新闻媒体自己是报道哪些事件和议题以及如何报道它们的最终裁定者。例如，对负面新闻的偏好[3]限制了媒介议程所涵盖的事件和议题的范围，而调查性新闻可以增加人们对新议题(如腐败)的知情，从而扩大媒介议程。然而，在通常情况下，拥有行政权力的人——国家元首和政府首脑——才被认为是一个国家新闻媒体最重要的议程设置者。

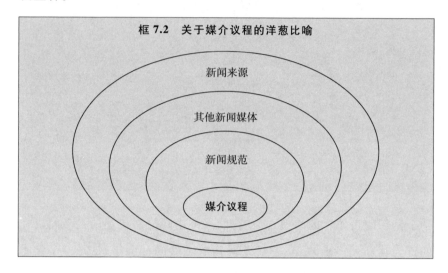

框 7.2　关于媒介议程的洋葱比喻
- 新闻来源
- 其他新闻媒体
- 新闻规范
- 媒介议程

一、总统与国家议程

描述和评估某个国家的政治领导人（例如美国总统）的一种方式，就是看他在设置国家议程方面所起的作用。影响新闻报道的关注点已日益成为美国总统的一项主要任务。这是一种营造支持性舆论的方式；然后，总统可以利用这些支持性舆论来影响国会。有相当多的轶事表明，总统是美国的头号新闻人物。从召开国际会议到在巡回竞选的路上停下来吃点东西，总统所做的几乎每一件事情都被认为具有新闻价值。

那么，成为媒体关注的焦点这个有利条件，也为总统设置媒介议程提供了重要机会吗？评估总统影响力的一个大好机会是一年一度的国情咨文。[4]根据美国宪法的要求，一个多世纪以来，总统都必须向国会递交此项书面报告。到了 20 世纪 60 年代，总统发布年度国情咨文成了一个重大的媒体事件，总统会于晚间在国会山向参众两院联席会议发表公开演讲,由所有电视网向全国直播。

国情咨文实际上是总统希望国会关注的议题的汇总清单,这种演讲的形式则为我们提供了一个测试总统议程设置影响力的理想机会。这里有一条消息(国情咨文),它是一份总统优先事项的清单,而这条消息是在几周时间里纳入了许多政治和政策顾问的建议才制作出来的。那么,总统议程上的这些优先考虑的议题会对其后的媒介议程产生任何明显的影响吗?除了发表国情咨文的时段之外,它们会对新闻报道的模式产生任何影响吗?

对这个问题的初步探究考察了卡特总统1978年发表的国情咨文。让人吃惊的是,这项研究发现,卡特总统的报告并没有对《纽约时报》《华盛顿邮报》和三家全国电视网次月在八个优先议题上的报道产生明显的影响[5],却有证据表明,《纽约时报》和几家全国电视网在国情咨文所发表之前一个月的报道影响了总统的议程。

在尼克松这个与卡特差别很大的美国总统身上,研究者使用了完全相同的研究设计,进行了重复验证。[6]在这个例子中,尼克松总统1970年国情咨文所承载的包含15个议题的议程,确实影响了《纽约时报》《华盛顿邮报》和三家全国电视网中的两家次月的新闻报道,却没有证据表明媒介议程对总统产生了任何影响。当然,在这类历史分析中,应当纳入考量的一个主要因素是总统与总统之间巨大的个性差别。然而,即便考虑到了这个因素,在某位总统的整个任期内,仍可发现总统议程与媒介议程之间关系转变的证据。分析富兰克林·罗斯福总统早期(1934—1940)的七次国情咨文,在新闻媒体与总统之间的关系上,发现的证据极为混杂。[7]在对里根总统1982年至1985年发表的国情咨文的分析中,也发现了类似的混合效果的证据。[8]

有的时候,总统能够将新闻媒体的注意力导向特定的议题,从而设置媒介与公众的议程;而在其他时候,是总统追随新闻媒体和公众的意见。[9]在美国之外进行的研究,也得到了相似的有力证据。在加拿大,斯图尔特·索罗卡分析了1985年至1995年的数据,结果发现,就财政政策等议题而言,御座致辞(Throne Speech;政府施政报告)对新闻媒体的议程发挥了相当大的影响。[10]在智利,塞巴斯蒂安·瓦伦苏埃拉和阿图罗·阿里亚加达(Arturo Arriagada)利用收集到的2000年至2005年的数据,研究了总统向国会发表的国情咨文对公众和新闻媒体的两种议程产生的影响。[11]他们指出,在五个议题上,即使控制了公众议程和现实世界指标的影响,总统的演讲都对后续的电视新闻报道产生了在统计上显著的正面效果。

这些关于施政演说的研究所提供的答案,远不只是回答了"是谁设置了媒介议程?"这个问题。这些研究还阐明了政策议程设置的一个方面,即政府决定将什么社会议题作为其关注焦点的过程。[12]但是,很少有考察新闻媒体如何塑造公共政策的实证研究,远远不如人们对新闻媒体如何塑造舆论的关注。[13]造成这个差异的主要原因可能是新闻媒体自身的特性。新闻媒体通常不可能长期将自己的注意力放在某个特殊议题上,而公共政策过程的演化却需要较长的时间。媒介议程的形成,更多的是由突发事件与紧急情况的新闻价值决定的,而不是由精心审议的社会价值塑造的。

然而,也有证据表明,媒介已经在政策议程方面发挥了很大的影响,不论是在全国范围,还是在地方层面。20世纪80年代到90年代的研究案例包括:《美国医学会杂志》上发表了一篇关于虐待儿童的原创文章,引来媒体相当大的关注,国会与许多州立法机构接着就采取了行动[14];《圣安东尼奥之光》社论版上的新年社区议程获得了当年大量后续新闻报道的支持,促使市政府极大地增加了在儿童项目上的支出[15];芝加哥电视台的两个系列调查报道,也引起了芝加哥市警察与消防部门的政策变化[16]。

最近,有一篇综述对2005年至2015年间发表的成果进行了回顾[17],发现有32项研究涉及媒介议程对政策议程的影响,涵盖的国家相当不同,有比利时、智利、丹麦、荷兰、西班牙、瑞士和美国。三分之二的研究是"客观性的",也就是说,研究者分析新闻报道的内容和决策者的行为,以检验议题的显著性从一个议程向另一个议程的转移。其余的研究是"主观性的",基于政治行动者对媒介影响的感知。这篇综述得出的结论是,媒介影响确实存在,不过,就客观研究而言,这是一种温和的效果,但就主观研究而言,却是一种强有力的效果。然而,政策制定过程的哪个方面最受媒介的影响,却是一目了然的:"媒体对政客们的言论比对他们的行为更重要。"[18]也就是说,与财政预算等实质性议程相比,新闻报道主要是对总统演讲等象征性议程产生了巨大的影响。

总括所有这些研究,非常明显的是,新闻报道与随时间而演变的公共政策之间的关系是循环的。在艾滋病[19]、全球变暖[20]、毒品[21]等各种议题上,学者们仔细研究并详细记录了这种循环关系。由于新闻媒体的作用时断时续,而且往往循环往复,对媒介传播与舆论的研究很少包括民主三要素中的第三个,即政府政策。

二、补贴媒介议程

新闻工作者只能观察到每日形势与事件中极少的一部分。即便很多地方例行排除了多种事件,也没有足够的记者去报道每日新闻中的重大话题的方方面面。我们所知道的许多事情,例如政府工作与企业经营,从国际层面直至地方层面,大都来自公共信息官员和其他公共关系从业者,他们代表重要的新闻来源。这些专业的传播者向新闻媒体提供大量组织好的信息,以"补贴"(subsidize)[22]新闻机构的新闻采写努力。他们通常采用这些方式:书面或视频形式的新闻通稿、新闻发布会、经过策划的事件、背景吹风,以及向脸书、推特和其他社交媒体投放消息。

一项原创性研究考察了二十年间《纽约时报》和《华盛顿邮报》的新闻报道,发现近半数的报道主要源自新闻通稿和其他直接的信息补贴。[23]在这两家报纸上出现的所有新闻报道中,大约17.5%的报道至少部分基于新闻通稿,而关于新闻发布会与背景吹风的报道又占了32%。《纽约时报》和《华盛顿邮报》是拥有大量员工和充足资源的重要报纸,它们对公关信息来源的这种严重依赖,彰显了这样的事实:信息补贴在所有媒介议程的日常构建方面都扮演着重要角色。

在2006年对英国五家主要报纸和四家电视新闻频道的广泛研究中,发现了更多的证据,表明公共关系在塑造新闻议程方面起到关键作用。19%的报纸报道和17%的广播电视新闻报道"可被证实主要或全部来自公关材料或活动"[24]。如果加上混合了公共关系和其他信息的报道,那么对于报纸来说,这个比例会增加到30%,对于电视台来说,则是31%。美国路易斯安那州的主要报纸关于六个州政府部门的新闻报道,也在很大程度上基于这些部门的公共信息官员提供的信息。[25]这些公共信息官员提供的信息补贴主要是书面新闻通稿,但偶尔也有个人谈话;有一半以上的内容后来出现在新闻报道中。信息补贴的话题议程,从州财政、总体经济状况到仪式性事件、庆祝活动等,涵盖广泛。尤其值得注意的是,在八周时间里,源于公共信息官员的议程与使用补贴信息的新闻报道的议程之间,相关系数为+0.84。而在那一时期,源自政府部门的议程与所有关于这些部门的新闻报道之间的相关系数为+0.57。深入探讨这种高度匹配的原因,可以清楚地看到新闻规范和传统的核心作用,它是洋葱的最内层,为塑造媒介议程设定基本规则。在82%的情况下,新闻价值是最重要的考虑因素。

公共关系发挥了实质上的议程设置作用,这在许多方面是一种不可避免的结果,因为新闻工作者的活动"受到经济、体制和组织方面的束缚,各方要求他们起草和处理太多报道,以供发表……"[26]一些观察者进行了这样的区分,即基于原创报道的"新闻业"(journalism)和内容来自不一定符合公众利益的组织的"搅拌新闻业"(churnalism)[27],透露出了他们对日益依赖公关新闻来源这种倾向的担忧。

关于艾滋病、小儿麻痹症等公共健康议题的新闻报道,同样反映出了信息补贴,这些信息主要由科学家和其他专家新闻来源提供。[28] 20世纪80年代艾滋病相关报道的兴起,是由科学议程启动的,但在80年代后半期,这种关注被保留下来,出现了一些讲述艾滋病故事的新框架。伴随着这些新框架的出现,生物医学界与新闻媒体的议程设置作用也发生了位移。正如总统、新闻媒体和公众之间的互动关系一样,就几乎每个议题的自然历史而言,我们都可以考虑一种时间上的动态关系。

本特·福莱伯格(Bent Flyvjberg)、托德·兰德曼(Todd Landman)和桑福德·施拉姆(Sanford Schram)的专著《真正的社会科学:应用实践智慧》(*Real Social Science: Applied Phronesis*)显示了社会科学家在塑造社会议题方面广泛的基础性作用。他们在书中详细描述了社会科学家对世界上二十个国家的重大公共工程项目的评估,以及在评估之后如何利用媒介影响公众对相关支出的看法。"phronesis"一词最初来自亚里士多德的伦理学,指实践智慧和政治能力。[29] 过去二十年,全球变暖是另一个重要的媒介议题,而科学家提供的信息补贴已被证明是关键的因素。[30] 围绕气候变化产生的政治冲突也表明,非政府组织、企业界甚至名人都常常瞄准新闻媒体,志在影响它们的报道。[31]

如果没有公共部门、非营利组织及私营领域的公关人士定期提供的信息补贴,媒介议程在范围与内容上都将大为不同。毕竟,议程设置是公共关系的重要组成部分。[32] 不仅如此,公共关系对媒介议程的影响,有时大大超过可以帮助新闻记者完成日常工作的简单信息补贴。有研究者考察了代表外国政府(很多政府在国际上形象高度负面)开展的专业公关活动,发现了两个表明这些公关活动取得了成功的指标:《纽约时报》对这些政府的总体报道减少了,意味着媒体对这些政府的关注变少了;而在"缩水"的新闻报道中,正面报道又增加了。[33]

三、俘获媒介议程

政治竞选是一种特殊的公共关系活动。在总统选举中,候选人在政治广告上花费巨资,力图设置选民的议程。此外,他们还为影响新闻媒体的议程作出了重大努力,因为新闻媒体报道消息的自利动机不太明显,因此对公众来说更加可信。在全国层面,这些竞选努力在选举年的最初几个月里相当成功地设置了媒介的议程。然而,随着选举日期临近,选举活动进入倒计时并吸引了新闻工作者越来越多的关注,这种影响逐渐减弱。[34]另一方面,在州和地方选举中,因为那里可供报道的新闻资源很少,候选人对媒介议程的影响更加稳定,而且影响力往往更加强大。

虽然任何政治竞选活动的最终目标都是在选举日那天获胜,但是俘获媒介议程日益成为竞选宣传的眼前目标。[35]这种竞选宣传思维隐含的是一种议程设置的想法,因为控制了媒介议程便意味着可以对公众议程施加重大影响。当然,传播议程的一部分处于竞选活动即刻和直接的控制之下。大量金钱花在媒体(在许多国家指的是电视)的政治广告上;然而,也有越来越多的金钱投入各种社交媒体渠道。[36]这些媒介消息准确地反映了竞选活动的议程。

在对1983年英国大选和1984年美国大选的一项比较分析中,研究者发现,两个国家的政党在影响新闻议程方面存在较大差异。[37]在1983年的英国大选中,各个政党相当成功地引导新闻媒体关注它们各自强调的议题。进一步将保守党、工党和联盟党(自由党和社会民主党的联合）对五个关键政策议题的关注，与英国广播公司（BBC）、独立电视公司（ITV）及五份报纸（既有大报也有小报）对这些议题的报道作比较，结果发现两者之间存在很高的相关性，相关系数中位数为+0.70。在将三个政党分别与七种不同新闻媒体配对所产生的21组数据中，相关系数范围在+0.30到1.0（完全匹配）之间。在这21项相关系数中，有六项正好为+0.70（中位数），只有五个相关系数低于+0.70。各政党针对报纸与电视的议程设置都同样成功。

1984年的美国总统竞选活动对新闻媒体的影响，没有英国那样成功。将民主党和共和党对六个关键政策议题的强调与三家全国电视网关于这些议题的新闻报道作比较，结果发现，相关系数均没有超过+0.31。六项比较中有三项为零或负数。另有证据表明，两党在影响报纸方面也没有更好的成绩。

在英美这两个国家，政治竞选活动作为媒介议程的设置者所取得的成功之所以明显不同，主要是因为两国的新闻工作者在对选举的态度上存在文化差异。换句话说，理论洋葱的最内层——社会规范与新闻传统——在英国与美国非常不同。美国选举新闻的报道模式来自一种规范性精确计算，也就是新闻工作者每天都在选举新闻与其他所有新闻故事的激烈竞争中衡量它的新闻价值。与此相反，英国新闻工作者具有圣职规范导向，认为选举活动本质上是盛大而重要的活动，对它们的报道不能仅仅取决于其新闻价值。两个国家在选举报道方式上的这种差异，可以明确地以议程设置的语言这样描述：

> 在英国，大部分电视新闻工作者不太情愿以"议程设置"这个术语来界定他们对竞选的贡献。在他们看来，这个词有一种"积极"干预的含义，他们有可能被指责说，只是自顾自地提出个人认为重要的议题，不顾政党的意愿，甚至与政党想要推进的议题背道而驰……而在美国，全国广播公司（NBC）的多数新闻工作者对他们的角色则不那么抵触。与

英国广播公司的同行相比,他们更愿意承认自己在议程设置过程中的主动作用。"[38]

在2000年的美国总统预选期间,《纽约时报》的编辑也反映出同样的美国观点,即媒体坚持不懈地追问乔治·W.布什年轻时是否吸过毒,而布什拒绝回答这个问题。该报执行主编约瑟夫·莱利维尔德(Joseph Lelyveld)说:"这里有一个由谁设置议程的问题——是政客还是新闻媒体。"[39]这是一个核心问题,我们将在这里详细探讨。

虽然总体证据表明,在冗长的总统选举中美国新闻媒体多数时间发挥了强大的议程设置作用,但政客们有时的确在开头略胜一筹。在第三章讨论属性与框架时,证据显示,对1996年共和党候选人竞争总统提名的活动,《纽约时报》《华盛顿邮报》《洛杉矶时报》从1995年12月26日(这一天《纽约时报》开始对竞选者进行系列人物深度报道)到1996年2月20日(新罕布什尔州预选的日期,亦即美国冗长的总统选举年中的第一次预选)的新闻报道,反映出候选人对新闻媒体的影响。[40]四个主要的共和党竞争者是亚历山大(Lamar Alexander)、布坎南(Pat Buchanan)、多尔和福布斯(Steve Forbes)。研究者把媒体对他们的描述与这些候选人网站上的新闻通稿进行比较。媒介属性议程与每个候选人自我描述之间的一致是惊人的,相关系数分别为:亚历山大,+0.74;布坎南,+0.75;福布斯,+0.78;多尔,+0.62。多尔的领跑者位置可以很好地解释他稍低但仍然稳健的相关关系。

然而,在新罕布什尔州预选期间,对本州预选新闻报道进行的一项更为聚焦的分析发现,电视新闻报道与候选人演讲话题之间的相关性仅为中等水平(+0.40)。[41]虽然几乎所有候选人的演讲都谈及公众议题,但是只有不到三分之一的电视新闻报道提到了议题。美国新闻工作者对"赛马"报道(即只关注竞选者的领先情况)的长期偏爱,以及对议题的兴趣不足,都非常明显。

另一项研究考察了四大电视网及《纽约时报》《华盛顿邮报》《洛

杉矶时报》对1996年秋季总统竞选的报道,发现了更多的证据表明"赛马"报道在媒介议程上的首席地位。[42]不管是在报纸上,还是在电视上,"赛马"报道均占据了大约一半的媒介议程。这项研究没有讨论竞选本身,而是特别聚焦于公众议题,研究者对新闻报道的分析表明,在秋季竞选中,对于任何媒介议程,候选人的议题议程最多只有不明显的影响。

然而,在选举年的早期阶段,候选人再一次显示出了影响力——在2000年的总统预选中,有证据表明,候选人的议题议程的确影响了电视网的新闻报道。[43]在四个候选人议程与三家主要电视网之间的12项比较中,有10项产生了显著相关性,中位数在+0.64到+0.68之间。进一步的研究采用了交叉时滞相关分析,考察总统竞选最初几个月的情况,结果发现,候选人议程影响媒介议程的情况,是后者影响前者的两倍。

在议程设置的第二层面,虽然议程设置效果的总体证据较少,但发现的显著相关的强度与基本议程设置研究的证据相比,似乎更胜一筹。一项研究对比了候选人与电视新闻对不同受众亚群体(年长者、少数族群、妇女等)的重视程度,结果发现,12项比较中只有6项发现了显著相关性。这6项比较都与共和党的布什或麦凯恩相关,而不涉及民主党的戈尔或布拉德利,它们的相关系数中位数在+0.77到+0.85之间。对于一系列竞选话题(民意测验、表态支持、竞选辩论等)来说,12项比较中只有3项发现了显著性。所有这三项都涉及共和党的挑战者麦凯恩,他凭压倒性的媒体叙事以小胜大,成为巨人歌利亚(布什)面前的大卫。在这三项显著相关性中,中位数为+0.69。

全民公投涉及的是类型非常不同的政治动员组织。2006年的瑞士公投要决定是否引入一项更严格的政治庇护法,参与辩论的有47个组织。[44]研究者将不同组织提出的赞成或者反对的议程,与电视和报纸关于拟议法律的七个关键论点的新闻报道相比较,结果发现,那些支持新法的组织在为其论点争取新闻报道的关注方面要比那些反对组织成功得多。在为期三个月的时间里,赞成新法的论点和新闻报道之间的相关系数中位数为+0.78。另一方面,这些报道也产生了强大的议程设置效果,虽然这种效果只体现在那些高度依赖媒介的公众身上。然而,在研究覆盖的三个月中,这些议程设置效果只出现在公投日之前的最后几个星期。到那时,媒介议程与经常使用媒介的公众的议程之间的相关系数高达+0.92。

转向议程设置的理论前沿,在2012年美国总统大选中期,研究者分析了奥巴马和罗姆尼的竞选活动所提供的信息补贴——新闻通稿、政党纲领、博客和候选人使用的其他社交媒体,考察了它们对报纸和电视报道的第一层面、第二层面和第三层面的议程设置效果。[45]与以前的研究结果相仿,竞选议程与媒介议程尤其是报纸议程之间存在很强的一致性,不管是在议题的显著性方面,还是在利益相关群体的显著性方面,群体范围从多名候选人及其团队直至活跃分子团体和社会机构。在议题属性议程和候选人属性议程方面也发现了同样的结果。

在探索新领域时,在竞选活动与媒介的议题网络和议题属性网络之间,亦即议程设置的第三层面,发现了更多微弱的相关。然而,在利益相关者网络的第三层面议程设置中,发现新闻通稿、博客和政党纲领与报纸报道(中位数为+0.66)和电视报道(中位数为+0.77)高度相关。就竞选活动所使用的四种社交媒体平台(脸书、优兔、谷歌+和推特)而言,利益相关者网络与报纸报道之间的相关系数中位数为+0.51,与电视报道之间的相关系数中位数为+0.88。

一项研究分析了奥地利从1970年到2008年的四次全国选举,发现主要政党新闻通稿的议题优先顺序在主要报纸的新闻报道中得到了反映。[46]为了考察这些效果对政治审议的作用,研究者还将分析延伸到了各政党和报纸的议题属性议程,评估了新闻通稿和新闻报道中有关信息质量的四个方面:所持议题立场的原因、提供解决方案的建议、文明程度和对各种议题立场的足够批评。在这些方面,报纸所表现出来的信息质量远不及政党的新闻通稿。进一步比较新闻工作者作为消息传播者和议题分析者的两种角色,结果揭示:直接新闻报道体现出来的质量水平要高于分析性文章。

这种对信息质量的分析,回答了一个关键的规范性问题的某个方面,即新闻媒体在呈现一种对公民有益的议程方面所起的作用。[47] 作为民主国家的公民对公共事务作出决策的基础,这些话题和属性的议程究竟有多大用处呢?

四、三种选举议程

新闻规范不仅在塑造媒介议题议程方面,而且在塑造随后的公众议题议程方面,都可能产生强烈的影响。这方面的充足证据来自对1992年和2000年美国总统竞选活动的全面的全国性分析。[48] 初看之下,1992年候选人竞选纲领的议程与媒介议程(+0.76)和公众议程(+0.78)这两方面的高度相关性,好像削弱了媒介具有议程设置作用的观点,甚至暗示媒介议程与公众议程之间的相关性(+0.94)被夸大了。但情况并非如此。如果同时考虑所有三个方面(候选人、媒介和公众)的议程,那么,媒介议程与公众议程之间的相关性依然强大,而候选人纲领与公众议程之间的相关性却大幅减弱。这可以通过几种方式观察到。

如果在分析媒介议程与公众议程之间的相关性(+0.94)时,同时考虑候选人纲领对媒介议程与公众议程的直接影响,那么最终的相关系数仍然是突出的+0.85。换一种方法,如果将媒介议程视作候选人与公众之间的重要干预因素,也就是说,作为候选人与公众之间的主要桥梁,那么最终产生的偏相关(partial correlation)便如预料中的那样会大幅度减少。如果剔除媒介的干扰影响,那么候选人纲领与公众议程之间的相关系数便由原先的+0.78减少至+0.33。当然,媒介议程绝不是凭空编造的——有大量来自媒体消息源的重要投入,相关系数高达+0.76证明了这一点——只不过,候选人的竞选活动所发出的光在到达公众之前,会被新闻规范的棱镜折射。

新闻媒体对议题议程具有足够的议程设置影响(在很大程度上独立于政治动员),对2000年秋季总统竞选的研究再次验证了这种效果。[49]在启动阶段,相关关系的基本模式与前面的大致相同,候选人的议题议程与媒介议程和公众议程之间的相关性均很高,相关系数分别为+0.79和+0.76。媒介议程与公众议程之间的相关系数则更是高达+0.92。

复制1992年发现的模式,在分析媒介议程与公众议程之间的相关关系时,也考虑到候选人对两者的影响,结果媒介议程与公众议程之间的相关仍然强劲,相关系数为+0.79。再者,将媒介议程视作候选人议程与公众议程之间的干预因素,那候选人议程与公众议程之间的相关系数便从原先的+0.76降至+0.15。分别对两个主要候选人——乔治·W.布什与阿尔·戈尔——的议程重复进行这种分析,结果发现了相同的情况。所有这些证据都强烈表明:新闻媒体在将公众的关注聚集到公众议题方面具有议程设置作用。

在对2000年总统竞选的分析中,研究者还探索了候选人和新闻媒体在界定公众如何认识社会福利议题上的属性议程设置影响,这个议题居于公众议程的首位。所获证据显然支持这样的说法:在2000年的秋季竞选中,竞选活动是这个议题的主要议程设置者。在社会福利议题的八个属性上,竞选议程与新闻媒体议程之间的相关系数为令人开心的+0.76,而与公众议程之间的相关系数甚至更为强大,达到+0.86。然而,与1992年和2000年研究中发现的在整体议题上的第一层面议程设置效果不同,在议程设置的第二层面,如果将媒介议程作为候选人与公众议程之间的干预因素引入分析,那么候选人与公众议程之间的相关系数只是稍有降低,为+0.78。但是,如果在分析媒介议程与公众议程之间的相关性时,考虑到候选人议程对它们的影响,那么媒介与公众的属性议程之间原先为+0.60的相关系数便会消失。

五、地方选举中的媒介议程

有研究者分析了2006年九场州级选举中各个竞选者发布的新闻通稿,发现在候选人的议题议程与各州发行量大的报纸的议题议程之间,相关系数中位数为+0.48。在第二层面,候选人的议题属性议程和报纸属性议程之间的相关系数中位数为+0.58。[50]

将2002年佛罗里达州长选举中共和党和民主党候选人新闻通稿中的议题议程,与本州六大报纸的议题议程相比较,得到的相关系数中位数为+0.78。[51]接下来,报纸的议题议程和公众议程之间的相关系数中位数为+0.74。候选人新闻通稿中的属性议程和他们在报纸中的形象也呈现出较明显的一致性。例如,在候选人的实质属性方面,相关系数中位数为+0.79;在负面语气方面,为+0.81,在正面语气方面,为+0.60。

1990年得克萨斯州长选举期间,在得克萨斯州首府奥斯汀市,研究者将民主党和共和党的付费电视广告的联合议题议程,与奥斯汀的报纸和三家地方电视台有关这些议题的新闻报道进行比较。[52]结果发现,竞选议程既对地方报纸施加了重要影响(+0.64),又对地方电视台施加了重要影响(+0.52)。即便将其他因素纳入考虑,这种影响的模式依然存在。

然而,这种影响的模式在四年后的得克萨斯州长选举中基本上被颠倒过来。这次选举标志着乔治 W.布什政治生涯的开端。将布什和时任州长理查兹(Ann Richards)在1994年秋季竞选期间的新闻通稿与本州三大报纸的报道进行比较,结果发现,报纸极大地影响了候选人的议题议程(+0.70),他们的新闻通稿对议题、个人形象及竞选活动本身的整体关注(+1.0),以及新闻通稿总体上正面或者负面的语气(+0.80)。[53]

在议程设置的第二层面,从1995年西班牙纳瓦拉省地方选举中得出的研究证据表明,政治广告影响了其后电视新闻对候选人的描绘(+0.99),但对报纸的效果则比较温和(+0.32)。[54]广告的主要作用表现在对候选人资质的描述上。在电视上,从竞选早期到后来,报道候选人资质的时间增长了八倍多。而在报纸上,整个竞选过程中提及这一属性的内容只增加了一倍。

六、地方议题的属性

在美国地方政治层面,研究者观察到了政治广告在得克萨斯州维多利亚市两次选举中的议程设置效果。[55]在1995年维多利亚市关于地方营业税的公投中,对注册选民的两次民意调查(一次在投票前一个月,一次在投票前一周)显示出两种明显的模式:在动员活动期间,选民的学习能力显著增强;在拟议的营业税会给维多利亚市带来什么影响方面,政治广告对塑造选民观点起到了非常重要的作用。

从第一次调查到第二次调查,选民头脑中关于营业税的图像与地方报纸对营业税的呈现之间,匹配度从+0.40增长到+0.65,与政治广告之间的匹配度从+0.80增长到+0.95。如果在考察这些得克萨斯选民与一个来源(例如报纸)的匹配度时,控制另一个来源(例如广告)的影响,那么公众与报纸之间的相关性会完全消失;但是对政治广告来讲,通过这种控制方法得到的两个相关系数却分别是+0.87(第一次调查,相比原先的+0.80)和+0.94(第二次调查,相比原先的+0.95)。可见,政治广告是学习这一地方经济议题的主要来源。

在那一年维多利亚市的市长选举中,两个候选人在选民心目中的形象与地方报纸报道的属性议程之间都存在显著的匹配性（两个候选人均为+0.60），而与每个候选人的政治广告之间的匹配度则更高（分别为+0.73和+0.85）。进一步分析得出结论：政治广告是这次地方选举中的主要议程设置者。如果将候选人对媒介议程与公众议程两者的影响都考虑进来，那么对于一个候选人来说，报纸议程与公众议程之间的匹配度便从+0.60减少到+0.46；而对于第二个候选人，两种议程则几乎没有相关性可言。然而，如果在考察政治广告议程与公众议程之间的关系时控制了媒介议程的作用，那么，根本没有证据表明媒介议程在竞选活动与公众认知之间充当了关键的桥梁，而候选人议程与公众议程之间的强烈相关性却没有改变。

七、选举三要素

这一系列证据的基础是政治竞选所有的三个关键要素，即候选人与政党、新闻媒体、公众，它们记录了复杂的组合方式，可以考察新闻媒体在全部背景下的议程设置作用。这种丰富的组合回应了早期对议程设置效果的批评，批评者认为媒介的议程设置效果证据零碎，因为那么多的证据一次只探究两个要素，例如，在议程设置研究的最初阶段是媒体与公众，其后自20世纪80年代开始，是新闻来源与媒体。特别是，这些证据也回答了一个基本问题，即谁是真正的议程设置者，是媒体还是政治动员。如果说竞选议程同样主导了媒介议程和公众议程的形成，那媒体最多不过是公众议程的近因而已。在英国，全国性政党在俘获媒介议程方面相当成功。但在美国却并非如此。美国的新闻规范使得总统竞选期间的媒介议程与全国性政党提出的议程只有微弱的对应关系。最重要的是，涵盖三要素的美国证据表明，直至目前，是媒介议程，而非候选人议程，对公众议程的影响最大。

总而言之，在美国整个选举年中，媒介是议程设置者。然而，在美国总统选举活动开跑时,以及在美国、西班牙的地方选举中,情况就比较混杂了。在这些情形下,政治竞选宣传通常能够成功地俘获媒介议程。

八、更广阔的图景

不管是检验新闻来源对媒介的影响,还是接下来媒介对公众的影响,选举都提供了一个非常集中的研究情境。然而,在更大的历史范围内,对于有关时下议题的公民意见的持续起伏,选举的影响却堪称微弱。议题的显著性如何从各种新闻来源流向新闻媒体,又如何从新闻媒体流向公众?有研究者详细分析了1985年至1995年在三个议题上的加拿大舆论,提供了议题显著性从多种新闻来源流向新闻媒体,又从新闻媒体流向公众的更广阔图景。[56]这次分析选择的三个议题是通货膨胀、环境、国债和财政赤字。这项研究也重新审视了前面几章提及的议程设置理论的各个方面,这次是在议程设置过程全面模型的背景下进行的。

首先,按照第五章讨论过的媒介效果及强制性和非强制性议题的概念,在这三个议题构成的连续体中有一个清晰的模式。在通货膨胀这个强制性议题上,研究结果与以前的证据一致,没有发现媒介对舆论产生了任何议程设置效果。对于环境议题,媒介议程与公众议程之间是相互影响的关系,其中公众对媒介的影响看起来更大一些。

而在最后一个议题,即加拿大国债和财政赤字这个非强制性的抽象议题上,证据显示,媒介对公众施加了显著的影响。这项全面的研究还为我们提供了新的机会,重新考察媒介议程与现实之间的关系。研究者在分析通货膨胀、环境以及加拿大国家财政的情况时发现,在这些年里,媒介议程的趋势与现实世界的测量之间并没有显著关系。原本按照常理,在通货膨胀与环境议题上,这些现实测量应该与公众议程和政策议程的趋势存在联系。而对于第三个议题，即国家财政，这些测量只与政策议程有关。在分析时，研究者利用加拿大议会质询期和委员会报告中出现的争议话题来界定政策议程。当然，选举也是现实的一个方面，而且是新闻的重大来源。但是，选举的发生并没有影响媒体在这些议题上的长期趋势，只是影响了公众对环境议题的关注趋势。

政府政策议程的各种表现也是媒体潜在的新闻来源。这方面的证据比较混杂。在通货膨胀议题上，有证据表明，政策议程对新闻媒介议程有一定的影响。但是就环境和加拿大财政的议题而言，证据表明，媒介议程与政策议程之间存在相互影响的关系，在环境议题上的相互作用较强，而在国家财政议题上则较弱。

对印第安纳州布卢明顿市议会活动与地方日报相关报道长达一年的比较研究，发现了同样混杂的情况。[57]虽然市议会的优先事项与媒介议程之间存在相当大的一致性(+0.84)，但进一步的分析发现，在19个类别中，七个类别的排名存在重要差异。在四个类别，即艺术和娱乐、"核冻结"、公用事业和选举上，报纸的强调要突出得多。在颁奖、动物保护和城市发展方面，报纸的强调则要少得多。即便是对政府正式会议的新闻报道，几乎可以预见主要是速记式报道，也显示出新闻规范与新闻事件之间的相互影响。一个负责报道市议会的记者说，他"喜欢那些涉及争议、辩论以及若干行动者的主题，因为这些特点使故事更精彩"[58]。他的这种观点反映了新闻叙事要求的规范性影响，也就是讲一个好故事。这种观点也至少部分说明了这样的事实，即市议会记录中描述的事项只有59%获得了地方报纸的报道。

最后，影响上述所有三种议程，即由各种政府活动反映出的政策议程、媒介议程和公众议程，通常是各种有组织的利益群体的目标。[59]这些利益群体的议题游说活动往往和竞选活动一样资金充足，而且有同样成功的设置记录。一项为期九年的分析考察了美国有关枪支管制的辩论,结果发现,在这个议题上,电视新闻网的注意与持正反立场的利益群体发布的大量新闻通稿之间存在较大的联系(+0.60),与国会讨论之间也有一定的联系(+0.32)。[60]研究者对这个议题的架构方式进行了分析,结果发现:在将近一半的新闻报道中,"暴力文化"主题占支配地位;在国会关于枪支管制的辩论中,只有不到四分之一的陈述使用"暴力文化"作为主导框架;而在利益群体的新闻通稿中,这个比例更是不到六分之一。简言之,新闻媒体在很大程度上是独立于这些新闻来源的,它注重叙事要求,因而更倾向于采用戏剧性的"暴力文化"框架。虽然这种现象可能会鼓励媒体保持声音的独立,但同时也是一种失败,因为新闻媒体未能"使讨论超越简单的情感框架,提升为更理性的政策辩论"[61]。

九、媒体间议程设置

精英新闻媒体经常对其他新闻媒体的议程施加足够的影响。在美国,《纽约时报》通常扮演这种媒体间议程设置者的角色。不管是纽约州西部爱河(Love Canal)的严重化学污染,还是邻近的宾夕法尼亚州和新泽西州的氡气威胁,虽然地方报纸连续多月进行了密集报道,但都没有引起全国关注,直到这些问题进入《纽约时报》的议程,情况才有所改观。[62]前面第二章也提到,《纽约时报》在1985年底发现了毒品问题,导致第二年全国各大报纸与全国电视新闻的密集报道,这种关注在1986年9月随着两个全国电视专题节目的播出而达到高潮。[63]有一项韩国研究也指出,在网络新闻环境中,主要新闻组织之间也存在这种媒体间议程设置的影响。[64]

社会学家沃伦·布里德(Warren Breed)将这种新闻故事从精英新闻媒体向其他新闻媒体扩散的现象,概念化为树枝状影响(dendritic influence)。[65]就像家谱一样,血从一个祖先流向了众多后裔。在很多情况下,这些新闻子嗣是绝对的克隆体。20 世纪中期,《纽约时报》与现已不存在的《纽约先驱论坛报》展开了激烈竞争,这两家报纸的执行主编经常在最后时刻命令下属更改头版,以便与竞争者一争高下。[66]

正如第一章关于新闻景观的讨论中提到的,新闻工作者也经常互相观察,随后照抄同行的新闻报道,以验证自己对每日事件的新闻判断。[67]个体记者这种做法的一个经典例子,来自 1972 年美国总统竞选期间。在那个美国选举年中,第一个重大政治事件是艾奥瓦州的党团会议,即为了选出参加州政党大会的代表而在本州各地举行的一系列地方政党会议。会上的形势非常模糊,很难抓住报道重点,因为参加这几十次地方会议的是一些自我选择(自愿参加)的选民,他们有足够的兴趣出席会议并参与讨论。同时,在这种选举年的早期阶段,总是有一大批候选人竞相争夺代表席位。记者在这些晚间党团会议上的任务就是理解这一切,并从中寻找新闻线索。

> 此时的情况是,《纽约时报》的艾珀尔(Johnny Apple)坐在角落,每个人都围在他的旁边,看他在写些什么……他坐下来,写下导语,别人就去写导语……最后到午夜,有人宣布马斯基(Muskie)得票 32%,而麦戈文(McGovern)得到了 26% 的票,艾珀尔就坐下来完成他的整篇报道。他将此描述为"乔治·麦戈文强劲的表现令人吃惊"。每个人又都从他的背后看到了这句话,并照抄下来。第二天,这句话出现在每份主要报纸的头版。[68]

从 1985 年至 1992 年报道全球变暖议题的过往中,研究者也发现了美国精英新闻媒体中的这种媒体间议程设置的大量写照。[69]随着对这个议题的报道稳步增加,直至 1989 年达到高峰,主要报纸(即《纽约时报》《华盛顿邮报》《华尔街日报》)明显地影响了三家全国电视网的议程。在这个复杂的科学议题上,科学出版物也扮演了一个重要的媒体间议程设置者的角色,科学作者与编辑会定期追踪这些关键的专业知识来源。

精英新闻媒体带领新闻界对新话题进行广泛报道,关键位置的新闻工作者建构新闻的报道框架,这些都是媒体间议程设置的突出例子。然而,由于地方新闻机构根据通讯社供给的海量新闻创建自己的每日议程,媒体间议程设置的普通版本实际上每天都在发生。一项研究考察了24份艾奥瓦州日报使用美联社新闻稿的情况,结果发现了通讯社新闻对地方新闻议程的主导影响。[70]虽然每份报纸都仅仅使用了很少一部分美联社的报道,但是它们的报道模式基本上反映了美联社各类新闻所占的比例。

在一项实验室研究中,研究者选择了经验丰富的负责选择通讯社稿件的报纸和电视编辑作为受试者,结果发现,比照通讯社提供的大量稿件和编辑选取的少量样本,各类新闻的比例呈现出高度的一致性(+0.62)。[71]在实验的控制条件下,即每类新闻都有相同数量的故事,也发现了通讯社的议程设置影响。在这种情况下,无论是选取的稿件与完全平衡而缺乏显著性线索的通讯社稿件相比,还是在可能分享类似新闻价值观的通讯社稿件编辑中,都没有发现共同的选择模式。

早期对把关问题的调查,探究的是本地新闻机构的新闻工作者对新闻通讯社稿件的取舍,强调把关人自己的心理特点。与此相反,议程设置理论要求关注把关任务的社会环境。[72]

重新分析[73]关于盖茨先生(Mr. Gates)的经典个案研究[74],结果发现,他所跟踪的各通讯社的综合议程与他为自家报纸作出的最终选择之间,存在较大的相关性(+0.64)。十七年后进行验证研究时,盖茨先生只采用了一家通讯社的稿件。[75]进一步考察可知,通讯社议程与他选择的新闻之间,相关系数为+0.80。[76]

转向地方新闻层面,研究者分析了得克萨斯州奥斯汀市1990年州长竞选期间的选举报道,结果发现,地方日报的议题议程影响了地方电视新闻的议题议程(+0.73)。[77]回顾本章前面的讨论,我们注意到候选人的议题议程既影响了报纸报道,也影响了电视报道。但是,即便将这种影响纳入考虑,仍有证据表明报纸对电视新闻施加了重要影响(+0.44)。

在西班牙,研究者开展了一项对1995年地方选举中报纸与电视之间的媒体间影响的研究,既考察了第一层面的议程设置效果,又考察了第二层面的议程设置效果。[78]在潘普洛纳发现的第一层面议程设置效果与在奥斯汀发现的结果非常相似。将两份潘普洛纳报纸在六个议题上的报道分别与其后的电视新闻议程相比较,各自的相关系数为+0.66与+0.70。在议程设置的第二层面,没有证据表明报纸与地方电视新闻在描述候选人的方式上存在属性议程设置的影响。但是,回顾前面关于政治广告的讨论,潘普洛纳报纸上的政治广告确实影响了其后报纸与电视对候选人的描述。

新闻工作者通过观察新闻同行的工作来验证自己对新闻的感觉。这些日常的、连续的观察及其产生的媒体间影响的结果,最终形成了一种高度重复的新闻议程。原创性的查普希尔研究发现所分析的九家传统媒体主要的议题议程之间的相关系数中位数为+0.78。[79]四十年后,卓越新闻项目对2008年美国大选的竞选报道进行了分析,发现了同样的强相关性。[80]例如,麦库姆斯与肖1972年发表的研究成果表明,《纽约时报》及CBS和NBC电视新闻节目在竞选议题议程上的等级相关系数中位数是+0.66。卓越新闻项目2008年的数据对15个广泛的新闻题材进行了编码,分析这些数据,结果显示这几家媒体的相关系数中位数为+0.68。

随着数字媒体的崛起,现在不同的媒体组织可以很容易地查验竞争对手所报道的议题,从而增加了新闻媒体议程的冗余度。这种"信息充裕时代的模仿"[81]过程导致全国媒介议程相当程度的同质化。回到2008年的卓越新闻项目数据,新闻网站(CNN.com、Yahoo!News、MSNBC.com、Google News和AOL News)议程之间的相关系数中位数,从早晨(上午 9 点)的平均+0.21 增加到晚间(下午 4 点)的+0.51。也就是说,由于数字记者和编辑在白天追踪和参考同行的工作,对什么是时下最重要的议题这个问题的回答不断趋同。[82]

媒体议程的高度一致性是一个世界性现象。在 1992 年中国台湾地区的"民意代表"选举中,研究者以相似的方法比较了台北三份主要日报与三家电视台的议题议程,发现相关系数中位数为+0.75。[83] 2000 年至 2005 年在智利进行的一项研究发现,电视新闻和报纸议题议程的相关系数中位数为+0.83。[84] 另一项研究采用时间序列分析,对 2013 年奥地利大选中 39 家新闻媒体的报道进行检验,发现了媒体间议程传染的强有力证据。[85]

在第二层面议程设置方面,第三章讨论过日本一家主要报纸即《每日新闻》关于日本经济问题的报道框架。该研究涉及两组属性,宏观的问题性情境框架和细描经济问题具体方面的属性。另一项验证和拓展研究比较了《朝日新闻》和《读卖新闻》经济报道的同样两组属性,结果发现,不论是在问题性情境框架的显著性方面(+0.93),还是在次级议题属性的显著性方面(+0.79),这两份报纸都非常相似。[86] 在一项对美国经济议题的属性的比较研究中,研究者发现报纸与电视议程之间的相关系数为+0.80。[87] 这种比较可以称为一种准比较,因为两份报纸的议程已合并为复合的报纸议程,三家电视台的议程则合并为复合的电视议程。

在调查媒介的议程设置作用时,将各种新闻机构的议程合并,以创建一个复合的媒介议程,是一种常见的做法,因为各种议程之间存在高度的同质性。用研究方法的语言来说,这种新闻媒体议程之间的高度相关性可以视为信度的测量,即独立的观察者采用同样的规则观察时所能达到的一致程度。新闻工作者将新闻规范与专业传统应用于每日可供观察的大量事件与情况(当然,也凭借他们对其他媒体的观察),创建了高度相似的议程。在议程设置的第二层面,议程的同质性超越了对特定客体的属性议程的认同,因此多个相关客体的属性议程也存在高度的相似性。比较台北主要报纸在三个市长候选人方面的属性议程,结果发现相关系数中位数为+0.93。[88]新闻规范对报道时下新闻施加了强大的同质化压力,而这种同质化接着又影响了新闻在一个主要的社交媒体渠道即推特上的传递方式。惠普实验室考察了2010年9月到10月关于3361个不同热门话题的1632万条推文,结果发现,这些热门话题"主要是来自传统媒体的新闻,这些新闻在推特平台经由持续转发而不断放大,从而形成了趋势"[89]。

在数字领域,媒体间议程设置变得更加细微。在相当大的程度上,政治博客与传统媒体的议程高度趋同,尤其体现在议程设置的第一层面。不过,鉴于这些博客的政治多样性,它们的属性议程呈现出较少的趋同趋势,这倒也不奇怪。就影响力而言,主流媒体仍然是主要推手;但不时地,政治博客和社交媒体确实能够成功地引领潮流。不管谁是领导者,谁是跟随者,主导模式都是一个高度同质化的议题议程和一个具有相当趋同性的属性议程。[90]

最后,转到新媒介景观的其他方面。在2008年美国总统选举初选期间,一项分析发现,与奥巴马官方或MoveOn.org的优兔广告的议题重点相比,"奥巴马30秒"在线广告竞赛所反映的积极活动分子的议题议程与党派新闻媒体报道的关系更为密切。[91]

小　结

是谁设置了媒介议程?这个关于哪些议题将会引起公众关注的问题非常关键。专栏作家皮茨(Leonard Pitts)指出:"在一个由传媒设置公众议程并推动对话的世界里,媒体所忽视的事情就像不存在一样。"[92]在回答是谁设置了媒介议程这个问题时,本章罗列的答案考虑了三个关键因素:为新闻报道提供信息的主要来源、其他新闻组织,以及新闻的规范和传统。

有时候，国家领导人能够成功地设置新闻议程。公共信息官员与其他公共关系专家在这方面的作用也很大。但是，所有这些影响都要经过新闻规范所建立的基本规则的过滤，而这些规则是非常强大的过滤器。新闻机构之间的互动则进一步塑造并规范每日及每周新闻议程的演变。在这种媒体间议程设置的过程中，诸如《纽约时报》这样的地位较高的新闻机构设置了其他新闻机构的议程。在城市层面，地方报纸与电视台也会影响它们的竞争对手的新闻议程。近些年来，各种社交媒体也加入了传播大合唱。在一些情况下，媒体间议程设置会以一种非常不同的形式发生，如娱乐媒体设置新闻媒体的议程。[93]

"是谁设置了媒介议程？"这是传播学者和专业人士最感兴趣的问题。除了探索这个问题之外，我们对外部议程的那些认识也说明了议程设置理论范围的扩展。虽然我们关于议程设置过程的大多数知识都集中于媒介议程与公众议程之间的关系，但这方面的研究只是议程设置理论的一种有限应用。议程设置理论是有关显著性从一个议程向另一个议程转移的理论。这个理论最发达的部分集中于媒介议程与公众议程之间的联系，因为议程设置理论植根于民意调查，而且建立这个理论的大多数学者对媒介效果特别感兴趣。本章也讨论了塑造媒介议程的其他各种因素。尽管有此转变，但是议程设置理论的总体关注始终是以媒介为中心的。当然，我们将看到，还有许多其他的议程设置关系需要去考虑。

从历史的角度看，对塑造媒介议程的影响来源的研究，开启了议程设置理论的新阶段，标志着超越媒介议程与公众议程之关系的重大扩展。议程设置理论的最初阶段从查普希尔研究开始，以媒介议题议程对公众议题议程的影响为核心。议程设置的第二个面向，是着力阐释新闻媒体的这种影响，探讨在公众中加强或者限制议程设置效果的各种偶发条件。第三个面向则扩展了媒介议程设置的影响范围，从对注意的影响(客体议程)到对理解的影响(属性议程)。最近,这一理论正在探索网络议程设置,亦即第三层面的议程设置效果。本章还介绍了另一种理论面向,亦即媒介议程的起源。虽然议程设置的这些面向最初显现时有一个明显的历史轮廓,但它们并不是历史分期,新面向的出现并不意味着之前的面向就关上了大门。所有这些议程设置的理论面向仍然是活跃的探索场所。而且,始终存在许多其他领地等待我们开发!

第八章　议程设置的后果

　　大多数社会科学的典型发展过程是渐进式的,与流行观念中科学因重大"发现"而进步形成了鲜明对比。在 20 世纪与 21 世纪之交,议程设置理论的渐进特点尤其明显。在前几章可见的以媒介议程和公众议程为中心的有序和简约的知识准则,现在正处于新关系与新场景扩张性爆发的边缘。然而,与其说这些新视角是关于媒介在塑造舆论中的作用的重大发现的曙光,不如说它们是学术研究持续积累的成果。作为锲而不舍的学术研究的结果,媒介议程设置作用的思想正与许多其他关于传播和人类行为的社会科学概念和研究兴趣相融合。从 1968 年至今,议程设置理论的知识历史反映了在绘制传播过程的图谱中分散但却稳定的进展。查普希尔研究首先描绘了基本的第一层面议程设置的效果,在此基础上,又增加了大量关于公众、媒介及其议程的额外细节,增进了我们对媒介的公众效果的理解。在此前的章节中,我们呈现了与议程设置理论核心有关的细节。现在,在这个理论地图的最新版本中,又添加了超出显著性转移范围的议程设置过程之后果的细节。议程设置理论的这一面向,即解释议程设置过程的后果,以前只是勾勒出了一个轮廓,正如尤金·肖(Eugene Shaw)在 1979 年指出的:

　　　　态度与行为通常受认知的支配,认知就是一个人知道什么,思考什么,相信什么。因此,新闻媒体的议程设置功能意味着一种潜在的巨大影响,其全部维度和各种后果有待进一步调查与领会。[1]

第三章最后指出,在属性议程设置中,认知与情感因素的结合促使人们重新思考传播对态度与观点的影响。那一章和第四章展示的公众对政治候选人的描述中情感属性的显著性(至少部分来自新闻媒体)的相关证据,重新开启了一个心理探索的领域。而在20世纪中期,面对基于坚固实证研究的媒介效果有限的论断,心理探索的领域基本上被抛弃了。

正如许多早期学者所相信的,有时媒介效果可能仅仅来自大量的媒介接触。第一层面的议程设置效果在某种程度上证明了这一点。但是,正如属性议程设置所表明的,进一步关注媒介消息的特定内容,可以更详细地了解我们头脑中的图像以及根植于这些图像的态度和意见。属性议程设置将我们带回到大众传播对人们的态度和意见的影响,而这正是大众传播理论在20世纪40—50年代的理论发源地。这是对卡尔·霍夫兰(Carl Hovland)的科学修辞的回归,即消息的特征与态度和意见的变化是对应的。[2]然而,与霍夫兰的先驱作品不同,现在指导我们探索的是,将媒介议程与公众联系起来的一幅详细的理论地图。

为了达到戏剧性效果,一些电影的开场片段是黑白或灰褐的色调,然后猛然从这些压抑的颜色转到充满活力的彩色,以加强它们的情感冲击力。同样,当媒介与公众的属性议程既包括实质属性又包含情感语气时,新闻中关于这些客体的图像会激起强烈的情绪与感情,亦即意见。简言之,公众属性议程与个人意见的概念趋于一致。然而,这并不是公众议程与个人意见唯一的交汇点,因此,在我们详细考察这些关系之前,我们需要先勾勒出议程设置理论地图的一些附加部分。

前面我们讨论了议程设置第一层面和第二层面的理论地图,框8.1

第八章 议程设置的后果

再现了客体显著性与属性显著性的图谱。这幅地图中的新元素是意见的两个方面,加上可以观察到的行为。框 8.1 中的第一个新元素是意见的强度(strength of opinion),从意见是否存在这一基本点开始。意见依据强度还可以分为弱意见与强意见,不管这种意见是正面的还是负面的。框 8.1 中的第二个新元素我们比较熟悉,它是意见的方向(direction of opinion),即对某个客体或属性的看法是正面的还是负面的。

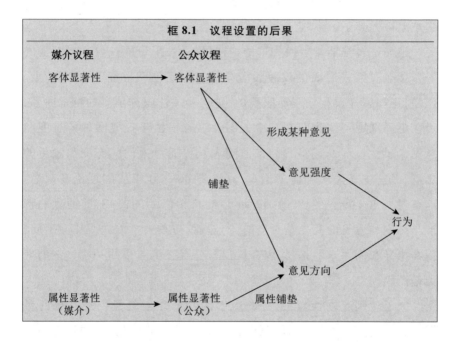

将意见的这两个方面与客体和属性的显著性联系起来,可以解释三种主要的关系。大量证据表明了媒介铺垫(priming,亦称启动)作用的存在,即公众议程上的客体显著性与意见方向之间的联系。探讨议程设置的第二层面,引出了属性铺垫(attribute priming),这是属性显著性与意见方向之间的联系。第三种关系则是意见的形成(forming an opinion),这是客体显著性与意见强度之间的联系。本章将讨论所有这三种关系,以及其后它们与个体行为之间的联系。

一、铺垫舆论

议程设置效果的突出后果之一,便是准备好观点,从而引导公众对公众人物形成某种意见。这一后果使媒介的议程设置影响成为舆论场的中心。的确,媒介的作用要比塑造我们头脑中的客体与属性议程多得多,"电视新闻(以及其他新闻媒体)通过将人们的注意力引至某些问题而忽视其他问题,影响人们在评判政府、总统、政策和公职候选人时所使用的标准",艾英戈(Shanto Iyengar)和金德(Donald Kinder)在他们的创新性著作《至关重要的新闻》中是如此解释的。[3]

议程设置效果(其结果是议题或其他元素在公众中的显著性)与随后对特定公众人物的意见表达之间的这种联系,叫作媒介铺垫。铺垫的心理学基础是公众的选择性注意。的确,人们并没有注意到所有的事情,事实上也不可能关注所有的事情,公众议程的有限容量已经表明了这种情况。不仅如此,人们在作出判断时,不管是在选举日投票,还是回答某个民意调查员的问题,都会使用简单的经验法则,走直觉捷径——这种认知方法被心理学者称为启发法(heuristics)。[4]大多数公民在必须作出判断时,并不会根据自己的全部信息储备进行全面分析,而总是利用那些特别显著的信息片段。[5]换句话说,公民依靠他们头脑中显著客体及属性的议程作出反应,而这个议程在很大程度上是由新闻媒体设置的。这种议程决定了公众在形成某种意见时所依据的标准,有时只是单一标准。

第一章中描述的一系列议程设置实验,也显示了电视新闻对人们形成关于总统执政总成绩的意见所发挥的铺垫效果。[6]为了证明特定议题的显著性变化能够影响人们对总统执政成绩的总体评判,这些实验比较了两个群体,即那些没有看过任何与特定议题相关的电视新闻报道的人和那些看过的人。在五个不同的议题(国防、通货膨胀、军备控制、公民权利和失业）上，较之没有看过任何新闻报道的人，接触过关于一个或多个议题的广泛新闻报道的人，对一个或多个受到大量报道的议题的评分，更可能影响其对总统执政表现的总体意见。不管新闻报道是否暗示总统在那个议题上负有重大责任，这种影响都存在。在其后的实验中，研究者明确操纵了总统在某个议题上应负责任的程度，结果发现，当新闻报道强调总统的责任时，代表表现有问题的得分对总统执政总体成绩的评判意见冲击更大。

这是实验室控制实验得出的强因果证据，表明新闻媒体的议程对一些议题在公众中的显著性的影响，为美国人评判总统执政的总体表现准备好了标准。[7]在美国的一个重要政治事件的背景下进行的经典研究，也发现了这种铺垫作用的证据，这一事件便是"伊朗—康特拉丑闻"（"伊朗门事件"）。[8]1986年11月25日，美国司法部长宣布，美国政府从对伊朗的秘密武器销售中得到的资金已被非法转给尼加拉瓜反政府武装"康特拉"，这是一支试图推翻尼加拉瓜"桑解阵"政府的武装力量，这场秘密交易是由国家安全委员会成员促成的。其后，里根总统透露，国家安全事务助理和该部门另外一名重要成员已被解职。不出所料，所有这些爆料都被媒体大量报道。巧合的是，在这些事件报道出来的时候，美国国家选举研究正在进行有关1986年总统选举的选后调查。这样，这一事件就创造了一个天然的机会，可以前后对比，考察影响美国人对里根总统的评价的舆论因素。

> 从事件揭露之前到揭露之后，就对总统总体执政表现的评价而言，援助尼加拉瓜反政府武装和美国干涉中美洲问题上的公众意见的重要性明显增长［……］采取干涉立场还是孤立主义的总体政策选择上的公众意见的重要性也是如此［……］与此同时，这次揭露显然没有影响公众对美国在世界上的实力的看法。这一结果确证了前面提到的实验中的发现。[9]

自这些初步探索以后,媒介铺垫效应已在广泛多样的议题上得到确认,包括对种族的态度[10]、经济[11]、腐败[12]和外交政策[13]。更重要的是,这些影响已经在全球范围内得到验证[14],并且在短期和长期内都是如此[15]。其中一些研究还提出了哪些公众更容易受媒介影响的问题。如果铺垫的发生是因为人们在政治上不够老练,那将是令人担忧的,这表明舆论很容易被主导新闻报道的媒体和精英集团左右。但是,如果铺垫作用发生在有政治经验的个人身上,这便意味着媒介的影响产生于一个更加审慎的新闻内容过滤的过程。这里存在一些共识,即在政治成熟度适中的人中,媒介铺垫作用表现得最强,这些人愿意关注政治新闻,但自身态度不定,因此不能轻易地拒绝媒体线索。[16]

与第一章讨论的公民渗透相一致,铺垫效果主要来自媒介创造的积累性信息环境。可见,媒介铺垫是议程设置的重要延伸[17],是媒介借以塑造公众态度与意见的路径之一[18]。有时,这些议程设置效果可以非常直接地影响个体的态度和意见。属性议程设置的情况尤其如此,其影响可能就像电影色调突然由暗转亮一样具有戏剧性。

二、属性议程与意见

在探测新闻媒体对意见的影响时,区分媒体对某个议题的总体关注(议程设置的第一层面),与媒体对这一议题的描述方式(议程设置的第二层面),是至关重要的。有关1990—1991年海湾战争的美国舆论,就说明了客体显著性与属性显著性的不同后果。[19]广泛的电视报道使海湾战争在公众议程上高度显著,公众视之为国家面临的最重要问题,这是第一层面的议程设置效果。而分析从1988年到1991年关于布什总统的公众意见,则进一步表明,他受欢迎的基础从经济问题转到了外交政策,这便是一种媒介铺垫效果。那些报告称自己较常收看电视新闻的公众,更倾向于用军事手段而非外交途径解决海湾地区问题;实际上,电视新闻提及战争时更强调军事解决办法,从而证明了属性议程设置对意见的影响。

对于核能、杀虫剂和吸烟等长期存在的议题,不仅新闻报道数量的增加提高了公众的意识,而且媒体报道还重新界定了这些议题,公众意见也随之发生了转变。[20]核能和杀虫剂从原先有益的科学应用,变成了对公众安全的主要威胁。吸烟日益被定义为危害个人健康的一种行为。随着这些议题的主导属性在公众议程上发生变化,公众意见也日渐负面。

媒介对某个议题各方面的报道,即媒介的属性议程,既影响我们看待事件的角度,也影响我们的观点。正如第三章我们在讨论属性议程设置时提到的,需要修改科恩那句经典总结,应该说,媒介不仅告诉我们想什么,而且告诉我们怎么想。有时候,媒介还告诉我们应该想它的什么(方面)。

例如,新闻报道的语气对公众意见的影响一直是学术界关注的问题。一个典型的发现是,媒体报道中正面和负面语气的变化模式可以解释政治领导人支持率的显著变化。[21]用议程设置的术语来说,这些结果是属性铺垫的证据。当媒体强调的某个客体的某些属性成为该客体的公共评价的重要维度时,就会出现这种情况。[22]这样,如果媒介成功地在使用者中铺垫了关于国家元首或政府首脑的正面(或负面)的考量,对候选人的正面(或负面)报道就会在民调中转化为正面(或负面)的支持率。[23]

在一项属性铺垫效果的详细分析中,研究者采用从"非常喜欢"到"非常不喜欢"的十点量表,要求西班牙公民给六个主要政治人物打分;随后,将得分与受访者对那些人的情感性描述(对那个广为应用的"你会告诉你的朋友什么"的开放式问题的回答)进行对比。[24]接着,对开放式问题的答案进行编码,将其定义为六个实质性类别和五个情感性类别,组成一个描述矩阵,比之此前的效果证据更能看到细微差别。对开放式问题的回答也提供了更丰富的细节,可以解释简约的评分后面隐藏着的各种图谱。在六个西班牙政治领袖身上,公民的各种情感描述与其评分之间的相关系数取值范围在+0.78 到+0.97 之间,中位数为+0.86。那些在十点量表中给出低分的公民对领导人的描述内容也很负面,而那些给出高分的公民对领导人的描述内容则高度正面。

在 2002 年得克萨斯州选举和联邦选举中,研究发现,对于州长和参议员候选人,新闻媒体的属性议程对公民的属性议程影响明显;而其后,在个体属性议程与他们对四个候选人的看法之间也发现了显著的相关性。与较少阅读报纸的人相比,更多的属性可以预测经常阅读报纸的人对候选人的个人看法。[25]

这些作用模式在 2006 年的以色列选举中得到了验证。在竞选期间,媒体报道中属性的显著性发生了变化,于是公众议程中属性的显著性也随之变化。并且,选民是根据最显著的属性来评价候选人的,对于经常阅读报纸的选民来说,这一点体现得更加明显。[26]

语气的影响并不仅限于人们对政治的态度和观点。一项对十四年里英国经济新闻报道的内容分析,结合了评估经济的两种测量与现实世界经济状况的两项指标。[27]统计分析的结果表明,媒体对经济的负面报道多于正面报道。更重要的是,研究发现,公众对这种报道模式的反应是不对称的,消费者对未来经济的预期受到了负面报道而非正面报道的影响。可见,英国媒体成功地铺垫了对经济形势更悲观而非乐观的评价。

某次操纵性实验对议题(全球变暖)的显著性和属性(人们对全球变暖的五种可能后果中的每一种是否会发生的看法)的显著性都进行了测试。结果发现,议题显著性对参与者支持遏制全球变暖的努力没有影响。但是,与雄辩论据的概念(客体的某个特殊属性会影响客体在公众中的显著性)相一致,实验中的一个属性(对生态系统的负面

第八章 议程设置的后果

影响)与受试者支持遏制全球变暖的努力之间关联显著。[28]

美国人对同性婚姻的态度变化令人印象深刻,这可能是属性铺垫效果的另一个例子。20世纪90年代后期,反对同性婚姻的人多于支持同性婚姻的人。到2013年,这一趋势已经完全扭转。2015年,同性婚姻在全美范围内合法化。一项研究[29]测量了2003年至2013年《纽约时报》上与同性婚姻议题相关的报道的实质属性和情感属性的显著性,无论是在宗教信仰、家庭价值观或法律权利的背景下讨论,无论是用正面还是负面的语气,并将其与公众对同性婚姻问题的意见相联系。结果显示出非常高的相关性,尤其是在长时段(一年的时间)内。

这些关于铺垫效果及媒介消息中实质和情感两种属性效果的合并证据表明,议程设置会对公众意见的正面或负面方向产生影响。

三、形成意见

让我们从头说起。新闻中客体的显著性与受众意见的形成之间存在一种基本的联系。例如,随着公众人物在新闻中显著性的提升,越来越多的人会对这些人产生看法。在1984年到2004年的六次美国总统选举中,新闻报道的数量存在相当大的差异。美国国家选举研究发现,这种报道模式与每次选举中对候选人发表意见的公民的比例之间,存在高度一致性。[30]如果某个候选人在媒体中的显著性高,那么就会有更多的人表达对这个候选人的观点。相反,如果候选人在媒体中的显著性低,那么相应地,对这些候选人不持有看法的人就会更多。在1996年的美国总统选举中,对11个政治人物持有观点的公众所占比例也呈现同样的模式。[31]如果某个政治人物在新闻中的可见度降低,那么对这个人物持有观点的公众人数也会随之下降。比较媒体对这11个人的报道频次和针对他们每一个人表达观点的公众的比例,发现两者之间的相关系数高达+0.81。

人们在民意测验中表达观点的意愿也遵循类似的路径。在2004年美国总统选举的几周内,在"安纳伯格选举研究"进行的全国调查中,拒访率与《纽约时报》和三大电视网新闻节目的竞选报道频次呈负相关关系。也就是说,关于选举的新闻报道越多,拒访率越低,人们越愿意参与民意测验。[32]

如果没有什么新闻报道,那么对于非强制性议题或者鲜为人知的公众人物,公众将倾向于持中立意见或者无意见。由此可见,议程设置可以间接地影响态度的形成和态度的强度。例如,在德国巴登-符腾堡州,两个主要议题(两德统一与东德移民)在个体议程上的显著性与个人意见的强度和方向都存在强相关。[33]就意见的强度而言,对于这两个议题,个体显著性是一个远比媒体报道或者人口特征更强的预测因素。就意见的方向而言,在德国统一议题上,个体显著性是比年龄稍强的预测因素;在东德移民议题上,个体显著性是与观看电视相当的预测因素,仅稍逊于受教育程度这个指标。

四、影响行为

影响人们的行为是媒介效果的顶峰。媒体是否能够说服人们以某种方式行事(从给某个政党投票到购买某种广告产品),自八十年前传播研究出现,这便是它的主要焦点。直到现在,影响人们的行为仍然是媒介的焦点,任何传播手册的普通读者都可以证明这一点。伊莱休·卡茨(Elihu Katz)注意到:

> 传播研究,或者说媒介研究,是有关效果的。否则它可能会是别的模样,比如艺术研究,但事实并非如此。不过,这个领域是细分的[……]其根本目标是解释媒介的力量,虽然这个目标并不总是被承认。[34]

媒介影响行为的许多案例广为人知。其中一个是,成功地利用娱乐电视节目在年轻人中传播"指定司机"的理念:每次聚会时,都指定一个人不喝酒,以便事后开车将朋友们安全地送回家。[35]另一个正面效果的案例是,关于流感的新闻报道促使家长决定让孩子接种疫苗[36],或者向医生报告流感样症状[37]。

在议程设置内部,最初的探索集中在研究媒介议程对公众行为的直接影响上。经典的例子是布洛伊(Alexander Bloj)于1973年对飞机失事和劫机新闻进行的调查,那是为雪城大学麦克斯韦尔·麦库姆斯的传播理论课程准备的作业。[38]该分析明确基于议程设置理论,假设死亡超过10人的坠机新闻或者劫机者控制飞行中的航班的新闻能够提升飞行危险问题的显著性。研究者在美国一个中等城市收集了两组关于人们行为的补充证据,即五年内购买机票的乘客人数和购买航空保险的乘客人数。框8.2比较了五年中每一年的高显著度周和低显著度周,高显著度周是指发生了致命坠机或劫机的一周。正如预期的那样,在高显著度周,机票销售减少,相反,航空保险销售增加。这些互补行为的差异惊人。媒介议程的确远远不止影响我们头脑中的图像。很多时候,媒介会影响我们的态度和意见,甚至我们的行为。

框8.2 对坠机与劫机新闻作出反应的个人行为

	平均机票销售		平均航空保险销售	
	低显著度周	高显著度周	低显著度周	高显著度周
1969	4493	4030	52	56
1970	4798	4302	58	63
1971	5014	4601	60	64
1972	5412	4789	63	69
1973	5667	5021	68	74

来源:这一研究由布洛伊实施,是为麦库姆斯的传播理论课做的作业。关于这一研究的报告可见:Maxwell McCombs and Donald Shaw, 'A progress report on agenda-setting research', paper presented at the Association for Education in Journalism, San Diego, CA, 1974。

随后,有研究考察了议题的显著性能否成为公民在选举日实际投票的重要预测因素。[39]除了对公众议程上的议题显著性施加影响之外,媒介议程有时也有利于特定政党,这是因为这个政党掌控着某些议题的话语权,选民会觉得它可能比另一个政党更善于处理这类议题。在美国,民主党手握更多的社会福利议题,而共和党则握有更多的防务议题。[40]媒体对其中某个议题的强调,不仅会影响这一议题的显著性(这是传统的议程设置效果),而且这种显著性还可以转化为行动,促使选民投票支持掌握这一议题的政党。[41]

然而,传播领域很久以前便承认,媒介对行为产生效果并不遵循简单的刺激—反应模式。据此,在这个领域里,当前多数的议程设置效果研究检验的是媒介影响的动力机制和非直接路径。一个好的例子是,使用议程设置理论去理解美国青少年政治社会化的一批研究成果。[42]基于对亚利桑那州、佛罗里达州和科罗拉多州的青少年及其父母的两轮调查,研究者发现,如果家庭谈论过2002年州长选举,青少年对2004年总统选举期间的新闻的关注度便会提升。新闻使用的增加强化了青少年对伊拉克战争的重视,最重要的是,他们对布什政府如何处理伊拉克议题有了更强烈的感受。接着,态度的强化促使青少年接受一种更为全球化的意识形态认同,并最终在2004年选举中投票。于是,经由具体的和一般的政治态度,从多个因果链条中产生了对投票率的基本议程设置效果。[43]

在另一项关于2004年美国大选的研究中,吴和科尔曼(Denis Wu and Renita Coleman)[44]探究了候选人的议题立场及其个人属性之于公民投票意向的相对优势,投票意向是与实际投票选择密切相关的前因。他们发现,首先,议题议程和属性议程在很大程度上是由新闻媒体设置的。其后,这些第一层面和第二层面的议程设置效果,尤其是受访者对候选人特质的感知,可以用来预测投票意向。

研究者也利用多重因果链,对属性议程设置的行为结果进行了探索。结合对科索沃新闻报道的内容分析与民意调查,林迪塔·卡马伊[45]发现,媒体在描述政治机构时所强调的方面影响了人们对机构的信心,而政治信任接下来又决定了公民参与常规政治活动(比如投票或为政党工作)的可能性。

在美国和日本进行的调查,记录了因媒介议程上的客体显著性而产生的一系列相互补充的认知与行为结果。框8.3记录了三种结果的细节:讨论,反思和对更多信息的渴望,注意和兴趣。在美国,研究者使用葛兰杰因果分析(Granger analysis),评估2000年美国总统竞选活动在全国电视新闻中每周的显著性对三种结果各自的影响,显著性以用于选举报道的时间来测量。[46]因为任何行为(如讨论选举)的主要决定因素是这种行为在前几周的水平,所以葛兰杰分析首先采用竞选期间29周的全国调查数据,分别测量了对这三种结果的影响。然后,将电视议程上选举议题的显著性加入分析,作为每种结果的额外预测因素,结果如框8.3所示。我们看到,媒介议程显著地影响了所有这三种结果。

在日本的实验中,媒介中客体显著性的效果体现为,与每个受试者在所测四个非强制性议题中认为优先级最低的议题相关的三种行为的变化程度。[47]研究者让一半受试者阅读优先级最低议题的相关文章,其中只有直白的事实,这种客观与松散的风格经常被记者用于现场报道。研究者让另一半受试者阅读关于优先级最低议题的阐释性文章,预想这些议题会对读者产生影响。结果发现,尽管阅读阐释性新闻报道的受试者一致发生了更大的变化,但采用陈述事实和进行解释两种框架的报道在三种行为结果方面都促成了大量变化。例如,据框8.3的报告,一半以上的受试者(不管他们阅读了哪种框架)都想要获得关于优先级最低议题的更多信息,并且希望进行更多的讨论。

> **框 8.3　媒介议程上的客体显著度对三种行为的影响**
>
> | 2000年美国总统选举[a] | 日本实验[b] | |
> |---|---|---|
> | [葛兰杰因果分析] | [改变了的受试者的百分比] | |
> | | 接触阐释框架 | 接触碎片框架 |
> | "讨论竞选" | "想要讨论这个议题" | |
> | $R^2 = +0.68$[c] | 58.3% | 50.2% |
> | 媒介作用 = +7% | | |
> | "思考竞选" | "想要获得关于这个议题的更多信息" | |
> | $R^2 = +0.65$ | 69.5% | 60.6% |
> | 媒介作用 = +7% | | |
> | "关注竞选" | "对这个议题有更大兴趣" | |
> | $R^2 = +0.54$ | 53.5% | 44.2% |
> | 媒介作用 = +4% | | |
>
> a（美国）客体＝总统竞选
>
> b（日本）客体＝优先级最低的议题
>
> c 这种葛兰杰分析使用 r 的平方，即本书经常引用的相关系数，来测量某个因变量（如最近讨论竞选的次数），在多大程度上可以被因变量以前的水平加上媒介接触等因素解释。因为 R^2 基于 r，所以取值范围是相同的，即从 1 到 0 再到 -1。
>
> 来源：Robert L. Stevenson, Rainer Böhme and Nico Nickel, 'The TV agenda-setting influence on campaign 2000', *Egyptian Journal of Public Opinion Research*, 2, 1 (2001): 29–50; Tsuneo Ogawa, 'Framing and agenda setting function', *Keio Communication Review*, 23 (2001): 71–80。

从美国和日本获得的两组互补的行为证据来自差别很大的两种文化，并且基于非常不同的调查方法，它们的相互印证，为议程设置后果的存在提供了强有力的支持。[48] 这些结果也可用以解释"导向需求"，我们在第五章中讨论过这个心理学概念。可以说，导向需求的两个组成部分都产生了影响：一个是某人认为某个话题在多大程度上与自己有关(感知到的个人关联性),另一个是某人对这个话题是否有充分的了解。感知到的个人关联性解释了日本实验中的发现,即阐释性文章对受试者的影响更大。简言之,这一证据从议程设置理论的部分核心观点延伸到了我们理论图谱的新的部分。

1988年美国印第安纳州的民意调查将议程设置效果及其后果的所有方面整合起来。[49]这次研究验证了我们熟悉的结论,即一个当时的主要议题(美国联邦预算赤字)在公众中的显著性,与公民接触报纸和电视新闻的频率之间存在明显的相关性。并且,议题显著性与使用单一媒介(电视新闻)相结合,可预测人们对这个议题所持意见的强度;而议题显著性与阅读报纸相结合,可预测实际行为的发生,例如就赤字议题写信或者参加会议。在单一媒介的情况下,有证据表明,在媒介接触和议题显著性之间存在明确的关系,并且随后也会影响到知识、意见及可观察到的行为。

五、财经新闻的议程设置作用

在投资人对《财富》杂志报道的反应中,研究者发现了议程设置效果与公众行为之间的联系。[50]在三年的时间里,当标准普尔500股票市场指数提升了2.3%时,《财富》杂志报道的54家公司的股票上涨了3.6%。虽然那些获得正面报道的公司股票涨得最多,达到4.7%,但只要公司的显著性提升了,就会有一些增长,如被负面报道的公司的股票上涨了1.9%,被中性报道的公司的股票上涨了1.7%。

这次调查打开了一个正在成长的新领域:财经新闻对公众的议程设置影响。在这个领域,一个发展良好的专业方向是公司声誉研究,特别是财经报道对企业及其CEO在公众中的认知度和声望的议程设置作用,媒体关于企业的描述对与公众有关的实质属性的影响,以及新闻报道的语气对公众有关个体企业的观点的作用。在针对世界上20个经济体(包括发达市场、新兴市场和前沿市场)的近期研究中,同样发现了第一层面和第二层面的议程设置效果。[51]随后,这些议程设置效果带来了明显的经济后果。[52]

从备受推崇的《金融时报》《华尔街日报》到大量新兴的有线电视财经频道,财经新闻能够产生非常广泛的属性议程设置效果,对意见和行为也有重大影响。对财经新闻这种细致入微和多重维度的焦点研究,展示了议程设置理论的微观世界,也包括新兴的第三层面的议程设置效果。[53]

议程设置理论的另一面向,即新闻来源对媒介议程的作用,在这个专业领域也非常关键。第七章以公共事务为语境,讨论了新闻通稿的影响。新闻通稿和公司网站是财经新闻的关键来源[54],它们涉及的内容非常广泛,从公司业绩的定期报告,到公司经营策略的重大转变,再到在投票代理权争夺和公司兼并中影响利益相关者议程的各种努力,无所不包。[55]财经新闻议程已经成为大众传播议程设置作用研究的一个重要方面。

小　结

媒介的议程设置效果不限于在公众头脑中创造图像,它还包含其他重要的意义。在最初的、传统的议程设置领域,亦即公众议题的显著性方面,有相当数量的证据表明,议题显著性的变化通常是公众对领导人的总体任职表现所持意见的基础。随之而来,某个公众人物在新闻中的显著性也关系到一般人对他是否持有意见。在议程设置的第二层面,情感属性的显著性与公众关于这些领导人的认知图式交织在一起,代表了属性议程设置与意见的形成和变化趋于一致。除了态度和意见之外,媒介创造的关于现实的图像对个人行为也有意义,作用范围从接种流感疫苗到在选举日投票等。不过,这些议程设置的行为效果并不是直接的,不像刺激—反应模式那样简单。相反,它们的发生是间接的,首先作用于认知、态度和意见,接下来认知、态度和意见就可能影响行为。

第九章 传播与社会

传播,特别是通过媒介渠道进行的传播,有三个广泛的社会作用:监控外界大环境,让社会各阶层达成共识,传承文化。[1]前面几章详细介绍的议程设置过程是监控作用的一个重要组成部分。我们头脑中大部分关于大环境的图像和想法来自这个过程。议程设置过程对缔造社会共识与传承文化也有重要意义,这使议程设置理论超越了传统的公共事务和政治传播的场景。

在监控环境的时候,媒介的聚光灯漫游在不同客体以及客体的不同属性之间,公众也由此获得了重要的知识。起初,通过接触媒介,人们开始意识到环境中超越个人直接经验的主要元素,并对其中一些给予特别重视。其后,作为媒介监控作用的进一步结果,公众头脑中形成了关于环境中重要元素的图像,包括关键的客体及这些客体最显著的属性。这方面的学习是议程设置过程的核心。

考虑到传播在缔造社会共识方面的作用,可以将这些议程设置效果与第六章的观察联系起来,其中提到:"媒介议程设置效果并非体现为在不同个体中创造出各异的显著性,而明显地表现在推动所有个体的显著性随着时间的推移提高或者降低。"[2]从这种结果可以得出一个合理的推论,即在民意调查中经常可以看到的不同人口群体之间的差异(例如,男性与女性之间,或者年轻人与老年人之间),会随着人们与新闻媒体的接触而减少。特别是,随着人们更多地接触新闻媒体,不同人口群体在议程上的一致性会增强。[3]

在北卡罗来纳州民意调查中发现的证据意义重大,支持了这种关于议程设置与共识之间关系的观点。[4]比较那些极少阅读日报的男性和女性的议题议程,发现两者之间的相关系数为+0.55。然而,那些偶尔阅读日报的男性和女性在对国家面临的最重要问题的认识上,议题议程之间的相关系数却高达+0.80。对于那些经常阅读报纸的男性和女性来说,议题议程之间的相关系数竟为完全相同的+1.0。比较年轻人与老年人,白人与黑人,都发现了这种相似的情况:由于更多接触报纸,人们对国家面临的最重要问题达成了共识。在对电视新闻观众的调查中,也发现了同样的结果,说明随着媒介接触行为的增加,不同人口群体之间达成共识的可能性也会提高。

在西班牙与中国台湾地区,也发现了相似的情况,表明接触新闻媒体能够缔造社会共识。[5]框9.1总结了不同人口群体之间的共识模式。当然,由于西班牙、中国台湾地区、美国等地之间存在极大的文化与政治差异,框9.1中所列举的模式并不完全相同,这并不让人吃惊。不过,在框9.1的19个比较中,有11个显示了因更多接触大众媒介而增加共识的模式。

在议程设置的第二层面,也发现了共识增加的相似情形。[6]在2001年9月11日纽约悲剧事件发生两个月后,研究者在15个欧洲国家调查了两组属性,即欧盟对"9·11"事件的反应的八个实质属性,以及有关欧洲穆斯林/阿拉伯社群的五个情感属性。结果发现,在其中绝大多数国家,经常观看全国电视新闻的人,不论是年轻人还是老年人,也不论受教育程度是高是低,在两组属性上都呈现出共识增加的情况。在大多数国家的两类人口群体中,阅读报纸的人在实质属性上有同样的模式,但在社群情感属性上则没有。比如,在三分之二的国家里,不论是年轻人还是老年人,报纸读者在实质属性上呈现出共识的增长;但只有不到一半的国家,在社群情感属性上显示出相同的模式。

框9.1　各种人口群体中随接触新闻媒体的增加而产生社会共识的情况
（西班牙、中国台湾地区与美国）

各种人口群体	西班牙		中国台湾地区	美国	
	报纸	电视新闻	电视新闻	报纸	电视新闻
性别	是*	否	是	是	否
受教育程度	是	是	是	否	否
年龄	否	否		是	是
收入			是	否	否
种族（黑/白）				是	是

*"是"的意思是，在以某一特征（例如男性和女性）界定的人口群体中，人们之间的相关程度随着接触报纸或电视新闻的增多而增加。"否"的意思是并不存在这种关系。

来源：Esteban López-Escobar, Juan Pablo Llamas and Maxwell McCombs, "Una dimensión social do los efectos dó los medios de difusión: agenda-setting y consenso", *Comunicación y Sociedad* IX (1996): 91-125; Ching-Yi Chiang, "Bridging and closing the gap of our society: social function of media agenda setting", unpublished master's thesis, University of Texas at Austin, 1995; Donald Shaw and Shannon Martin, "The function of mass media agenda setting", *Journalism Quarterly*, 69 (1992): 902-920.

媒介的议程设置作用在多大程度上促进了社会共识？对各种人口群体进行比较是探讨这个问题的一个有用的出发点。大家都很熟悉在民意调查报告中经常可以看到的这种对人口特征的比较。进一步细究媒介对社会共识的贡献，应该将心理特征包括进来，更好地挖掘个体差异及社会参与的情况。人口特征统计最多只能算是对人们生活状况的粗略描摹。

一、传承文化

传播的第三方面的社会作用，即传承文化，也与议程设置过程有关。媒介与公众关于议题、政治候选人及其属性（所有这些要素都是本书关注的焦点)的议程,都建立在范围更大的公民文化之基础上,而这种文化是由关于民主和社会的规范信念的基本议程来定义的。议程设置理论迷人的新案例还探讨了其他议程设置机构,如学校和宗教组织,它们也是公民文化的组成部分。

对媒介在传播其他文化议程方面所起作用的探讨,将议程设置理论推向新的学术前沿,远远超出了公共事务这一传统的领域。这些文化探求的新路线无所不至,从定义一个社会对过往的集体记忆的历史议程,到参观当代希腊博物馆的活动和全球对职业篮球赛的兴趣。

从关注公众议题的传统议程设置开始,媒介议题议程往往同时传达了关于公民文化的重要消息,也就是一系列界定议题产生并演化于其间的环境的信念和行为。从更宏观的方面来看,媒介对这些广泛的公民态度的议程设置影响,远比对特定议题和意见的议程设置效果更重要。例如,任何民主社会健康与否,都在很大程度上取决于有关选举参与的公民文化。

在美国,政治并不占据大多数公民个人议程的显著位置。媒介最明显的议程设置作用可能就是每四年激发一次人们对政治的兴趣,并将总统选举置于公民议程之上。早在1976年美国总统选举期间,对议程设置作用的早期考察便发现,在春季末尾接触电视新闻会激发人们对政治的兴趣,经历夏秋两季,一直持续到11月的选举日。[7]遗憾的是,电视新闻对公民文化的这种积极贡献被一系列其他证据所抵消,这些证据表明,美国政治记者向来喜欢强调政治的负面属性,这对公民文化产生了重大的负面影响。两本关于政治新闻与选民反应的书总结了媒介议程设置的这种缺点,被人们广为引用。它们是约瑟夫·卡佩拉(Joseph Cappella)、凯瑟琳·霍尔·贾米森(Kathleen Hall Jamieson)的《愤世嫉俗的螺旋》(*Spiral of Cynicism*)和托马斯·帕特森(Thomas Patterson)的《失序》(*Out of Order*)。[8]从议程设置理论的角度看,这些结果并不让人吃惊。年复一年地在公民中重复这些负面话题,使得这些关于政治的负面观点在公众中非常显著。

二、议程设置的新战场

在定义文化和传承文化方面起主要作用的另外一个重要机构是宗教组织。即便是在公共事务这个相对狭窄的公民领域,宗教议程也能发挥重大的影响。[9]在1992年的总统竞选中,虽然新闻媒体对堕胎议题关注极少,但是宗教传播却将这个议题置于公众议程之上。对少数受试者(他们所在的教会敦促成员将某些话题视作对他们自由的威胁)来说,从在公立学校中祈祷到支持拥有枪支的宪法议题,即便关于总统选举的媒体话语并不包括这些内容,但这些议题对他们而言却是最重要的议题。[10]

宗教议程离公共事务相当遥远,但却能对信徒的个人生活产生重大影响。迄今为止的经验证据仅仅暗示了宗教消息对人们过去和现在的行为模式的议程设置影响。[11]在中世纪的德国和法国,个体可以通过推迟犹太会堂的祈祷仪式,将某个议题带入犹太社区的公众议程。海灵格和拉什(Moshe Hellinger and Tsuriel Rashi)从议程设置理论的角度进行分析,讨论了催生这种做法的习俗与议程设置理论所描述的传播过程之间的相似之处[12]。

集体记忆有时与公民议程有所重合,但它占据了一个更广泛的文化生态点位。集体记忆是有关过去事件和场景的高度选择性的议程,它主导着公众对自己的历史身份的认识。[13]这些文化神话,在一个群体、地区或国家回忆自身过往的过程中往往非常显著,但通常与实际的历史情况没什么相似之处。要理解我们的集体记忆的本质与起源,尤其需要考察媒介叙事对个人回忆的影响。

在许多国家,深刻的个人记忆塑造了对经济大萧条、第二次世界大战及其他情绪激昂的时代的集体记忆。但是,随着新的世代加入经历过这些年代的年龄组,媒介叙事就走向了中心舞台。[14]在非常真实的意义上,每一代人都在书写他们自己的历史,并且发展他们自己关于过去的集体记忆。对于数百万美国人来说,他们对约翰·肯尼迪总统遇刺事件的看法,在很大程度上是由电影制片人斯通(Oliver Stone)的议程塑造的。在这些人对将尼克松总统赶下台的水门事件的印象中,演员罗伯特·雷德福(Robert Redford)就是《华盛顿邮报》的记者鲍勃·伍德沃德(Bob Woodward)。

再往历史的深处走去,媒介叙事,包括流行书籍、学校教科书,还有电影和新闻媒体对过去事件的选择性纪念,对公众议程的影响甚至更大。对于第一层面的议程设置(哪些过去的事件更为显著)和第二层面的议程设置(这些事件的哪些方面与细节在我们的记忆中是鲜明的),都是如此。以色列学者约拉姆·佩里(Yoram Peri)指出,"媒体知道如何讲故事,并且它们比传统的记忆载体更擅长创造传奇"[15]。

在以色列建国六十周年之际,有一个例子能够说明媒介的这种惊人的能力。[16]在两项连续的调查中,研究者询问具有代表性的全国样本,让受访者指出他们认为过去一百年里以色列和世界上最重要的两个事件;同时,对主要的报纸和电视频道进行内容分析,检验媒介的历史议程。从第一次调查(为期一周的常规新闻)到第二次调查(紧接六十年庆典之后),受访者提到的事件数量增加了五倍。媒介议程和公众议程在第一次调查时的匹配度为+0.62,到了第二次调查,相关系数增加到+0.83。最重要的是,在这个过程中,受访者提到国际事件和以色列国内小事件的次数减少了,而提及以色列国内重大事件的次数增加了六倍多——与媒体的报道一致。

从过去的形象转到当前的形象,新闻报道影响了2004年美国人和英国人对九个国家的看法,从德国到土耳其再到朝鲜。[17]美英两国的结果十分相似,新闻报道的语气和以百分点感情温度计测量的舆论之间的一致性,在美国是+0.72,在英国为+0.73。再分别分析正面和负面报道,美国的两种影响模式相似,舆论和正面报道之间的一致性为+0.87,和负面报道之间的一致性为+0.85。但是在英国,负面报道比正面报道的影响力更大,舆论和负面报道之间的一致性为+0.84,和正面报道之间的一致性为+0.56。[18]

学校是我们集体记忆的另一个重要的议程设置者。对学校教科书进行内容分析,能够确认一个社会希望强调或者忽视的过去事件的某些方面。在这里,关注的现象仍然是显著性从一个议程向另一个议程的转移。在教育工作者与公众不时就学校教科书和课程应该如何记忆过去进行辩论时,这种议程设置作用至少得到了含蓄的承认。当然,学校所影响的文化议程与个人议程,远远不止集体记忆这一种。在西班牙,研究者创造性地应用议程设置理论考察新闻专业价值观的议程,这是大学课堂上对未来的新闻工作者进行教育的核心。[19]

三、其他文化议程

劳伦斯·温纳(Lawrence Wenner)指出:"我们对新事物和重要事物的文化感觉,亦即我们的文化议程,在很大程度上来自电视上播放的内容。"[20]今天,在世界范围内,电视议程的一个重要组成部分是职业体育。有个典型的例子能够很好地说明这种电视议程所产生的效果,那就是美国职业篮球赛近几十年的疯狂流行。在《最后助攻》(*The Ultimate Assist*)一书中,约翰·福尔图纳托(John Fortunato)详细介绍了美国男子篮球职业联赛(NBA)与美国电视网之间的商业合作关系,他们吸引观众的策略主要基于议程设置的第一层面与第二层面。[21]第一层面的效果是指增加美国男子篮球职业联赛的显著性,通过在全国电视时间表上精心安排最佳球队和球员的比赛场次,至少部分地实现了这一目标。第二层面的效果是指提升职业篮球的形象,采用的方式包括创造性地制作球员与教练的访谈,解说员点评球赛,引入说明性图表,运用即时回放技术,以及其他能够使篮球运动更加精彩的框架建构方式。结果是,这些做法无论是在电视上,还是在球赛现场,均获得了成功。在1969—1970年赛季,14支NBA球队共进行了574场比赛,吸引了430万球迷到体育馆看球;三十年后,在1999—2000年赛季,29支NBA球队共进行了1198场比赛,吸引了2010万球迷到体育馆看球。在这三十年时间里,NBA从电视台获得的收入从每个赛季不到1000万美元增加到20多亿美元。议程设置,既可以是一种理论,也可以是一个商业计划。

新闻也会影响个人的文化议程。以希腊博物馆为例,那些在主要的雅典报纸上享有较高可见度的博物馆,比可见度较低的博物馆接待的参观人数更多。媒体可见度对当月和次月的参观人数都有影响,而对后者的影响则更大。观察报纸的情感属性议程,新闻报道更多正面提及的博物馆接待的参观者更多,而负面提及的博物馆接待的参观者则较少。正面报道对当月和次月的参观流量都产生了正面的效果;而负面报道的负面影响主要是对次月,而非当月。[22]

在其后的一项研究中,同一组作者将第一层面和第二层面的文化议程设置概念应用于希腊的艺术电影市场。他们用影片的每周票房收入衡量公众议程,发现媒体报道影片的篇幅和语气对票房有显著的影响。更进一步,电影评论家对影片正面、中性和负面的评价对影片在公众中的显著性有更多独立的效果。[23]

个人文化议程的另一个方面,对饮酒的看法,也反映出议程设置的效果。研究发现,俄勒冈酒庄发送给主要杂志和报纸的葡萄酒专栏作者的新闻通稿、宣传册和试饮评论,亦即属性议程,明显反映到了新闻工作者关于俄勒冈葡萄酒的文章中(+0.67)。接着,将这些媒介属性议程与美国五个主要都市地区接受调查的消费者对俄勒冈葡萄酒的描述进行比较,也发现了一种显著的一致性(+0.44)。[24]

在当代议程设置研究中,有两种相反的趋势。一种是前几章描述的向心趋势,指的是学者们进一步阐释关键的理论概念;另一种趋势是本章所讨论的离心趋势,指的是议程设置研究拓展到了更多的新领域。尽管许多持保守的正统观点的学者反对这种偏离议程设置理论原始领域的做法,但这种性质的探究未来必然会继续下去。回到20世纪80年代初,在面对"是谁设置了媒介议程?"这个问题时,也曾经有学者宣称这个领域超出了议程设置理论的范畴,但现实是,这个理论在新的场景和领域中不断开花结果。

四、概念、领域和场景

为了充分理解庞大且不断扩展的议程设置文献,掌握已经考察过的内容和未来可能的研究方向,分清作为议程设置调查研究焦点的概念(concepts)、领域(domains)和场景(settings)是非常有用的。议程设置理论的核心概念是客体议程、属性议程以及显著性在议程之间的转移。同时,网状结构的客体和属性,再加上显著性转移时的关键偶发条件,即导向需求,也应该包括在内。

研究者可以在许多不同的领域和场景中研究这些理论概念。从查普希尔研究开始,直到今天,议程设置研究的主导领域都是公共事务,尤其是公众议题。本章则回顾了过去十几年里议程设置研究所涉及的一系列非常不同的领域,每个领域都有很重要的学术文献。这些公民领域和文化领域涵盖广泛,从教育和宗教机构,到一个社会对自己过往的集体记忆,当代希腊博物馆的接待人数和电影票房,以及全球对职业篮球的关注。

在每个领域,又可以在许多背景下研究议程设置。也就是说,议程设置理论核心概念的操作性定义可以是许多不同领域的特定方面。在公共事务这个传统领域,研究最多的场景是新闻媒体与公众之间的关系。但是,在传统的议程设置研究文献中发现的场景包括:各种新闻媒体之间的联系、消息来源和新闻媒体之间的联系,以及私人谈话对公众议程的影响。这些领域的其他方面也包含所研究的议程项目的种类(例如,议题和候选人)。最后,利用议程设置理论的概念调查研究各个领域,是在世界范围内广泛多样的地理环境中及不同的时间点上进行的。新兴的议程设置文化领域引入了一大批新的操作性定义,来解释议程的来源和界定这些议程的项目,它们所处的场景均远离公共事务。

将议程设置理论的核心概念与它们的操作性定义分开,会在文献中发现丰富的领域和场景,这有助于我们更好地认清过去并展望未来研究的新方向。这种区分还澄清了不同学者提出的关于议程设置的各种各样(有时是令人困惑的)的定义。有些人坚守议程设置研究的原初领域和场景,将议程设置狭义地界定为议题显著性从媒介议程向公众议程的转移。这方面的证据是,研究者继续引用1972年最初的查普希尔研究的实践方法。有些人将议程设置更广地界定为媒介议程上凸显的要素通常会变成公众议程上凸显的要素,这种被广为引述的定义仍然坚持了原始的领域和场景。这两种定义都是正确的,但都无法涵盖当下议程设置理论和研究的全部内容。

认识到概念、领域和场景之间的区别,为我们定义议程设置并理解广泛的议程设置现象提供了一种有用的语境。在如此多样的领域和场景中,议程设置理论关于显著性从一个议程转移到另一个议程的核心命题,使我们的理论词汇变得简洁。虽然在文献中不时有人将议程设置与议程建构(agenda-building)两个词并列使用,但是两者之间并不存在根本的差异。这是一种没有差别的区分。从根本上讲,议程设置理论就是关于显著性在议程之间的转移,不论是在何种领域或场景中。在当代世界,有许多议程,也有许多议程设置者。然而,就像古罗马时代的凯撒,新闻媒体在塑造当代议程方面居于领先地位。

新闻媒体在设置公众议程和政策议程方面发挥的重要作用并非一成不变,它当然可能减弱。许多当代观察家将推特、脸书、照片墙、瓦次普(WhatsApp)及其他大批社交媒体渠道赞为新的主要议程设置者。但正如我们在第一章所讨论的,迄今为止,关于这种可能性的经验证据莫衷一是。当然,也不排除这样一种事实:对于某些群体,或者在某些语境下,社交媒体已经以传统媒体所未曾使用过的方式设置了议程。在这种情形下,议程设置理论的概念、领域和场景仍然很有价值。议程设置很有可能经得起时间的考验,即使是新的最小效果论的当代倡导者也承认这一点:

> 因此,越来越多的选择性接触预示着一个最小效果的新时代的到来,至少就说服力而言是如此。但是其他形式的媒介影响,如议程设置或铺垫,可能仍然很重要。[25]

五、议程设置理论的继续演化

议程设置的理论地图始自五十多年前的查普希尔研究,研究者当时调查了新闻媒体对选民关于最重要议题的认知的影响。几十年后,议程设置已经扩展为一种拥有几个不同方面的多重理论。伴随议程设置的理念在广泛的国际场景中扩展到不同的领域,所有这些方面都会继续成为富有成效的研究区域。随着研究的深入,对议程设置过程的阐释会更加细化,对议程设置应用的探索将远远超出原先关注的公共事务领域,议程设置未来有望在当代理论地图之外继续发展。议程设置研究既向内回归理论基础,同时也向外开拓新的领域,为学术活动提供了一个引人入胜的议程。借用福尔摩斯那句号召冒险的话,就是——"来吧,游戏开始了。"

注　释

序　言

[1] Alan Cowell, 'New owner struggles at a London tabloid', *New York Times*, 26 February 2001, p. C15.

[2] Max Frankel, *The Times of My Life and My Life with The Times* (New York: Random House, 1999), pp. 414-415.

[3] Theodore White, *The Making of the President, 1972* (New York: Bantam, 1973), p. 327.

[4] Maxwell McCombs and Donald Shaw, 'The agenda-setting function of mass media', *Public Opinion Quarterly*, 36 (1972): 176-187. 这一研究的早期历史提供了一种关于理论新视角的有益注解。1968年选举结束几个月后，麦库姆斯与肖向新闻教育协会的年会提交了这篇论文，但被草率地拒绝了。后来他们的论文发表在《舆论季刊》(*Public Opinion Quarterly*)上。这也解释了为何在总统选举到1972年文章发表之间存在四年的间隔。

[5] 有一种公开的陈述是，"议程设置"一词是由一个匿名审稿人在审阅发表在1972年夏季《舆论季刊》上的原稿时提出的建议。与此说法相反，麦库姆斯与肖在1969年6月提交给全美广播业者协会的报告的第一部分，标题就是"大众传播媒介的议程设置功能"。整篇报告的名字叫作《获取政治信息》。直到几年之后，这份报告的修改稿才被提交给《舆论季刊》。关于"议程设置"术语起源的这种错误说法出现在史蒂文森、博希姆与尼克尔的文章中。Robert L. Stevenson, Rainer Böhme, and Nico Nikel, 'The TV agenda-setting influence on campaign 2000', *Egyptian Journal of Public Opinion Research*, 2,

1 (2001): 29.

[6] Maxwell McCombs and Jian-Hua Zhu, 'Capacity, diversity, and volatility of the public agenda: trends from 1954 to 1994', *Public Opinion Quarterly*, 59 (1995): 495-525; Jill A. Edy and Patrick C. Meirick, 'The fragmenting public agenda: capacity, diversity, and volatility in responses to the "most important problem" question', *Public Opinion Quarterly*, 82 (2018): 661-685.

[7] 2003年9月12日,在德国波恩,约翰·帕夫利克(John Pavlik)在提及本书第一版的谈话中,提到了"格氏解剖学"这个隐喻性比较。我在此向他表示感谢。

[8] 在1968年查普希尔研究之后不久,戴维·韦弗来到北卡罗来纳大学攻读博士学位,并迅速成为发展议程设置理论的主要人物。在1972年美国总统选举中,他以研究生的身份参与调查,第七章对这个研究作了详细介绍;在1976年美国总统选举中,他以印第安纳大学教员的身份参与调查,第一章对这个研究作了介绍。除了他在北卡罗来纳大学查普希尔进行的研究之外,其他章节还提到他之后多年在印第安纳大学继续作出的许多其他贡献。

[9] Michael Gurevitch and Jay Blumler, 'Political communication systems and democratic values', in *Democracy and the Mass Media*, ed. Judith Lichtenberg (Cambridge: Cambridge University Press, 1990), pp. 269-289.

[10] Tom Bettag, 'What's news? Evolving definitions of news', *Harvard International Journal of Press/Politics*, 5, 3 (2000): 105.

[11] Davis Merritt and Maxwell McCombs, *The Two W's of Journalism: The Why and What of Public Affairs Reporting* (Mahwah, NJ: Lawrence Erlbaum, 2003).

第一章 影响舆论

[1] Walter Lippmann, *Public Opinion* (New York: Macmillan, 1922), p. 29.

[2] Robert Park, 'News as a form of knowledge', *American Journal of Sociology*, 45 (1940): 667-686.

[3] 然而,宣传也可能具有议程设置效果。例如,有证据显示,"假新闻"网站,即那些故意散布误解和捏造内容的网站,在2016年美国总统选举期间影响了

基于事实的媒体议程；见 Chris J. Vargo, Lei Guo, and Michelle A. Amazeen, 'The agenda-setting power of fake news: a big data analysis of the online media landscape from 2014 to 2016', *New Media and Society*, 20 (2018): 2028–2049。

［4］Bernard Cohen, *The Press and Foreign Policy* (Princeton, NJ: Princeton University Press, 1963), p. 13.

［5］Lippmann, *Public Opinion*, p. 3.

［6］Ibid., p. 4.

［7］Paul Lazarsfeld, Bernard Berelson, and Hazel Gaudet, *The People's Choice* (New York: Duell, Sloan, and Pearce, 1944).

［8］Joseph Klapper, *The Effects of Mass Communication* (New York: Free Press, 1960), p. 8.

［9］例如，Robert E. Park, 'The city: suggestions for investigation of human behavior in the urban environment', in Robert E. Park and Ernest W. Burgess, eds., *The City* (Chicago, IL: University of Chicago Press, 1925), pp. 1–46; Paul F. Lazarsfeld and Robert K. Merton, 'Mass communication, popular taste and organized social action', in Guy E. Swanson, Theodore M. Newcomb, and Eugene L. Hartley, eds., *Readings in Social Psychology* (rev. edn) (New York, NY: Henry Holt and Company, 1952), pp. 74–85。

［10］Maxwell McCombs and Donald Shaw, 'The agenda setting function of mass media', *Public Opinion Quarterly*, 36 (1972): 176–187.

［11］Yeojin Kim, Youngju Kim, and Shuhua Zhou, 'Theoretical and methodological trends of agenda-setting theory: a thematic analysis of the last four decades of research', *Agenda Setting Journal*, 1 (2017): 5–22.

［12］Stanley Presser, 'Substance and method in *Public Opinion Quarterly*, 1937–2010', *Public Opinion Quarterly*, 75 (2011): 839–845. 详细内容见文章中的表2 (p. 843)。关于引证查普希尔研究的更多背景，见 W. Russell Neuman and Lauren Guggenheim, 'The evolution of media effects theory: a six-stage model of cumulative research', *Communication Theory*, 21 (2011): 169–196。

详细内容见 p. 180。

[13] W. Lance Bennett and Shanto Iyengar, 'A new era of minimal effects? The changing foundations of political communication', *Journal of Communication*, 58 (2008): 707-731. 引自 p. 708。

[14] Yunjuan Luo, Hansel Burley, Alexander Moe, and Mingxiao Sui, 'A meta-analysis of news media's public agenda-setting effects, 1972-2015', *Journalism and Mass Communication Quarterly*, 96 (2019): 150-172.

[15] Stephen A. Rains, Timothy R. Levine, and Rene Weber, 'Sixty years of quantitative communication research summarized: lessons from 149 meta-analyses', *Annals of the International Communication Association*, 42 (2018): 105-124.

[16] Donald Shaw and Maxwell McCombs, eds., *The Emergence of American Political Issues* (St Paul, MN: West, 1977).

[17] David H. Weaver, Doris A. Graber, Maxwell E. McCombs, and Chaim H. Eyal, *Media Agenda Setting in a Presidential Election: Issues, Images and Interest* (Westport, CT: Greenwood, 1981).

[18] James Winter and Chaim Eyal, 'Agenda setting for the civil rights issue', *Public Opinion Quarterly*, 45 (1981): 376-383.

[19] Stuart N. Soroka, 'Media, public opinion, and foreign policy', *Harvard International Journal of Press/Politics*, 8 (2003): 27-48.

[20] Hans-Bernd Brosius and Hans Mathias Kepplinger, 'The agenda setting function of television news: static and dynamic views', *Communication Research*, 17 (1990): 183-211.

[21] Adam Shehata, 'Unemployment on the agenda: a panel study of agenda setting effects during the 2006 Swedish national election campaign', *Journal of Communication*, 60 (2010): 182-203.

[22] Kim Smith, 'Newspaper coverage and public concern about community issues', *Journalism Monographs*, 101 (1987).

[23] Maria José Canel, Juan Pablo Llamas, and Federico Rey, 'El primer nivel del efecto agenda setting en la información local: los "problemas más importantes" de

la ciudad de Pamplona' ['The first level agenda setting effect on local information: the "most important problems" of the city of Pamplona'], *Comunicación y Sociedad*, 9, 1 and 2 (1996): 17-38.

[24] Toshio Takeshita, 'Agenda setting effects of the press in a Japanese local election', *Studies of Broadcasting*, 29 (1993): 193-216.

[25] Federico Rey Lennon, *Los Diarios Nacionales y la Campaña Electoral: Argentina, 1997 Elecciones* [The national press and the electoral campaign: Argentina, the 1997 elections] (Buenos Aires: Freedom Forum and Universidad Austral, 1998).

[26] Alicia Casermeiro de Pereson, Los medios en las elecciones: la agenda setting en la ciudad de Buenos Aires [The media in the elections: Agenda setting in the city of Buenos Aires] (Buenos Aires, Argentina, EDUCA, 2003).

[27] Howard Eaton Jr, 'Agenda setting with bi-weekly data on content of three national media', *Journalism Quarterly*, 66 (1989): 942-948.

[28] McCombs and Shaw, 'The agenda setting function of mass media.'

[29] Shaw and McCombs, *The Emergence of American Political Issues*.

[30] Weaver, Graber, McCombs and Eyal, *Media Agenda Setting in a Presidential Election*.

[31] Winter and Eyal, 'Agenda setting for the civil rights issue.'

[32] Eaton, 'Agenda setting with bi-weekly data on content of three national media.'

[33] Brosius and Kepplinger, 'The agenda setting function of television news.'

[34] Smith, 'Newspaper coverage and public concern about community issues.'

[35] Shanto Iyengar and Donald R. Kinder, *News That Matters: Television and American Opinion* (Chicago: University of Chicago Press, 1987).

[36] Scott L. Althaus and David Tewksbury, 'Agenda setting and the "new" news: patterns of issue importance among readers of the paper and online versions of the *New York Times*', *Communication Research*, 29 (2002): 180-207. 引自 p. 199。

[37] Michael Conway and J. R. Patterson, 'Today's top story? An agenda setting and

recall experiment involving television and Internet news', *Southwestern Mass Communication Journal*, 24 (2008): 31-48.

[38] Gary King, Benjamin Schneer, and Ariel White, 'How the news media activate public expression and influence national agendas', *Science*, 358 (2017): 776-780.

[39] Matthew Gentzkow, 'Small media, big impact: Randomizing news stories reveals broad public impacts', *Science*, 358 (2017): 726-727. 引自 p. 727。

[40] Mike Gruszczynski and Michael W. Wagner, 'Information flow in the 21st century: the dynamics of agenda-uptake', *Mass Communication and Society*, 20 (2017): 378-402; Sharon Meraz, 'Using time series analysis to measure intermedia agenda-setting influence in traditional media and political blog networks', *Journalism and Mass Communication Quarterly*, 88 (2011): 176-194; Kevin Wallsten, 'Agenda setting and the blogosphere: An analysis of the relationship between mainstream media and political blogs', *Review of Policy Research*, 24 (2007): 567-587.

[41] 特定个案研究可见: Jacob Groshek and Megan Clough Groshek, 'Agenda-trending: reciprocity and the predictive capacity of social networking sites in intermedia agenda-setting across topics over time', *Media and Communication*, 1, 1, 2013: 15-27; Raymond A. Harder, Julie Sevenans, and Peter Van Aelst, 'Intermedia agenda setting in the social media age: How traditional players dominate the news agenda in election times', *International Journal of Press/Politics*, 22, 3 (2017): 275-293; Ingrid Rogstad, 'Is Twitter just rehashing? Intermedia agenda setting between Twitter and mainstream media', *Journal of Information Technology and Politics*, 13, 2 (2016): 142-158; Ben Sayre, Leticia Bode, Dhavan Shah, Dave Wilcox, and Chirag Shah, 'Agenda setting in a digital age: tracking attention to California Proposition 8 in social media, online news and conventional news', *Policy and Internet*, 2, 2 (2010): 7-32; Kathleen Searles and Glen Smith, 'Who's the boss? Setting the agenda in a fragmented media environment', *International Journal of Communication*, 10 (2016): 2074-2095; Sebas-

tián Valenzuela, Soledad Puente, and Pablo M. Flores, 'Comparing disaster news on Twitter and television: An intermedia agenda setting perspective', *Journal of Broadcasting and Electronic Media*, 61 (2017): 615-637; Chris J. Vargo and Lei Guo, 'Networks, big data, and intermedia agenda setting: an analysis of traditional, partisan, and emerging online US news', *Journalism and Mass Communication Quarterly*, 94 (2017): 1031-1055。

[42] Hai Tran, 'Online agenda setting: a new frontier for theory development', in *Agenda Setting in a 2.0 World*, ed. Thomas J. Johnson (New York: Routledge, 2013), pp. 205-229.

[43] Jason Martin, 'Agenda setting, elections and the impact of information technology', in *Agenda Setting in a 2.0 World*, ed. Thomas J. Johnson (New York: Routledge, 2013), pp. 28-52.

[44] Conway and Patterson, 'Today's top story?'; Althaus and Tewksbury, 'Agenda setting and the "new" news.'

[45] Yonghoi Song, 'Internet news media and issue development: a case study on the roles of independent online news services as agenda-builders for anti-US protests in South Korea', *New Media and Society*, 9 (2007): 71-92.

[46] Jae Kook Lee, 'The effect of the Internet on homogeneity of the media agenda: a test of the fragmentation thesis', *Journalism and Mass Communication Quarterly*, 84 (2007): 745-760.

[47] Ana S. Cardenal, Carol Galais, and Silvia Majó-Vázquez, 'Is Facebook eroding the public agenda? Evidence from survey and web-tracking data', *International Journal of Public Opinion Research*, 31, (2019): 589-608.

[48] Pablo Barberá, Andreu Casas, Jonathan Nagler, Patrick J. Egan, Richard Bonneau, John T. Jost, and Joshua A. Tucker, 'Who leads? Who follows? Measuring issue attention and agenda setting by legislators and the mass public using social media data', *American Political Science Review*, 113 (2019): 883-901.

[49] Ibid., p. 897.

[50] G. R. Boynton and Glenn W. Richardson, Jr, 'Agenda setting in the twenty-first

century', *New Media and Society*, 18 (2016): 1916-1934.

[51] Steven H. Chaffee and Miriam J. Metzger, 'The end of mass communication?', *Mass Communication and Society*, 4 (2001): 365-379; Bennett and Iyengar, 'A new era of minimal effects?'; Bruce A. Williams and Michael X. Delli Carpini, 'Monica and Bill all the time and everywhere: The collapse of gatekeeping and agenda setting in the new media environment', *American Behavioral Scientist*, 47 (2004): 1208-1230.

[52] 很少有人认为,由于高选择的媒介环境,人们的注意力已经减弱。比如,见 Philipp Lorenz-Spreen, Bjarke Mørch Mønsted, Philipp Hövel, and Sune Lehmann, 'Accelerating dynamics of collective attention', *Nature Communications*, 10, 1759 (2019)。然而,主动关注媒介内容并不是人们学习媒介议程的唯一途径;因为也有证据显示,这种过程同样可能通过相关线索偶然产生。见 Maxwell McCombs and Natalie J. Stroud, 'Psychology of agenda-setting effects: Mapping the paths of information processing', *Review of Communication Research*, 2 (2014): 68-93; Elizabeth Stoycheff, Raymond J. Pingree, Jason T. Peifer, and Mingxiao Sui, 'Agenda cueing effects of news and social media', *Media Psychology*, 21, 2 (2018): 182-201。

[53] Yue Tan and David Weaver, 'Agenda diversity and agenda setting from 1956 to 2004: what are the trends over time?', *Journalism Studies*, 14, (2013): 773-789.

[54] Monika Djerf-Pierre and Adam Shehata, 'Still an agenda setter: traditional news media and public opinion during the transition from low to high choice media environments', *Journal of Communication*, 67 (2017): 733-757.

[55] Daniela Grassau, 'Has TV decreased impact on public opinion due to the transformations of the media environment in the 21st century?', paper presented to the International Association for Media and Communication Research, Madrid, 2019.

[56] Renita Coleman and Maxwell McCombs, 'The young and agenda-less? Age-related differences in agenda setting on the youngest generation, baby boomers, and the

civic generation', *Journalism and Mass Communication Quarterly*, 84 (2007): 495-508.

[57] Jae Kook Lee and Renita Coleman, 'Testing generational, life cycle, and period effects of age on agenda setting', *Mass Communication and Society*, 17, 1 (2014): 3-25.

[58] Yunjuan Luo, Hansel Burley, Alexander Moe, and Mingxiao Sui, 'A meta-analysis of news media's public agenda-setting effects, 1972-2015.'

[59] Pablo Boczkowski, *News at Work: Imitation in an Age of Information Abundance* (Chicago: University of Chicago Press, 2010).

[60] Maxwell McCombs, 'Civic osmosis: the social impact of media', *Communication and Society*, 25 (2012): 7-14.

[61] James Webster and Thomas Ksiazek, 'The dynamics of audience fragmentation: public attention in an age of digital media', *Journal of Communication*, 62 (2012): 39-56. 引自 p. 39。

[62] Hyun, Ki Deuk, and Soo Jung Moon, 'Agenda setting in the partisan TV news context: attribute agenda setting and polarized evaluation of presidential candidates among viewers of NBC, CNN, and Fox News', *Journalism and Mass Communication Quarterly*, 93 (2016): 509-529.

[63] Lazarsfeld, Berelson and Gaudet, *The People's Choice*, p. 122.

[64] Maxwell McCombs, Esteban López-Escobar, and Juan Pablo Llamas, 'Setting the agenda of attributes in the 1996 Spanish general election', *Journal of Communication*, 50, 2 (2000): 77-92.

[65] Coleman and McCombs, 'The young and agenda-less?.' 引自 p. 503。

[66] Jesper Stromback and Spiro Kiousis, 'A new look at agenda setting effects-Comparing the predictive power of overall political news consumption and specific news media consumption across different media channels and media types', *Journal of Communication*, 60 (2010): 271-292. 引自 p. 288。

[67] Steven Chaffee and Donna Wilson, 'Media rich, media poor: two studies of diversity in agenda-holding', *Journalism Quarterly*, 54 (1977): 466-476. 也见

Peter Jochen and Claes H. de Vreese, 'Agenda-rich, agenda-poor: a cross-national comparative investigation of nominal and thematic public agenda diversity', *International Journal of Public Opinion Research*, 15 (2003): 44–64。

[68] 例如，见 Mark Boukes, 'Agenda-setting with satire: how political satire increased TTIP'S saliency on the public, media, and political agenda', *Political Communication*, 36 (2019): 426–451; Xiaoxia Cao, 'Hearing it from Jon Stewart: the impact of The Daily Show on public attentiveness to politics', *International Journal of Public Opinion Research*, 22 (2010): 26–46; J. Carroll Glynn, Michael Huge, James Reineke, Bruce Hardy and James Shanahan, 'When Oprah intervenes: political correlates of daytime talk show viewing', *Journal of Broadcasting and Electronic Media*, 51 (2007): 228–244。

[69] William Gamson, *Talking Politics* (New York: Cambridge University Press, 1992).

[70] William G. Mayer, *The Changing American Mind: How and Why American Public Opinion Changed between 1960 and 1988* (Ann Arbor: University of Michigan Press, 1992).

第二章 现实与新闻

[1] Ray Funkhouser, 'The issues of the sixties', *Public Opinion Quarterly*, 37 (1973): 62–75.

[2] Ibid., p. 72.

[3] Hans Mathias Kepplinger and Herbert Roth, 'Creating a crisis: German mass media and oil supply in 1973–1974', *Public Opinion Quarterly*, 43 (1979): 285–296.

[4] Maxwell McCombs, Edna Einsiedel, and David Weaver, *Contemporary Public Opinion: Issues and the News* (Hillsdale, NJ: Lawrence Erlbaum, 1991), pp. 43–45. 也参见 Pamela Shoemaker, ed., *Communication Campaigns about Drugs* (Hillsdale, NJ: Lawrence Erlbaum, 1989)。特别是这本书中的：Stephen Reese and Lucig Danielian, 'Intermedia influence and the drug issue: converging

on cocaine', pp. 29-46; Danielian and Reese, 'A closer look at intermedia influences on agenda setting: the cocaine issue of 1986', pp. 47-66; Pamela Shoemaker, Wayne Wanta, and Dawn Leggett, 'Drug coverage and public opinion, 1972-1986', pp. 67-80。

[5] William Gonzenbach, *The Media, the President, and Public Opinion: A Longitudinal Analysis of the Drug Issue, 1984-1991* (Mahwah, NJ: Lawrence Erlbaum, 1996). 这项对毒品议题的纵向研究将政策议程添加到了对媒介议程—公众议程的传统分析中。虽然主要证据表明，显著性的转移主要是从媒介到公众，但在政策议程与媒介议程之间，影响流动的波动性要大得多。又见 James Dearing and Everett Rogers, *Agenda Setting* (Thousand Oaks, CA: Sage, 1996)。迪林和罗杰斯，还有其他一些人提出，大多数涉及政策议程的研究都是在脱离本书讨论的以媒介为中心的议程设置理论的情况下发展起来的。

[6] Anthony Downs, 'Up and down with ecology: the "issue-attention cycle"', *The Public Interest*, 28 (1972): 38-50.

[7] Salma Ghanem, 'Media coverage of crime and public opinion: an exploration of the second level of agenda setting', unpublished doctoral dissertation, University of Texas at Austin, 1996. 加尼姆研究了得克萨斯州媒体报道与犯罪统计数字所反映出来的现实情况之间的不匹配，这是全国状况的一个详细缩影。见 Richard Morin, 'Crime time: the fear, the facts: how the sensationalism got ahead of the stats', *Outlook, Washington Post* (30 January 1994), p. C1; Dennis Lowry, Tam Ching, Josephine Nio, and Dennis Leitner, 'Setting the public fear agenda: a longitudinal analysis of network TV crime reporting, public perceptions of crime, and FBI crime statistics', *Journal of Communication*, 53, (2003): 61-73。

[8] Margaret T. Gordon and Linda Heath, 'The news business, crime and fear', in *Reactions to Crime*, ed. Dan Lewis (Beverly Hills, CA: Sage, 1981). 节选转载于 *Agenda Setting: Readings on Media, Public Opinion, and Policymaking*, eds. David Protess and Maxwell McCombs (Hillsdale, NJ: Lawrence Erlbaum, 1991), pp. 71-74。另一个例子说明了新闻报道和现实之间的不一致，在这个案例

中,对比的是地方电视新闻与美国 19 个不同社区的实际犯罪情况,见 James T. Hamilton, *Channeling Violence: The Economic Market for Violent Television Programming* (Princeton, NJ: Princeton University Press, 1998)。

[9] George Gerbner, Larry Gross, Michael Morgan, Nancy Signorielli, and James Shanahan, 'Growing up with television: cultivation processes', in *Media Effects: Advances in Theory and Research*, 2nd edn, eds. Jennings Bryant and Dolf Zillmann (Mahwah, NJ: Lawrence Erlbaum, 1994), pp. 43–68. 也见 R. Andrew Holbrook and Timothy Hill, 'Agenda setting and priming in prime time television: crime dramas as political cues', *Political Communication*, 22 (2005): 277–295。

[10] Kimberly Gross and Sean Aday, 'The scary world in your living room and neighborhood: using local broadcast news, neighborhood crime rates, and personal experience to test agenda setting and cultivation', *Journal of Communication*, 53 (2003): 411–426.

[11] Magdalena Browne and Sebastián Valenzuela, 'Temor a la delincuencia en Chile: [Fear of crime in Chile], in (*In*)*seguridad, medios y miedos* [(In)security, media and fears], eds. Brenda Focás and Omar Rincón (Buenos Aires: Ediciones Imago Mundi, 2018), pp. 63–84.

[12] 'The statistical shark', *New York Times*, 6 September 2001, p. A26.

[13] Christine Ader, 'A longitudinal study of agenda setting for the issue of environmental pollution', *Journalism and Mass Communication Quarterly*, 72 (1995): 300–311.

[14] Stuart N. Soroka, *Agenda-Setting Dynamics in Canada* (Vancouver: UBC Press, 2002).

[15] Downs, 'Up and down with ecology: the "issue-attention cycle".'

[16] 早期研究个体议题议程的一个极好范例,见 Jack McLeod, Lee B. Becker, and J. E. Byrnes, 'Another look at the agenda setting function of the press', *Communication Research*, 1 (1974): 131–166。

[17] 有一本书大量引用了基于注意的研究,见 Wayne Wanta, *The Public and the*

National Agenda (Mahwah, NJ: Lawrence Erlbaum, 1997)。

[18] Jesper Stromback and Spiro Kiousis, 'A new look at agenda setting effects-Comparing the predictive power of overall political news consumption and specific news media consumption across different media channels and media types', *Journal of Communication*, 60 (2010): 271-292. 引自 p. 288。

[19] Magdalena Browne and Sebastián Valenzuela, 'Temor a la delincuencia en Chile' [Fear of crime in Chile].

[20] Richard L. Merritt, *Symbols of American Community, 1735-1775* (New Haven, CT: Yale University Press, 1966).

[21] David Paul Nord, 'The politics of agenda setting in late 19th century cities', *Journalism Quarterly*, 58 (1981): 563-574, 612.

[22] Ibid., p. 570.

[23] Jean Lange Folkerts, 'William Allen White's anti-populist rhetoric as an agenda setting technique', *Journalism Quarterly*, 60 (1983): 28-34.

[24] Funkhouser, 'The issues of the sixties.'

[25] James Winter and Chaim Eyal, 'Agenda setting for the civil rights issue', *Public Opinion Quarterly*, 45 (1981): 376-383.

[26] Edward Caudill, 'An agenda setting perspective on historical public opinion', in *Communication and Democracy: Exploring the Intellectual Frontiers in Agenda setting Theory*, eds. Maxwell McCombs, Donald Shaw, and David Weaver (Mahwah, NJ: Lawrence Erlbaum, 1997), p. 179.

[27] Ibid., p. 181.

[28] Chris J. Vargo, Lei Guo, and Michelle Amazeen, 'The agenda-setting power of fake news: A big data analysis of the online media landscape from 2014 to 2016', *New Media and Society*, 20 (2018): 2028-2049.

[29] William Safire, 'Like father, unlike son', *New York Times*, 2 September 2002, p. A17.

第三章 我们头脑中的图像

[1] Walter Lippmann, *Public Opinion* (New York: Macmillan, 1922).

[2] Maxwell McCombs and Donald Shaw, 'The agenda-setting function of mass media', *Public Opinion Quarterly*, 36 (1972): 176–187.

[3] Maxwell McCombs, 'Explorers and surveyors: expanding strategies for agenda setting research', *Journalism Quarterly*, 69 (1992): 815.

[4] Stuart N. Soroka, *Agenda-Setting Dynamics in Canada* (Vancouver: UBC Press, 2002). 在以色列进行的类似研究,见 Dan Caspi, 'The agenda-setting function of the Israeli press', *Knowledge: Creation, Diffusion, Utilization*, 3 (1982): 401–414。

[5] William J. McGuire, 'Theoretical foundations of campaigns', in *Public Communication Campaigns*, 2nd edn., eds. Richard E. Rice and Charles K. Atkin (Newbury Park, CA: Sage, 1989): 43–65.

[6] *New York Times*, 1 November 2002, p. A28.

[7] Bernard Cohen, *The Press and Foreign Policy* (Princeton, NJ: Princeton University Press, 1963), p. 13.

[8] David Swanson and Paolo Mancini, eds., *Politics, Media, and Modern Democracy: An International Study of Innovations in Electoral Campaigning and their Consequences* (Westport, CT: Praeger, 1996).

[9] Maxwell McCombs, 'The future agenda for agenda setting research', *Journal of Mass Communication Studies* [Japan], 45 (1994): 171–181; Maxwell McCombs and Dixie Evatt, 'Los temas y los aspectos: explorando una nueva dimensión de la agenda setting' ['Objects and attributes: exploring a new dimension of agenda setting'], *Comunicación y Sociedad*, 8, 1 (1995): 7–32.

[10] Lee Becker and Maxwell McCombs, 'The role of the press in determining voter reactions to presidential primaries', *Human Communication Research*, 4 (1978): 301–307.

[11] David H. Weaver, Doris A. Graber, Maxwell E. McCombs, and Chaim H. Eyal, *Media Agenda Setting in a Presidential Election: Issues, Images and Interest* (Westport, CT: Greenwood, 1981).

[12] Maxwell McCombs, Esteban López-Escobar, and Juan Pablo Llamas, 'Setting

the agenda of attributes in the 1996 Spanish general election', *Journal of Communication*, 50, 2 (2000): 77-92.

[13] Rosa Berganza and Marta Martin, 'Selective exposure to highly politicized media'; José Javier Sánchez-Aranda, María José Canel, and Juan Pablo Llamas, 'Framing effects of television political advertising and the selective perception process', papers presented at the World Association for Public Opinion Research regional conference, Pamplona, Spain, 1997.

[14] Pu-Tsung King, 'The press, candidate images, and voter perceptions', in *Communication and Democracy*, eds. Maxwell McCombs, Donald Shaw, and David Weaver (Mahwah, NJ: Lawrence Erlbaum, 1997), pp. 29-40.

[15] Esteban López-Escobar, Juan Pablo Llamas, and Maxwell McCombs, 'Una dimensión social de los efectos de los medios de difusión: agenda-setting y consenso' ['A social dimension of media effects: agenda-setting and consensus'] *Comunicación y Sociedad*, Ⅸ (1996): 91-125. 也参见 Maxwell McCombs, Juan Pablo Llamas, Esteban López-Escobar, and Federico Rey, 'Candidate images in Spanish elections: second-level agenda setting effects', *Journalism and Mass Communication Quarterly*, 74 (1997): 703-717.

[16] Soo Jung Moon, 'Attention, attitude, and behavior: second-level agenda-setting effects as a mediator of media use and political participation', *Communication Research*, 40 (2013): 698-719.

[17] Spiro Kiousis, Philemon Bantimaroudis and Hyun Ban, 'Candidate image attributes: experiments on the substantive dimension of second-level agenda setting', *Communication Research*, 26, 4 (1999): 414-428.

[18] Renita Coleman and Stephen Banning, 'Network TV news' affective framing of the presidential candidates: evidence for a second-level agenda-setting effect through visual framing', *Journalism and Mass Communication Quarterly*, 83 (2006): 313-328.

[19] Ibid., p. 321. 在进一步分析视觉资料的情感议程设置效果的基础上,科尔曼和吴在理论上区分了作为情绪的情感与作为积极和消极的认知评价的情

感。他们对布什和戈尔在电视新闻镜头中的非语言行为的测量,与公众对候选人特质的认知评价或公众对候选人的积极情绪反应之间没有发现明显的关联。在负面情绪反应方面则发现了显著的关系。参见 Renita Coleman and H. Denis Wu,'Proposing emotion as a dimension of affective agenda setting: separating affect into two components and comparing their second-level effects', *Journalism and Mass Communication Quarterly*, 87 (2010): 315-327。

[20] Hyun, Ki Deuk and Soo Jung Moon, 'Agenda setting in the partisan TV news context: attribute agenda setting and polarized evaluation of presidential candidates among viewers of NBC, CNN, and Fox News', *Journalism and Mass Communication Quarterly*, 93 (2016): 509-529.

[21] Toshio Takeshita and Shunji Mikami, 'How did mass media influence the voters' choice in the 1993 general election in Japan?: a study of agenda setting', *Keio Communication Review*, 17 (1995): 27-41.

[22] Marc Benton and P. Jean Frazier, 'The agenda-setting function of the mass media', *Communication Research*, 3 (1976): 261-274.

[23] Mikami, Shunji, Toshio Takeshita, Makoto Nakada and Miki Kawabata, 'The media coverage and public awareness of environmental issues in Japan', *International Communication Gazette*, 54 (1995), 209-226.

[24] Michael Salwen, 'Effects of accumulation of coverage on issue salience in agenda setting', *Journalism Quarterly*, 65 (1988): 100-106,130.

[25] Maxwell McCombs and John Smith, 'Perceptual selection and communication', *Journalism Quarterly*, 46 (1969): 352-355.

[26] Salma Ghanem, 'Filling in the tapestry: the second level of agenda-setting', in *Communication and Democracy*, eds. Maxwell McCombs, Donald Shaw and David Weaver (Mahwah, NJ: Lawrence Erlbaum, 1997), pp. 3-14.

[27] Salma Ghanem, 'Media coverage of crime and public opinion: an exploration of the second level of agenda setting', unpublished doctoral dissertation, University of Texas at Austin, 1996.

[28] Amy Jasperson, Dhavan Shah, Mark Watts, Ronald Faber, and David Fan,

'Framing and the public agenda: media effects on the importance of the federal budget deficit', *Political Communication*, 15 (1998): 205-224. 又见 David Fan, Kathy Keltner and Robert Wyatt, 'A matter of guilt or innocence: how news reports affect support for the death penalty in the United States', *International Journal of Public Opinion Research*, 14 (2002): 439-452。

[29] Klaus Schoenbach and Holli Semetko, 'Agenda setting, agenda reinforcing or agenda deflating? A study of the 1990 German national election', *Journalism Quarterly*, 68 (1992): 837-846.

[30] Thomas Birkland, *After Disaster: Agenda Setting, Public Policy, and Focusing Events* (Washington, DC: Georgetown University Press, 1997).

[31] Jan Váně and František Kalvas, 'Focusing events and their effect on agenda setting', paper presented to the World Association for Public Opinion Research, Hong Kong, China, 2012.

[32] Spiro Kiousis, 'Compelling arguments and attitude strength-exploring the impact of second-level agenda setting on public opinion of presidential candidate images', *Harvard International Journal of Press/Politics*, 10 (2005): 3-27.

[33] W. Russell Neuman, Marion Just, and Ann Crigler, *Common Knowledge: News and the Construction of Political Meaning* (Chicago: University of Chicago Press, 1992).

[34] 麦库姆斯进行原始分析的数据来自 Neuman, Just and Crigler, *Common Knowledge*。

[35] Paul F. Lazarsfeld and Robert Merton, 'Mass communication, popular taste and organized social action', in *The Communication of Ideas*, ed. Lyman Bryson (New York: Institute for Religious and Social Studies, 1948): 95-118.

[36] Walter Lippmann, *Public Opinion*; Dan Nimmo and Robert L. Savage, *Candidates and their Images* (Pacific Palisades, CA: Goodyear, 1976).

[37] Pamela Shoemaker and Tim Vos, *Gatekeeping Theory* (New York: Routledge, 2009).

[38] George Gerbner, Larry Gross, Michael Morgan, Nancy Signorielli, and James

Shanahan, 'Growing up with television', in *Media Effects*, 2nd edn, eds. Jennings Bryant and Dolf Zillmann (Mahwah, NJ: Lawrence Erlbaum, 1994), pp. 43-68.

[39] 又见 Margaret T. Gordon and Linda Heath, 'The news business, crime and fear', in *Reactions to Crime*, ed. Dan Lewis (Beverly Hills, CA: Sage, 1981)。

[40] Elisabeth Noelle-Neumann, *The Spiral of Silence: Our Social Skin*, 2nd edn (Chicago: University of Chicago Press, 1993).

[41] Maxwell McCombs and David Weaver, 'Toward a merger of gratifications and agenda-setting research', in *Media Gratifications Research*, eds. K. E. Rosengren, L. Wenner and P. Palmgreen (Beverly Hills, CA: Sage, 1985), pp. 95-108.

[42] Mark Miller, Julie Andsager, and Bonnie Riechert, 'Framing the candidates in presidential primaries: issues and images in press releases and news coverage', *Journalism and Mass Communication Quarterly*, 75 (1998): 312-324. 此处报告的相关系数是2000年春季在得克萨斯大学奥斯汀分校由麦库姆斯组织的议程设置理论研讨班计算得出的。

[43] Toshio Takeshita, 'Expanding attribute agenda setting into framing: an application of the problematic situation scheme', paper presented to the International Communication Association, Seoul, Korea, 2002.

[44] Alex Edelstein, Youichi Ito, and Hans Mathias Kepplinger, *Communication and Culture: A Comparative Approach* (New York: Longman, 1989). 虽然文章作者并未明确地将问题性情境的概念与架构联系起来,但后来加尼姆指出了这种联系的有用性。见 Salma Ghanem, 'Filling in the tapestry: the second level of agenda setting', in *Communication and Democracy*, eds. Maxwell McCombs, Donald Shaw, and David Weaver (Mahwah, NJ: Lawrence Erlbaum, 1997), p. 13。

[45] Michael Cacciatore, Dietram Scheufele, and Shanto Iyengar, 'The end of framing as we know it ... and the future of media effects', *Mass Communication and Society*, 19 (2016): 7-23. 引自 p. 20。

[46] Daniel Kahneman and Amos Tversky,'Choices, values and frames', *American Psychologist*, 39 (1984): 341-350.

[47] McGuire,'Theoretical foundations of campaigns.'对于大众传播媒介的主要效果是强化了流行观点还是创造了新的观点,仍然存在一些争论。第一层面与第二层面议程设置的区分对处理这些争论具有启发性。结合卡特从显著性和相关性这两个心理相关方面出发对媒介效果的观察,这种区分就更加具有启发意义了:

> 如果一个人所寻找的只是价值方面的显著性证据,那么价值的强化很可能就是他所找到的全部。另一方面,如果一个人要寻找的是个体如何根据他分配给各种元素的价值来构建他的认知环境,就必须通过处理与价值相关的信息来完成。于是,这种明显的悖论可以通过这种区分来解决。(Richard Carter,'Communication and affective relations', *Journalism Quarterly*, 57 (1866): 108.)

[48] Frank R. Baumgartner and Bryan D. Jones, *Agendas and Instability in American Politics*, 2nd edn (Chicago: University of Chicago Press, 2009).

第四章 议题和属性的网络

[1] Y. J. Son and David Weaver,'Another look at what moves public opinion: media agenda setting and polls in the 2000 US election', *International Journal of Public Opinion Research*, 18 (2006): 174-197.

[2] Lei Guo,'Toward the third level of agenda setting theory: A network agenda setting model', in Thomas J. Johnson, ed., *Agenda Setting in a 2.0 World* (New York: Routledge, 2013), pp. 112-133.

[3] John R. Anderson, *The Architecture of Cognition* (Cambridge, MA: Harvard University Press, 1983).

[4] Stephen Kaplan,'Cognitive maps in perception and thought', in *Image and Environment: Cognitive Mapping and Spacial Behavior*, eds. Roger M. Downs and David Stea (Chicago: Aldine, 1973), pp. 63-78.

[5] Allan M. Collins and Elizabeth F. Loftus,'A spreading activation theory of se-

mantic processing', *Psychological Review*, 82 (1975): 402-408.

[6] Daniel S. Levine, 'Neural population modeling and psychology: A review', *Mathematical Biosciences*, 66 (1983): 1-86.

[7] Peter H. Lindsay and Donald A. Norman, *Human Information Processing: An Introduction to Psychology* (New York: Academic Press, 1977); Vincent Price and David Tewksbury, 'News values and public opinion: a theoretical account of media priming and framing' in *Progress in Communication Sciences: Advances in Persuasion*, eds. G. A. Barnett and F. J. Boster (Greenwich, CT: Ablex, 1997), pp. 173-212; David E. Rumelhart and Donald A. Norman, 'Accretion, tuning and restructuring: Three modes of learning', in *Semantic Factors in Cognition*, eds. John Wealdon Cotton and Roberta L. Klatzky (Hillsdale, NJ: Lawrence Erlbaum, 1978).

[8] Lei Guo and Maxwell McCombs, 'Network agenda setting: a third level of media effects', paper presented to the International Communication Association, Boston, 2011.

[9] Kihan Kim and Maxwell McCombs, 'News story descriptions and the public's opinions of political candidates', *Journalism and Mass Communication Quarterly*, 84 (2007): 299-314.

[10] Lei Guo and Maxwell McCombs, 'Toward the third-level agenda setting theory: a network agenda setting model', paper presented to the Association for Education in Journalism and Mass Communication, St Louis, 2011.

[11] Lei Guo and Maxwell McCombs, 'Network agenda setting: A third level of media effects.'

[12] Hong Vu, Lei Guo, and Maxwell McCombs, 'Exploring "the world outside and the pictures in our heads": a network agenda setting study', *Journalism and Mass Communication Quarterly*, 91 (2014): 669-686.

[13] Chris Vargo, Lei Guo, Maxwell McCombs, and Donald L. Shaw, 'Network issue agendas on Twitter during the 2012 US presidential election', *Journal of Communication*, 64 (2014): 296-316.

[14] Spiro Kiousis, Ji Young Kim, Matt Ragas, Gillian Wheat, Sarab Kochhar, Emma Svensson, and Maradith Miles, 'Exploring new frontiers of agenda building during the 2012 US presidential election pre-convention period', *Journalism Studies*, 16 (2015): 363-382.

[15] H. Denis Wu and Lei Guo, 'Beyond salience transmission: linking agenda networks between media and voters', *Communication Research* (2017): Advance online publication.

[16] Lei Guo, Yi-Ning Katherine Chen, Radoslaw Aksamit, Damian Guzek, Qian Wang, Hong Vu, and Maxwell McCombs, 'How the world pictured the Iraq War: a transnational network analysis', *Journalism Studies*, 16 (2015): 343-362.

[17] Nirit Weiss-Blatt, 'Role of tech bloggers in the flow of information', in *The Power of Information Networks*, eds. Lei Guo and Maxwell McCombs (New York: Routledge, 2016), pp. 88-103.

[18] Michael Etter and Anne Vestergaard, 'Third level of agenda building and agenda setting during a corporate crisis', in *The Power of Information Networks*, eds. Lei Guo and Maxwell McCombs (New York: Routledge, 2016), pp. 175-189.

[19] Funkhouser, 'The issues of the sixties.'

[20] Stromback and Kiousis, 'A new look at agenda setting effects.'

[21] Chris J. Vargo and Lei Guo, 'Networks, big data, and intermedia agenda setting: an analysis of traditional, partisan, and emerging online US news', *Journalism and Mass Communication Quarterly*, 94 (2017): 1031-1055.

[22] 关于其他研究的详细综述，见 Lei Guo and Maxwell McCombs, eds. *The Power of Information Networks: New Directions for Agenda Setting* (New York: Routledge, 2016).

第五章 议程设置为何发生

[1] Pamela Shoemaker, 'Hardwired for news: using biological and cultural evolution to explain the surveillance function', *Journal of Communication*, 46, 3 (1996):

32–47.

[2] David Weaver, 'Political issues and voter need for orientation', in *The Emergence of American Political Issues*, eds. Donald Shaw and Maxwell McCombs (St Paul, MN: West, 1977), pp. 107–119; David Weaver, 'Audience need for orientation and media effects', *Communication Research*, 7 (1980): 361–376; Bruce Westley and Lee Barrow, 'An investigation of news seeking behavior', *Journalism Quarterly*, 36 (1959): 431–438; Maxwell McCombs, 'Editorial endorsements: a study of influence', *Journalism Quarterly*, 44 (1967): 545–548; J. E. Mueller, 'Choosing among 133 candidates', *Public Opinion Quarterly*, 34 (1970): 395–402.

[3] Edward C. Tolman, *Purposive Behavior in Animals and Men* (New York: Appleton-Century-Crofts, 1932). 又见 Tolman, 'Cognitive maps in rats and men', *Psychological Review*, 55 (1948): 189–208; W. J. McGuire, 'Psychological motives and communication gratification', in *The Uses of Mass Communication: Current Perspectives on Gratifications Research*, eds. J. G. Blumler and Elihu Katz (Beverly Hills, CA: Sage, 1974), pp. 167–196。

[4] Robert E. Lane, *Political Life: Why and How People Get Involved in Politics* (New York: Free Press, 1959), p. 12.

[5] Davis Merritt and Maxwell McCombs, *The Two W's of Journalism* (Mahwah, NJ: Lawrence Erlbaum, 2003), chapter 6. 又见 Michael Schudson, *The Good Citizen: A History of American Civic Life* (New York: Free Press, 1998), pp. 310–311.

[6] 在为议程设置的失败提供深度解释时,尤塔斯和舍格维奇超越了导向需求的概念,借鉴了议程设置理论的其他两个方面,亦即我们在第三章中讨论过的主题:雄辩论据的概念及属性议程设置与框架融合的思路。见 Julie Yioutas and Ivana Segvic, 'Revisiting the Clinton/Lewinsky scandal: the convergence of agenda setting and framing', *Journalism and Mass Communication Quarterly*, 80 (2003): 567–582。

[7] Jeffrey M. Jones, 'As Senate Trial Begins, 44% Approve of Trump', Gallup.com, https://news.gallup.com/poll/283364/senate-trial-begins-approve-trump.aspx.

[8] Weaver, 'Political issues and voter need for orientation', p. 112.

[9] Paula Poindexter, Maxwell McCombs, Laura Smith, and others, 'Need for orientation in the new media landscape', unpublished paper, University of Texas at Austin, 2002.

[10] Weaver, 'Political issues and voter need for orientation', pp. 113, 115.

[11] Toshio Takeshita, 'Agenda-setting effects of the press in a Japanese local election', *Studies of Broadcasting*, 29 (1993): 193-216.

[12] Maxwell McCombs and Donald Shaw, 'The agenda-setting function of mass media', *Public Opinion Quarterly*, 36 (1972): 176-187.

[13] David Weaver and Maxwell McCombs, 'Voters' need for orientation and choice of candidate: mass media and electoral decision making', paper presented to the American Association for Public Opinion Research, Roanoke, VA, 1978.

[14] David Cohen, 'A report on a non-election agenda setting study', paper presented to the Association for Education in Journalism, Ottawa, Canada, 1975.

[15] Dixie Evatt and Salma Ghanem, 'Building a scale to measure salience', paper presented to the World Association for Public Opinion Research, Rome, Italy, 2001.

[16] Fermín Bouza, 'The impact area of political communication: citizenship faced with public discourse', *International Review of Sociology*, 14 (2004): 245-259. 引自 p. 250。

[17] Maxwell McCombs, 'Personal involvement with issues on the public agenda', *International Journal of Public Opinion Research*, 11 (1999): 152-168.

[18] Ronald Inglehart, *Culture Shift in Advanced Industrial Society* (Princeton, NJ: Princeton University Press, 1990).

[19] Sebastián Valenzuela, 'Materialism, post-materialism and agenda-setting effects: the values-issues consistency hypothesis', *International Journal of Public Opinion Research*, 23 (2011): 437-463.

[20] 关于价值观在解释议程设置上的作用的进一步讨论,可见 Sebastián Valenzuela and Gennadiy Chernov, 'Explicating the values-issue consistency hypothesis

through need for orientation', *Canadian Journal of Communication*, 41, 1 (2016); Sebastián Valenzuela, 'Value resonance and the origins of issue salience', in *Agenda Setting in a 2.0 World*, ed. Thomas J. Johnson (New York: Routledge, 2013), pp. 53-64.

[21] Joanne Miller, 'Examining the mediators of agenda setting: A new experimental paradigm reveals the role of emotions', *Political Psychology*, 28 (2007): 689-717.

[22] Jörg Matthes, 'The need for orientation towards news media: revising and validating a classic concept', *International Journal of Public Opinion Research*, 18 (2006): 422-444.

[23] Jörg Matthes, 'Need for orientation as a predictor of agenda-setting effects: causal evidence from a two-wave panel study', *International Journal of Public Opinion Research*, 20 (2008): 440-453.

[24] Gennadiy Chernov, Sebastián Valenzuela and Maxwell McCombs, 'An experimental comparison of two perspectives on the concept of need for orientation in agenda-setting theory', *Journalism and Mass Communication Quarterly*, 88 (2011): 142-155.

[25] Harold Zucker, 'The variable nature of news media influence', in *Communication Yearbook 2*, ed. Brent Ruben (New Brunswick, NJ: Transaction Books, 1978), pp. 225-240.

[26] James Winter, Chaim Eyal and Ann Rogers, 'Issue-specific agenda setting: the whole as less than the sum of the parts', *Canadian Journal of Communication*, 8, 2 (1982): 1-10.

[27] Zucker, 'The variable nature of news influence.'

[28] Kim Smith, 'Newspaper coverage and public concern about community issues: a time-series analysis', *Journalism Monographs*, 101 (1987): 13.

[29] David H. Weaver, Doris A. Graber, Maxwell E. McCombs, and Chaim H. Eyal, *Media Agenda Setting in a Presidential Election: Issues, Images and Interest* (Westport, CT: Greenwood, 1981).

[30] Warwick Blood, 'Unobtrusive issues in the agenda setting role of the press', unpublished doctoral dissertation, Syracuse University, 1981.

[31] 关于失业议题(尤其是作为一个全国性议题)的非强制性特点的更多证据,参见 Donald Shaw and John Slater, 'Press puts unemployment on agenda: Richmond community opinion, 1981-1984', *Journalism Quarterly*, 65 (1988): 407-411。

[32] Warwick Blood, 'Competing models of agenda-setting: issue obtrusiveness vs. media exposure', paper presented to the Association for Education in Journalism, Boston, 1980. 这是对帕特森报告原始数据的二度分析,原始数据见 Thomas Patterson, *The Mass Media Election: How Americans Choose Their President* (New York: Praeger, 1980)。

[33] Edna F. Einsiedel, Kandice L. Salomone, and Frederick Schneider, 'Crime: effects of media exposure and personal experience on issue salience', *Journalism Quarterly*, 61 (1984): 131-136; Dominic Lasorsa and Wayne Wanta, 'Effects of personal, interpersonal and media experiences on issue saliences', *Journalism Quarterly*, 67 (1990): 804-813.

[34] Elisabeth Noelle-Neumann, 'The spiral of silence: a response', in *Political Communication Yearbook 1984*, eds. Keith Sanders, Lynda Lee Kaid, and Dan Nimmo (Carbondale: Southern Illinois University Press, 1985), pp. 66-94. 又见 Lutz Erbring, Edie Goldenberg and Arthur Miller, 'Front-page news and real-world cues', *American Journal of Political Science*, 24 (1980): 16-49。

[35] Lasorsa and Wanta, 'Effects of personal, interpersonal and media experiences on issue saliences.'

[36] Jin Yang and Gerald Stone, 'The powerful role of interpersonal communication on agenda setting', *Mass Communication and Society*, 6 (2003): 57-74.

[37] James P. Winter, 'Contingent conditions in the agenda-setting process', in *Mass Communication Review Yearbook*, eds. G. C. Wilhoit and Harold de Bock (Beverly Hills, CA: Sage, 1981), pp. 235-243; G. Gumpert and R. Cathcart, eds., *Inter/Media: Interpersonal Communication in a Media World* (New York: Oxford

University Press, 1986).

[38] 关于交谈的强化作用,有一个例子,见 Wayne Wanta, *The Public and the National Agenda* (Mahwah, NJ: Lawrence Erlbaum, 1997), p. 59。在此处,交谈对议程设置过程的影响远远超过接触媒介。另一个不同的视角是,新闻媒体是主要的推动力。媒介的这种"培育交谈"(The cultivation of conversation)作用是苏珊·赫布斯特在讨论法国社会学家塔尔德(Gabriel Tarde)的意见形成模式时提出的。见 Susan Herbst, 'The cultivation of conversation', in *The Poll with a Human Face: The National Issues Convention Experiment in Political Communication*, eds. Maxwell McCombs and Amy Reynolds (Mahwah, NJ: Lawrence Erlbaum, 1999), esp. pp. 201-204; Joohan Kim, Robert Wyatt and Elihu Katz, 'News, talk, opinion, participation: the part played by conversation in deliberative democracy', *Political Communication*, 16 (1999): 361-385。

[39] Hong Nga Nguyen Vu and Volker Gehrau, 'Agenda diffusion: an integrated model of agenda setting and interpersonal communication', *Journalism and Mass Communication Quarterly*, 87 (2010): 100-116.

[40] Tony Atwater, Michael Salwen and Ronald Anderson, 'Interpersonal discussion as a potential barrier to agenda setting', *Newspaper Research Journal*, 6, 4 (1985): 37-43.

[41] Jessica T. Feezell, 'Agenda setting through social media: the importance of incidental news exposure and social filtering in the digital era', *Political Research Quarterly*, 71 (2018): 482-494.

[42] Peter A. Frensch, 'One concept, multiple meanings: on how to define the concept of implicit learning', in *Handbook of Implicit Learning*, eds. Michael A. Stadler and Peter A. Frensch (Thousand Oaks, CA: Sage, 1998), pp. 47-104.

[43] Kristin Bulkow, Juliane Urban, and Wolfgang Schweiger, 'The duality of agenda-setting: The role of information processing', *International Journal of Public Opinion Research*, 25 (2012): 43-63.

[44] Gary King, Benjamin Schneer, and Ariel White, 'How the news media activate

public expression and influence national agendas', *Science*, 358 (2017): 776-780.

[45] Donald L. Shaw, Milad Minooie, Deb Aikat, and Chris J. Vargo, *Agendamelding: News, Social Media, Audiences and Civic Community* (New York: Peter Lang, 2019).

[46] Donald L. Shaw, Bradley J. Hamm, and Thomas C. Terry, 'Vertical vs. horizontal media: Using agenda setting and audience agenda-melding to create public information strategies in the emerging Papyrus Society', *Military Review*, 86, 6 (2006): 13-25.

[47] Shaw, Minooie, Aikat, and Vargo, p. 194.

[48] Yunjuan Luo, Hansel Burley, Alexander Moe, and Mingxiao Sui, 'A meta-analysis of news media's public agenda-setting effects, 1972-2015', *Journalism and Mass Communication Quarterly*, 96 (2019): 150-172; Wayne Wanta and Salma Ghanem, 'Effects of agenda setting', in *Mass Media Effects Research: Advances through Meta-Analysis*, eds. Raymond W. Preiss, Barbara Mae Gayle, Nancy Burrell, Mike Allen, and Jennings Bryant (Mahwah, NJ: Lawrence Erlbaum, 2006), pp. 37-51.

[49] Shaw, Minooie, Aikat, and Vargo, Chapter 4.

[50] Ibid., Chapter 5.

[51] Richard F. Carter, 'Communication and affective relations', *Journalism Quarterly*, 42 (1965): 203-212. 关于卡特的显著性和相关性概念与议程设置理论之间的联系的进一步讨论，见 Maxwell McCombs, 'Myth and reality in scientific discovery: The case of agenda setting theory', in *Communication: A Different Kind of Horse Race*, eds. Brenda Dervin and Steven Chaffee (Cresskill, NJ: Hampton Press, 2003), pp. 25-37。

[52] 关于导向需求与另一种传播理论(沉默的螺旋)之间关联的进一步讨论，见 Maxwell McCombs and David Weaver, 'Toward a merger of gratifications and agenda-setting research', in *Media Gratifications Research: Current Perspectives*, eds. Karl Erik Rosengren, Lawrence Wenner, and Philip Palmgreen (Beverly

Hills, CA: Sage, 1985), pp. 95-108。

[53] 又见 Jay Blumler, 'The role of theory in uses and gratifications research', *Communication Research*, 6 (1979): 9-36。

第六章 议程设置如何起作用

[1] Yeojin Kim, Youngju Kim, and Shuhua Zhou, 'Theoretical and methodological trends of agenda-setting theory: a thematic analysis of the last four decades of research', *Agenda Setting Journal*, 1 (2017): 5-22.

[2] Larry M. Bartels, *Unequal Democracy: The Political Economy of the New Gilded Age*, 2nd edn (New York, NY: Russell Sage Foundation, 2016); Kay Lehman Schlozman, Sidney Verba, and Henry E. Brady, *The Unheavenly Chorus: Unequal Political Voice and the Broken Promise of American Democracy* (Princeton, NJ: Princeton University Press, 2013).

[3] 关于这种系统视角,有一个重要的推论,即认为新闻报道本身并不是产生议程设置效果的充分条件。研究者聚焦于欧洲一体化议题,比较分析了1999年6月欧洲选举活动的相关电视新闻报道和选举后在所有欧盟国家做的选后调查。结果发现,对欧盟报道的增加并未自动提升欧洲一体化议题在公众心中的重要性。在那些政治精英对欧洲一体化议题意见不同的国家,人们观看的欧盟报道越多,就越认为欧洲一体化议题重要。如果政治精英在欧洲一体化议题上的看法一致,那么这种效果就不会出现。见 Jochen Peter, 'Country characteristics as contingent conditions of agenda setting: the moderating influence of polarized elite opinion', *Communication Research*, 30 (2003): 683-712。

[4] Pu-Tsung King, 'The press, candidate images, and voter perceptions', in *Communication and Democracy*, eds. Maxwell McCombs, Donald Shaw, and David Weaver (Mahwah, NJ: Lawrence Erlbaum, 1997), pp. 29-40.

[5] V. O. Key, *The Responsible Electorate: Rationality in Presidential Voting 1936-1960* (Cambridge, MA: Belknap Press of Harvard University Press, 1966). 最初引自 p. 7。

[6] George A. Miller, 'The magic number seven, plus or minus two: some limits on

our capacity for processing information', *Psychological Review*, 63 (1956): 81-97.

[7] W. Russell Neuman, 'The threshold of public attention', *Public Opinion Quarterly*, 54 (1990): 159-176.

[8] Maxwell McCombs and Jian-Hua Zhu, 'Capacity, diversity and volatility of the public agenda: trends from 1954-1994', *Public Opinion Quarterly*, 59 (1995): 495-525.

[9] Jill A. Edy and Patrick C. Meirick, 'The fragmenting public agenda: capacity, diversity, and volatility in responses to the "most important problem" question', *Public Opinion Quarterly*, 82, (2018): 661-685.

[10] Sebastián Valenzuela, 'Agenda setting and journalism', in *Oxford Research Encyclopedia of Communication*, ed. Jon F. Nussbaum (New York, NY: Oxford University Press, 2019).

[11] Ibid.

[12] Jian-Hua Zhu, 'Issue competition and attention distraction: a zero-sum theory of agenda setting', *Journalism Quarterly*, 68 (1992): 825-836.

[13] Tom Smith, 'America's most important problems—a trend analysis, 1946-1976', *Public Opinion Quarterly*, 44 (1980): 164-180.

[14] McCombs and Zhu, 'Capacity, diversity and volatility of the public agenda'; Edy and Meirick, 'The fragmenting public agenda: capacity, diversity, and volatility in responses to the "most important problem" question.'

[15] Mike Gruszczynski, 'Evidence of partisan agenda fragmentation in the American public, 1959-2015', *Public Opinion Quarterly*, 83 (2020): 749-781.

[16] Jong-Wha Lee and Hanol Lee, 'Human capital in the long run', *Journal of Development Economics*, 122 (2016): 147-169; Robert J. Barro and Jong-Wha Lee, 'A new data set of educational attainment in the world, 1950-2010', *Journal of Development Economics*, 104 (2013): 184-198.

[17] Samuel Popkin, *The Reasoning Voter* (Chicago: University of Chicago Press, 1991), p. 36.

[18] Ibid., p. 43.

[19] McCombs and Zhu, 'Capacity, diversity and volatility of the public agenda'; Edy and Meirick, 'The fragmenting public agenda: capacity, diversity, and volatility in responses to the "most important problem" question.'

[20] Edy and Meirick, 'The fragmenting public agenda', p. 674.

[21] Wayne Wanta, *The Public and the National Agenda: How People Learn about Important Issues* (Mahwah, NJ: Lawrence Erlbaum, 1997), pp. 22-24.

[22] Philip E. Converse, 引自 Jian-Hua Zhu, with William Boroson, 'Susceptibility to agenda setting: a cross-sectional and longitudinal analysis of individual differences', in *Communication and Democracy*, eds. Maxwell McCombs, Donald Shaw, and David Weaver (Mahwah, NJ: Lawrence Erlbaum, 1997), p. 71。一项研究进一步阐释了康夫斯关于"概念老练度"的引言,发现媒介对候选人形象的属性议程设置效果受选民政治成熟程度的调节。政治上非常成熟的公民,尽管高度接触媒介信息,但较少受到影响;而对接触政治消息有足够的兴趣且政治成熟度中等的选民,最容易受到媒介信息的影响。见 Sungtae Ha, 'Attribute priming effects and presidential candidate evaluation: the conditionality of political sophistication', *Mass Communication and Society*, 14 (2011): 315-342。

[23] Michael MacKuen, 'Social communication and the mass policy agenda', in *More Than News: Media Power in Public Affairs*, eds. Michael MacKuen and Steven Coombs (Beverly Hills, CA: Sage, 1981), pp. 19-144.

[24] Zhu with Boroson, 'Susceptibility to agenda setting.'

[25] Ibid., p. 82.

[26] Toshio Takeshita, 'Current critical problems in agenda-setting research', *International Journal of Public Opinion Research*, 18 (2006): 275-276.

[27] Richard E. Petty and John T. Cacioppo, *Communication and Persuasion: Central and Peripheral Routes to Attitude Change* (New York, NY: Springer, 1986).

[28] 虽然关于议程设置双轨路径的提法越来越常见,但这些路线的标签名依然未定,如"随意"(casual)与"刻意"(deliberative)、"消极"(passive)与"积极"

(active)、"提示"(cueing)与"推理"(reasoning)等。见 Na Yeon Lee, 'How agenda setting works: a dual path model and motivated reasoning', *Journalism* (2019); Raymond Pingree and Elizabeth Stoycheff, 'Differentiating cueing from reasoning in agenda setting effects', *Journal of Communication*, 63 (2013): 852–872。

[29] Kristin Bulkow, Juliane Urban, and Wolfgang Schweiger, 'The duality of agenda-setting: the role of information processing', *International Journal of Public Opinion Research*, 25 (2013): 43–63.

[30] Ibid., p. 17.

[31] Raymond Pingree, Andrea Quenette, John Tchernev, and Ted Dickinson, 'Effects of media criticism on gatekeeping trust and implications for agenda setting', *Journal of Communication*, 63 (2013): 351–372; Pingree and Stoycheff, 'Differentiating cueing from reasoning in agenda setting effects.'

[32] David Weaver, 'Audience need for orientation and media effects', *Communication Research*, 7 (1980): 361–376.

[33] Lindita Camaj, 'Need for orientation, selective exposure, and attribute agenda-setting effects', *Mass Communication and Society*, 17 (2014): 689–712.

[34] Natalie Stroud, *Niche News: The Politics of News Choice* (New York: Oxford University Press, 2011).

[35] Lindita Camaj, 'Motivational theories of agenda-setting effects: an information selection and processing model of attribute agenda-setting', *International Journal of Public Opinion Research*, 31 (2019): 441–462.

[36] Joseph Klapper, *The Effects of Mass Communication* (New York: Free Press, 1960), p. 8.

[37] James Winter and Chaim Eyal, 'Agenda setting for the civil rights issue', *Public Opinion Quarterly*, 45 (1981): 376–383.

[38] Shanto Iyengar and Donald R. Kinder, *News That Matters: Television and American Opinion* (Chicago, IL: University of Chicago Press, 1987); Pingree and Stoycheff, 'Differentiating cueing from reasoning in agenda setting effects.'

[39] Harold Zucker, 'The variable nature of news media influence', in *Communication Yearbook 2*, ed. Brent Ruben (New Brunswick, NJ: Transaction Books, 1978), pp. 225–240.

[40] Michael Salwen, 'Effects of accumulation of coverage on issue salience in agenda setting', *Journalism Quarterly*, 65 (1988): 100–106, 130.

[41] Marilyn Roberts, Wayne Wanta, and Tzong-Houng (Dustin) Dzwo, 'Agenda setting and issue salience online', *Communication Research*, 29 (2002): 452–465.

[42] 关于用数字数据资料作为公众议程代表的其他研究,可见 Gary King, Benjamin Schneer and Ariel White, 'How the news media activate public expression and influence national agendas', *Science*, 358 (2017): 776–780; Michael Scharkow and Jens Vogelgesang, 'Measuring the public agenda using search engine queries', *International Journal of Public Opinion Research*, 23 (2011): 104–113; Brian Weeks and Brian Southwell, 'The symbiosis of news coverage and aggregate online search behavior: Obama, rumors, and presidential politics', *Mass Communication and Society*, 13 (2010): 341–360.

[43] Wayne Wanta and Y. Hu, 'Time-lag differences in the agenda setting process: an examination of five news media', *International Journal of Public Opinion Research*, 6 (1994): 225–240.

[44] Stefan Geiß, 'The media's conditional agenda setting power: how baselines and spikes of issue salience affect likelihood and strength of agenda setting', *Communication Research* (2019). 引自 p. 22。

[45] 议程设置效果削减的类似变化,见 James H. Watt, Mary Mazza and Leslie Synder, 'Agenda-setting effects of television news coverage and the memory decay curve', *Communication Research*, 20 (1993): 408–435。

[46] Geiß, 'The media's conditional agenda setting power.'

[47] Don W. Stacks, Michael B. Salwen, and Kristen C. Eichhorn, eds., *An Integrated Approach To Communication Theory And Research*, 3rd edn (New York, NY: Routledge, 2019); Mary Beth Oliver, Arthur A. Raney, and Jennings Bryant,

eds., *Media Effects: Advances in Theory and Research*, 4th edn (New York, NY: Routledge, 2020).

[48] Chaim Eyal, James Winter, and William DeGeorge, 'The concept of time frame in agenda setting', in *Mass Communication Review Yearbook*, vol. 2, eds. G. Cleveland Wilhoit and Harold de Bock (Beverly Hills, CA: Sage, 1981), pp. 212-218.

[49] 以一整章讨论议程设置时间框架问题的文献,可见 Stuart N. Soroka, *Agenda-Setting Dynamics in Canada* (Vancouver: UBC Press, 2002)。

[50] Zhu, 'Issue competition and attention distraction.'

[51] Gerald Kosicki, 'Problems and opportunities in agenda setting research', *Journal of Communication*, 43 (1993): 117.

[52] Maxwell McCombs and Jian-Hua Zhu, 'Capacity, diversity, and volatility of the public agenda', *Public Opinion Quarterly*, 59 (1995): 495-525. 另见 Smith, 'America's most important problem-a trend analysis, 1946-1976', *Public Opinion Quarterly*, 44 (1980): 164-180。一些议程设置研究改述了盖洛普调查关于"最重要问题"的问法,而非使用原来的措辞。

[53] Will Jennings and Christopher Wlezien, 'Distinguishing between most important problems and issues?', *Public Opinion Quarterly*, 75 (2011): 545-555.

[54] Young Min, Salma Ghanem and Dixie Evatt, 'Using a split-ballot survey to explore the robustness of the "MIP" question in agenda setting research: a methodological study', *International Journal of Public Opinion Research*, 19 (2007): 221-236.

[55] Scott L. Althaus and David Tewksbury, 'Agenda setting and the "new" news: patterns of issue importance among readers of the paper and online versions of the *New York Times*', *Communication Research*, 29 (2002): 180-207.

[56] Tai-Li Wang, 'Agenda setting online: an experiment testing the effects of hyperlinks in online newspapers', *Southwestern Mass Communication Journal*, 15, 2 (2000): 59-70.

[57] Dixie Evatt and Salma Ghanem, 'Building a scale to measure salience', paper

presented to the World Association for Public Opinion Research, Rome, Italy, 2001.

[58] Brian Weeks and Brian Southwell, 'The symbiosis of news coverage and aggregate online search behavior: Obama, rumors, and presidential politics', *Mass Communication and Society*, 13 (2010): 341-360.

[59] Edna F. Einsiedel, Kandice L. Salomone and Frederick Schneider, 'Crime: effects of media exposure and personal experience on issue salience', *Journalism Quarterly*, 61 (1984): 131-136.

[60] David Cohen, 'A report on a non-election agenda setting study', paper presented to the Association for Education in Journalism, Ottawa, Canada, 1975.

[61] David H. Weaver, Doris A. Graber, Maxwell E. McCombs and Chaim H. Eyal, *Media Agenda Setting in a Presidential Election: Issues, Images and Interest* (Westport, CT: Greenwood, 1981).

[62] Spiro Kiousis and Maxwell McCombs, 'Agenda-setting effects and attitude strength: political figures during the 1996 presidential election', *Communication Research*, 31 (2004): 36-57.

[63] Sei-Hill Kim, Dietram Scheufele, and James Shanahan, 'Think about it this way: attribute agenda-setting function of the press and the public's evaluation of a local issue', *Journalism and Mass Communication Quarterly*, 79 (2002): 7-25.

[64] Joe Bob Hester and Rhonda Gibson, 'The agenda setting function of national versus local media: a time-series analysis for the issue of same sex marriage', *Mass Communication and Society*, 10 (2007): 299-317.

[65] Lori Young and Stuart Soroka, 'Affective news: the automated coding of sentiment in political texts', *Political Communication*, 29 (2012): 205-231.

[66] Chris J. Vargo and Lei Guo, 'Networks, big data, and intermedia agenda setting: an analysis of traditional, partisan, and emerging online US news', *Journalism and Mass Communication Quarterly*, 94 (2017): 1031-1055; Chris J. Vargo and Lei Guo, 'Exploring the network agenda setting model with big social data', in Lei Guo and Maxwell McCombs, eds. *The Power of Information*

Networks: *New Directions for Agenda Setting* (New York, Routledge: 2016), pp. 55-65.

第七章　塑造媒介议程

[1] Pamela Shoemaker and Stephen D. Reese, *Mediating the Message in the 21st Century: A Media Sociology Perspective* (New York, NY: Routledge, 2014). 将这一影响层次模型应用于当前新闻媒介环境的案例,可见: Stephen D. Reese and Pamela J. Shoemaker, 'A media sociology for the networked public sphere: the hierarchy of influences model', *Mass Communication and Society*, 19 (2016): 389-410。

[2] 在大量相关文献中,经常被引用的经典研究包括: Warren Breed, 'Social control in the newsroom', *Social Forces*, 33 (May 1955): 326-335; Gaye Tuchman, 'Telling stories', *Journal of Communication*, 26, 4 (1976): 93-97; Herbert Gans, *Deciding What's News: A Study of CBS Evening News, NBC Nightly News, Newsweek and Time* (New York: Pantheon, 1979)。

[3] Stuart Soroka and Stephen McAdams, 'News, politics, and negativity', *Political Communication*, 32, 1 (2015): 1-22.

[4] 在其他国家,也有与国情咨文功能相当的演说,如女王的演讲(英国)、御座致辞(加拿大)、国会致辞(巴西与智利)。这些演说中的一部分适于编码,可在比较议程研究项目网站(https://www.comparativeagendas.net/)上获得,并用于议程设置研究。

[5] Sheldon Gilberg, Chaim Eyal, Maxwell McCombs, and David Nicholas, 'The State of the Union address and the press agenda', *Journalism Quarterly*, 57 (1980): 584-588.

[6] Maxwell McCombs, Sheldon Gilberg and Chaim Eyal, 'The State of the Union address and the press agenda: a replication', paper presented to the International Communication Association, Boston, 1982.

[7] Thomas J. Johnson and Wayne Wanta, with John T. Byrd and Cindy Lee, 'Exploring FDR's relationship with the press: a historical agenda-setting study', *Politi-

cal Communication, 12 (1995): 157-172.

[8] Wayne Wanta, Mary Ann Stephenson, Judy VanSlyke Turk, and Maxwell Mc-Combs, 'How president's State of Union talk influenced news media agendas', *Journalism Quarterly*, 66 (1989): 537-541. 关于总统新闻发布会和演说对国家议程产生影响的证据,可见 Spiro Kiousis and Jesper Stromback, 'The White House and public relations: examining the linkages between presidential communications and public opinion', *Public Relations Review*, 36 (2010): 7-14。

[9] William Gonzenbach, *The Media, the President and Public Opinion* (Mahwah, NJ: Lawrence Erlbaum, 1996); Wayne Wanta and Joe Foote, 'The president-news media relationship: a time-series analysis of agenda setting', *Journal of Broadcasting and Electronic Media*, 38 (1994): 437-448. 又见 Wayne Wanta, *The Public and the National Agenda* (Mahwah, NJ: Lawrence Erlbaum, 1997), 这本书的第七章将分析扩展到国情咨文演讲对公众议程的影响。一项设计精巧的研究,比较了四组议题——总统强调但新闻媒体没有强调的议题、只有新闻媒体强调的议题、两者都强调的议题、两者都没有强调的议题。结果发现,通过媒体报道获知(媒介接触),而非实际收看电视上的总统国情咨文演讲,是预示所有其他议题(除了只有总统强调的那些议题之外)显著性的关键要素。对于那些两者都强调的议题,媒介接触本身就可以成为重要预测变量。这意味着,媒介议程冗余的影响超过了总统的权威。

[10] Stuart N. Soroka, *Agenda-Setting Dynamics in Canada* (Vancouver: UBC Press, 2002).

[11] Sebastián Valenzuela and Arturo Arriagada, 'Politics without citizens? Public opinion, television news, the president, and real-world factors in Chile, 2000-2005', *Harvard International Journal of Press/Politics*, 16 (2011): 357-381.

[12] R. W. Cobb and C. D. Elder, *Participation in American Politics: The Dynamics of Agenda-Building* (Baltimore: Johns Hopkins University Press, 1972).

[13] Peter van Aelst and Stefaan Walgrave, 'Political agenda setting by the mass media: ten years of research, 2005-2015', in *Handbook of Public Policy Agenda Setting*, ed. Nikolaos Zahariadis (Cheltenham, UK: Edward Elgar, 2016),

pp. 157-178.

[14] Barbara Nelson, *Making an Issue of Child Abuse: Political Agenda Setting for Social Problems* (Chicago: University of Chicago Press, 1984).

[15] Marcus Brewer and Maxwell McCombs, 'Setting the community agenda', *Journalism and Mass Communication Quarterly*, 73 (1996): 7-16.

[16] David Protess, Fay Cook, Jack Doppelt, James Ettema, Margaret Gordon, Donna Leff, and Peter Miller, *The Journalism of Outrage: Investigative Reporting and Agenda Building in America* (New York: Guilford, 1991). 也可见 David Protess and Maxwell McCombs, eds., *Agenda Setting: Readings on Media, Public Opinion, and Policymaking* (Hillsdale, NJ: Lawrence Erlbaum, 1991), esp. part Ⅳ。

[17] Peter van Aelst and Stefaan Walgrave, 'Political agenda setting by the mass media.'

[18] Ibid., p. 174.

[19] Everett Rogers, James Dearing, and Soonbum Chang, 'AIDS in the 1980s: the agenda-setting process for a public issue', *Journalism Monographs*, 126 (1991).

[20] Craig Trumbo, 'Longitudinal modelling of public issues: an application of the agenda-setting process to the issue of global warming', *Journalism Monographs*, 152 (1995).

[21] Gonzenbach, *The Media, the President and Public Opinion*.

[22] Oscar J. Gandy, *Beyond Agenda Setting: Information Subsidies and Public Policy* (Norwood, NJ: Ablex, 1982); Jarol B. Manheim, *Strategic Public Diplomacy and American Foreign Policy: The Evolution of Influence* (New York: Oxford University Press, 1994), chapter 8; Judy VanSlyke Turk, 'Information subsidies and media content: a study of public relations influence on the news', *Journalism Monographs*, 100 (1986).

[23] Leon Sigal, *Reporters and Officials: The Organization and Politics of Newsmaking* (Lexington, MA: D. C. Heath, 1973), p. 121.

[24] Justin Lewis, Andrew Williams, and Bob Franklin, 'A compromised Fourth Estate? UK news journalism, public relations and news sources', *Journalism*

Studies, 9 (2008): 1–20. 引自 p. 7. 对于英国新闻业依赖公关材料的更多负面评估, 可见 Nick Davies, *Flat Earth News: An Award-winning Reporter Exposes Falsehood, Distortion and Propaganda in the Global Media* (London: Chatto and Windus, 2008)。

[25] Judy VanSlyke Turk, 'Public relations influence on the news', *Newspaper Research Journal*, 7 (1986): 15–27; Judy VanSlyke Turk, 'Information subsidies and influence', *Public Relations Review*, 11 (1985): 10–25.

[26] Ibid., 引自 p. 18。

[27] Daniel Jackson and Kevin Moloney, 'Inside churnalism: PR, journalism and power relationships in flux', *Journalism Studies*, 17 (2015): 1–18.

[28] Rogers, Dearing, and Chang, 'AIDS in the 1980s'; Liz Watts, 'Coverage of polio and AIDS: agenda setting in reporting cure research on polio and AIDS in newspapers, news magazines and network television', *Ohio Journalism Monograph Series* [School of Journalism, Ohio University], 4 (1993).

[29] Bent Flyvbjerg, Todd Landman, and Sanford Schram, eds., *Real Social Science: Applied Phronesis* (Cambridge: Cambridge University Press, 2012), chapter 7.

[30] Helen Ingram, H. Brinton Milward, and Wendy Laird, 'Scientists and agenda setting: advocacy and global warming', in *Risk and Society: The Interaction of Science, Technology and Public Policy*, ed. Marvin Waterstone (Dordrecht, the Netherlands: Springer, 1992); Spencer R. Weart, *The Discovery of Global Warming* (Cambridge, MA: Harvard University Press, 2008).

[31] Alison Anderson, 'Sources, media, and modes of climate change communication: the role of celebrities', *Wiley Interdisciplinary Reviews: Climate Change*, 2, (2011): 535–546.

[32] John V. Pavlik, *Public Relations: What Research Tells Us* (Newbury Park, CA: Sage, 1987), chapter 4.

[33] Jarol B. Manheim and R. B. Albritton, 'Changing national images: international public relations and media agenda setting', *American Political Science Review*, 73 (1984): 641–647. 另见 Spiro Kiousis and Xu Wu, 'International agenda-

building and agenda setting: exploring the influence of public relations counsel on US news media and public perceptions of foreign nations', *International Communication Gazette*, 70 (2008): 58-75。

[34] John C. Tedesco, 'Intercandidate agenda setting in the 2004 Democratic presidential primary', *American Behavioral Scientist*, 49 (2005): 92-113.

[35] *Political Public Relations: Principles and Applications*, eds. Jesper Stromback and Spiro Kiousis (New York: Routledge, 2011); Kathleen Hall Jamieson and Karlyn Kohrs Campbell, *The Interplay of Influence: News, Advertising, Politics and the Mass Media* (Belmont, CA: Wadsworth, 1992).

[36] Nicholas O'Shaughnessy, *The Phenomenon of Political Marketing* (London: Macmillan, 1990).

[37] Holli Semetko, Jay Blumler, Michael Gurevitch, and David Weaver, with Steve Barkin and G. C. Wilhoit, *The Formation of Campaign Agendas: A Comparative Analysis of Party and Media Roles in Recent American and British Elections* (Hillsdale, NJ: Lawrence Erlbaum, 1991).

[38] Semetko, Blumler, Gurevitch, and Weaver, *The Formation of Campaign Agendas*, p. 49. 引用材料来自 Michael Gurevitch and Jay Blumler, 'The construction of election news at the BBC: an observation study', in *Individuals in Mass Media Organizations: Creativity and Constraint*, eds. James Ettema and Charles Whitney (Beverly Hills, CA: Sage, 1982): 179-204。又见 Heinz Brandenburg, 'Who follows whom? The impact of parties on media agenda formation in the 1997 British general elections campaign', *Harvard International Journal of Press/Politics*, 7, 3 (2002): 34-54。

[39] Joseph Lelyveld, *New York Times*, 22 August 1999, p. 18.

[40] Mark Miller, Julie Andsager, and Bonnie Riechert, 'Framing the candidates in presidential primaries', *Journalism and Mass Communication Quarterly*, 75 (1998): 312-324. 这里和第三章报告的相关系数数据,均是2000年春季在得克萨斯大学奥斯汀分校由麦库姆斯组织的议程设置理论研讨班计算得到的。

[41] Robert Lichter and Ted Smith, 'Why elections are bad news: media and candidate discourse in the 1996 presidential primaries', *Harvard International Journal of Press/Politics*, 1, 4 (1996): 15–35.

[42] Thomas P. Boyle, 'Intermedia agenda setting in the 1996 presidential primaries', *Journalism and Mass Communication Quarterly*, 78 (2001): 26–44.

[43] John Tedesco, 'Issue and strategy agenda setting in the 2000 presidential primaries', unpublished paper, Virginia Technological University, 2001.

[44] Werner Wirth, Jörg Matthes, Christian Schemer, Martin Wettstein, Thomas Friemel, Regula Hänggli, and Gabriele Siegert, 'Agenda building and setting in a referendum campaign: investigating the flow of arguments among campaigners, the media, and the public', *Journalism and Mass Communication Quarterly*, 87 (2010): 328–345.

[45] Spiro Kiousis, Ji Young Kim, Matt Ragas, Gillian Wheat, Sarab Kochhar, Emma Svensson, and Maradith Miles, 'Exploring new frontiers of agenda building during the 2012 US presidential election pre-convention period: examining linkages across three levels', paper presented to the International Communication Association convention, London, 2013.

[46] Roland Burkart and Uta Russmann, 'Quality of understanding in political campaign communication: an analysis of political parties' press releases and media coverage in Austria (1970–2008)', working paper, University of Vienna, 2013.

[47] Michael Gurevitch and Jay Blumler, 'Political communication systems and democratic values', in *Democracy and the Mass Media*, ed. Judith Lichtenberg (Cambridge: Cambridge University Press, 1990), pp. 269–289. 另见 Davis Merritt and Maxwell McCombs, *The Two W's of Journalism* (Mahwah, NJ: Lawrence Erlbaum, 2003), chapter 6。

[48] Russell Dalton, Paul Allen Beck, Robert Huckfeldt, and William Koetzle, 'A test of media-centered agenda setting: newspaper content and public interests in a presidential election', *Political Communication*, 15 (1998): 463–481. 这篇文

章报告了在各种议程之间的原始零阶相关。在本章中,麦库姆斯引入了各种控制变量,计算得出了偏相关系数。

[49] Sungtae Ha, 'The intermediary role of news media in the presidential campaign: a mediator, moderator, or political agent?', unpublished paper, University of Texas at Austin, 2001. 关于这一模式在一次美国参议院选举中的重复验证,见 Jason Martin, 'Agenda setting, elections, and the impact of information technology', in *Agenda Setting in a 2.0 World*, ed. T. Johnson (New York: Routledge, 2013)。

[50] Spiro Kiousis, Soo-Yeon Kim, Michael McDevitt, and Ally Ostrowski, 'Competing for attention: information subsidy influence in agenda building during election campaigns', *Journalism and Mass Communication Quarterly*, 86 (2009): 545–562.

[51] Spiro Kiousis, Michael Mitrook, Xu Wu, and Trent Seltzer, 'First-and second-level agenda-building and agenda-setting effects: exploring the linkages among candidate news releases, media coverage, and public opinion during the 2002 Florida gubernatorial election', *Journal of Public Relations Research*, 18 (2006): 265–285.

[52] Marilyn Roberts and Maxwell McCombs, 'Agenda setting and political advertising: origins of the news agenda', *Political Communication*, 11 (1994): 249–262.

[53] Dixie Evatt and Tamara Bell, 'Upstream influences: the early press releases, agenda setting and politics of a future president', *Southwestern Mass Communication Journal*, 16, 2 (2001): 70–81. 又见 S. W. Dunn, 'Candidate and media agenda setting in the 2005 Virginia gubernatorial Election', *Journal of Communication*, 59 (2009): 635–652。

[54] Esteban López-Escobar, Juan Pablo Llamas, Maxwell McCombs, and Federico Rey Lennon, 'Two levels of agenda setting among advertising and news in the 1995 Spanish elections', *Political Communication*, 15 (1998): 225–238.

[55] Kenneth Bryan, 'Political communication and agenda setting in local races',

unpublished doctoral dissertation, University of Texas at Austin, 1997.

[56] Stuart Soroka, 'Issue attributes and agenda setting by media, the public, and policymakers in Canada', *International Journal of Public Opinion Research*, 14 (2002): 264-285. 关于加拿大八个主要议题的更广泛、更详细的分析,见 Stuart Soroka, *Agenda-Setting Dynamics in Canada* (Vancouver: UBC Press, 2002)。

[57] David Weaver and Swanzy Nimley Elliot, 'Who sets the agenda for the media? A study of local agenda-building', *Journalism Quarterly*, 62 (1985): 87-94.

[58] Ibid., p. 93.

[59] 也可见 Kyle Huckins, 'Interest-group influence on the media agenda: a case study', *Journalism and Mass Communication Quarterly*, 76 (1999): 76-86。

[60] Karen Callaghan and Frauke Schnell, 'Assessing the democratic debate: how the news media frame elite policy discourse', *Political Communication*, 18 (2001): 183-212.

[61] Ibid., p. 197.

[62] Penelope Ploughman, 'The creation of newsworthy events: an analysis of newspaper coverage of the man-made disaster at Love Canal', unpublished doctoral dissertation, State University of New York at Buffalo, 1984; Allen Mazur, 'Putting radon on the public risk agenda', *Science, Technology, and Human Values*, 12, 3-4 (1987): 86-93.

[63] Stephen Reese and Lucig Danielian, 'Intermedia influence and the drug issue', in *Communication Campaigns about Drugs*, ed. P. Shoemaker (Hillsdale, NJ: Lawrence Erlbaum, 1989), pp. 29-46.

[64] Jeongsub Lim, 'A cross-lagged analysis of agenda setting among online news media', *Journalism and Mass Communication Quarterly*, 83 (2006): 298-312.

[65] Warren Breed, 'Newspaper opinion leaders and the process of standardization', *Journalism Quarterly*, 32 (1955): 277-284, 328.

[66] Richard Kluger, *The Paper: The Life and Death of the New York Herald Tribune* (New York: Alfred A. Knopf, 1986).

[67] 例如,《今日美国》(*USA Today*)1A 版讲述的某个故事后来一跃而成"CBS 晚间新闻"的头条报道。见 Peter Pritchard, 'The McPapering of America: an insider's candid account', *Washington Journalism Revue* (1987): 32-37。还有一项个案研究,调查了关于某天主教神父不良行为的一篇新闻报道如何引发了其后四年潮水般的神职人员负面报道,见 Michael J. Breen, 'A cook, a cardinal, his priests, and the press: deviance as a trigger for intermedia agenda setting', *Journalism and Mass Communication Quarterly*, 74 (1997): 348-356。

[68] Timothy Crouse, *The Boys on the Bus* (New York: Ballantine, 1973), pp. 84-85.

[69] Trumbo, 'Longitudinal modelling of public issues.'

[70] David Gold and Jerry Simmons, 'News selection patterns among Iowa dailies', *Public Opinion Quarterly*, 29 (1965): 425-430.

[71] D. Charles Whitney and Lee Becker, '"Keeping the gates" for gatekeepers: the effects of wire news', *Journalism Quarterly*, 59 (1982): 60-65.

[72] Lee Becker, Maxwell McCombs, and Jack McLeod, 'The development of political cognitions', in *Political Communication: Issues and Strategies for Research*, ed. Steven Chaffee (Beverly Hills, CA: Sage, 1975), p. 39.

[73] 唐纳德·肖对经典把关研究中媒体间议程设置的相关系数进行了计算,报告见 Maxwell McCombs and Donald Shaw, 'Structuring the unseen environment', *Journal of Communication*, 26, spring (1976): 18-22。

[74] David Manning White, 'The "gate keeper": a case study in the selection of news', *Journalism Quarterly*, 27 (1950): 383-390.

[75] Paul Snider, 'Mr Gates revisited: a 1966 version of the 1949 case study', *Journalism Quarterly*, 44 (1967): 419-427.

[76] 关于肖的计算,见 McCombs and Shaw, 'Structuring the unseen environment'。

[77] Roberts and McCombs, 'Agenda setting and political advertising.'

[78] López-Escobar, Llamas, McCombs, and Lennon, 'Two levels of agenda setting among advertising and news in the 1995 Spanish elections.'

[79] Maxwell McCombs and Donald Shaw,'The agenda-setting function of mass media', *Public Opinion Quarterly*, 36 (1972): 183.

[80] Sebastián Valenzuela,'Agenda setting and journalism', in *Oxford Research Encyclopedia of Communication*, ed. Jon F. Nussbaum (New York, NY: Oxford University Press, 2019).

[81] Pablo Boczkowski, *News at Work: Imitation in an Age of Information Abundance* (Chicago: University of Chicago Press, 2010).

[82] Valenzuela,'Agenda setting and journalism.'

[83] Pu-Tsung King,'Issue agendas in the 1992 Taiwan legislative election', unpublished doctoral dissertation, University of Texas at Austin, 1994.

[84] Sebastián Valenzuela and Arturo Arriagada,'Competencia por la uniformidad en noticieros y diarios chilenos 2000–2005'[The competition for similarity in Chilean news broadcasts and newspapers 2000–2005], *Cuadernos. info*, 24 (2009): 41–52.

[85] Ramona Vonbun, Katharina Kleinen-von Königslöw, and Klaus Schoenbach,'Intermedia agenda-setting in a multimedia news environment', *Journalism*, 17 (2016): 1054–1073.

[86] Toshio Takeshita,'Agenda setting and framing: two dimensions of attribute agenda-setting', *Mita Journal of Sociology* [Japan], 12 (2007): 4–18. 这项调查重复并拓展了竹下的另一项研究,见 Takeshita,'Expanding attribute agenda setting into framing', paper presented to the International Communication Association, Seoul, Korea, 2002。第三章讨论过这篇文章。

[87] Marc Benton and P. Jean Frazier,'The agenda-setting function of the mass media at three levels of information-holding', *Communication Research*, 3 (1976): 2261–2274.

[88] Pu-Tsung King,'The press, candidate images, and voter perceptions', in *Communication and Democracy*, eds. M. McCombs, D. Shaw, and D. Weaver (Mahwah, NJ: Lawrence Erlbaum, 1997), pp. 29–40.

[89] Sitaram Asur, Bernardo A. Huberman, Gabor Szabo, and Chunyan Wang,

'Trends in social media: persistence and decay', Social Computing Lab Hewlett Packard, Palo Alto, CA (2011). 引自 p. 8。http://mashable.com/2011/02/14/twitter-trending-topics-hp/.

[90] 关于近期对博客和其他在线媒体的研究,有一篇全面回顾的文章,见 Hai Tran, 'Online agenda setting: a new frontier for theory development', in *Agenda Setting in a 2.0 World*, ed. T. Johnson (New York: Routledge, 2013)。关于媒介议程分殊与合流的研究案例,可见 Sharon Meraz, 'The fight for how to think: traditional media, social networks, and issue interpretation', *Journalism: Theory, Practice, and Criticism*, 12 (2011): 107-127; Jae Kook Lee, 'The effect of the internet on homogeneity of the media agenda: a test of the fragmentation thesis', *Journalism and Mass Communication Quarterly*, 84 (2007): 745-760。

[91] Matthew Ragas and Spiro Kiousis, 'Intermedia agenda-setting and political activism: MoveOn.org and the 2008 presidential election', *Mass Communication and Society*, 13 (2010): 560-583.

[92] Leonard Pitts, 'Objectivity might be impossible, so we strive for fairness', *Austin American-Statesman*, 17 December 2001, p. A13.

[93] Stuart N. Soroka, 'Schindler's List's intermedia influence: exploring the role of "entertainment" in media agenda-setting', *Canadian Journal of Communication*, 25 (2000): 211-230.

第八章 议程设置的后果

[1] Eugene F. Shaw, 'Agenda-setting and mass communication theory', *International Communication Gazette*, 25, 2 (1979): 101. 在这一领域中很早就开始尝试探索的一个创造性例子是,Lee Becker, 'The impact of issue saliences', in *The Emergence of American Political Issues*, eds. Donald Shaw and Maxwell McCombs (St Paul, MN: West, 1977), pp. 121-132。

[2] Carl Hovland, Irving Janis, and Harold Kelley, *Communication and Persuasion* (New Haven, CT: Yale University Press, 1953). 又见 Nathan Maccoby, 'The

new "scientific" rhetoric', in *The Science of Human Communication*, ed. Wilbur Schramm (New York: Basic Books, 1963), pp. 41-53。

[3] Shanto Iyengar and Donald R. Kinder, *News That Matters: Television and American Opinion* (Chicago: University of Chicago Press, 1987), p. 63. 虽然这本书中报告的证据只与电视新闻有关,但在括号中插入了"以及其他新闻媒体",这是因为,有充足的证据表明,在公众对公共部门表现的判断上,所有新闻媒体都可以发挥铺垫作用。

[4] Gerd Gigerenzer, Ralph Hertwig, and Thorsten Pachur, eds., *Heuristics: The Foundations of Adaptive Behavior* (New York: Oxford University Press, 2011).

[5] 对于启发式信息处理的一个经典陈述,见 Amos Tversky and Daniel Kahneman, 'Availability: a heuristic for judging frequency and probability', *Cognitive Psychology*, 5 (1973): 207-232。

[6] Iyengar and Kinder, *News That Matters*, chapters 7-11.

[7] 对媒介铺垫作用的另一种解释是"投射"假设,这种假说预测:接触议题相关新闻的公民对总统在此项议题上的评分,会向他们此前对总统表现的总体评价看齐。有研究者进行了一项基于人口的调查实验,以检验这些相互竞争的假设,结果显示:"因果箭头是从支持议题指向支持总体(亦即媒介铺垫),而非相反,从支持总体指向支持议题(亦即投射作用)。"见 Austin Hart and Joel A. Middleton, 'Priming under fire: reverse causality and the classic media priming hypothesis', *Journal of Politics*, 76 (2014): 581-592。引自 p. 581。

[8] Jon A. Krosnick and Donald R. Kinder, 'Altering the foundations of support for the president through priming', *American Political Science Review*, 84 (1990): 497-512.

[9] Ibid., p. 505.

[10] Nicholas A. Valentino, Vincent L. Hutchings, and Ismail K. White, 'Cues that matter: how political ads prime racial attitudes during campaigns', *American Political Science Review*, 96 (2002): 75-90.

[11] Diana C. Mutz, *Impersonal Influence: How Perceptions of Mass Collectives Affect Political Attitudes* (Cambridge, UK: Cambridge University Press, 1998).

[12] Sebastián Valenzuela, 'Variations in media priming: the moderating role of knowledge, interest, news attention, and discussion', *Journalism and Mass Communication Quarterly*, 86 (2009): 756-774.

[13] Jon A. Krosnick and Laura Brannon, 'The impact of war on the ingredients of presidential evaluations: George Bush and the Gulf conflict', *American Political Science Review*, 87 (1993): 963-975; Shanto Iyengar and Adam Simon, 'News coverage of the Gulf crisis and public opinion', in *Do the Media Govern?*, eds. Shanto Iyengar and Richard Reeves (Thousand Oaks, CA: Sage, 1997), pp. 248-257.

[14] 在美国之外进行的研究包括：Robert Anderson, 'Do newspapers enlighten preferences? Personal ideology, party choice, and the electoral cycle: the United Kingdom, 1992-1997', *Canadian Journal of Political Science*, 36 (2003): 601-619; David Nicolas Hopmann, Rens Vliegenthart, Claes de Vreese, and Erik Albaek, 'Effects of television news coverage: how visibility and tone influence party choice', *Political Communication*, 27 (2010): 389-405; Tamir Sheafer and Gabriel Weimann, 'Agenda building, agenda setting, priming, individual voting intentions, and the aggregate results: an analysis of four Israeli elections', *Journal of Communication*, 55 (2005): 347-365; Gunnar Thesen, Christoffer Green-Pedersen, and Peter B. Mortensen, 'Priming, issue ownership, and party support: the electoral gains of an issue-friendly media agenda', *Political Communication*, 34 (2017): 282-301。

[15] Scott L. Althaus and Young Mie Kim, 'Priming effects in complex information environments: reassessing the impact of news discourse on presidential approval', *Journal of Politics*, 68 (2006): 960-976.

[16] 见 Sungtae Ha, 'Attribute priming effects and presidential candidate evaluation: the conditionality of political sophistication', *Mass Communication and Society*, 14 (2011): 315-342; Sebastián Valenzuela, 'Variations in media priming'。

[17] Iyengar and Simon, 'News coverage of the Gulf crisis and public opinion', p. 250.

[18] 更多的讨论见 Lars Willnat, 'Agenda setting and priming: conceptual links and differences', in *Communication and Democracy*, eds. M. McCombs, D. Shaw, and D. Weaver (Mahwah, NJ: Lawrence Erlbaum, 1997), pp. 51-66。

[19] Iyengar and Simon, 'News coverage of the Gulf crisis and public opinion.'

[20] Frank R. Baumgartner and Bryan D. Jones, *Agendas and Instability in American Politics*, 2nd edn (Chicago: University of Chicago Press, 2009).

[21] Hans Mathias Kepplinger, Wolfgang Donsbach, Hans Bernd Brosius, and Joachim Friedrich Staab, 'Media tone and public opinion: a longitudinal study of media coverage and public opinion on Chancellor Kohl', *International Journal of Public Opinion Research*, 1 (1989): 326-342; Daron R. Shaw, 'The impact of news media favorability and candidate events in presidential campaigns', *Political Communication*, 16 (1999): 183-202.

[22] Sungtae Ha, 'Attribute priming effects and presidential candidate evaluation: the conditionality of political sophistication', *Mass Communication and Society*, 14 (2011): 315-342.

[23] 新闻报道与好评度的关系是或然而非必然的。如我们在第五章中看到的，对于克林顿/莱温斯基丑闻与特朗普弹劾案，媒介的属性铺垫影响未能奏效。见 Spiro Kiousis, 'Job approval and favorability: the impact of media attention to the Monica Lewinsky scandal on public opinion of President Bill Clinton', *Mass Communication and Society*, 6 (2003): 435-451。

[24] Esteban López-Escobar, Maxwell McCombs, and Antonio Tolsá, 'Measuring the public images of political leaders: a methodological contribution of agenda-setting theory', paper presented to the Congress for Political Communication Investigation, Madrid, 2007.

[25] Kihan Kim and Maxwell McCombs, 'News story descriptions and the public's opinions of political candidates', *Journalism and Mass Communication Quarterly*, 84 (2007): 299-314.

[26] Meital Balmas and Tamir Sheafer, 'Candidate image in election campaigns: attribute agenda setting, affective priming, and voting intentions', *International*

[27] *Journal of Public Opinion Research*, 22 (2010): 204-229. 又可见 Tamir Sheafer, 'How to evaluate it: the role of story-evaluation tone in agenda setting and priming', *Journal of Communication*, 57 (2007): 21-39。

[27] Stuart Soroka, 'Good news and bad news: asymmetric responses to economic information', *Journal of Politics*, 68 (2006): 372-385. 针对经济议题的其他一些研究,见 Deborah J. Blood and Peter C. B. Phillips, 'Economic headline news on the agenda: new approaches to understanding causes and effects', in *Communication and Democracy*, eds. McCombs, Shaw, and Weaver, pp. 97-114; Joe Bob Hester and Rhonda Gibson, 'The economy and second-level agenda setting: a time-series analysis of economic news and public opinion about the economy', *Journalism and Mass Communication Quarterly*, 80 (2003): 73-90。

[28] Gunho Lee, 'Who let priming out? Analysis of first and second-level agenda-setting effects on priming', *International Communication Gazette*, 72 (2010): 759-776.

[29] Victoria Y. Chen and Paromita Pain, 'What changed public opinion on the same-sex marriage issue? New implications of attribute measures and attribute priming in media agenda setting', *Newspaper Research Journal*, 39 (2018): 453-469.

[30] Spiro Kiousis, 'Agenda-setting and attitudes: exploring the impact of media salience on perceived salience and public attitude strength of US presidential candidates from 1984 to 2004', *Journalism Studies*, 12 (2011): 359-374.

[31] Spiro Kiousis and Maxwell McCombs, 'Agenda-setting effects and attitude strength: political figures during the 1996 presidential election', *Communication Research*, 31 (2004): 36-57.

[32] Natalie J. Stroud and Kate Kenski, 'From agenda setting to refusal setting: survey nonresponse as a function of media coverage across the 2004 election cycle', *Public Opinion Quarterly*, 71 (2007): 539-559.

[33] Patrick Rössler and Michael Schenk, 'Cognitive bonding and the German reunification: agenda-setting and persuasion effects of mass media', *International*

Journal of Public Opinion Research, 12 (2000): 29-47.

[34] Elihu Katz, 'Media effects', in *International Encyclopedia of the Social and Behavioral Sciences*, eds. Neil J. Smelser an Paul B. Baltes (Oxford, UK: Elsevier, 2001), pp. 9472-9479. 引自 p. 9472。

[35] *New York Times*, 17 January 1989, p. 22. 在国际层面,国际人口传播协会(PCI)曾经协助制作一系列电视节目,涉及全球发展中国家的计划生育、艾滋病预防、性别平等,以及其他各种社会话题。见 Doris A. Graber, *Processing Politics: Learning from Television in the Internet Age* (Chicago: University of Chicago Press, 2001), p. 127。

[36] Kimberly K. Ma, William Schaffner, C. Colmenares, J. Howser, J. Jones, and K. A. Poehling, 'Influenza vaccinations of young children increased with media coverage in 2003', *Pediatrics*, 117 (2006): 157-163.

[37] Craig Trumbo, 'The effect of newspaper coverage of influenza on the rate of physician visits for influenza 2002-2008', *Mass Communication and Society*, 15 (2012): 718-738.

[38] 调查报告见 Maxwell McCombs and Donald Shaw, 'A progress report on agenda-setting research', paper presented to the Association for Education in Journalism, San Diego, CA, 1974。

[39] Marilyn Roberts, 'Predicting voter behavior via the agenda setting tradition', *Journalism Quarterly*, 69 (1992): 878-892; Marilyn Roberts, Ronald Anderson, and Maxwell McCombs, '1990 Texas gubernatorial campaign influence of issues and images', *Mass Communication Review*, 21 (1994): 20-35. 关于美国之外的应用研究,见 Sebastián Valenzuela and Maxwell McCombs, 'Agenda-setting effects on vote choice: evidence from the 2006 Mexican election', paper presented to the annual meeting of the International Communication Association, San Francisco, 2007。

[40] John R. Petrocik, 'Issue ownership in presidential elections with a 1980 case study', *American Journal of Political Science*, 40 (1996): 825-850. 又见 John Petrocik, William Benoit, and G. J. Hansen, 'Issue ownership and presidential

campaigning, 1952 – 2000', *Political Science Quarterly*, 118 (2003): 599 – 626。

[41] Riccardo Puglisi, 'The spin doctor meets the rational voter: electoral competition with agenda-setting effects', available at SSRN: https://ssrn.com/abstract = 581881(2004).

[42] Spiro Kiousis, Mike McDevitt, and Xu Wu, 'The genesis of civic awareness: agenda setting in political socialization', *Journal of Communication*, 55 (2005): 756 – 774; Spiro Kiousis and Michael McDevitt, 'Agenda setting in civic development: effects of curricula and issue importance on youth voter turnout', *Communication Research*, 35 (2008): 481 – 502.

[43] 有一项关于议程设置对选举之外的政治参与的非直接效果的研究，见 Soo Jung Moon, 'Attention, attitude, and behavior: second-level agenda-setting effects as a mediator of media use and political participation', *Communication Research*, 40 (2013): 698 – 719。

[44] H. Denis Wu and Renita Coleman, 'Advancing agenda-setting theory: the comparative strength and new contingent conditions of the two levels of agenda-setting effects', *Journalism and Mass Communication Quarterly*, 86 (2009): 775 – 789.

[45] Lindita Camaj, 'The consequences of attribute agenda-setting effects for political trust, participation, and protest behaviour', *Journal of Broadcasting and Electronic Media*, 58 (2014): 634 – 654.

[46] Robert L. Stevenson, Rainer Böhme, and Nico Nickel, 'The TV agenda-setting influence on campaign 2000', *Egyptian Journal of Public Opinion Research*, 2, 1 (2001): 29 – 50.

[47] Tsuneo Ogawa, 'Framing and agenda setting function', *Keio Communication Review*, 23 (2001): 71 – 80.

[48] 关于媒体报道的数量与人们讨论和思考选举新闻的程度的变化的一致性，进一步的证据可见 Thomas E. Patterson, *The Vanishing Voter: Public Involvement in an Age of Uncertainty* (New York: Alfred A. Knopf, 2002)。

[49] David H. Weaver, 'Issue salience and public opinion: are there consequences

of agenda-setting?', *International Journal of Public Opinion Research*, 3 (1991):53-68.

[50] Nancy Kieffer, 'Agenda-setting and corporate communication issues: can the mass media influence corporate stock prices?', unpublished master's thesis, Syracuse University, 1983.

[51] Craig Carroll, ed., *Corporate Reputation and the News Media: Agenda-setting within News Coverage in Developed, Emerging, and Frontier Markets* (New York: Routledge, 2011). 又见 M. M. Meijer and Jan Kleinnijenhuis, 'Issue news and corporate reputation: applying the theories of agenda setting and issue ownership in the field of business communication', *Journal of Communication*, 56 (2006): 543-559; Craig Carroll, 'The relationship between media favorability and firms' public esteem', *Public Relations Journal*, 3-4 (2010): 1-32。

[52] Spiro Kiousis, Cristina Popescu, and Michael Mitrook, 'Understanding influence on corporate reputation: an examination of public relations efforts, media coverage, public opinion, and financial performance from an agenda building and agenda-setting perspective', *Journal of Public Relations Research*, 19 (2007): 147-165.

[53] 由网络分析定义的第三层面议程设置的根源,可见于 Craig Carroll, 'How the mass media influence perceptions of corporate reputation: exploring agenda-setting effects within business news coverage', unpublished doctoral dissertation, University of Texas at Austin, 2004。

[54] Coy Callison, 'Media relations and the internet: how Fortune 500 company websites assist journalists in news gathering', *Public Relations Review*, 29 (2003): 29-41.

[55] Matthew Ragas, 'Issue and stakeholder intercandidate agenda setting among corporate information subsidies', *Journalism and Mass Communication Quarterly*, 89 (2012): 91-111; Coral Ohl, J. David Pincus, Tony Rimmer and Denise Harison, 'Agenda building role of news releases in corporate takeovers', *Public Relations Review*, 21 (1995): 89-101.

第九章 传播与社会

[1] Harold Lasswell, 'The structure and function of communication in society', in *The Communication of Ideas*, ed. Lyman Bryson (New York: Institute for Religious and Social Studies, 1948), pp. 37-51.

[2] Jian-Hua Zhu with William Boroson, 'Susceptibility to agenda setting', in *Communication and Democracy*, eds. M. McCombs, D. Shaw, and D. Weaver (Mahwah, NJ: Lawrence Erlbaum, 1997), p. 82.

[3] 对那些熟悉涵化理论的学者而言,这一过程与"主流化"类似。它发生于接触电视和其他媒介之后,从而减少了"不同群体的回答中发现的差异,而这些差异与不同群体的文化、社会和政治特征相关"。Nancy Signorielli, Michael Morgan, and James Shanahan, 'Cultivation analysis: research and practice', in *An Integrated Approach to Communication Theory and Research*, 3rd edn, eds., Don W. Stacks, Michael B. Salwen, and Kristen C. Eichhorn (New York, NY: Routledge, 2019), pp. 113-125. 引自 p. 121。不过,在议程设置理论看来,"主流化"的过程是有益的,它使共识得以建立。但在涵化理论中,"主流化"却与同质化的、常常扭曲公众感知的扩散相联系。

[4] Donald Shaw and Shannon Martin, 'The function of mass media agenda setting', *Journalism Quarterly*, 69 (1992): 902-920.

[5] Ching-Yi Chiang, 'Bridging and closing the gap of our society: social function of media agenda setting', unpublished master's thesis, University of Texas at Austin, 1995; Esteban López-Escobar, Juan Pablo Llamas, and Maxwell McCombs, 'Una dimensión social de los efectos de los medios de difusión: agenda-setting y consenso' ['A social dimension of media effects: agenda-setting and consensus'] *Comunicación y Sociedad* IX (1996): 91-125; Esteban López-Escobar, Juan Pablo Llamas, and Maxwell McCombs, 'Agenda setting and community consensus: first and second level effects', *International Journal of Public Opinion Research*, 10 (1998): 335-348.

[6] Vanessa de Macedo Higgins Joyce, 'Consensus-building function of agenda setting in times of crisis: substantive and affective dimensions', in *Agenda Setting in a 2.0 World*, ed. Thomas J. Johnson (New York: Routledge, 2013).

[7] David Weaver, Doris Graber, Maxwell McCombs, and Chaim Eyal, *Media Agenda Setting in a Presidential Election: Issues, Images and Interest* (Westport, CT: Greenwood, 1981).

[8] Joseph Cappella and Kathleen Hall Jamieson, *Spiral of Cynicism: The Press and the Public Good* (New York: Oxford University Press, 1997); Thomas E. Patterson, *Out of Order* (New York: Random House Vintage Books, 1993).

[9] Kyle Huckins, 'Interest-group influence on the media agenda', *Journalism and Mass Communication Quarterly*, 76 (1999): 76–86.

[10] Judith Buddenbaum, 'The media, religion, and public opinion: toward a unified theory of cultural influence', in *Religion and Popular Culture: Studies in the Interaction of Worldviews*, eds. Daniel A. Stout and Judith Buddenbaum (Ames: Iowa State University Press, 2001), p. 27.

[11] Jacqueline Harris and Maxwell McCombs, 'The interpersonal/mass communication interface among church leaders', *Journal of Communication*, 22 (1972): 257–262.

[12] Moshe Hellinger and Tsuriel Rashi, 'The Jewish custom of delaying communal prayer: a view from communication theory', *Review of Rabbinic Judaism*, 12 (2009): 189–203.

[13] 例如,见 Michael Robinson, 'Collective memory: from the 20s through the 90s: the way we think we were', *Public Perspective*, 11, 1 (2000): 14–19, 44–47。

[14] Kurt Lang, Gladys Engel Lang, Hans Mathias Kepplinger, and Simone Ehmig, 'Collective memory and political generations: a survey of German journalists', *Political Communication*, 10 (1993): 211–229.

[15] Yoram Peri, 'The media and collective memory of Yitzhak Rabin's remembrance', *Journal of Communication*, 49, 3 (1999): 106–124.

[16] Neta Kliger-Vilenchik, 'Memory setting: applying agenda setting theory to the

study of collective memory' in *On Media Memory: Collective Memory in a New Media Age*, eds. Motti Neiger, Oren Meyers and Eyal Zandberg (London: Palgrave Macmillan, 2011), pp. 226-237.

[17] Asya Besova and Skye Chance Cooley, 'Foreign news and public opinion: attribute agenda-setting theory revisited', *Ecquid Novi: African Journalism Studies*, 30 (2009): 219-242.

[18] 一项分析国家层面议程设置的早期研究,可见 Wayne Wanta, Guy Golan, and Cheolhan Lee, 'Agenda setting and international news: media influence on public perception of foreign nations', *Journalism and Mass Communication Quarterly*, 81 (2004): 364-377。

[19] Raquel Rodriguez Díaz, 'Los profesores universitarios como medios de comunicación: la agenda setting de los alumnos y profesores' [University professors as communication media: agenda setting of students and professors], unpublished doctoral dissertation, Complutense University of Madrid, 2000.

[20] 引自 John Fortunato, *The Ultimate Assist: The Relationship and Broadcasting Strategies of the NBA and Television Networks* (Cresskill, NJ: Hampton Press, 2001), p. 2。

[21] Fortunato, *The Ultimate Assist*.

[22] Philemon Bantimaroudis, Stelios Zyglidopoulos, and Pavlos Symeou, 'Greek museum media visibility and museum visitation: an exploration of cultural agenda setting', *Journal of Communication*, 60 (2010): 743-757; Stelios Zyglidopoulos, Pavlos Symeou, Philemon Bantimaroudis, and Eleni Kampanellou, 'Cultural agenda setting: media attributes and public attention of Greek museums', *Communication Research*, 39 (2012): 480-498.

[23] Pavlos C. Symeou, Philemon Bantimaroudis and Stelios C. Zyglidopoulos, 'Cultural agenda setting and the role of critics: an empirical examination in the market for art-house films', *Communication Research*, 42 (2015): 732-754.

[24] Lisa Weidman, 'Consumer knowledge about Oregon wines: applying agenda setting theory to the dissemination of information about consumer products', paper

presented to the Midwest Association for Public Opinion Research, Chicago, 2011.

[25] Shanto Iyengar, 'A typology of media effects', in the *Oxford Handbook of Political Communication*, eds., Kate Kenski and Kathleen Hall Jamieson (New York: Oxford University Press, 2017), pp. 59-68. 引自 p. 66。

参 考 文 献

Ader, Christine, 'A longitudinal study of agenda setting for the issue of environmental pollution', *Journalism and Mass Communication Quarterly*, 72 (1995): 300–11.
Althaus, Scott L. and David Tewksbury, 'Agenda setting and the "new" news: patterns of issue importance among readers of the paper and online versions of the *New York Times*', *Communication Research*, 29 (2002): 180–207.
Althaus, Scott L. and Young Mie Kim, 'Priming effects in complex information environments: reassessing the impact of news discourse on presidential approval', *Journal of Politics*, 68 (2006): 960–76.
Anderson, Alison, 'Sources, media, and modes of climate change communication: the role of celebrities', *Wiley Interdisciplinary Reviews: Climate Change*, 2 (2011): 535–46.
Anderson, John R., *The Architecture of Cognition* (Cambridge, MA: Harvard University Press: 1983).
Anderson, Robert, 'Do newspapers enlighten preferences? Personal ideology, party choice, and the electoral cycle: the United Kingdom, 1992–1997', *Canadian Journal of Political Science*, 36 (2003): 601–619.
Asur, Sitaram, Bernardo A. Huberman, Gabor Szabo, and Chunyan Wang, 'Trends in social media: persistence and decay', Social Computing Lab Hewlett Packard, Palo Alto, CA (2011).
Atwater, Tony, Michael Salwen, and Ronald Anderson, 'Interpersonal discussion as a potential barrier to agenda setting', *Newspaper Research Journal*, 6, 4 (1985): 37–43.
Balmas, Meital and Tamir Sheafer, 'Candidate image in election campaigns: attribute agenda setting, affective priming, and voting intentions', *International Journal of Public Opinion Research*, 22 (2010): 204–29.
Bantimaroudis, Philemon, Stelios Zyglidopoulos, and Pavlos Symeou, 'Greek museum media visibility and museum visitation: an exploration of cultural agenda setting', *Journal of Communication*, 60 (2010): 743–57.
Barberá, Pablo, Andreu Casas, Jonathan Nagler, Patrick J. Egan, Richard Bonneau, John T. Jost,, and Joshua A. Tucker, 'Who leads? Who follows? Measuring issue attention and agenda setting by legislators and the mass public using social media data', *American Political Science Review*, 113 (2019): 883–901.

Barro, Robert J. and Jong-Wha Lee, 'A new data set of educational attainment in the world, 1950–2010', *Journal of Development Economics*, 104 (2013): 184–98.

Bartels, Larry M., *Unequal Democracy: The Political Economy of the New Gilded Age*, 2nd edn (New York: Russell Sage Foundation, 2016).

Baumgartner, Frank R. and Bryan D. Jones, *Agendas and Instability in American Politics*, 2nd edn (Chicago: University of Chicago Press, 2009).

Becker, Lee, 'The impact of issue saliences', in *The Emergence of American Political Issues*, eds. Donald Shaw and Maxwell McCombs (St Paul, MN: West, 1977), pp. 121–32.

Becker, Lee, Maxwell McCombs and Jack McLeod, 'The development of political cognitions', in *Political Communication: Issues and Strategies for Research*, ed. Steven Chaffee (Beverly Hills, CA: Sage, 1975), pp. 21–63.

Becker, Lee and Maxwell McCombs, 'The role of the press in determining voter reactions to presidential primaries', *Human Communication Research*, 4 (1978): 301–7.

Bennett, W. Lance and Shanto Iyengar, 'A new era of minimal effects? The changing foundations of political communication', *Journal of Communication*, 58 (2008): 707–31.

Benton, Marc and P. Jean Frazier, 'The agenda-setting function of the mass media at three levels of information-holding', *Communication Research*, 3 (1976): 261–74.

Besova, Asya and Skye Chance Cooley, 'Foreign news and public opinion: attribute agenda-setting theory revisited', *Ecquid Novi: African Journalism Studies*, 30 (2009): 219–42.

Bettag, Tom, 'What's news? Evolving definitions of news', *Harvard International Journal of Press/Politics*, 5, 3 (2000): 105–107.

Birkland, Thomas, *After Disaster: Agenda Setting, Public Policy, and Focusing Events* (Washington, DC: Georgetown University Press, 1997).

Blood, Warwick, 'Competing models of agenda setting: issue obtrusiveness vs. media exposure', paper presented to the Association for Education in Journalism, Boston, 1980.

Blood, Warwick, 'Unobtrusive issues in the agenda-setting role of the press', unpublished doctoral dissertation, Syracuse University, 1981.

Blumler, Jay G., 'The role of theory in uses and gratifications research', *Communication Research*, 6 (1979): 9–36.

Boczkowski, Pablo J., *News at Work: Imitation in an Age of Information Abundance* (Chicago: University of Chicago Press, 2010).

Boukes, Mark, 'Agenda setting with satire: how political satire increased TTIP'S saliency on the public, media, and political agenda', *Political Communication*, 36 (2019): 426–51.

Bouza, Fermín, 'The impact area of Political Communication: citizenship faced with public discourse', *International Review of Sociology*, 14 (2004): 245–59.

Boyle, Thomas P., 'Intermedia agenda setting in the 1996 presidential primaries', *Journalism and Mass Communication Quarterly*, 78 (2001): 26–44.

Boynton, G. R. and Glenn W. Richardson, Jr, 'Agenda setting in the twenty-first century', *New Media and Society*, 18 (2016): 1916–34.

Brandenburg, Heinz, 'Who follows whom? The impact of parties on media agenda formation in the 1997 British general elections campaign', *Harvard International Journal of Press/Politics*, 7, 3 (2002): 34–54.

Breed, Warren, 'Newspaper opinion leaders and the process of standardization', *Journalism Quarterly*, 32 (1955): 277–84, 328.

Breed, Warren, 'Social control in the newsroom', *Social Forces*, 33 (May 1955): 326–35.

Breen, Michael J., 'A cook, a cardinal, his priests, and the press: deviance as a trigger for intermedia agenda setting', *Journalism and Mass Communication Quarterly*, 74 (1997): 348–56.

Brewer, Marcus and Maxwell McCombs, 'Setting the community agenda', *Journalism and Mass Communication Quarterly*, 73 (1996): 7–16.

Brosius, Hans Bernd and Hans Mathias Kepplinger, 'The agenda setting function of television news: static and dynamic views', *Communication Research*, 17 (1990): 183–211.

Browne, Magdalena and Sebastián Valenzuela, 'Temor a la delincuencia en Chile' ['Fear of crime in Chile'], in *Seguridad, medios y miedos [(In)Security, media and fears]*, eds. Brenda Focás and Omar Rincón (Buenos Aires: Ediciones Imago Mundi, 2018), pp. 63–84.

Bryan, Kenneth, 'Political Communication and agenda setting in local races', unpublished doctoral dissertation, University of Texas at Austin, 1997.

Buddenbaum, Judith, 'The media, religion, and public opinion: toward a unified theory of cultural influence', in *Religion and Popular Culture: Studies in the Interaction of Worldviews*, eds. Daniel A. Stout and Judith Buddenbaum (Ames: Iowa State University Press, 2001).

Bulkow, Kristin, Juliane Urban, and Wolfgang Schweiger, 'The duality of agenda-setting: the role of information processing', *International Journal of Public Opinion Research*, 25 (2012): 43–63.

Burkart, Roland and Uta Russmann, 'Quality of understanding in political campaign communication: an analysis of political parties' press releases and media coverage in Austria (1970–2008)', working paper, University of Vienna, 2013.

Cacciatore, Michael, Dietram Scheufele, and Shanto Iyengar, 'The end of framing as we know it…and the future of media effects', *Mass Communication and Society*, 19 (2016): 7–23.

Callaghan, Karen and Frauke Schnell, 'Assessing the democratic debate: how the news media frame elite policy discourse', *Political Communication*, 18 (2001): 183–212.

Callison, Coy, 'Media relations and the internet: how *Fortune* 500 company websites assist journalists in news gathering', *Public Relations Review*, 29 (2003): 29–41.

Camaj, Lindita, 'Need for orientation, selective exposure, and attribute agenda-setting effects', *Mass Communication and Society*, 17 (2014): 689–712.

Camaj, Lindita, 'The consequences of attribute agenda-setting effects for political trust, participation, and protest behaviour', *Journal of Broadcasting and Electronic Media*, 58 (2014): 634–54.

Camaj, Lindita, 'Motivational theories of agenda-setting effects: an information selection and processing model of attribute agenda-setting', *International Journal of Public Opinion Research*, 31 (2019): 441–62.

Canel, Maria José, Juan Pablo Llamas, and Federico Rey, 'El primer nivel del efecto agenda setting en la información local: los "problemas más importantes" de la ciudad de Pamplona' ['The first level agenda setting effect on local information: the "most important problems" of the city of Pamplona'], *Comunicación y Sociedad*, 9, 1 and 2 (1996): 17–38.

Cao, Xiaoxia, 'Hearing it from Jon Stewart: the impact of The Daily Show on public attentiveness to politics', *International Journal of Public Opinion Research*, 22 (2010): 26–46.

Cappella, Joseph and Kathleen Hall Jamieson, *Spiral of Cynicism: The Press and the Public Good* (New York: Oxford University Press, 1997).

Cardenal, Ana S., Carol Galais, and Silvia Majó-Vázquez, 'Is Facebook eroding the public agenda? Evidence from survey and web-tracking data', *International Journal of Public Opinion Research*, 31 (2019): 589–608.

Carroll, Craig E., 'How the mass media influence perceptions of corporate reputation: exploring agenda-setting effects within business news coverage', unpublished doctoral dissertation, University of Texas at Austin, 2004.

Carroll, Craig E., 'The relationship between media favorability and firms' public esteem', *Public Relations Journal*, 3–4 (2010): 1–32.

Carroll, Craig E., ed., *Corporate Reputation and the News Media: Agenda-setting within News Coverage in Developed, Emerging, and Frontier Markets* (New York: Routledge, 2011).

Carter, Richard F., 'Communication and affective relations', *Journalism Quarterly*, 42 (1965): 203–212.

Casermeiro de Pereson, Alicia, *Los medios en las elecciones: la agenda setting en la ciudad de Buenos Aires* [The media in the elections: agenda setting in the city of Buenos Aires] (Buenos Aires, Argentina, EDUCA, 2003).

Caspi, Dan, 'The agenda-setting function of the Israeli press', *Knowledge: Creation, Diffusion, Utilization*, 3 (1982): 401–14.

Caudill, Edward, 'An agenda-setting perspective on historical public opinion', in *Communication and Democracy*, eds. Maxwell McCombs, Donald Shaw, and David Weaver (Mahwah, NJ: Lawrence Erlbaum, 1997), p. 179.

Chaffee, Steven H. and Donna G. Wilson, 'Media rich, media poor: two studies of diversity in agenda-holding', *Journalism Quarterly*, 54 (1977): 466–76.

Chaffee, Steven H. and M. Metzger, 'The end of mass communication?', *Mass Communication and Society*, 4 (2001): 365–79.

Chen, Victoria Y. and Paromita Pain, 'What changed public opinion on the same-sex marriage issue? New implications of attribute measures and attribute priming in media agenda setting', *Newspaper Research Journal*, 39 (2018): 453–69.

Chernov, Gennadiy, Sebastián Valenzuela, and Maxwell McCombs, 'An experimental comparison of two perspectives on the concept of need for orientation in agenda-setting theory', *Journalism and Mass Communication Quarterly*, 88 (2011): 142–55.

Chiang, Ching-Yi, 'Bridging and closing the gap of our society: social function of media agenda setting', unpublished master's thesis, University of Texas at Austin, 1995.

Cobb, Roger W., and Charles D. Elder, *Participation in American Politics: The Dynamics of Agenda-Building* (Baltimore: Johns Hopkins University Press, 1972).

Cohen, Bernard C., *The Press and Foreign Policy* (Princeton, NJ: Princeton University Press, 1963).

Cohen, David, 'A report on a non-election agenda setting study', paper presented to the Association for Education in Journalism, Ottawa, Canada, 1975.

Coleman, Renita and Stephen Banning, 'Network TV news' affective framing of the presidential candidates: evidence for a second-level agenda-setting effect through visual framing', *Journalism and Mass Communication Quarterly*, 83 (2006): 313–28.

Coleman, Renita and Maxwell McCombs, 'The young and agenda-less? Age-related differences in agenda setting on the youngest generation, baby boomers, and the civic generation', *Journalism and Mass Communication Quarterly*, 84 (2007): 495–508.

Coleman, Renita and H. Denis Wu, 'Proposing emotion as a dimension of affective agenda setting: separating affect into two components and comparing their second-level effects', *Journalism and Mass Communication Quarterly*, 87 (2010): 315–27.

Collins, Allan M. and Elizabeth F. Loftus, 'A spreading activation theory of semantic processing', *Psychological Review*, 82 (1975): 402–8.

Conway, Michael and Jeffrey R. Patterson, 'Today's top story? An agenda setting and recall experiment involving television and Internet news', *Southwestern Mass Communication Journal*, 24 (2008): 31–48.

Crouse, Timothy, *The Boys on the Bus* (New York: Ballantine, 1973).

Dalton, Russell J., Paul Allen Beck, Robert Huckfeldt, and William Koetzle, 'A test of media-centered agenda setting: newspaper content and public interests in a presidential election', *Political Communication*, 15 (1998): 463–81.

Davies, Nick, *Flat Earth News: An Award-Winning Reporter Exposes Falsehood, Distortion and Propaganda in the Global Media* (London: Chatto and Windus, 2008).

Dearing, James W. and Everett M. Rogers, *Agenda Setting* (Thousand Oaks, CA: Sage, 1996).

Djerf-Pierre, Monika and Adam Shehata, 'Still an agenda setter: Traditional news media and public opinion during the transition from low to high choice media environments', *Journal of Communication*, 67 (2017): 733–57.

Downs, Anthony, 'Up and down with ecology: the "issue-attention cycle"', *The Public Interest*, 28 (1972): 38–50.

Dunn, Scott W., 'Candidate and media agenda setting in the 2005 Virginia gubernatorial election', *Journal of Communication*, 59 (2009): 635–52.

Eaton, Jr, Howard, 'Agenda setting with bi-weekly data on content of three national media', *Journalism Quarterly*, 66 (1989): 942–8.

Edelstein, Alex, Youichi Ito, and Hans Mathias Kepplinger, *Communication and Culture: A Comparative Approach* (New York: Longman, 1989).

Edy, Jill A. and Patrick C. Meirick, 'The fragmenting public agenda: capacity, diversity, and volatility in responses to the "most important problem" question', *Public Opinion Quarterly*, 82 (2018): 661–85.

Einsiedel, Edna F., Kandice L. Salomone, and Frederick Schneider, 'Crime: effects of media exposure and personal experience on issue salience', *Journalism Quarterly*, 61 (1984): 131–6.

Erbring, Lutz, Edie Goldenberg and Arthur Miller, 'Front-page news and real-world cues', *American Journal of Political Science*, 24 (1980): 16–49.

Etter, Michael and Anne Vestergaard, 'Third level of agenda building and agenda setting during a corporate crisis', in *The Power of Information Networks*, eds. Lei Guo and Maxwell McCombs (New York: Routledge, 2016), pp. 175–89.

Evatt, Dixie and Salma Ghanem, 'Building a scale to measure salience', paper presented to the World Association for Public Opinion Research, Rome, Italy, 2001.

Evatt, Dixie and Tamara Bell, 'Upstream influences: the early press releases, agenda setting and politics of a future president', *Southwestern Mass Communication Journal*, 16, 2 (2001): 70–81.

Eyal, Chaim, James Winter, and William DeGeorge, 'The concept of time frame in agenda setting', in *Mass Communication Review Yearbook*, vol. 2, eds. G. Cleveland Wilhoit and Harold de Bock (Beverly Hills, CA: Sage, 1981), pp. 212–18.

Fan, David P., Kathy Keltner, and Robert Wyatt, 'A matter of guilt or innocence: how news reports affect support for the death penalty in the United States', *International Journal of Public Opinion Research*, 14 (2002): 439–52.

Feezell, Jessica T., 'Agenda setting through social media: the importance of incidental news exposure and social filtering in the digital era', *Political Research Quarterly*, 71 (2018): 482–94.

Flyvbjerg, Bent, Todd Landman, and Sanford Schram, eds., *Real Social Science: Applied Phronesis* (Cambridge: Cambridge University Press, 2012).

Folkerts, Jean Lange, 'William Allen White's anti-populist rhetoric as an agenda-setting technique', *Journalism Quarterly*, 60 (1983): 28–34.

Fortunato, John A., *The Ultimate Assist: The Relationship and Broadcasting Strategies of the NBA and Television Networks* (Cresskill, NJ: Hampton Press, 2001).

Frankel, Max, *The Times of My Life and My Life with The Times* (New York: Random House, 1999).

Frensch, Peter A., 'One concept, multiple meanings: on how to define the concept of implicit learning', in *Handbook of Implicit Learning*, eds. Michael A. Stadler and Peter A. Frensch (Thousand Oaks, CA: Sage, 1998), pp. 47–104.

Funkhouser, G. Ray, 'The issues of the sixties', *Public Opinion Quarterly*, 37 (1973): 62–75.

Gamson, William A., *Talking Politics* (New York: Cambridge University Press, 1992).

Gandy, Oscar J., *Beyond Agenda Setting: Information Subsidies and Public Policy* (Norwood, NJ: Ablex, 1982).

Gans, Herbert J., *Deciding What's News: A Study of CBS Evening News, NBC Nightly News, Newsweek and Time* (New York: Pantheon, 1979).

Geiß, Stefan, 'The media's conditional agenda setting power: how baselines and spikes of issue salience affect likelihood and strength of agenda setting', *Communication Research* (2019).

Gentzkow, Matthew, 'Small media, big impact: randomizing news stories reveals broad public impacts', *Science*, 358 (2017): 726–7.

Gerbner, George, Larry Gross, Michael Morgan, Nancy Signorielli, and James Shanahan, 'Growing up with television: cultivation processes', in *Media Effects: Advances in Theory and Research*, 2nd edn, eds. Jennings Bryant and Dolf Zillmann (Mahwah, NJ: Lawrence Erlbaum, 1994), pp. 43–68.

Gigerenzer, Gerd, Ralph Hertwig, and Thorsten Pachur, eds., *Heuristics: The Foundations of Adaptive Behavior* (New York: Oxford University Press, 2011).

Ghanem, Salma, 'Media coverage of crime and public opinion: an exploration of the second level of agenda setting', unpublished doctoral dissertation, University of Texas at Austin, 1996.

Ghanem, Salma, 'Filling in the tapestry: the second level of agenda-setting', in *Communication and Democracy*, eds. Maxwell McCombs, Donald Shaw, and David Weaver (Mahwah, NJ: Lawrence Erlbaum, 1997), pp. 3–14.

Gilberg, Sheldon, Chaim Eyal, Maxwell McCombs, and David Nicholas, 'The State of the Union address and the press agenda', *Journalism Quarterly*, 57 (1980): 584–8.

Glynn, J. Carroll, Michael Huge, James Reineke, Bruce Hardy, and James Shanahan, 'When Oprah intervenes: political correlates of daytime talk show viewing', *Journal of Broadcasting and Electronic Media*, 51 (2007): 228–44.

Gold, David, and Jerry Simmons, 'News selection patterns among Iowa dailies', *Public Opinion Quarterly*, 29 (1965): 425–30.

Gonzenbach, William, *The Media, the President, and Public Opinion: A Longitudinal Analysis of the Drug Issue, 1984–1991* (Mahwah, NJ: Lawrence Erlbaum, 1996).

Gordon, Margaret T. and Linda Heath, 'The news business, crime and fear', in *Reactions to Crime*, ed. Dan Lewis (Beverly Hills, CA: Sage, 1981).

Graber, Doris A., *Processing Politics: Learning from Television in the Internet Age* (Chicago: University of Chicago Press, 2001).

Grassau, Daniela, 'Has TV decreased impact on public opinion due to the transformations of the media environment in the 21st century?', paper presented to the International Association for Media and Communication Research, Madrid, 2019.

Groshek, Jacob and Megan Clough Groshek, 'Agenda-trending: reciprocity and the predictive capacity of social networking sites in intermedia agenda-setting across topics over time', *Media and Communication*, 1, 1, 2013: 15–27.

Gross, Kimberly and Sean Aday, 'The scary world in your living room and neighborhood: using local broadcast news, neighborhood crime rates, and personal experience to test agenda setting and cultivation', *Journal of Communication*, 53 (2003): 411–26.

Gruszczynski, Mike, 'Evidence of partisan agenda fragmentation in the American public, 1959–2015', *Public Opinion Quarterly*, 83 (2020): 749–81.

Gruszczynski, Mike and Michael W. Wagner, 'Information flow in the 21st century: the dynamics of agenda-uptake', *Mass Communication and Society*, 20 (2017): 378–402.

Gumpert, Gary and Robert Cathcart, eds., *Inter/Media: Interpersonal Communication in a Media World* (New York: Oxford University Press, 1986).

Guo, Lei, 'Toward the third level of agenda setting theory: A network agenda setting model', in Thomas J. Johnson, ed., *Agenda Setting in a 2.0 World* (New York: Routledge, 2013), pp. 112–33.

Guo, Lei and Maxwell McCombs, 'Network agenda setting: A third level of media effects', paper presented to the International Communication Association, Boston, 2011.

Guo, Lei and Maxwell McCombs, 'Toward the third-level agenda setting theory: A network agenda setting model', paper presented to the Association for Education in Journalism and Mass Communication, St Louis, 2011.

Guo, Lei, Yi-Ning Katherine Chen, Radoslaw Aksamit, Damian Guzek, Qian Wang, Hong Vu, and Maxwell McCombs, 'How the world pictured the Iraq War: a transnational network analysis', *Journalism Studies*, 16 (2015): 343–62.

Guo, Lei and Maxwell McCombs, eds. *The Power of Information Networks*: New Directions for Agenda Setting (New York: Routledge, 2016)

Gurevitch, Michael and Jay Blumler, 'The construction of election news at the BBC: an observation study', in *Individuals in Mass Media Organizations: Creativity and Constraint*, eds. James Ettema and Charles Whitney (Beverly Hills, CA: Sage, 1982): 179–204.

Gurevitch, Michael and Jay Blumler, 'Political communication systems and democratic values', in *Democracy and the Mass Media*, ed. Judith Lichtenberg (Cambridge: Cambridge University Press, 1990), pp. 269–89.

Ha, Sungtae, 'The intermediary role of news media in the presidential campaign: a mediator, moderator, or political agent?', unpublished paper, University of Texas at Austin, 2001.

Ha, Sungtae, 'Attribute priming effects and presidential candidate evaluation: the conditionality of political sophistication', *Mass Communication and Society*, 14 (2011): 315–42.

Hamilton, James T., *Channeling Violence: The Economic Market for Violent Television Programming* (Princeton, NJ: Princeton University Press, 1998).

Harder, Raymond A., Julie Sevenans, and Peter Van Aelst, 'Intermedia agenda setting in the social media age: How traditional players dominate the news agenda in election times', *Harvard International Journal of Press/Politics*, 22, 3 (2017): 275–293.

Harris, Jacqueline J. and Maxwell E. McCombs, 'The interpersonal/mass communication interface among church leaders', *Journal of Communication*, 22 (1972): 257–62.

Hart, Austin, and Joel A. Middleton, 'Priming under fire: reverse causality and the classic media priming hypothesis', *Journal of Politics*, 76 (2014): 581–92.

Hellinger, Moshe and Tsuriel Rashi, 'The Jewish custom of delaying communal prayer: a view from communication theory', *Review of Rabbinic Judaism*, 12 (2009): 189–203.

Herbst, Susan, 'The cultivation of conversation', in *The Poll with a Human Face: The National Issues Convention Experiment in Political Communication*, eds. Maxwell McCombs and Amy Reynolds (Mahwah, NJ: Lawrence Erlbaum, 1999).

Hester, Joe Bob and Rhonda Gibson, 'The economy and second-level agenda setting: a time-series analysis of economic news and public opinion about the economy', *Journalism and Mass Communication Quarterly*, 80 (2003): 73–90.

Hester, Joe Bob and Rhonda Gibson, 'The agenda setting function of national versus local media: a time-series analysis for the issue of same sex marriage', *Mass Communication and Society*, 10 (2007): 299–172.

Higgins Joyce, Vanessa de Macedo, 'Consensus-building function of agenda setting in times of crisis: substantive and affective dimensions', in *Agenda Setting in a 2.0 World*, ed. Thomas J. Johnson (New York: Routledge, 2013).

Holbrook, R. Andrew and Timothy Hill, 'Agenda setting and priming in prime time television: crime dramas as political cues', *Political Communication*, 22 (2005): 277–95.

Hopmann, David Nicolas, Rens Vliegenthart, Claes de Vreese, and Erik Albaek, 'Effects of television news coverage: how visibility and tone influence party choice', *Political Communication*, 27 (2010): 389–405.

Hovland, Carl, Irving Janis, and Harold Kelley, *Communication and Persuasion* (New Haven, CT: Yale University Press, 1953).

Huckins, Kyle, 'Interest-group influence on the media agenda: a case study', *Journalism and Mass Communication Quarterly*, 76 (1999): 76–86.

Hyun, Ki Deuk, and Soo Jung Moon, 'Agenda setting in the partisan TV news context: attribute agenda setting and polarized evaluation of presidential candidates among viewers of NBC, CNN, and Fox News', *Journalism and Mass Communication Quarterly*, 93 (2016): 509–29.

Inglehart, Ronald, *Culture Shift in Advanced Industrial Society* (Princeton, NJ: Princeton University Press, 1990).

Ingram, Helen, H. Brinton Milward, and Wendy Laird, 'Scientists and agenda setting: advocacy and global warming', in *Risk and Society: The Interaction of Science, Technology and Public Policy*, ed. Marvin Waterstone (Dordrecht, the Netherlands: Springer, 1992).

Iyengar, Shanto, 'A typology of media effects', in the *Oxford Handbook of Political Communication*, eds., Kate Kenski and Kathleen Hall Jamieson (New York: Oxford University Press, 2017), pp. 59–68.

Iyengar, Shanto and Donald R. Kinder, *News That Matters: Television and American Opinion* (Chicago, IL: University of Chicago Press, 1987).

Iyengar, Shanto and Adam Simon, 'News coverage of the Gulf crisis and public opinion', in *Do the Media Govern?*, eds. S. Iyengar and R. Reeves (Thousand Oaks, CA: Sage, 1997), pp. 248–57.

Jackson, Daniel and Kevin Moloney, 'Inside churnalism: PR, journalism and power relationships in flux', *Journalism Studies*, 17 (2015): 1–18.

Jamieson, Kathleen Hall and Karlyn Kohrs Campbell, *The Interplay of Influence:*

News, Advertising, Politics and the Mass Media (Belmont, CA: Wadsworth, 1992).

Jasperson, Amy, Dhavan Shah, Mark Watts, Ronald Faber, and David Fan, 'Framing and the public agenda: media effects on the importance of the federal budget deficit', *Political Communication*, 15 (1998): 205–24.

Jennings, Will and Christopher Wlezien, 'Distinguishing between most important problems and issues', *Public Opinion Quarterly*, 75 (2011): 545–55.

Johnson, Thomas J. and Wayne Wanta, with John T. Byrd and Cindy Lee, 'Exploring FDR's relationship with the press: a historical agenda-setting study', *Political Communication*, 12 (1995): 157–172.

Kahneman, Daniel, and Amos Tversky, 'Choices, values and frames', *American Psychologist*, 39 (1984): 341–50.

Kaplan, Stephen, 'Cognitive maps in perception and thought', in *Image and Environment: Cognitive Mapping and Spacial Behavior*, eds. Roger M. Downs and David Stea (Chicago: Aldine, 1973), pp. 63–78.

Katz, Elihu, 'Media effects', in *International Encyclopedia of the Social and Behavioral Sciences*, eds. Neil J. Smelser and Paul B. Baltes (Oxford, UK: Elsevier, 2001), pp. 9472–9.

Kepplinger, Hans Mathias and Herbert Roth, 'Creating a crisis: German mass media and oil supply in 1973–1974', *Public Opinion Quarterly*, 43 (1979): 285–96.

Kepplinger, Hans Mathias, Wolfgang Donsbach, Hans Bernd Brosius, and Joachim Friedrich Staab, 'Media tone and public opinion: a longitudinal study of media coverage and public opinion on Chancellor Kohl', *International Journal of Public Opinion Research*, 1 (1989): 326–42.

Key, V. O., *The Responsible Electorate: Rationality in Presidential Voting 1936–1960* (Cambridge, MA: Belknap Press of Harvard University Press, 1966).

Kieffer, Nancy, 'Agenda-setting and corporate communication issues: can the mass media influence corporate stock prices?', unpublished master's thesis, Syracuse University, 1983.

Kim, Joohan, Robert O. Wyatt, and Elihu Katz, 'News, talk, opinion, participation: the part played by conversation in deliberative democracy', *Political Communication*, 16 (1999): 361–85.

Kim, Kihan and Maxwell McCombs, 'News story descriptions and the public's opinions of political candidates', *Journalism and Mass Communication Quarterly*, 84 (2007): 299–314.

Kim, Sei-Hill, Dietram Scheufele, and James Shanahan, 'Think about it this way: Attribute agenda-setting function of the press and the public's evaluation of a local issue', *Journalism and Mass Communication Quarterly*, 79 (2002): 7–25.

Kim, Yeojin, Youngju Kim, and Shuhua Zhou, 'Theoretical and methodological trends of agenda-setting theory: A thematic analysis of the last four decades of research', *Agenda Setting Journal*, 1 (2017): 5–22.

King, Gary, Benjamin Schneer, and Ariel White, 'How the news media activate public expression and influence national agendas', *Science*, 358 (2017): 776–80.

King, Pu-Tsung, 'The press, candidate images, and voter perceptions', in *Communication and Democracy*, eds. Maxwell McCombs, Donald Shaw, and David Weaver (Mahwah, NJ: Lawrence Erlbaum, 1997), pp. 29–40.

Kiousis, Spiro, 'Job approval and favorability: the impact of media attention to the Monica Lewinsky scandal on public opinion of President Bill Clinton', *Mass Communication and Society*, 6 (2003): 435–51.

Kiousis, Spiro, 'Compelling arguments and attitude strength – exploring the impact of second-level agenda setting on public opinion of presidential candidate images', *Harvard International Journal of Press/Politics*, 10 (2005): 3–27.

Kiousis, Spiro, 'Agenda-setting and attitudes: exploring the impact of media salience on perceived salience and public attitude strength of US presidential candidates from 1984 to 2004', *Journalism Studies*, 12 (2011): 359–74.

Kiousis, Spiro, Philemon Bantimaroudis, and Hyun Ban, 'Candidate image attributes: experiments on the substantive dimension of second-level agenda setting', *Communication Research*, 26, 4 (1999): 414–28.

Kiousis, Spiro and Maxwell McCombs, 'Agenda-setting effects and attitude strength: political figures during the 1996 presidential election', *Communication Research*, 31 (2004): 36–57.

Kiousis, Spiro, Mike McDevitt, and Xu Wu, 'The genesis of civic awareness: agenda setting in political socialization', *Journal of Communication*, 55 (2005): 756–74.

Kiousis, Spiro, Michael Mitrook, Xu Wu, and Trent Seltzer, 'First and second-level agenda-building and agenda-setting effects: exploring the linkages among candidate news releases, media coverage, and public opinion during the 2002 Florida gubernatorial election', *Journal of Public Relations Research*, 18 (2006): 265–85.

Kiousis, Spiro, Cristina Popescu, and Michael Mitrook, 'Understanding influence on corporate reputation: an examination of public relations efforts, media coverage, public opinion, and financial performance from an agenda building and agenda-setting perspective', *Journal of Public Relations Research*, 19 (2007): 147–65.

Kiousis, Spiro and Michael McDevitt, 'Agenda setting in civic development: effects of curricula and issue importance on youth voter turnout', *Communication Research*, 35 (2008): 481–502.

Kiousis, Spiro and Xu Wu, 'International agenda-building and agenda setting: exploring the influence of public relations counsel on US news media and public perceptions of foreign nations', *International Communication Gazette*, 70 (2008): 58–75.

Kiousis, Spiro, Soo-Yeon Kim, Michael McDevitt, and Ally Ostrowski, 'Competing for attention: information subsidy influence in agenda building during election campaigns', *Journalism and Mass Communication Quarterly*, 86 (2009): 545–62.

Kiousis, Spiro and Jesper Stromback, 'The White House and public relations: examining the linkages between presidential communications and public opinion', *Public Relations Review*, 36 (2010): 7–14.

Kiousis, Spiro, Ji Young Kim, Matt Ragas, Gillian Wheat, Sarab Kochhar, Emma

Svensson, and Maradith Miles, 'Exploring new frontiers of agenda building during the 2012 US presidential election pre-convention period', *Journalism Studies*, 16 (2015): 363–82.

Klapper, Joseph T., *The Effects of Mass Communication* (New York: Free Press, 1960).

Kliger-Vilenchik, Neta, 'Memory setting: applying agenda setting theory to the study of collective memory' in *On Media Memory: Collective Memory in a New Media Age*, eds. Motti Neiger, Oren Meyers, and Eyal Zandberg (London: Palgrave Macmillan, 2011), pp. 226–37.

Kluger, Richard, *The Paper: The Life and Death of the New York Herald Tribune* (New York: Alfred A. Knopf, 1986).

Kosicki, Gerald M., 'Problems and opportunities in agenda setting research', *Journal of Communication*, 43 (1993): 100–27.

Krosnick, Jon A. and Donald R. Kinder, 'Altering the foundations of support for the president through priming', *American Political Science Review*, 84 (1990): 497–512.

Krosnick, Jon A. and Laura Brannon, 'The impact of war on the ingredients of presidential evaluations: George Bush and the Gulf conflict', *American Political Science Review*, 87 (1993): 963–75.

Lane, Robert E., *Political Life: Why and How People Get Involved in Politics* (New York: Free Press, 1959), p. 12.

Lang, Kurt, Gladys Engel Lang, Hans Mathias Kepplinger, and Simone Ehmig, 'Collective memory and political generations: a survey of German journalists', *Political Communication*, 10 (1993): 211–29.

Lasorsa, Dominic L. and Wayne Wanta, 'Effects of personal, interpersonal and media experiences on issue saliences', *Journalism Quarterly*, 67 (1990): 804–13.

Lasswell, Harold D., 'The structure and function of communication in society', in *The Communication of Ideas*, ed. Lyman Bryson (New York: Institute for Religious and Social Studies, 1948), pp. 37–51.

Lazarsfeld, Paul F., Bernard Berelson, and Hazel Gaudet, *The People's Choice* (New York: Duell, Sloan, and Pearce, 1944).

Lazarsfeld, Paul F. and Robert K. Merton, 'Mass communication, popular taste and organized social action', in Guy E. Swanson, Theodore M. Newcomb, and Eugene L. Hartley, eds., *Readings in Social* Psychology (rev. edn) (New York: Henry Holt and Company, 1952), pp. 74–85.

Lee, Gunho, 'Who let priming out? Analysis of first and second-level agenda-setting effects on priming', *International Communication Gazette*, 72 (2010): 759–76.

Lee, Jae Kook, 'The effect of the Internet on homogeneity of the media agenda: a test of the fragmentation thesis', *Journalism and Mass Communication Quarterly*, 84 (2007): 745–60.

Lee, Jae Kook, and Renita Coleman, 'Testing generational, life cycle, and period effects of age on agenda setting', *Mass Communication and Society*, 17, 1 (2014): 3–25.

Lee, Jong-Wha and Hanol Lee, 'Human capital in the long run', *Journal of Development Economics*, 122 (2016): 147–69.

Lee, Na Yeon, 'How agenda setting works: a dual path model and motivated reasoning', *Journalism* (2019).

Lennon, Federico Rey, *Los Diarios Nacionales y la Campaña Electoral: Argentina, 1997 Elecciones* [The national press and the electoral campaign: Argentina, the 1997 elections] (Buenos Aires: Freedom Forum and Universidad Austral, 1998).

Levine, Daniel S., 'Neural population modeling and psychology: a review', *Mathematical Biosciences*, 66 (1983): 1–86.

Lewis, Justin, Andrew Williams, and Bob Franklin, 'A compromised Fourth Estate? UK news journalism, public relations and news sources', *Journalism Studies*, 9 (2008): 1–20.

Lichter, Robert and Ted Smith, 'Why elections are bad news: media and candidate discourse in the 1996 presidential primaries', *Harvard International Journal of Press/Politics*, 1, 4 (1996): 15–35.

Lim, Jeongsub, 'A cross-lagged analysis of agenda setting among online news media', *Journalism and Mass Communication Quarterly*, 83 (2006): 298–312.

Lindsay, Peter H. and Donald A. Norman, *Human Information Processing: An Introduction to Psychology* (New York: Academic Press, 1977).

Lippmann, Walter, *Public Opinion* (New York: Macmillan, 1922).

López-Escobar, Esteban, Juan Pablo Llamas, and Maxwell McCombs, 'Una dimensión social de los efectos de los medios de difusión: agenda-setting y consenso' ['A social dimension of media effects: agenda-setting and consensus'] *Comunicación y Sociedad* IX (1996): 91–125.

López-Escobar, Esteban, Juan Pablo Llamas, and Maxwell McCombs, 'Agenda setting and community consensus: first and second level effects', *International Journal of Public Opinion Research*, 10 (1998): 335–48.

López-Escobar, Esteban, Juan Pablo Llamas, Maxwell McCombs, and Federico Rey Lennon, 'Two levels of agenda setting among advertising and news in the 1995 Spanish elections', *Political Communication*, 15 (1998): 225–38.

López-Escobar, Esteban, Maxwell McCombs, and Antonio Tolsá, 'Measuring the public images of political leaders: a methodological contribution of agenda-setting theory', paper presented to the Congress for Political Communication Investigation, Madrid, 2007.

Lorenz-Spreen, Philipp, Bjarke Mørch Mønsted, Philipp Hövel, and Sune Lehmann, 'Accelerating dynamics of collective attention', *Nature Communications*, 10, 1759 (2019).

Lowry, Dennis T., Tarn Ching Josephine Nio, and Dennis W. Leitner, 'Setting the public fear agenda: a longitudinal analysis of network TV crime reporting, public perceptions of crime, and FBI crime statistics', *Journal of Communication*, 53 (2003): 61–73.

Luo, Yunjuan, Hansel Burley, Alexander Moe, and Mingxiao Sui, 'A meta-analysis of news media's public agenda-setting effects, 1972–2015', *Journalism and Mass Communication Quarterly*, 96 (2019): 150–72.

Ma, Kimberly K., William Schaffner, C. Colmenares, J. Howser, J. Jones, and K. A. Poehling, 'Influenza vaccinations of young children increased with media coverage in 2003', *Pediatrics*, 117 (2006): 157–63.

Maccoby, Nathan, 'The new "scientific" rhetoric', in *The Science of Human*

Communication, ed. Wilbur Schramm (New York: Basic Books, 1963), pp. 41–53.

McCombs, Maxwell, 'Editorial endorsements: a study of influence,' *Journalism Quarterly*, 44 (1967): 545–8.

McCombs, Maxwell, 'Explorers and surveyors: expanding strategies for agenda setting research,' *Journalism Quarterly*, 69 (1992): 815.

McCombs, Maxwell, 'The future agenda for agenda setting research,' *Journal of Mass Communication Studies* [Japan], 45 (1994): 171–81.

McCombs, Maxwell, 'Personal involvement with issues on the public agenda,' *International Journal of Public Opinion Research*, 11 (1999): 152–68.

McCombs, Maxwell, 'Myth and reality in scientific discovery: The case of agenda setting theory,' in *Communication: A Different Kind of Horse Race*, eds. Brenda Dervin and Steven Chaffee (Cresskill, NJ: Hampton Press, 2003), pp. 25–37.

McCombs, Maxwell, 'Civic osmosis: the social impact of media,' *Comunicación y Sociedad*, 25 (2012): 7–14.

McCombs, Maxwell and John Smith, 'Perceptual selection and communication,' *Journalism Quarterly*, 46 (1969): 352–5.

McCombs, Maxwell and Donald Shaw, 'The agenda setting function of mass media,' *Public Opinion Quarterly*, 36 (1972): 176–87.

McCombs, Maxwell and Donald Shaw, 'A progress report on agenda-setting research,' paper presented to the Association for Education in Journalism, San Diego, CA, 1974.

McCombs, Maxwell and Donald Shaw, 'Structuring the unseen environment,' *Journal of Communication*, 26, Spring (1976): 18–22.

McCombs, Maxwell, Sheldon Gilberg, and Chaim Eyal, 'The State of the Union address and the press agenda: a replication,' paper presented to the International Communication Association, Boston, 1982.

McCombs, Maxwell and David Weaver, 'Toward a merger of gratifications and agenda-setting research,' in *Media Gratifications Research: Current Perspectives*, eds. Karl Erik Rosengren, Lawrence Wenner and Philip Palmgreen (Beverly Hills, CA: Sage, 1985), pp. 95–108.

McCombs, Maxwell, Edna Einsiedel, and David Weaver, *Contemporary Public Opinion: Issues and the News* (Hillsdale, NJ: Lawrence Erlbaum, 1991).

McCombs, Maxwell and Dixie Evatt, 'Los temas y los aspectos: explorando una nueva dimensión de la agenda setting' ['Objects and attributes: exploring a new dimension of agenda setting'], *Comunicación y Sociedad*, 8, 1 (1995): 7–32.

McCombs, Maxwell and Jian-Hua Zhu, 'Capacity, diversity and volatility of the public agenda: trends from 1954–1994,' *Public Opinion Quarterly*, 59 (1995): 495–525.

McCombs, Maxwell, Juan Pablo Llamas, Esteban López-Escobar, and Federico Rey, 'Candidate images in Spanish elections: second-level agenda setting effects,' *Journalism & Mass Communication Quarterly*, 74 (1997): 703–17.

McCombs, Maxwell, Esteban López-Escobar, and Juan Pablo Llamas, 'Setting the agenda of attributes in the 1996 Spanish general election,' *Journal of Communication*, 50, 2 (2000): 77–92.

McCombs, Maxwell and Natalie J. Stroud, 'Psychology of agenda-setting effects: Mapping the paths of information processing,' *Review of Communication Research*, 2 (2014): 68–93.

McGuire, William J., 'Psychological motives and communication gratification', in *The Uses of Mass Communication: Current Perspectives on Gratifications Research*, eds. J. G. Blumler and Elihu Katz (Beverly Hills, CA: Sage, 1974), pp. 167–96.

McGuire, William J. 'Theoretical foundations of campaigns', in *Public Communication Campaigns*, 2nd edn, eds. Richard E. Rice and Charles K. Atkin (Newbury Park, CA: Sage, 1989), pp. 43–65.

MacKuen, Michael, 'Social communication and the mass policy agenda', in *More Than News: Media Power in Public Affairs*, eds. Michael MacKuen and Steven Coombs (Beverly Hills, CA: Sage, 1981), pp. 19–144.

McLeod, Jack M., Lee B. Becker, and James E. Byrnes, 'Another look at the agenda setting function of the press', *Communication Research*, 1 (1974): 131–66.

Manheim, Jarol B. and Robert B. Albritton, 'Changing national images: international public relations and media agenda setting', *American Political Science Review*, 73 (1984): 641–7.

Martin, Jason, 'Agenda setting, elections and the impact of information technology', in *Agenda Setting in a 2.0 World*, ed. Thomas J. Johnson (New York: Routledge, 2013), pp. 28–52.

Matthes, Jörg, 'The need for orientation towards news media: revising and validating a classic concept', *International Journal of Public Opinion Research*, 18 (2006): 422–44.

Matthes, Jörg, 'Need for orientation as a predictor of agenda-setting effects: causal evidence from a two-wave panel study', *International Journal of Public Opinion Research*, 20 (2008): 440–53.

Mayer, William G., *The Changing American Mind: How and Why American Public Opinion Changed between 1960 and 1988* (Ann Arbor: University of Michigan Press, 1992).

Mazur, Allen, 'Putting radon on the public risk agenda', *Science, Technology, and Human Values*, 12, 3–4 (1987): 86–93.

Meijer, May-May and Jan Kleinnijenhuis, 'Issue news and corporate reputation: applying the theories of agenda setting and issue ownership in the field of business communication', *Journal of Communication*, 56 (2006): 543–59.

Meraz, Sharon, 'The fight for how to think: traditional media, social networks, and issue interpretation', *Journalism: Theory, Practice, and Criticism*, 12 (2011): 107–27.

Meraz, Sharon, 'Using time series analysis to measure intermedia agenda-setting influence in traditional media and political blog networks', *Journalism and Mass Communication Quarterly*, 88 (2011): 176–94.

Merritt, Davis and Maxwell McCombs, *The Two W's of Journalism: The Why and What of Public Affairs Reporting* (Mahwah, NJ: Lawrence Erlbaum, 2003).

Merritt, Richard L., *Symbols of American Community, 1735–1775* (New Haven, CT: Yale University Press, 1966).

Mikami, Shunji, Toshio Takeshita, Makoto Nakada, and Miki Kawabata, 'The media coverage and public awareness of environmental issues in Japan', *International Communication Gazette*, 54 (1995), 209–26.

Miller, George A., 'The magic number seven, plus or minus two: some limits on our capacity for processing information', *Psychological Review*, 63 (1956): 81–97.

Miller, Joanne M., 'Examining the mediators of agenda setting: A new experimental paradigm reveals the role of emotions', *Political Psychology*, 28 (2007): 689–717.

Miller, Mark, Julie Andsager, and Bonnie Riechert, 'Framing the candidates in presidential primaries: issues and images in press releases and news coverage', *Journalism and Mass Communication Quarterly*, 75 (1998): 312–24.

Min, Young, Salma Ghanem, and Dixie Evatt, 'Using a split-ballot survey to explore the robustness of the "MIP" question in agenda setting research: a methodological study', *International Journal of Public Opinion Research*, 19 (2007): 221–36.

Moon, Soo Jung, 'Attention, attitude, and behavior: second-level agenda-setting effects as a mediator of media use and political participation', *Communication Research*, 40 (2013): 698–719.

Mueller, John E., 'Choosing among 133 candidates', *Public Opinion Quarterly*, 34 (1970): 395–402.

Mutz, Diana C., *Impersonal Influence: How Perceptions of Mass Collectives Affect Political Attitudes* (Cambridge, UK: Cambridge University Press, 1998).

Nelson, Barbara, *Making an Issue of Child Abuse: Political Agenda Setting for Social Problems* (Chicago: University of Chicago Press, 1984).

Neuman, W. Russell, 'The threshold of public attention', *Public Opinion Quarterly*, 54 (1990): 159–76.

Neuman, W. Russell, and Lauren Guggenheim, 'The evolution of media effects theory: a six-stage model of cumulative research', *Communication Theory*, 21 (2011): 169–96.

Neuman, W. Russell, Marion R. Just, and Ann N. Crigler, *Common Knowledge: News and the Construction of Political Meaning* (Chicago: University of Chicago Press, 1992).

Nimmo, Dan and Robert L. Savage, *Candidates and their Images* (Pacific Palisades, CA: Goodyear, 1976).

Noelle-Neumann, Elisabeth, 'The spiral of silence: a response', in *Political Communication Yearbook 1984*, eds. Keith Sanders, Lynda Lee Kaid, and Dan Nimmo (Carbondale: Southern Illinois University Press, 1985), pp. 66–94.

Noelle-Neumann, Elisabeth, *The Spiral of Silence: Our Social Skin*, 2nd edn (Chicago: University of Chicago Press, 1993).

Nord, David Paul, 'The politics of agenda setting in late 19th century cities', *Journalism Quarterly*, 58 (1981): 563–74, 612.

O'Shaughnessy, Nicholas, *The Phenomenon of Political Marketing* (London: Macmillan, 1990).

Ogawa, Tsuneo, 'Framing and agenda setting function', *Keio Communication Review*, 23 (2001): 71–80.

Ohl, Coral, J. David Pincus, Tony Rimmer, and Denise Harison, 'Agenda building role of news releases in corporate takeovers', *Public Relations Review*, 21 (1995): 89–101.

Oliver, Mary Beth, Arthur A. Raney, and Jennings Bryant, eds., *Media Effects: Advances in Theory and Research*, 4th edn (New York: Routledge, 2020).

Park, Robert E., 'News as a form of knowledge', *American Journal of Sociology*, 45 (1940): 667–86.

Park, Robert E., 'The city: suggestions for investigation of human behavior in the urban environment', in Robert E. Park and Ernest W. Burgess, eds., *The City* (Chicago, IL: University of Chicago Press, 1925), pp. 1–46.

Patterson, Thomas E., *The Mass Media Election: How Americans Choose Their President* (New York: Praeger, 1980).

Patterson, Thomas E., *Out of Order* (New York: Random House Vintage Books, 1993).

Patterson, Thomas E., *The Vanishing Voter: Public Involvement in an Age of Uncertainty* (New York: Alfred A. Knopf, 2002).

Pavlik, John V., *Public Relations: What Research Tells Us* (Newbury Park, CA: Sage, 1987).

Peri, Yoram, 'The media and collective memory of Yitzhak Rabin's remembrance', *Journal of Communication*, 49 (1999): 106–24.

Peter, Jochen and Claes H. de Vreese, 'Agenda-rich, agenda-poor: a cross-national comparative investigation of nominal and thematic public agenda diversity', *International Journal of Public Opinion Research*, 15 (2003): 44–64.

Peter, Jochen, 'Country characteristics as contingent conditions of agenda setting: the moderating influence of polarized elite opinion', *Communication Research*, 30 (2003): 683–712.

Petrocik, John R., 'Issue ownership in presidential elections with a 1980 case study', *American Journal of Political Science*, 40 (1996): 825–50.

Petrocik, John R., William L. Benoit, and Glenn J. Hansen, 'Issue ownership and presidential campaigning, 1952–2000', *Political Science Quarterly*, 118 (2003): 599–626.

Petty, Richard E. and John T. Cacioppo, *Communication and Persuasion: Central and Peripheral Routes to Attitude Change* (New York: Springer, 1986).

Pingree, Raymond J. and Elizabeth Stoycheff, 'Differentiating cueing from reasoning in agenda setting effects', *Journal of Communication*, 63 (2013): 852–72.

Pingree, Raymond J., Andrea Quenette, John Tchernev, and Ted Dickinson, 'Effects of media criticism on gatekeeping trust and implications for agenda setting', *Journal of Communication*, 63 (2013): 351–72.

Ploughman, Penelope, 'The creation of newsworthy events: an analysis of newspaper coverage of the man-made disaster at Love Canal', unpublished doctoral dissertation, State University of New York at Buffalo, 1984.

Poindexter, Paula, Maxwell McCombs, Laura Smith, and others, 'Need for orientation in the new media landscape', unpublished paper, University of Texas at Austin, 2002.

Popkin, Samuel L., *The Reasoning Voter: Communication and Persuasion in Presidential Campaigns* (Chicago: University of Chicago Press, 1991).

Presser, Stanley, 'Substance and method in *Public Opinion Quarterly*, 1937–2010', *Public Opinion Quarterly*, 75 (2011): 839–45.

Price, Vincent and David Tewksbury, 'News values and public opinion: a theoretical account of media priming and framing' in *Progress in Communication Sciences: Advances in Persuasion*, eds. G. A. Barnett and F. J. Boster (Greenwich, CT: Ablex, 1997), pp. 173–212.

Pritchard, Peter, 'The McPapering of America: an insider's candid account', *Washington Journalism Revue* (1987): 32–7.

Protess, David L. and Maxwell McCombs, eds., *Agenda Setting: Readings on Media, Public Opinion, and Policymaking* (Hillsdale, NJ: Lawrence Erlbaum, 1991).

Protess, David L., Fay L. Cook, Jack C. Doppelt, James S. Ettema, Margaret T. Gordon, Donna R. Leff and Peter Miller, *The Journalism of Outrage: Investigative Reporting and Agenda Building in* America (New York: Guilford, 1991).

Puglisi, Riccardo, 'The spin doctor meets the rational voter: electoral competition with agenda-setting effects', available at SSRN: https://ssrn.com/abstract=581881 (2004).

Ragas, Matthew, 'Issue and stakeholder intercandidate agenda setting among corporate information subsidies', *Journalism and Mass Communication Quarterly*, 89 (2012): 91–111.

Ragas, Matthew and Spiro Kiousis, 'Intermedia agenda-setting and political activism: MoveOn.org and the 2008 presidential election', *Mass Communication and Society*, 13 (2010): 560–83.

Rains, Stephen A., Timothy R. Levine, and Rene Weber, 'Sixty years of quantitative Communication Research summarized: lessons from 149 meta-analyses', *Annals of the International Communication Association*, 42 (2018): 105–24.

Reese, Stephen D. and Lucig Danielian, 'Intermedia influence and the drug issue', in *Communication Campaigns about Drugs*, ed. P. Shoemaker (Hillsdale, NJ: Lawrence Erlbaum, 1989), pp. 29–46.

Reese, Stephen D. and Pamela J. Shoemaker, 'A media sociology for the networked public sphere: the hierarchy of influences model', *Mass Communication and Society*, 19 (2016): 389–410.

Roberts, Marilyn, 'Predicting voter behavior via the agenda setting tradition', *Journalism Quarterly*, 69 (1992): 878–92.

Roberts, Marilyn and Maxwell McCombs, 'Agenda setting and political advertising: origins of the news agenda', *Political Communication*, 11 (1994): 249–62.

Roberts, Marilyn, Ronald Anderson, and Maxwell McCombs, '1990 Texas gubernatorial campaign influence of issues and images', *Mass Communication Review*, 21 (1994): 20–35.

Roberts, Marilyn, Wayne Wanta, and Tzong-Houng (Dustin) Dzwo, 'Agenda setting and issue salience online', *Communication Research*, 29 (2002): 452–65.

Robinson, Michael, 'Collective memory: from the 20s through the 90s: the way we think we were', *Public Perspective*, 11, 1 (2000): 14–19, 44–7.

Rodríguez Díaz, Raquel, 'Los profesores universitarios como medios de comunicación: la agenda setting de los alumnos y profesores' [University professors as communication media: agenda setting of students and professors], unpublished doctoral dissertation, Complutense University of Madrid, 2000.

Rogers, Everett M., James W. Dearing, and Soonbum Chang, 'AIDS in the 1980s: the agenda-setting process for a public issue', *Journalism Monographs*, 126 (1991).

Rogstad, Ingrid, 'Is Twitter just rehashing? Intermedia agenda setting between Twitter and mainstream media', *Journal of Information Technology and Politics*, 13, 2 (2016): 142–58.

Rössler, Patrick and Michael Schenk, 'Cognitive bonding and the German reunification: agenda-setting and persuasion effects of mass media', *International Journal of Public Opinion Research*, 12 (2000): 29–47.

Rumelhart, David E. and Donald A. Norman, 'Accretion, tuning and restructuring: Three modes of learning', in *Semantic Factors in Cognition*, eds. John Wealdon Cotton and Roberta L. Klatzky (Hillsdale, NJ: Lawrence Erlbaum, 1978).

Salwen, Michael, 'Effects of accumulation of coverage on issue salience in agenda setting', *Journalism Quarterly*, 65 (1988): 100–6, 130.

Sánchez-Aranda, José Javier, María José Canel, and Juan Pablo Llamas, 'Framing effects of television political advertising and the selective perception process', papers presented at the World Association for Public Opinion Research regional conference, Pamplona, Spain, 1997.

Sayre, Ben, Leticia Bode, Dhavan Shah, Dave Wilcox, and Chirag Shah, 'Agenda setting in a digital age: tracking attention to California Proposition 8 in social media, online news and conventional news', *Policy and Internet*, 2, 2 (2010): 7–32.

Scharkow, Michael and Jens Vogelgesang, 'Measuring the public agenda using search engine queries', *International Journal of Public Opinion Research*, 23 (2011): 104–113.

Schlozman, Kay Lehman, Sidney Verba, and Henry E. Brady, *The Unheavenly Chorus: Unequal Political Voice and the Broken Promise of American Democracy* (Princeton, NJ: Princeton University Press, 2013).

Schoenbach, Klaus and Holli A. Semetko, 'Agenda setting, agenda reinforcing or agenda deflating? A study of the 1990 German national election', *Journalism Quarterly*, 68 (1992): 837–46.

Schudson, Michael, *The Good Citizen: A History of American Civic Life* (New York: Free Press, 1998), pp. 310–11.

Searles, Kathleen, and Glen Smith, 'Who's the boss? Setting the agenda in a fragmented media environment', *International Journal of Communication*, 10 (2016): 2074–95.

Semetko, Holli A., Jay G. Blumler, Michael Gurevitch, and David H. Weaver, with Steve Barkin and G. Cleveland Wilhoit, *The Formation of Campaign Agendas: A Comparative Analysis of Party and Media Roles in Recent American and British Elections* (Hillsdale, NJ: Lawrence Erlbaum, 1991).

Shaw, Daron R., 'The impact of news media favorability and candidate events in presidential campaigns', *Political Communication*, 16 (1999): 183–202.

Shaw, Donald L. and Maxwell E. McCombs, eds., *The Emergence of American Political Issues* (St Paul, MN: West, 1977).

Shaw, Donald L. and John Slater, 'Press puts unemployment on agenda: Richmond community opinion, 1981–1984', *Journalism Quarterly*, 65 (1988): 407–11.

Shaw, Donald L. and Shannon Martin, 'The function of mass media agenda setting', *Journalism Quarterly*, 69 (1992): 902–20.

Shaw, Donald L., Bradley J. Hamm, and Thomas C. Terry, 'Vertical vs. horizontal media: Using agenda setting and audience agenda-melding to create public information strategies in the emerging Papyrus Society', *Military Review*, 86, 6 (2006): 13–25.

Shaw, Donald L., Milad Minooie, Deb Aikat, and Chris J. Vargo, *Agendamelding: News, Social Media, Audiences and Civic Community* (New York: Peter Lang, 2019).

Shaw, Eugene F., 'Agenda-setting and mass communication theory', *International Communication Gazette*, 25, 2 (1979): 101.

Sheafer, Tamir, 'How to evaluate it: the role of story-evaluation tone in agenda setting and priming', *Journal of Communication*, 57 (2007): 21–39.

Sheafer, Tamir and Gabriel Weimann, 'Agenda building, agenda setting, priming individual voting intentions and the aggregate results: an analysis of four Israeli elections', *Journal of Communication*, 55 (2005): 347–65.

Shehata, Adam, 'Unemployment on the agenda: A panel study of agenda setting effects during the 2006 Swedish national election campaign', *Journal of Communication*, 60 (2010): 182–203.

Shoemaker, Pamela, ed., *Communication Campaigns about Drugs* (Hillsdale, NJ: Lawrence Erlbaum, 1989).

Shoemaker, Pamela, 'Hardwired for news: using biological and cultural evolution to explain the surveillance function', *Journal of Communication*, 46, 3 (1996): 32–47.

Shoemaker, Pamela and Tim Vos, *Gatekeeping Theory* (New York: Routledge, 2009).

Shoemaker, Pamela and Stephen D. Reese, *Mediating the Message in the 21st Century: A Media Sociology Perspective* (New York: Routledge, 2014).

Sigal, Leon V. *Reporters and Officials: The Organization and Politics of Newsmaking* (Lexington, MA: D. C. Heath, 1973).

Signorielli, Nancy, Michael Morgan, and James Shanahan, 'Cultivation analysis: research and practice', in *An Integrated Approach To Communication Theory And Research*, 3rd edn, eds., Don W. Stacks, Michael B. Salwen, and Kristen C. Eichhorn (New York: Routledge, 2019), pp. 113–25.

Smith, Kim, 'Newspaper coverage and public concern about community issues', *Journalism Monographs*, 101 (1987).

Smith, Tom W., 'America's most important problems – a trend analysis, 1946–1976', *Public Opinion Quarterly*, 44 (1980): 164–80.

Snider, Paul, 'Mr Gates revisited: a 1966 version of the 1949 case study', *Journalism Quarterly*, 44 (1967): 419–27.

Son, Young Jun, and David H. Weaver, 'Another look at what moves public opinion: media agenda setting and polls in the 2000 US election', *International Journal of Public Opinion Research*, 18 (2006): 174–97.

Song, Yonghoi, 'Internet news media and issue development: a case study on the roles of independent online news services as agenda-builders for anti-US protests in South Korea', *New Media and Society*, 9 (2007): 71–92.

Soroka, Stuart N., 'Schindler's List's intermedia influence: exploring the role of "entertainment" in media agenda-setting', *Canadian Journal of Communication*, 25 (2000): 211–30.

Soroka, Stuart N., *Agenda-Setting Dynamics in Canada* (Vancouver: UBC Press, 2002).

Soroka, Stuart N., 'Issue attributes and agenda setting by media, the public, and policymakers in Canada', *International Journal of Public Opinion Research*, 14 (2002): 264–85.

Soroka, Stuart N., 'Media, public opinion, and foreign policy', *Harvard International Journal of Press/Politics*, 8 (2003): 27–48.

Soroka, Stuart N., 'Good news and bad news: asymmetric responses to economic information', *Journal of Politics*, 68 (2006): 372–85.

Soroka, Stuart N. and Stephen McAdams, 'News, politics, and negativity', *Political Communication*, 32, 1 (2015): 1–22.

Stacks, Don W., Michael B. Salwen, and Kristen C. Eichhorn, eds., *An Integrated Approach to Communication Theory and Research*, 3rd edn (New York: Routledge, 2019).

Stevenson, Robert L., Rainer Böhme, and Nico Nickel, 'The TV agenda-setting influence on campaign 2000', *Egyptian Journal of Public Opinion Research*, 2, 1 (2001): 29–50.

Stoycheff, Elizabeth, Raymond J. Pingree, Jason T. Peifer, and Mingxiao Sui, 'Agenda cueing effects of news and social media', *Media Psychology*, 21, 2 (2018): 182–201.

Stromback, Jesper and Spiro Kiousis, 'A new look at agenda setting effects – Comparing the predictive power of overall political news consumption and specific news media consumption across different media channels and media types', *Journal of Communication*, 60 (2010): 271–92.

Stromback, Jesper and Spiro Kiousis, eds., *Political Public Relations: Principles and Applications* (New York: Routledge, 2011).

Stroud, Natalie J., *Niche News: The Politics of News Choice* (New York: Oxford University Press, 2011).

Stroud, Natalie J. and Kate Kenski, 'From agenda setting to refusal setting: survey nonresponse as a function of media coverage across the 2004 election cycle', *Public Opinion Quarterly*, 71 (2007): 539–59.

Swanson, David and Paolo Mancini, eds., *Politics, Media, and Modern Democracy: An International Study of Innovations in Electoral Campaigning and their Consequences* (Westport, CT: Praeger, 1996).

Symeou, Pavlos C., Philemon Bantimaroudis, and Stelios C. Zyglidopoulos, 'Cultural agenda setting and the role of critics: an empirical examination in the market for art-house films', *Communication Research*, 42 (2015): 732–54.

Takeshita, Toshio, 'Agenda setting effects of the press in a Japanese local election', *Studies of Broadcasting*, 29 (1993):193–216.

Takeshita, Toshio, 'Expanding attribute agenda setting into framing: an application of the problematic situation scheme', paper presented to the International Communication Association, Seoul, Korea, 2002.

Takeshita, Toshio, 'Current critical problems in agenda-setting research', *International Journal of Public Opinion Research*, 18 (2006): 275–96.

Takeshita, Toshio, 'Agenda setting and framing: two dimensions of attribute agenda-setting', *Mita Journal of Sociology* [Japan], 12 (2007): 4–18.

Takeshita, Toshio and Shunji Mikami, 'How did mass media influence the voters' choice in the 1993 general election in Japan?: a study of agenda setting', *Keio Communication Review*, 17 (1995): 27–41.

Tan, Yue and David H. Weaver, 'Agenda diversity and agenda setting from 1956 to 2004: what are the trends over time?', *Journalism Studies*, 14 (2013): 773–89.

Tedesco, John C., 'Issue and strategy agenda setting in the 2000 presidential primaries', unpublished paper, Virginia Technological University, 2001.

Tedesco, John C., 'Intercandidate agenda setting in the 2004 Democratic presidential primary', *American Behavioral Scientist*, 49 (2005): 92–113.

Thesen, Gunnar, Christoffer Green-Pedersen, and Peter B. Mortensen, 'Priming, issue ownership, and party support: the electoral gains of an issue-friendly media agenda', *Political Communication*, 34 (2017): 282–301.

Tolman, Edward C., *Purposive Behavior in Animals and Men* (New York: Appleton-Century-Crofts, 1932).

Tolman, Edward C., 'Cognitive maps in rats and men', *Psychological Review*, 55 (1948): 189–208.

Tran, Hai, 'Online agenda setting: a new frontier for theory development', in *Agenda Setting in a 2.0 World*, ed. Thomas J. Johnson (New York: Routledge, 2013), pp. 205–29.

Trumbo, Craig, 'Longitudinal modelling of public issues: an application of the agenda-setting process to the issue of global warming', *Journalism Monographs*, 152 (1995).

Trumbo, Craig, 'The effect of newspaper coverage of influenza on the rate of physician visits for influenza 2002–2008', *Mass Communication and Society*, 15 (2012): 718–38.

Tuchman, Gaye, 'Telling stories', *Journal of Communication*, 26, 4 (1976): 93–7.

Tversky, Amos and Daniel Kahneman, 'Availability: a heuristic for judging frequency and probability', *Cognitive Psychology*, 5 (1973): 207–32.

Valentino, Nicholas A., Vincent L. Hutchings, and Ismail K. White, 'Cues that matter: How political ads prime racial attitudes during campaigns', *American Political Science Review*, 96 (2002): 75–90.

Valenzuela, Sebastián, 'Variations in media priming: the moderating role of knowledge, interest, news attention, and discussion', *Journalism and Mass Communication Quarterly*, 86 (2009): 756–74.

Valenzuela, Sebastián, 'Materialism, post-materialism and agenda-setting effects: the values-issues consistency hypothesis', *International Journal of Public Opinion Research*, 23 (2011): 437–63.

Valenzuela, Sebastián, 'Value resonance and the origins of issue salience', in *Agenda Setting in a 2.0 World*, ed. Thomas J. Johnson (New York: Routledge, 2013), pp. 53–64.

Valenzuela, Sebastián, 'Agenda setting and journalism', in *Oxford Research Encyclopedia of Communication,* ed. Jon F. Nussbaum (New York: Oxford University Press, 2019).

Valenzuela, Sebastián and Maxwell McCombs, 'Agenda-setting effects on vote choice: evidence from the 2006 Mexican election', paper presented to the annual meeting of the International Communication Association, San Francisco, 2007.

Valenzuela, Sebastián and Arturo Arriagada, 'Competencia por la uniformidad en noticieros y diarios chilenos 2000–2005' ['The competition for similarity in Chilean news broadcast and newspapaers 2000–2005'], *Cuadernos.info,* 24 (2009): 41–52.

Valenzuela, Sebastián and Arturo Arriagada, 'Politics without citizens? Public opinion, television news, the president, and real-world factors in Chile, 2000–2005', *Harvard International Journal of Press/Politics,* 16 (2011): 357–81.

Valenzuela, Sebastián and Gennadiy Chernov, 'Explicating the values-issue consistency hypothesis through need for orientation', *Canadian Journal of Communication,* 41, 1 (2016).

Valenzuela, Sebastián, Soledad Puente, and Pablo M. Flores, 'Comparing disaster news on Twitter and television: an intermedia agenda setting perspective', *Journal of Broadcasting and Electronic Media,* 61 (2017): 615–37.

van Aelst, Peter and Stefaan Walgrave, 'Political agenda setting by the mass media: ten years of research, 2005–2015', in *Handbook of Public Policy Agenda Setting,* ed. Nikolaos Zahariadis (Cheltenham, UK: Edward Elgar, 2016), pp. 157–78.

Váně, Jan and František Kalvas, 'Focusing events and their effect on agenda setting', paper presented to the World Association for Public Opinion Research, Hong Kong, 2012.

VanSlyke Turk, Judy, 'Information subsidies and influence', *Public Relations Review,* 11 (1985): 10–25.

VanSlyke Turk, Judy, 'Information subsidies and media content: a study of public relations influence on the news', *Journalism Monographs,* 100 (1986).

VanSlyke Turk, Judy, 'Public relations influence on the news', *Newspaper Research Journal,* 7 (1986): 15–27.

Vargo, Chris J., Lei Guo, Maxwell McCombs, and Donald L. Shaw, 'Network issue agendas on Twitter during the 2012 US presidential election', *Journal of Communication,* 64 (2014): 296–316.

Vargo, Chris J. and Lei Guo, 'Exploring the network agenda setting model with big social data', in Lei Guo and Maxwell McCombs, eds. *The Power of Information Networks*: New Directions for Agenda Setting (New York, Routledge: 2016), pp. 55–65.

Vargo, Chris J. and Lei Guo, 'Networks, big data, and intermedia agenda setting: an analysis of traditional, partisan, and emerging online US news', *Journalism and Mass Communication Quarterly,* 94 (2017): 1031–55.

Vargo, Chris J., Lei Guo, and Michelle A. Amazeen, 'The agenda-setting power of fake news: A big data analysis of the online media landscape from 2014 to 2016', *New Media and Society,* 20 (2018): 2028–49.

Vonbun, Ramona, Katharina Kleinen-von Königslöw, and Klaus Schoenbach,

'Intermedia agenda-setting in a multimedia news environment', *Journalism*, 17 (2016): 1054–73.

Vu, Hong, Nga Nguyen, and Volker Gehrau, 'Agenda diffusion: an integrated model of agenda setting and interpersonal communication', *Journalism and Mass Communication Quarterly*, 87 (2010): 100–16.

Vu, Hong Tien, Lei Guo, and Maxwell E. McCombs, 'Exploring "the world outside and the pictures in our heads": A network agenda setting study', *Journalism and Mass Communication Quarterly*, 91 (2014): 669–86.

Wallsten, Kevin, 'Agenda setting and the blogosphere: an analysis of the relationship between mainstream media and political blogs', *Review of Policy Research*, 24 (2007): 567–87.

Wang, Tai-Li, 'Agenda setting online: an experiment testing the effects of hyperlinks in online newspapers', *Southwestern Mass Communication Journal*, 15, 2 (2000): 59–70.

Wanta, Wayne, *The Public and the National Agenda: How People Learn about Important Issues* (Mahwah, NJ: Lawrence Erlbaum, 1997).

Wanta, Wayne and Joe Foote, 'The president–news media relationship: a time-series analysis of agenda setting', *Journal of Broadcasting and Electronic Media*, 38 (1994): 437–48.

Wanta, Wayne and Salma Ghanem, 'Effects of agenda setting', in *Mass Media Effects Research: Advances through Meta-Analysis*, eds. Raymond W. Preiss, Barbara Mae Gayle, Nancy Burrell, Mike Allen, and Jennings Bryant (Mahwah, NJ: Lawrence Erlbaum, 2006), pp. 37–51.

Wanta, Wayne, Guy Golan and Cheolhan Lee, 'Agenda setting and international news: media influence on public perception of foreign nations', *Journalism and Mass Communication Quarterly*, 81 (2004): 364–77.

Wanta, Wayne and Yu-Wei Hu, 'Time-lag differences in the agenda setting process: an examination of five news media', *International Journal of Public Opinion Research*, 6 (1994): 225–40.

Wanta, Wayne, Mary Ann Stephenson, Judy VanSlyke Turk, and Maxwell McCombs, 'How president's State of Union talk influenced news media agendas', *Journalism Quarterly*, 66 (1989): 537–41.

Watt, James H., Mary Mazza, and Leslie Synder, 'Agenda-setting effects of television news coverage and the memory decay curve', *Communication Research*, 20 (1993): 408–35.

Watts, Liz, 'Coverage of polio and AIDS: agenda setting in reporting cure research on polio and AIDS in newspapers, news magazines and network television', *Ohio Journalism Monograph Series* [School of Journalism, Ohio University], 4 (1993).

Weart, Spencer R., *The Discovery of Global Warming* (Cambridge, MA: Harvard University Press, 2008).

Weaver, David H., 'Political issues and voter need for orientation', in *The Emergence of American Political Issues*, eds. Donald Shaw and Maxwell McCombs (St Paul, MN: West, 1977), pp. 107–19.

Weaver, David H., 'Audience need for orientation and media effects', *Communication Research*, 7 (1980): 361–76.

Weaver, David H., 'Issue salience and public opinion: are there consequences of agenda-setting?', *International Journal of Public Opinion Research*, 3 (1991): 53–68.

Weaver, David H. and Maxwell McCombs, 'Voters' need for orientation and choice of candidate: mass media and electoral decision making', paper presented to the American Association for Public Opinion Research, Roanoke, VA, 1978.

Weaver, David H., Doris A. Graber, Maxwell E. McCombs, and Chaim H. Eyal, *Media Agenda Setting in a Presidential Election: Issues, Images and Interest* (Westport, CT: Greenwood, 1981).

Weaver, David H. and Swanzy Nimley Elliot, 'Who sets the agenda for the media? A study of local agenda-building', *Journalism Quarterly*, 62 (1985): 87–94.

Webster, James G. and Thomas B. Ksiazek, 'The dynamics of audience fragmentation: public attention in an age of digital media', *Journal of Communication*, 62 (2012): 39–56.

Weeks, Brian and Brian Southwell, 'The symbiosis of news coverage and aggregate online search behavior: Obama, rumors, and presidential politics', *Mass Communication and Society*, 13 (2010): 341–60.

Weidman, Lisa, 'Consumer knowledge about Oregon wines: applying agenda setting theory to the dissemination of information about consumer products', paper presented to the Midwest Association for Public Opinion Research, Chicago, 2011.

Weiss-Blatt, Nirit, 'Role of tech bloggers in the flow of information', in *The Power of Information Networks*, eds. Lei Guo and Maxwell McCombs (New York: Routledge, 2016), pp.88–103.

Westley, Bruce and Lee Barrow, 'An investigation of news seeking behavior', *Journalism Quarterly*, 36 (1959): 431–8.

White, David Manning, 'The "gate keeper": a case study in the selection of news', *Journalism Quarterly*, 27 (1950): 383–90.

White, Theodore, *The Making of the President, 1972* (New York: Bantam, 1973).

Whitney, D. Charles and Lee Becker, '"Keeping the gates" for gatekeepers: the effects of wire news', *Journalism Quarterly*, 59 (1982): 60–5.

Williams, Bruce A. and Michael X. Delli Carpini, 'Monica and Bill all the time and everywhere: the collapse of gatekeeping and agenda setting in the new media environment', *American Behavioral Scientist*, 47 (2004): 1208–30.

Willnat, Lars, 'Agenda setting and priming: conceptual links and differences', in *Communication and Democracy*, eds. M. McCombs, D. Shaw, and D. Weaver (Mahwah, NJ: Lawrence Erlbaum, 1997), pp. 51–66.

Winter, James P., 'Contingent conditions in the agenda-setting process', in *Mass Communication Review Yearbook*, eds. G. Cleveland Wilhoit and Harold de Bock (Beverly Hills, CA: Sage, 1981), pp. 235–43.

Winter, James P., and Chaim H. Eyal, 'Agenda setting for the civil rights issue', *Public Opinion Quarterly*, 45 (1981): 376–83.

Winter, James P., Chaim H. Eyal, and Ann Rogers, 'Issue-specific agenda setting: the whole as less than the sum of the parts', *Canadian Journal of Communication*, 8, 2 (1982): 1–10.

Wirth, Werner, Jörg Matthes, Christian Schemer, Martin Wettstein, Thomas Friemel, Regula Hänggli, and Gabriele Siegert, 'Agenda building and setting in a referendum campaign: investigating the flow of arguments among campaigners, the media, and the public', *Journalism and Mass Communication Quarterly*, 87 (2010): 328–45.

Wu, H. Denis and Renita Coleman, 'Advancing agenda-setting theory: the comparative strength and new contingent conditions of the two levels of agenda-setting effects', *Journalism and Mass Communication Quarterly*, 86 (2009): 775–89.

Wu, H. Denis and Lei Guo, 'Beyond salience transmission: linking agenda networks between media and voters', *Communication Research* (2017).

Yang, Jin, and Gerald Stone, 'The powerful role of interpersonal communication on agenda setting', *Mass Communication and Society*, 6 (2003): 57–74.

Yioutas, Julie, and Ivana Segvic, 'Revisiting the Clinton/Lewinsky scandal: the convergence of agenda setting and framing', *Journalism and Mass Communication Quarterly*, 80 (2003): 567–82.

Young, Lori and Stuart Soroka, 'Affective news: the automated coding of sentiment in political texts', *Political Communication*, 29 (2012): 205–31.

Zhu, Jian-Hua with William Boroson, 'Susceptibility to agenda setting', in *Communication and Democracy*, eds. M. McCombs, D. Shaw, and D. Weaver (Mahwah, NJ: Lawrence Erlbaum, 1997).

Zhu, Jian-Hua, 'Issue competition and attention distraction: a zero-sum theory of agenda setting', *Journalism Quarterly*, 68 (1992): 825–36.

Zucker, Harold, 'The variable nature of news media influence', in *Communication Yearbook 2*, ed. Brent Ruben (New Brunswick, NJ: Transaction Books, 1978), pp. 225–40.

Zyglidopoulos, Stelios, Pavlos Symeou, Philemon Bantimaroudis, and Eleni Kampanellou, 'Cultural agenda setting: media attributes and public attention of Greek museums', *Communication Research*, 39 (2012): 480–98.

索 引

此处页码为本书边码。

9/11 terrorist attacks "9·11"事件 151

A

ABC News 美国广播公司新闻节目 xviii
Acapulco typology 阿卡普尔科模型 36–38
    automaton 机械/机器人角度 37
    cognitive portrait 认知画像角度 37, 41
    competition 竞争角度 37–38, 41, 83, 104
    natural history 自然历史角度 37, 38, 41, 83, 104, 105, 116
advertising 广告 24, 46, 48, 77, 117, 118, 124, 125, 130
affective attributes/tone 情感属性/情感语气 23, 47–48, 49–50, 51, 65, 81, 109, 136, 141, 142, 151, 156
African Americans 非洲裔美国人 xi
age *see* generational differences 年龄 可见 代际差异

agenda of attributes *see* attribute agenda-setting 属性议程 也见 属性议程设置
agenda building 议程建构 159
agenda of candidates 候选人议程 43, 45, 46–51
agenda cutting 议程削减 xi
agenda deflating effect 议程缩减效果 58
agenda of objects 客体议程 43, 138
agenda of questions 问题的议程 43
agenda-cueing 议程提示 101, 102
agenda-melding 议程融合 xi, 88–90, 91
agenda-reasoning 议程推理 101, 102
agenda-setting 议程设置
    cause and effect 原因和结果 16–19
    centrifugal trend 离心趋势 100, 157
    centripetal trend 向心趋势 80–81, 100, 157
    concepts 概念 157–159

content vs exposure 内容相对于接触 38

development of theory 理论发展 x-xii, xiv-xviii,39-40,133-134,159-160

domains and settings 领域和场景 157-159

dual process approach 双轨路径思路 100-102

education and 教育和议程设置 98-100

empirical evidence 经验证据 4-15

experimental evidence 实验证据 17-19,50-51

field experiments 实地/田野实验 18, 87,101,102

history of 议程设置的历史 39-40

intermedia agenda-setting 媒体间议程设置 xi,19,111,128-132,133

methodology 方法论 106-109

new arenas 新领域/新战场 153-156

other communication theories and 其他传播理论和议程设置 59-60

second level see attribute agenda-setting 第二层面 可见 属性议程设置

terminology 术语 xvi,39,159

third-level 第三层面 65,66-69,70, 121,134,149

timeframe for effects 效果的时间框架/时间表 103-106

as zero-sum game 如零和博弈 95,106

see also correlation statistic; transfer of salience 也见 相关性统计；显著性转移

The Agenda-Setting Journal 《议程设置杂志》8

AIDS coverage 艾滋病报道 116

airlines 航班 60

alarmed discovery 警报发觉 35-36

Alexander, Lamar 拉马尔·亚历山大 119

American National Election Studies(ANES) 美国国家选举研究 51,52,139,143

Anguita, Julio 胡里奥·安奎塔 47,48

Annenberg Election Study 安纳伯格选举研究 143

Apple, Johnny 约翰尼·艾珀尔 129

Argentina 阿根廷 15,22

Aristotle 亚里士多德 117

Arriagada, Arturo 阿图罗·阿里亚加达 114

Asahi 《朝日新闻》54,131

Associated Press 美联社 21,129

Association for Education in Journalism 新闻教育协会 xi,xv

associative network models 联想网状模型 66

attention/comprehension distinction 注意/理解区分 44-45,134

attribute agenda-setting 属性议程设置 23,59,81,120,149

attribute priming 属性铺垫 136-137, 141,142

attributes of issues 议题属性 53-55

behavioural outcomes 行为结果 146

candidate images in local elections 地方选举中的候选人形象 49-51

candidate images in national elections 全国选举中的候选人形象 46-48, 108

compelling arguments 雄辩论据 55-59

comprehension and 理解和属性议程设置 44-45,134

corruption 腐败 47

cultural agendas 文化议程 156-157

environmental issues 环境议题 54-55

framing and 框架建构/架构和属性议程设置 60-62

homogeneity of agendas 议程的同质性 131,132

image building 形象塑造 59

increased consensus 增加共识 151

intermedia agenda-setting and 媒体间议程设置和属性议程设置 130, 132

local elections 地方选举 123-125

media agendas and 媒介议程和属性议程设置 119,121,123

networks of candidates and 候选人网络和属性议程设置 66-69

opinions and 意见和属性议程设置 140-142

partisan media and 党派媒体和属性议程设置 52

political candidates 政治候选人 46-52,60-61,119-120

political polarization and 政治极化和属性议程设置 23

political reform 政治改革 53-54

possible range of scores 可得数值范围 10-11

salience measures 显著性测量 108

stereotyping 刻板印象形成 59

visual images 视觉形象 51-53,143

attribute priming 属性铺垫 136-137, 141,142

audience fragmentation 受众碎片化 23

Austria 奥地利 121

automaton perspective 机械/机器人角度 37

Aznar, José María 何塞·玛丽亚·阿斯纳尔 47,48

B

Baier, Bret 布雷特·拜尔 52

Banning, Stephen 斯蒂芬·班宁 51

Barnum, P. T. P. T. 巴纳姆 ix

basketball 篮球 156

Baumgartner, Frank 弗兰克·鲍姆加特纳 63

BBC 英国广播公司 118,119

Beaverbrook, Lord 比弗布鲁克男爵 xiii

Bias, Len 伦·拜亚斯 30

Bild《图片报》58

blogs 博客 132

Bloj, Alexander 亚历山大·布洛伊 144

Boczkowski, Pablo 巴勃罗·博奇科夫斯基 22

Bouza, Fermín 费尔明·博萨 79

Bradlee, Benjamin C. 本杰明·布拉德利 8

Bradley, Bill 比尔·布拉德利 120

Buchanan, Pat 帕特·布坎南 119

Bush administration 布什政府 31,145

Bush, George W. 乔治·W. 布什 51,119,120,123,124,140

business news 财经新闻 148–149

C

Camaj, Lindita 林迪塔·卡马伊 102,146

Canada 加拿大 80,82,84–85,126

Cappella, Joseph 约瑟夫·卡佩拉 153

Carter, Jimmy 吉米·卡特 46–47,78,113

Caudill, Edward 爱德华·考迪尔 40

causality 因果关系 16–19

    time-order 时间先后顺序（时间序列）9,12,16

CBS 哥伦比亚广播公司 7,131

celebrity 名人 59

Chaffee, Steve 史蒂夫·查菲 xv, xvi

Chapel Hill study 查普希尔研究 xi, xv–xvi, 5–7, 22, 90, 159

    citations 引证 8,158

    competition perspective 竞争角度 36,41

    findings 发现 7,16,131

    influence of 查普希尔研究的影响 7–8,92,134

    issues 议题 6,42,45

    methodology 方法论 5–6,7

    need for orientation 导向需求 77–78

Charlotte study 夏洛特研究 xii, 9, 16, 74, 76, 77

The Charlotte Observer《夏洛特观察家报》xv, 9

Chicago Tribune《芝加哥论坛报》47

Chile 智利 21, 33–34, 38, 114

civic osmosis 公民渗透 22, 23–25, 140

civil rights issue 公民权利议题 12, 16, 103

Clinton, Bill 比尔·克林顿 76

Clinton, Hilary 希拉里·克林顿 89

CNN 美国有线电视新闻网 23, 52, 131

    online version 网络版 18, 19

cognitive maps/mapping 认知地图/认知

图绘 3,66,71-72,74

cognitive portrait perspective 认知画像角度 37,41

Cohen, Bernard 伯纳德·科恩 3,45

cohort analysis 群组分析 21

Cold War 冷战 96

Coleman, Renita 雷尼塔·科尔曼 51,146

Colistra, Rita 丽塔·科利斯特拉 xi

collective memory 集体记忆 154-155

communication gestalt 传播格式塔/完形 23-25

communicator-to-message-to-audience model 消息传递模式/传播者—消息—受众模式 x,xi-xii

compelling arguments 雄辩论据 55-59,64,65,142

competition perspective 竞争角度 37-38,41,83,104

comprehension/attention distinction 理解/注意区分 44-45,134

consensus 共识 150-152

Cooper, Anderson 安德森·库珀 52

coronavirus crisis 冠状病毒危机 xvii

correlation statistic 相关性统计 9,10-11,28,58-59,89,116,127,151

    agenda-melding and 议程融合和相关性统计 89,90

    attributes of issues 议题属性 53-55

    candidate images 候选人形象 46-51

cause and effect 原因和结果 16-19

civil rights issues 公民权利议题 12

crime coverage 犯罪报道 32-33,57

cultural agendas 文化议程 155,157

drugs 毒品 30-31

economic issues 经济议题 61

environmental issues 环境议题 34-35,103

foreign affairs issues 外交事务议题 13

general/national elections 普选/大选/全国选举 13-14,47-48,118,141

generational differences 代际差异 21-22,24

gun control 枪支管制 127-128

intermedia agenda-setting 媒体间议程设置 129-132

levels of exposure 接触程度 61

local elections 地方选举 123-124

local public issues 地方公众议题 13,14-15,125

need for orientation and 导向需求和相关性统计 77-79,80,84

network analysis 网络分析 66,67,69,71

obtrusive and unobtrusive issues 强制性与非强制性议题 82-84,126

online media 网络媒体 20,21-22

political reform 政治改革 53-54

possible range of scores 可得数值范围

10-11

　　presidential elections 总统选举 9,11,
　　　46-47,118,119,122-123,143

　　press releases 新闻通稿 61,128

　　replication with other issues 其他议题
　　　的验证研究 15-16

　　Rozelle-Campbell baseline 罗泽尔-坎
　　　贝尔基线 11

　　　as spurious 虚假的 27

　　timeframe for effects 效果的时间框
　　　架/时间表 103

　　visual images 视觉形象 51-52,143

crime 犯罪

　　emotions towards 感情指向 80

　　mean world syndrome 邪恶世界综合
　　　征 33,60

　　measuring salience 测量显著性 107

　　media coverage 媒体报道 31-34,35,56

　　personal experience and 个人经验和
　　　犯罪 85-86

cultivation analysis 涵化分析 33,59-60

culture 文化

　　cultural agendas 文化议程 156-157

　　transmission of 传承文化 150,152-153

　　validity of agenda-setting across cultures
　　　跨文化议程设置的有效性 53-55

Czech Republic 捷克共和国 58

D

Dallas Morning News《达拉斯晨报》31-32

Danielson, Wayne 韦恩·丹尼尔森 x

defence issues 国防议题 17

demographic groups 人口群体 150-152

　　generational differences 代际差异 21-
　　　22,24

Diario de Navarra《纳瓦拉日报》24,48

digital channels see online media 数字渠
　　道 可见 网络媒体

Dole, Robert 罗伯特·多尔 61,119

domains and settings 领域和场景 157-
　　159

Downs, Anthony 安东尼·唐斯 35

drugs issue 毒品议题 30-31

dual process approach 双轨路径思路
　　100-102

E

economic issues 经济议题 61,81-82,96

education, influence of 教育的影响 74,
　　76-77,86,96,97,98-100,151

El Pais《国家报》48

elaboration likelihood model of persua-
　　sion 说服的详尽可能性模型 100

elections 选举

　　campaign agendas 竞选活动议程
　　　121,122-123,124

　　elements of 选举的要素 125-126

　　gubernatorial elections 州长选举 45,
　　　67,123-124

　　mayoral elections 市长选举 15,39,

49,77,93,125,132

US Senate election 2010 2010年美国参议院选举 19

see also general/national elections; local elections; presidential elections 也见 普选/大选/全国选举；地方选举；总统选举

emphasis frames 强调性框架 61-62

employment/unemployment issues 就业/失业议题 14,20,81,84-85

Emporia Gazette《恩波里亚公报》39-40

energy crisis 能源危机 13,29-30,35

environmental issues 环境议题 34-35,54-55,78-79,103,107-108

equivalence frames 等值性框架 61-62

Erie County Study (1940) 伊利县研究 (1940) 4,12,24

experimental evidence 实验证据 17-19,50-51

F

Facebook 脸书 xiv,20,70,121

'fake news'"假新闻" 2,41

federal budget deficit 联邦预算赤字 57,148

field experiments 实地/田野实验 18,87,101,102

film 电影 154,157

Flyvjberg, Bent 本特·福莱伯格 117

focusing events 焦点事件 58

Folkerts, Jean Lange 珍·福克茨 39-40

Forbes, Steve 史蒂夫·福布斯 119

Ford, Gerald 杰拉尔德·福特 46,47,78

foreign/international affairs 外交/国际事务 13,82,96,97

Fortunato, John 约翰·福尔图纳托 156

Fortune magazine《财富》杂志 148

Fox News 福克斯新闻 23,52,70

framing 框架建构/架构 60-62,131

Frankel, Max 麦克斯·弗兰克尔 xiii

Funkhouser, Ray 雷·芬克豪泽 28,29,71

G

Gallup polls 盖洛普民意调查（测验）

MIP question 国家面临的最重要问题 xvi-xvii,12,15,21,28,31,34,69,80,94-95,107

gatekeeping 把关 59,101,130

general/national elections 普选/大选/全国选举

Austria 奥地利 121

candidate images in 全国选举中的候选人形象 46-48,108

Germany 1990 1990年德国选举 57-58

Israel 2006 2006年以色列选举 142

Japan 1993 1993年日本选举 53-55

Spain 1996 1996年西班牙选举 24,47-48

Sweden 2006 2006年瑞典选举 13-14, 24, 38

UK 1983 1983年英国选举 118-119, 125-126

see also presidential elections 也见 总统选举

generational differences 代际差异 21-22, 24

Gentzkow, Matthew 马修·根茨科 18

Gerbner, George 乔治·格伯纳 33

Germany 德国 100, 101, 102, 105

    1990 national election 1990年全国选举 57-58

    energy crisis 1973 1973年能源危机 13, 29-30, 35

    incidental learning 顺带学习 87

    longitudinal study 历时性研究 16-17

    nuclear reactor shut-down 2011 2011年决定关停核反应堆 58

    public opinion 舆论/公众意见 13, 143

    Second World War and 第二次世界大战和德国 xi

    unemployment issue 失业议题 81

gestalt perspective 格式塔/完形角度

    communication gestalt 传播格式塔 23-25

    network agenda-setting 网络议程设置 70-71

    relevance and 关联性和格式塔 80-81

global warming issue 全球变暖议题 62, 117, 129, 142

González, Felipe 费利佩·冈萨雷斯 47, 48

Gore, Al 阿尔·戈尔 51, 120, 123

government policy 政府政策 58, 114, 127, 159

Granger analysis 格兰杰因果分析 146

Greece 希腊 156-157

gubernatorial elections 州长选举 45, 67, 123-124

Gulf War 海湾战争 140

gun control issue 枪支管制议题 127-128

H

Hellinger, Moshe 摩西·海灵格 154

Hewlett Packard Labs 惠普实验室 132

Holmes, Sherlock 夏洛克·福尔摩斯 xvi, 160

Houston Chronicle《休斯敦纪事报》 31-32

Hovland, Carl 卡尔·霍夫兰 136

The Huffington Post《赫芬顿邮报》 18

hypodermic needle theory of media effects 媒介效果的皮下注射理论 6, 37, 103

I

idiosyncratic pictures 怪异的图像 28

alarmed discovery 警报发觉 35-36

decade of US public opinion 美国舆论的十年 28-29

energy crisis in Germany 德国的能源危机 29-30, 35

environmental issues 环境议题 34-35

fear of crime 罪行恐惧 31-34

national concern about drugs 全国对毒品问题的担忧 30-31

psychological maps 心理图式 28, 72

shark attacks 鲨鱼袭人 34, 35

image building 形象塑造 59

incidental learning 顺带学习 87-88

individual differences 个体差异 84-87

information vs persuasion 告知信息相对于说服 2, 4-5, 144

Inglehart, Ronald 罗纳德·英格尔哈特 80

intermedia agenda-setting 媒体间议程设置 xi, 19, 111, 128-132, 133

International Communication Association 国际传播协会 36

international/foreign affairs 国际/外交事务 13, 82, 96, 97

internet 互联网 24, 95, 104

    see also online media; social media 也见 网络媒体;社交媒体

Iran-Contra scandal "伊朗-康特拉"丑闻("伊朗门"事件) 139

Iraq War 伊拉克战争 145

Israel 以色列 142, 155

issue attention cycle 议题关注周期 35-36

ITV 独立电视公司 118

Iyengar, Shanto 仙托·艾英戈 138

J

Jamieson, Kathleen Hall 凯瑟琳·霍尔·贾米森 153

Japan 日本

    1993 general election 1993年大选 53-55

    earthquake 2011 2011年地震 58

    economic difficulties 经济困难 61, 130

    environmental issues 环境议题 54-55

    influencing behaviour 影响行为 146-148

    local public opinion 地方舆论 15

    mayoral elections 市长选举 15, 77

    Second World War and 第二次世界大战和日本 xi

Jaws《大白鲨》34

Johnson, Lyndon B. 林登·约翰逊 xiv

Jones, Bryan 布莱恩·琼斯 63

Journal of the American Medical Association《美国医学会杂志》114

K

Kahneman, Daniel 丹尼尔·卡尼曼 62

Katz, Elihu 伊莱休·卡茨 144
Kennedy, John F. 约翰·肯尼迪 154
Key, V. O. V. O. 科依 93
Kinder, Donald 唐纳德·金德 138
King, Gary 加里·金 18, 87
Kiousis, Spiro 斯皮罗·基欧瑟斯 24, 71
Klapper, Joseph 约瑟夫·克拉珀 4
Kosovo 科索沃 101-102, 146
Ksiazek, Thomas 托马斯·克西翁热克 22

L

Landman, Todd 托德·兰德曼 117
Lane, Robert 罗伯特·莱恩 74, 86
Latinobarometer 拉丁美洲晴雨表 95
Law of Minimal Consequences 最小后果定律 4-5, 103, 159
Lazarsfeld, Paul 保罗·拉扎斯菲尔德 4, 12, 24, 105
Lelyveld, Joseph 约瑟夫·莱利维尔德 119
Lewinsky, Monica 莫妮卡·莱温斯基 76
Lexicoder Sentiment Dictionary 自动编码情感辞典 109
Lind, Jenny 珍妮·林德 ix, x
Lippmann, Walter 沃尔特·李普曼 1, 4, 5, 6
 the pictures in our heads 我们头脑中的图像 27, 42, 43, 44, 45, 62, 65
 pseudo-environment 拟态环境 3, 27,
29, 41, 74
Public Opinion《舆论》1, 3, 4
local elections 地方选举
 attribute agenda-setting 属性议程设置 123-125
 candidate images in 地方选举中的候选人形象 49-51
 media agendas in 地方选举中的媒介议程 123-124
 Spain 西班牙 14-15, 49-50, 124
 see also mayoral elections 也见 市长选举
longitudinal analysis 历时性分析 16-17, 21, 103-104
time-order 时间先后顺序 9, 12, 16
Los Angeles Times《洛杉矶时报》xiv-xv, 60, 119, 120
Louisville 路易维尔 14, 16-17, 83
Louisville Times《路易维尔时报》14

M

McCain, John 约翰·麦凯恩 120
McCall, H. Carl H. 卡尔·麦考尔 45
McGovern, George 乔治·麦戈文 129
Mainichi Shimbun《每日新闻》61, 131
Matthes, Jörg 约尔格·马特斯 81
mayoral elections 市长选举 15, 39, 49, 77, 93, 125, 132
 see also local elections 也见 地方选举
mean world syndrome 邪恶世界综合征

33,60

media agenda 媒介议程

  capturing 俘获 117-121

  election agendas 选举议程 122-123

  homogeneity 同质性 22

  limits on size 容量限制 95

  local elections 地方选举 123-124

  onion metaphor 洋葱比喻 111-112,116,118

  policy agenda and 政策议程和媒介议程 58,114,127,159

  shaping 塑造媒介议程 110-134

  subsidizing 补贴媒介议程 115-117

media exposure 媒介接触 49,143,148,151

media organizations 媒体组织/机构 59,115,131

media use 媒介使用 21,22,24,38,71-72,85-86

memory 记忆

  associative network model 联想网状模型 66

  collective 集体记忆 154-155

Miller,George 乔治·米勒 94

Miller,Joanne 乔安妮·米勒 80

Milton,John 约翰·弥尔顿 xi

Most Important Problem (MIP) question 国家面临的最重要问题 20,25,56,57,69,85,140,151

crime 犯罪 31,33,34,38

drugs 毒品 31

environment 环境 34-35

Gallup polls 盖洛普民意调查 xvi-xvii,12,15,21,28,31,34,39,69,80,94-95,107

natural history perspective 自然历史角度 37

MoveOn.org 132

MSNBC 微软全国广播公司 70,131

museums 博物馆 156

N

National Association of Broadcasters (NAB) 全美广播业者协会 xvi

National Basketball Association (NBA) 美国男子职业篮球联盟 156

national elections *see* general/national elections 全国选举 可见 普选/大选/全国选举

The Nation《国家》杂志 18

natural history perspective 自然历史角度 37,38,41,83,104,105,116

NBC 美国全国广播公司 7,23,52,70,119,131

need for orientation (NFO) 导向需求 xii,73-74,90

  Chapel Hill study 查普希尔研究 77-78

  definition 定义 74

mass media and 大众媒介和导向需求 76–79

measuring 测量 81

relevance 关联性 74–76, 79–81

transfer of salience 显著性转移 101–102

uncertainty 不确定性 74–76

network agenda-setting 网络议程设置 64–72, 134

 accumulated evidence on 积累的证据 69–70

 associative memory 联想式记忆 66

 associative network models 联想网状模型 66

 candidate attributes 候选人属性 66–69

 gestalt perspective 格式塔/完形角度 70–71

 networks of candidates 候选人网络 66–69

 network analysis 网络分析 22, 66–67, 69, 70, 71, 89

New York Herald-Tribune《纽约先驱论坛报》128

New York Times《纽约时报》xiii, 7, 41, 45, 60, 107, 115, 117, 131, 143

 civil rights issues 公民权利议题 12

 crime coverage 犯罪报道 34

 drug problems 毒品问题 30, 31

 environmental stories 环境新闻故事 34–35

 foreign affairs coverage 外交事务报道 13

 generational differences 代际差异 22

 intermedia agenda setting 媒体间议程设置 128–129

 longitudinal analysis 历时性分析 21

 moral/leadership attributes of candidates 候选人的道德/领导力属性 58

 presidential elections 总统选举 119, 120

 print vs online version 印刷版相对于网络版 17–18, 19

 State of the Union address 国情咨文 113

The New Yorker《纽约客》8, 28

News Coverage Index 2012 2012年新闻报道指数 95

news media 新闻媒体

 agendas of 新闻媒体的议程 2–3, 123–124

 alarmed discovery 警报发觉 35–36

 crime coverage 犯罪报道 31–34, 56–57

 drug problem 毒品问题 30–31

 environmental issues 环境议题 34–35

 expansion 扩展 xiii–xiv

 influence on behaviour 对行为的影响 144–148

information vs persuasion 告知信息相对于说服 2,4-5,144

intermedia agenda-setting 媒体间议程设置 128-132,133

issue attention cycle 议题关注周期 35-36

partisan media 党派媒体 2,52

persuasion vs information 说服相对于告知信息 2,4-5,144

political campaigns 政治活动 117-126

power of the news 新闻的权力 8

president and national 总统和全国新闻媒体 112-115

 as primary source of information 作为主要信息来源 13,24,42,59,84

salience of topics 话题的显著性 2

signal function of 信号功能 1

wire services 通讯社 129-130

see also newspapers; television 也见 报纸；电视

newspapers 报纸 xi,1,24

 1972 presidential election 1972年总统选举 9

 1976 presidential election 1976年总统选举 10-12

 Chapel Hill study 查普希尔研究 6

 civil rights issues 公民权利议题 12

 crime coverage 犯罪报道 31-33,56-57

 foreign affairs coverage 外交事务报道 13

 generational differences 代际差异 21-22,24

 political reform issue 政治改革议题 53-54

 power of the press 新闻的权力 8

 print vs online versions 印刷版相对于网络版 17-18,19

 Southern white newspapers 南方的白人报纸 xi

 State of the Union address 1978 1978年国情咨文 113

 subsidizing 补贴 115-117

 wire services 通讯社 129-130

 see also news media 也见 新闻媒体

Newsweek《新闻周刊》28,30,46,58

Nicaragua 尼加拉瓜 139

Nielsen data 尼尔森数据 22

Nightline《夜线》xviii

Nixon, Richard 理查德·尼克松 113,154

O

Obama, Barack 巴拉克·奥巴马 52,70,89-90,121,132

obtrusive and unobtrusive issues 强制性和非强制性议题 82-87,126,146

OhmyNews 哦！我的新闻 19

oil crisis *see* energy crisis 石油危机 可见 能源危机

One World 寰宇一家 60
onion metaphor 洋葱比喻 111-112,116,118
online media 网络媒体 19-23
    candidates' websites 候选人网站 19
    CNN 美国有线电视新闻网 18,19
    correlation statistic 相关性统计 20,21-22
    generational differences 代际差异 21-22,24
    longitudinal analysis 历时性分析 21
    New York Times《纽约时报》17-18,19
    news websites 新闻网站 131
    proliferation of 网络媒体激增 21-23
    traditional media and 传统媒体和网络媒体 17-18,19,21-23
    see also social media 也见 社交媒体
open-ended questions 开放式问题 50,51,108,141
    see also Most Important Problem question 也见 国家面临的最重要问题
opinion polls/surveys 民意调查/问卷调查 2,17,43,50
    see also Gallup polls 也见 盖洛普民意调查（测验）
Orwell, George 乔治·奥威尔 55

P

paired comparisons 成对比较 108

Park, Robert 罗伯特·帕克 1
partisan media 党派媒体 2,52
Patterson, Thomas 托马斯·帕特森 153
Pavlik, John 约翰·帕夫利克 xvii
Peri, Yoram 约拉姆·佩里 155
personal experience 个人经验 25,90,94
    importance of 个人经验的重要性 10
    individual differences 个体差异 84-87
    need for orientation and 导向需求和个人经验 81-84
    obtrusive and unobtrusive issues 强制性和非强制性议题 82-87
    with public issues 个人经验和公众议题 81-84
persuasion 说服
    elaboration likelihood model of 详尽可能性模型 100
    news media 新闻媒体 2,4-5,144
    persuasion vs information 说服相对于告知信息 2,4-5,144
phronesis 实践智慧 117
pictures in our heads 我们头脑中的图像 136,144
    Lippmann 李普曼 27,42,43,44,45,62,65
    political candidates 政治候选人 45-51
Pitts, Leonard 伦纳德·皮茨 133
Plato 柏拉图 3
policy agenda 政策议程 58,114,127,159

political campaigns 政治活动
- advertising 广告 24, 46, 48, 77, 117, 118, 124, 125, 130
- attributes of local issues 地方议题的属性 124-125
- campaign agendas 竞选活动议程 121, 122-123, 124
- capturing the media agenda 俘获媒介议程 117-121
- election agendas 选举议程 122-4
- elements of elections 选举的要素 125-126
- intermedia agenda-setting 媒体间议程设置 128-132, 133
- local issues 地方议题 124-125
- media and local elections 媒体和地方选举 123-124
- obtrusive and unobtrusive issues 强制性和非强制性议题 126
- referendums 全民公投 120-121
- US and UK compared 美国和英国的比较 118-119, 125-126

political candidates 政治候选人 44, 45
- attributes 属性 46-52, 60-61, 119-120, 123-124
- images in local elections 在地方选举中的形象 49-51
- images in national elections 在全国选举中的形象 46-48, 108
- influence on news coverage 对新闻报道的影响 119-120
- moral quality and leadership 道德品质和领导力 58
- as objects 作为客体 43, 45-46
- pictures in our heads 我们头脑中的图像 45-51

political communication 政治传播 12, 48, 50, 66

political reform issue 政治改革议题 53-54

polls see opinion polls/surveys 调查 可见 民意调查/问卷调查

Popkin, Samuel 塞缪尔·波普金 96

post-factual society 后真相社会 xi

president 总统
- national agenda and 国家议程和总统 112-115
- State of the Union address 国情咨文 112-113

presidential elections 总统选举
- 1940 4, 12, 24
- 1948 12
- 1968 see Chapel Hill study 可见 查普希尔研究
- 1972 xii, 9, 16, 74, 76, 77
- 1976 10-12, 16, 46-47, 78-79, 153
- 1984 118-119
- 1992 122-123

索引   275

1996 60-61,104,119,143

2000 51-52,76,119-120,122-123,146

2004 143

2012 23,52,70,89,90,102,121

2016 89-90

caucuses 党团会议 129

primaries 初选 10,11,43,46,76,119

Twitter and 推特和总统 70,89

press releases 新闻通稿 60-61,115,119,121,123-124,128,149

PRESSian 报料人（新闻网站名）19

priming 铺垫 137,138-140,141,142

Project for Excellence in Journalism (PEJ) 卓越新闻项目 69,95,131

pseudo-environment 拟态环境 3,27,29,41,74

psychological maps 心理图式 28,72

 see also idiosyncratic pictures 也见 怪异的图像

public agenda 公众议程

 carrying capacity of 承载能力/容量 94-95

 Chapel Hill study 查普希尔研究 5-7

 diversity of 公众议程的多样性 95-96

 duration of major issues on 主要议题的停留时间 97-98

 education and 教育和公众议程 96,97,98-100

 limited size of 有限容量 94-95

 volatility of 公众议程的暂时性 97

public opinion 舆论/公众意见

 alarmed discovery 警报发觉 35-36

 America, 1960s 美国20世纪60年代的舆论 28-29

 Argentina 阿根廷 15

 attribute agendas and 属性议程和舆论/公众意见 140-142

 behaviour and 行为和舆论/公众意见 144-148

 crime 犯罪 31-34,56-57

 demographic groups 人口群体 150-152

 distribution of 舆论/公众意见的分布 2,43

 drugs 毒品 30-31

 energy crisis 能源危机 13,29-30,35

 environmental issues 环境议题 34-35

 formation 形成 4-7,143

 Germany 德国 13,29-30,35

 Japan 日本 15,61

 Louisville 路易维尔 14,17,83

 major shifts in 主要转移 63

 personal experience and *see* personal experience 个人经验 可见 个人经验

 polls *see* opinion polls/surveys 调查 可见 民意调查/问卷调查

 priming 铺垫 137,138-140,141,142

Spain 西班牙 14-15

Public Opinion（Lippmann）《舆论》（李普曼）1,3,4

Public Opinion Quarterly《舆论季刊》8

public relations 公共关系 115-117

R

ranking of issues 议题排序 6,10-11,37,53,64

Rashi, Tsuriel 崔瑞尔·拉什 154

Reagan, Ronald 罗纳德·里根 113,139

Redford, Robert 罗伯特·雷德福 154

Reese, Stephen 斯蒂芬·里斯 111

referendums 全民公投 120-121

relevance 关联性 74-76,79-81

religion 宗教 154

Richards, Ann 安·理查兹 124

Rogers, Don 唐·罗杰斯 30

Rogers, Everett 艾弗里特·罗杰斯 36

Rogers, Will 威尔·罗杰斯 1

Romney, Mitt 米特·罗姆尼 52,70,89,121

Roosevelt, Franklin D. 富兰克林·D. 罗斯福 113

Roper, Elmo 埃尔莫·罗珀 4

Rozelle-Campbell baseline 罗泽尔-坎贝尔基线 11

S

Safire, William 威廉·萨菲尔 41

Selena murder case 赛琳娜谋杀案 32

salience measures, diversity of 显著性测量的多样性 106-109

salience transfer *see* transfer of salience 显著性转移 可见 显著性转移

same-sex marriage 同性婚姻 109,142

San Antonio Light《圣安东尼奥之光》114

schools 中小学 155-156

Schram, Sanford 桑福德·施拉姆 117

Schramm, Wilbur 威尔伯·施拉姆 x,103

Science magazine《科学》杂志 18

second level agenda-setting *see* attribute agenda-setting 第二层面议程设置 可见 属性议程设置

Second World War 第二次世界大战 xi

selective perception 选择性认知 6-7,48,101

September 11, 2001 tragedy 2001年"9·11"悲剧 151

shark attacks 鲨鱼袭人 34,35

Sharknado《鲨卷风》34

Shaw, Donald 唐纳德·肖 x,xi,xii,xv,xvi,xvii,5,88,131

Shaw, Eugene 尤金·肖 135-136

Shoemaker, Pamela 帕梅拉·休梅克 111

Simpson, O. J. O. J. 辛普森 32

SkyTeam 天合联盟 60

smoking 吸烟 140,141

social media 社交媒体 ix,2,88,108–109,111,115,118,159

 blogs 博客 132

 expansion in 扩展 xiii–xiv

 Facebook 脸书 xiv,20,70,121

 manipulation of 操纵社交媒体 xi

 rise of 社交媒体的兴起 20,21,87

 Twitter 推特 xi,18,20,70,71,89,121,132

 YouTube 优兔 121,132

social welfare issue 社会福利议题 123,145

Socrates 苏格拉底 3

Son, Y. J. 孙英俊 65

Soroka, Stuart 斯图尔特·索罗卡 113–114

South Korea 韩国 19,128

Spain 西班牙 92,93,130,151,156

 intermedia agenda-setting 媒体间议程设置 130

 local elections 地方选举 49–50

 local public opinion 地方舆论 14–15

 national election 1996 1996 年全国选举 24,47–48

 social media 社交媒体 20

spiral of silence 沉默的螺旋 59,60

sport 运动 156

Standard and Poor 标准普尔 149

Star Alliance 星空联盟 60

state government agencies 州政府机构 116

State of the Union address 国情咨文 112–113

status conferral 地位授予 59

Stempel, Guido 吉多·斯坦普尔 x

stereotyping 刻板印象形成 58

Stone, Oliver 奥利弗·斯通 154

Stromback, Jesper 杰斯珀·斯特龙巴克 24,71

substantive attributes 实质属性 47–48,49–50,81,123,136,141,142,148,151

surveillance 监控 150

surveys 问卷调查

 see also opinion polls/surveys 也见 民意调查/问卷调查

Sweden 瑞典 13–14,21,24,38

Switzerland 瑞士 120–121

T

Takeshita, Toshio 竹下俊郎 100

television 电视 xi

 crime coverage 犯罪报道 33–34,56–57

 exposure to violence on 接触电视上的暴力内容 33

 mean world syndrome and 邪恶世界综

合征 33,60

presidential elections 总统选举 9,10-12,51

US and UK elections compared 美国和英国选举的比较 118-119,125-126

see also news media 也见 新闻媒体

third-level agenda-setting 第三层面议程设置 65,66-69,70,121,134,149

see also network agenda-setting 也见 网络议程设置

time lags 时滞 55,103,105,106

Time magazine 《时代》杂志 28,34

time-order 时间先后顺序 9,12,16

time-series analysis 时间序列分析 20,21,33-34,105,109,131

timeframe for effects 效果的时间框架/时间表 103-106

Tolman, Edward 爱德华·托尔曼 74

tone see affective attributes/tone 语气 可见 情感属性/语气

transfer of salience 显著性转移 44,133,155,157,159

    Acapulco typology 阿卡普尔科模型 36-38

    attention and comprehension distinguished 注意与理解的区分 44-45,134

    compelling arguments 雄辩论据 55-59

digital platforms 数字平台 20

    explaining 解释 100-102

    incidental learning 顺带学习 87-88

    issue salience 议题显著性 103,114

    need for orientation and 导向需求和显著性转移 101-102

    networks 网络 65

    political system and 政治系统和显著性转移 93

    timeframe 时间框架/时间表 103

    transmission of culture 传承文化 150,152-153

Trump, Donald 唐纳德·特朗普 76,89-90

Tversky, Amos 阿莫斯·特沃斯基 62

Twain, Mark 马克·吐温 21

Twitter see social media 推特 可见 社交媒体

U

unemployment/employment issues 失业/就业议题 14,20,81,84-85

United Kingdom 英国

    foreign affairs issues 外交事务议题 13

    general elections 大选 118-119,125-126

    political parties 政党 125

United Nations Conference on 联合国大会 Environment and Development 联合国环境与发展会议 54

unobtrusive issues *see* obtrusive and unobtrusive issues 非强制性议题 可见 强制性和非强制性议题

US News and World Report《美国新闻与世界报道》28, 58

USINET 67, 69

V

Vietnam 越南 29, 96

violence 暴力

 crime coverage 犯罪报道 31–34, 56–57

 mean world syndrome 邪恶世界综合征 33, 60

 television entertainment 电视娱乐节目 33–34

visual images 视觉形象 51–53, 143

W

Wall Street Journal《华尔街日报》129

Wallace, George 乔治·华莱士 7

Washington Post《华盛顿邮报》8, 58, 60, 113, 115, 119, 120, 129, 154

Watergate 水门事件 154

Weaver, David 戴维·韦弗 xii, xvii, 65, 74

Webster, James 詹姆斯·韦伯斯特 22

Wenner, Lawrence 劳伦斯·温纳 156

White, Theodore 西奥多·怀特 xiv, 7, 8

White, William Allen 威廉·艾伦·怀特 39–40

wine 葡萄酒 157

Winfrey, Oprah 奥普拉·温弗里 25

wire services 通讯社 129–130

Woodward, Bob 鲍勃·伍德沃德 154

Wu, Denis 丹尼斯·吴 146

Y

Yomiuri《读卖新闻》54, 131

YouTube 优兔 121, 132

Z

Zuckerberg, Mark 马克·扎克伯格 xiv

第三版译后记

一

马克斯韦尔·麦库姆斯博士的英文原著 Setting the Agenda: the Mass Media and Public Opinion（《议程设置：大众媒介与舆论》）的中译本第一版出版于2008年，第二版出版于2018年，这里翻译的是第三版（原著出版于2020年）。第三版原书名改为 Setting the Agenda: The News Media and Public Opinion，中译本相应改成《议程设置：新闻媒体与舆论》，以下简称《议程设置》。在正文中，"大众媒介""大众传媒"等译文也遵照原文的改动（mass media 变为 news media），多数改为"新闻媒体"。

第三版的作者增加了一位，是塞巴斯蒂安·瓦伦苏埃拉。依据网络资料，塞巴斯蒂安·瓦伦苏埃拉本科毕业于智利天主教大学，在美国得克萨斯大学奥斯汀分校获得硕士和博士学位，麦库姆斯是他的两位博士生指导教授之一。研究生毕业前，他曾在智利圣地亚哥担任过几年报纸的财经新闻记者，后担任天主教大学传播学院副教授。2018—2019年，大约是在他协助麦库姆斯完成《议程设置》第三版修订工作的同时，他在美国威斯康星大学麦迪逊分校新闻与大众传播学院担任汀克尔访问教授（Tinker Visiting Professor），并应"拉丁美洲、加勒比和伊比利亚研究计划"（Latin American, Caribbean &

Iberian Studies Program，LACIS)邀请作访问研究。他勤奋、多产,在议程设置研究方面有一些学术贡献;但显然,议程设置只是他的研究领域之一。《议程设置》第三版的灵魂人物仍然是麦库姆斯。

议程设置领域的第二位重要人物唐纳德·肖(Donald L. Shaw)于2021年10月19日逝世。议程设置研究传统是麦库姆斯与肖一道开启的,最初的研究也是他们俩一同完成的。只是肖虽然始终坚守在议程设置理论的诞生地北卡罗来纳大学,却并未一直以议程设置研究为主业。他是一位历史学者,而议程设置研究从本质上说是一种实证研究,主要采用量化方法,需要精细的测量技术。麦库姆斯虽然后来移师得克萨斯大学奥斯汀分校,却始终专注地看护着议程设置的理论阵地,并将议程设置研究的种子撒播到全球各地。在议程设置领域,麦库姆斯无疑是"教父"一样的存在。在他的指导下,主要是由他的学生——亲炙的或者私淑的——将议程设置理论研究的星星之火点燃于美国各地、西班牙、中国、韩国,以及世界上许许多多的地区。

虽然我算不上麦库姆斯的学生,也没有亲身从事议程设置的实证研究,但1996年在得克萨斯大学访学期间,我很幸运地获得了在麦库姆斯教授的指导下学习传播学理论知识的机会,并在教授那里接触到议程设置理论的"真经"。正是通过麦库姆斯教授,我才了解了议程设置这个研究领域,也才开始理解传播学研究。

1996年正值美国总统选举年(比尔·克林顿不出意外再次当选)。那一学期,麦库姆斯教授开设了一门名为"大众传播与全国选举"的研究生课程,我在课堂上听到了学生的讨论和教授的点评,也为此阅读了教授提供的关于议程设置研究的大量文献。我自己对"大选"本来是没有多少兴趣的——毕竟它与中国的实践距离很远,但在认真阅读文献的基础上,在与教授经常性的讨论过程中,我对议程设置研究渐生好奇。其后,经教授推荐,我着手翻译当时他与学生刚刚写好而尚未刊登的一篇关于议程设置的文章。这篇译文后来经张国良教授推荐,刊登在《新闻大学》上,开启了国内传播学学者对"议程设置"研究的关注。

那个时候,也就是20世纪90年代中期,传播学在中国还不是一个被承认的"学科"。虽然自从80年代初,国内学者便听说了"mass communication"这个名词,但了解传播学的人极少。直到1997年,传播学才被列入国家的学科目录,算是有了一个合法的学术身份。

第一版译本出版之前,我是临时加入译者队伍的,比较匆忙,没有写诸如"译后记"之类的文字。第二版翻译完成后,出版社编辑提醒我写一篇"导读"式的介绍,我也自觉有一些话需要交代,算是对多年关注议程设置研究领域的一个自我小结。于是有了第一次"译后记",第三版译后记则是在第二版译后记的基础上修订的。

二

议程设置是麦库姆斯倾注了一辈子心血的传播理论和研究。在该理论得到学界公认之后,麦库姆斯又为这个领域的丰富与发展进行了不遗余力的推广工作,使之向广袤与纵深前行——他亲自参与了全球多项议程设置研究,并亲自指导、培育了全球各地区的议程设置研究。麦库姆斯对这一理论领域的理解之深入及对研究细节掌握之熟稔,充分体现在这部全面介绍议程设置理论发展的概览性著述中。同时,作为国际知名学者,麦库姆斯所写的文字反而简明易懂,他娓娓而谈,如数家珍,信手拈来,相信阅读过原文的中国学者都深有体会。

在翻译过程中,我们力求在充分理解原著的基础上尽可能明白晓畅地表达文字——仅此而已。

议程设置理论起源于一个相当简单的假设,那就是:大众媒介关于世界的图像是建构的;而不论这种建构离真实的世界多远,它还是被视为"现实"。这个最初来自李普曼的思想被议程设置的研究者通过量化的途径加以证实,并以实证研究的方法论呈现于世。也就是说,由于新闻传媒通过新闻报道对现实进行选择性建构,它们挑选的"重要事实"会被公众所接受,成为社会的显著"议程"。从本质上说,议程设置属于"效果"研究的路径。

议程设置理论最初来自 20 世纪 60 年代末期对美国总统选举的传播学研究,测量选民对美国面临的最重要问题的感觉与媒体报道的契合程度。其后,议程设置研究的对象从"议题"转为"属性",深入到第二层面(如候选人属性)的议程设置效果。研究取向则从显著性转移的外在过程进入心理因素的影响过程(如导向需求),从对传媒"引导"作用的确认,扩展到转移的面向和时序(如时滞现象)。再后来,议程设置从"媒介—公众"关系扩大到"政府—媒介"关系、媒介间关系,以及新闻媒体与几乎所有社会集团和个人的关系;研究的问题也涉及安全、环境、金融、毒品等系列社会问题和公共政策。最新的研究领域已扩展到与互联网等新媒介相关的议程设置现象,研究范围不断扩大,研究问题日益丰富。

三

不过,随着议程设置理论领域的扩大与深入,特别是,与许多学科交叉,也引发一些学术争议。议程设置的若干假定面临挑战。

例如,议程设置与框架建构两种取向的学者之间曾就框架分析的学术归属发生争议。对此,我倾向于认为,就议程设置而言,框架的建构和议程显著性的转移可能发生于不同的阶段——(内在的)心理过程和(外显的)舆论过程。框架建构(框选)与"导向需求"一样,也是解释议程设置的心理机制中的一种。最初的议程设置研究之所以一经发表,顷刻成为公认的成功的大众传播理论,就在于它简单的因果假设和几乎无懈可击的测量方法,而一旦进入心理层面(框架建构属于心理过程),问题和因素就复杂到难以确定的程度,也就不易形成共识了。

与此同时,人们也不能不感叹时代的变化和理论的变迁。诞生于大众传播鼎盛时期的议程设置理论在新兴的网络传播时代面临着更大的挑战。传统的议程设置效果发生于有限渠道(亦即大众传播媒介)的传播,极有利于舆论的整合及共识的缔造。而互联网时代却是一个碎片时代,面对言论的汪洋大海和信息的真假难辨,持续产生断裂的社会,不断催生破碎的舆论,新闻传播传统的三大功能——监控环境、缔造共识和传承文化——无不经受着严峻的考验。

正如我们前面提到的,在《议程设置》第三版中,"新闻传播"已经取代了"大众传播",这说明,议程设置的基本条件——有限的新闻信息来源和大众传播媒介的可信度及权威性——已经改变。我们看到,群体变得疏离,观点日益极化,社会在分裂,共识的建立越来越遥远。这已经不再是某个国家面临的最重要的问题,而是整个世界面临的最严峻的挑战。在一个交流日益便捷的即时沟通时代,面对竞争日趋激烈的全球媒介社会,人们将何以自处及相处?共识的建立、人类的团结是一个重大的时代命题,也是当今议程设置研究需要回答的理论诘问。新一代理论研究者任重而道远。

郭镇之
2022 年 2 月 25 日